THE CIVIL WAR SOCIETY'S
ENCYCLOPEDIA
OF THE
CIVIL WAR

PRODUCED BY THE PHILIP LIEF GROUP, INC.

Principal Writer and Researcher:	Suzanne LeVert
Project Editors:	Stephen Francoeur and Gary M. Sunshine
Production Coordinator:	Laura-Ann Robb
Design Consultants:	Emma Crawford, H. Nolan
Photographic Research	Diane Hamilton
Additional Photography:	Michael Campbell
Additional Writing and Research:	Sharon Henderson
Additional Research:	Anne Pierce
Editorial Assistant:	Linda Barth
Typesetting:	NK Graphics

THE CIVIL WAR SOCIETY'S

ENCYCLOPEDIA

OF THE

CIVIL WAR

Published by arrangement with
The Philip Lief Group, Inc.
130 Wall Street
Princeton, NJ 08540

The Civil War Society gratefully acknowledges the National Archives in Washington, D.C., for
making available photographs appearing on pages 4, 8, 65, 68, 163, 182, 185, 195, 202, 217,
233, 245, 249, 250, 256, 275, 278, 284, 286, 304, 305, 315, 320, 386

All other photographs appear courtesy of the Library of Congress in Washington, D.C.

This 1997 edition is published by Wings Books, a division of Random House Value Publishing, Inc.,
201 East 50th Street, New York, New York 10022.

Wings Books and colophon are trademarks of Random House Value Publishing, Inc.

Random House
New York • Toronto • London • Sydney • Auckland
http://www.randomhouse.com/

Printed and bound in the United States of America

Library of Congress Cataloging-in-Publication Data
The Civil War Society's Encyclopedia of the Civil War
p.   cm.
Includes bibliographical references (p. 409).
ISBN 0-517-14983-4
1. United States—History—Civil War, 1861–1865—Encyclopedias.
I. Civil War Society.
E468.A49   1996
973.7'03—dc20   96-31219
CIP

8   7   6   5   4   3   2   1

Contents

Map: A Land Divided: 1861–1865   vi

Introduction   vii

Entries A–Z   1

Appendix 1: President Abraham Lincoln's First Inaugural Address   399

Appendix 2: The Emancipation Proclamation   405

Appendix 3: The Gettysburg Address   407

Sources   409

Further Reading   410

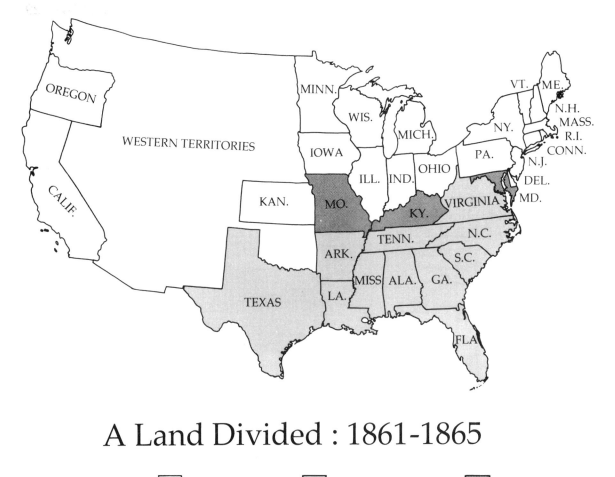

A Land Divided : 1861-1865

Union □   Confederate ■   Border States ■

Introduction

In the autumn of 1858, Abraham Lincoln, campaigning to become Illinois' next senator, declared that "a house divided against itself cannot stand," that "this government cannot endure permanently half slave and half free." Although Lincoln continued to believe that either all of the states would eventually forbid slavery or that all would allow it, the shelling of Fort Sumter from April 12 to April 13, 1861, led the nation onto a third, bloody path, one that in four years took the lives of more than 800,000 Americans and forced Lincoln as the newly elected President to focus on winning a war that divided the nation in two.

The American Civil War Encyclopedia explores this dark and fascinating period in United States history. This vividly illustrated compendium of useful and fascinating information about the Civil War presents over 250 alphabetical entries that explain why the war began, where and how the war was fought, and how the war shaped the lives of soldiers and civilians. Woven into the accounts of famous heroes and military clashes are stories of African-Americans, Native Americans, women, and people of many different ethnic groups. Research into these traditionally ignored areas is crucial to understanding how diverse the people and concerns of the Civil War actually were.

This encyclopedia surveys the most important battles of the war, from the first shots fired at Fort Sumter, through Bull Run, Shiloh, Antietam, Gettysburg, Vicksburg, and up to the final cavalry fight at Appomatox Station. Scores of entries feature military leaders, like the legendary generals Robert E. Lee, Thomas "Stonewall" Jackson, Ulysses S. Grant, and Philip Sheridan. Politicians appear throughout, including such important figures as Judah Philip Benjamin, a member of Jefferson Davis' cabinet and one of the most prominent Jewish-American statesmen of the nineteenth century, and William Henry Seward, one of Lincoln's cabinet members who was known by some as the "evil genius" of that administration.

This encyclopedia illuminates the crucial roles African-Americans played in the war, from Frederick Douglass' impassioned pleas for the immediate emancipation of slaves to the distinguished service of the 54th Massachusetts Regiment, a Union volunteer force composed of African-Americans from the North. Dred Scott's attempt to sue for his freedom is here examined to show how the affair's outcome deepened the rift between the North and the South.

By the mid-nineteenth century, American women were just beginning to gain independence and work outside the home. The stories of women are told throughout the encyclopedia, which recounts the contributions of such important figures as Mary Ann "Mother" Bickerdyke, who took medical supplies to the Union front lines; Belle Boyd, a daring Confederate spy; and Harriet Tubman, who helped hundreds of slaves escape to the North via the Underground Railroad.

Information on family life explains the many difficulties civilians endured on the home front, from the psychological effects of losing a loved one to the scarcity of supplies caused by the Union blockade of Southern ports. An entry on diarist Mary Chesnut provides a firsthand account of the particular hardships felt by Southerners, who watched as the majority of battles were fought on their own territory. An essay on camp life details the day-to-day travails of a Civil War soldier, while entries on medical care and prison life highlight the often unlivable conditions awaiting soldiers off the battlefield.

A close study of the Civil War will reveal the many different political, economic, moral, social, and cultural forces that shaped the period, and better enable today's reader to understand and confront the issues facing our diverse society today. For example, the decades leading up to the Civil War saw politicians clashing over whether the federal government had any right to interfere with a state's decision to allow slave trade. The eloquent and sometimes outrageous pleas in favor of or against this issue by such figures as Daniel Webster, John Calhoun, Stephen Douglas, and Abraham Lincoln, are echoed in today's congressional battles over the validity of all kinds of federal legislation that affects states, such as the Endangered Species Act of 1971, or, more pointedly, the Civil Rights Act of 1964. The issue of slavery itself still remains a fiercely contested topic, as some argue that the economic plight of African-Americans is due to the legacy of servitude and that reparations are due. Despite the long passage of time, the Civil War remains deeply imprinted in American culture.

THE CIVIL WAR SOCIETY'S
ENCYCLOPEDIA
OF THE
CIVIL WAR

A

Abolitionists

A vocal minority of black and white, male and female Northerners who demanded the eradication of slavery. Antislavery sentiments had existed in America since colonial days, but the abolitionist movement did not start in force until the 1830s, when the Second Great Awakening brought new spiritual fervor to the land. Motivated largely by Christian precepts espousing the equality of all, many white Northern-

The Liberator, an abolitionist newspaper.

ers, as concerned about their own souls as about blacks suffering in bondage, came to regard slavery as a religious and moral sin that needed to be expiated without delay.

In December 1833, members of the emerging abolition movement, including editor William Lloyd Garrison and industrialists Arthur and Lewis Tappan, founded the American Anti-Slavery Society. Scorning limited reforms that merely sought to prevent slavery's expansion, and opposing the financial compensation of ex-slaveholders and the colonization of free blacks in Africa, the organization insisted on the immediate abolition of the institution altogether and the granting of full political rights to blacks. Within five years, there were over 1,000 chapters in the North with a quarter million members, who spread the society's message through antislavery tracts, lecture tours, and massive petition drives.

Militant abolitionists faced strong and even violent opposition in the North and South alike; their presses were seized and buildings destroyed, and in 1837, Illinois editor Reverend Elijah Lovejoy was killed by a proslavery mob. They faced arrest in several Southern states, and they met antagonism from the federal government as well, with Congress passing a "gag rule" that forbade consideration of their petitions. Debates over tactics and ideology, meanwhile, split the Anti-Slavery Society, as Garrison and his followers continued to bypass traditional politics, while another wing ran former slaveowner James Birney as the Liberty party presidential candidate in 1840 and 1844.

Abolitionism gained new support among Northern whites after the enactment of the Fugitive Slave Law in 1850 and the 1852 publication of Harriet Beecher Stowe's incendiary novel, *Uncle Tom's Cabin*. Still, from operating the Underground Railroad to offering their more accurate, first-person accounts of the horrors of slavery, blacks remained the core of the abolitionist movement, and some, notably author and orator Frederick Douglass, were among its most renowned figures. Women were the mainstay of hundreds of local antislavery organizations.

Angelina and Sarah Grimké went on the lec-

ture circuit and coauthored with Angelina's husband, Theodore Weld, *American Slavery As It Is*, next to Stowe's book perhaps the most famous antislavery work of its day, while charismatic former slave and spiritual leader Sojourner Truth inspired whites as well as blacks in revival-like meetings across the country. Despite some patronizing and disdain—an 1840 international antislavery convention tried to exclude women entirely—there was unprecedented social interaction between the races and sexes in the abolition movement, with blacks and women treated as relative equals. Such progressiveness limited the general appeal of abolitionism, though there was some guarded opposition to slavery even in slave states, expressed by politicians like Kentuckian Cassius Clay, who called for gradual, compensated emancipation.

As sectional tensions seethed, however, most moderate Southern antislavery voices grew quiet while Northern abolitionists became more militant. Garrison protégé Wendell Phillips was one of many who advocated expelling the slave states from the Union. Others, like Frederick Douglass, grew willing to consider armed rebellion, while rejecting suicidal schemes like John Brown's Harpers Ferry Raid. With the outbreak of the Civil War, most abolitionists rallied to the Union cause, though they remained wary of Abraham Lincoln. By 1862, they seemed to gain, for the first time, real influence in Congress, which they used to lobby for making emancipation an explicitly declared war goal and for allowing blacks to serve in the military.

While Lincoln's Emancipation Proclamation technically failed to actually free any slaves, it was welcomed by the majority of abolitionists as the most solid indication yet that the war meant to end slavery. Movement leaders such as Garrison considered ratification of the 13th Amendment in 1865 the final victory and took up new causes, while others continued working in the Reconstruction era to guarantee citizenship, enfranchisement, education, and economic assistance for the newly freed slaves. Several prominent women abolitionists, including Susan B. Anthony and Elizabeth Cady

Stanton, resented being denied the civil rights newly obtained by black *men*, and concentrated their further efforts on women's suffrage.

By the time the American Anti-Slavery Society was disbanded in 1870, blacks' freedom from bondage was assured, though their freedom from oppression clearly had not been won.

African-Americans in the Civil War

In 1861, at the onset of the Civil War there were just under four million human beings held in slavery between the Northern, or "free" states, the border states, and the Southern states. Historian E. B. Long has called these people "more-than-interested spectators, and occasionally participants." Brought to the United States from Africa and the Caribbean in the years before the importation of human chattel was forbidden by law, African peoples from a broad spectrum of nations and tribal territories found themselves in this frightening situation for a number of reasons. Most were kidnapped from their homes, both as individuals and as families, by slavers once the demand for slave labor outstripped the other markets of the world. Some others were actually the victims of their own race; on the losing side of a tribal war, they were sold to white and Hispanic slave traders by their victorious enemies. At the time of our nation's first census (1790) the slave population of the United States was nearly seven hundred thousand, compared to approximately sixty thousand free Africans: about half a million persons of color out of a total population then approaching four million. By April 1861, the enslaved black population of North America had all but surpassed the previous total human population on the tax rolls.

By the beginning of the Civil War, the free black population in the Northern states and the border areas—territories such as New Mexico and the District of Columbia, and states on the fringe of larger sections, like Delaware and Maryland—far outstripped the free black population in the Southern states. For Southern blacks—free or slave—life was difficult, and full of reversals and danger. From one month to the next, they could never be sure that their situation would remain intact. Even if they lived with or worked for a family that was kind and compassionate, there could be no guarantee that their white owner would remain financially capable of sustaining both his own family and the wider family of slaves or freedmen for whom she or he was responsible. If someone started a school for blacks, it might be shut down at any moment. If freedom papers were issued, they might be revoked, stolen or ignored. If a slaveowner decided to sell someone, he generally did so without regard to breaking up families. The life of a slave, therefore, was usually one of unremitting tension, fear and insecurity; the life of a free black was not all that more certain. There were some examples of kindness between whites and enslaved African-Americans. Some whites taught blacks to read and write in violation of laws to suppress such activities. Some white children, cared for by slaves who showed them great affection, grew to adulthood and worked toward freedom for blacks. There are many more stories, however, of great cruelty practiced against the blacks, slave and free alike, for reasons that seem unbelievable and inhumane to modern eyes. Anyone who has ever felt pain must sympathize with a human being who is whipped until her or his back is raw and bloody, simply because they disagreed with their master or took some desperately needed food. Anyone who has ever loved another person or been a parent can understand and share the agony of standing by, helpless to intercede, while a sibling, spouse, or child is taken away to become the property of another, perhaps never to be seen again. When the war began, Confederate officers usually took one or two servants or freedmen off to battle, serving as cooks, body servants, or companions. Their masters gone, many enslaved African-Americans fled to the North via the Underground Railroad. Many free blacks remained in embattled Southern cities and countrysides to spy on Confederate troops for the

Union, or clandestinely aid runaways. Other blacks, slave and free alike, stayed to help white families; there are instances of blacks protecting the women and children whose men had gone off to war, and other tales of servants who placed their own lives in jeopardy in order to protect a master from being taken prisoner. Black men served the armies on both sides as cooks, farriers, hospital orderlies, and drivers; men and women alike worked in munitions plants and other factories producing war materials.

The Union army recruited all-black regiments with white officers as early as 1862. Casualty rates in these regiments were comparatively very high, because the soldiers knew execution or life imprisonment awaited them, should they be captured. For the black soldiers

of the Union army, then, battle was literally a matter of succeed or die.

Less known is the fact that the Confederacy also recruited black troops, though far later in the war than the North. Alabama voted to recruit slaves in the fall of 1863. General Robert E. Lee advocated the use of freedmen and slaves alike in the Confederate army late in the winter of 1864–65, with freedom offered as a reward to slaves willing to help defend the nation, but the idea got bogged down in the Confederate Congress until mid-March of 1865. On March 13, the Congress finally voted their approval, and President Jefferson Davis signed the bill immediately; training began literally on the heels of approval, fueled by Lee's backing of the idea. For the short time remaining to the Confederacy, the black troops of the Southern army la-

A family fleeing from slavery.

bored against the same difficulties and prejudices that hampered their Northern counterparts—but there is evidence to show they were as courageous under fire as their blue-coated brethren.

In the aftermath of the war, African Americans discovered the Emancipation Proclamation had not changed as many things as they had hoped. Only a handful of those professing antislavery sentiments during the war years were willing to continue the far more difficult work of helping the blacks get on their feet. Up North, blacks had to compete with immigrants for jobs in the cities. While Scandinavian and German immigrants had headed for the farmlands so like their native countries, Italian and Irish immigrants largely remained in the urban environment. In the nineteenth century, a high level of anti-Irish bias could be found in American cities. Many jobs that were closed to Irish people went to African-Americans, contributing to the great tension between these groups. On the whole, blacks working in the North were paid far lower wages than similarly skilled whites.

The Freedman's Bureau was established in the South during the Reconstruction years, originally to protect the new rights of the free blacks. Unfortunately, though some of the employees of the bureau were honest, upright men and women with a genuine desire to help, many of them were opportunists who took advantage of the blacks they were supposed to be helping. During the Civil War era, many African-Americans took great strides toward improving conditions for blacks. To read about some of them, see entries on Harriet Tubman, Frederick Douglass, the Colonization Movement, and Sojourner Truth.

Alabama Claims

The financial restitution package demanded by the United States for an array of what were perceived as England's neutrality violations during the war. The term referred to the Confederacy's most successful raiding vessel, an ironclad cruiser built in private British shipyards and launched from Liverpool on a "trial voyage" in February 1862.

Instead of returning to port, however, the CSS *Alabama* was outfitted at the Azores with guns and a state-of-the-art ram sent separately from England. The ship, captained by Raphael Semmes, successfully ran the Federal blockade of Galveston, Texas, and over the next two years wrecked or captured 64 merchant ships across the Atlantic, worth over $6.5 million, until June 1864, when it was sunk itself by the USS *Kearsarge* off the coast of Cherbourg.

The *Alabama* was only one of several ships obtained through similar means that menaced Union boats, requiring a diversion of ships from the blockade and driving insurance rates for Federal vessels up 900 percent. Early in the war, the Lincoln administration put a price on the damage inflicted by eleven British-built ships, along with other indirect costs it attributed to England's illegal activities on the Confederacy's behalf. Secretary of State William H. Seward instructed Charles Francis Adams, minister to Britain, to demand over $19 billion in compensation.

Although the claims were ignored while the war continued, Confederate shipbuilding in Britain was curtailed. To settle the issue, which became an ongoing strain on relations between the two countries, Britain offered some restitution in 1868, but refused to acknowledge responsibility for the *Alabama*. This proposal was refused by the U.S. Congress. Negotiations continued for another three years, stalled by American officials insisting on vastly inflated figures, and were finally resolved by the 1871 Treaty of Washington.

The agreement established a multinational court of arbitration, which ruled that Britain indeed had not adequately maintained its neutrality. The United States was awarded over $15 million in gold, paid by Britain in 1873, but in turn had to pay Britain $2 million for unlawful Union blockade seizures and other improper wartime actions.

The crew aboard the USS Kearsarge *sinks the CSS* Alabama.

Amish in the Civil War, the

The Amish are an Anabaptist separatist sect of mostly German and Dutch origin, who emigrated to the United States beginning in about the 1830s and largely settled in eastern Pennsylvania and the Middle Atlantic region. From the beginning, they were subsistence farmers; then and now, they have always been a people who prefer the uncomplicated, hard-working life they had in Europe. The Industrial Revolution largely left them behind; they do not, even now, believe in modern machines of almost any sort. To be called "simple" by the Amish is a great compliment. To the Amish, a simple person lives without fancy, mechanized things that draw the attention from the everyday pleasures and tasks of life, and take one's mind off contemplation of God.

These peaceful farmers were caught up, as were many other groups, in the destruction and horror of the Civil War. However, they kept to themselves as best they could. When the war came to them, as it did from time to time in the mid-eastern theater of operations, they played no favorites. They looked beyond the color of a uniform or the conformation of a flag, and fed Union and Confederate alike. They did not attempt to strike back when the armies appropriated their horses, wagons, or harvests; they sought no revenge or repayment for destroyed homes or fields. They prayed for both sides and went on with their lives when it was over—for, after all, in their minds, the war was a matter of concern only to the "English," their term for all non-Amish.

Nowadays, curiously enough, to look upon the Amish way of life is to see preserved, in far more lively a fashion than any time capsule could have done, the way our ancestors lived around the time of the Civil War. Still getting about by means of horse and buggy, wearing clothing made only from natural fibers they sew themselves; farming enough to live on with a little left over to sell, making what they need by way of furniture, toys, and farm implements, the Amish are a living heritage and reminder of a time when life was simpler with perhaps more obvious rewards.

Anaconda Plan

Widely ridiculed when it was first revealed, Union General-in-Chief Winfield Scott's 1861 strategy for defeating the South was essentially the approach that ultimately led to the North's victory. The 75-year-old commander had honed the plan by early May and presented it for Lin-

coln's consideration. Recognizing that it would take time to raise and train an army large and strong enough to successfully invade rebel territory, believing that anti-Union sentiment in most of the South was shaky, and wanting to limit the bloodshed if possible, Scott recommended enveloping the Confederacy by blockading its seacoast and gaining control of the Mississippi River with troops and gunboats. The goal was to squeeze the South into suing for peace. Only if that did not work should an army of invasion be sent in.

The general's subordinate, George McClellan, labeled the strategy Scott's "Boa Constrictor Plan"; the Northern press derisively affixed the modified "Anaconda" nickname that stuck. Scott's strategy, it was thought, was far too slow and cautious, altogether going against the popular "On to Richmond!" six-week war sentiment. Some critics suggested Scott's plan was selfishly concocted to avoid bringing war to the general's home state of Virginia. Yet even as the Anaconda Plan was technically rejected, hopes

Controlling the Mississippi with gunboats.

for an instant victory were dashed at Bull Run, while the blockade and Mississippi Valley campaigns were being readied.

Ultimately, although a war of conquest proved necessary, it indeed took that slow stranglehold to sap the Confederacy's strength.

Andersonville Prison

FEBRUARY 1864–APRIL 1865

Officially named Camp Sumter, the most notorious Civil War stockade was hastily constructed in early 1864 near the town of Andersonville in southwest Georgia. The number of Union soldiers held near Richmond had swelled with the breakdown of prisoner exchange agreements, posing a threat to the Con-

federate capital's security and taxing Virginia's already limited resources.

In late February, Federal prisoners began to be transferred to the still-unfinished Georgia facility. By July, Andersonville, built to accommodate up to 10,000 captured soldiers, was jammed with over 32,000, almost all enlisted men. The open-air stockade, enclosed by 20-foot-high log walls, grew to 26 acres, but remained horribly overcrowded and conditions became more and more intolerable. Running in the middle of the camp was a stagnant, befouled stream, absurdly named Sweet Water Branch, used as a sewer as well as for drinking and bathing. There were no barracks; prisoners were forbidden to construct shelters, and while some did erect tents and flimsy lean-tos, most were left fully exposed to the elements. Medical treatment was virtually nonexistent.

With the South barely able to feed its own men, the prisoners, who were supposed to get

Rations issued to Union prisoners at Andersonville.

the same rations as Confederate soldiers, starved—receiving rancid grain and perhaps a few tablespoons a day of mealy beans or peas.

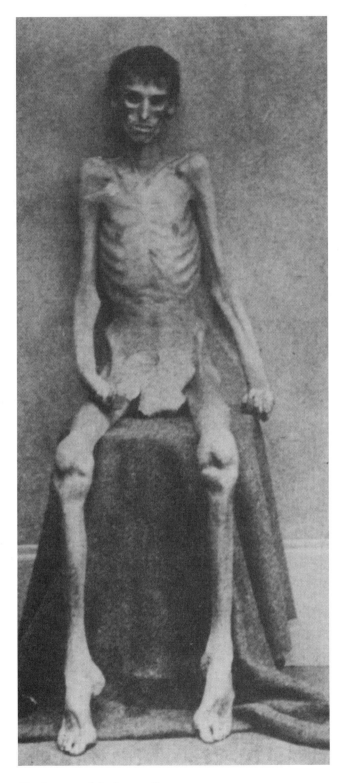

The horrors of Andersonville.

The poor food and sanitation, the lack of shelter and health care, the crowding, and the hot Georgia sun all took their toll in the form of dysentery, scurvy, malaria, and exposure.

During the summer months, more than 100 prisoners died every day. Others fell victim to thieves and marauders among their fellow captives. The desperate situation led a Confederate medical commission to recommend relocating those prisoners who were not too ill to move, and in September 1864, as William T. Sherman's advancing army approached, most of Andersonville's able-bodied inmates were sent to other camps.

Remaining in operation until the end of the war, Andersonville held more captured Union soldiers than any other Confederate camp, a total of more than 45,000, nearly 30 percent of whom died in captivity. The North had learned of the camp's appalling conditions well before the emaciated survivors were released in 1865, and outraged citizens urged retribution on Southern prisoners of war. That was hardly necessary: the Union had its own wretched prison camps, including Elmira, New York, where the death rate approached Andersonville's, even though the North was far better equipped to cope with captured soldiers. Mismanagement and severe shortages were more to blame for the horrors of Andersonville than any deliberate attempt to mistreat prisoners.

Nevertheless, many Northerners insisted that the abuse was deliberate and demanded vengeance. Consequently, after being tried by a U.S. military court and convicted of war crimes, the prison's commander, Captain Henry Wirz, was hanged in November 1865 for "impairing the health and destroying the lives of prisoners." Meanwhile, Clara Barton and other government workers compiled a list of 12,912 prisoners who had died at the camp. Andersonville's mass graves were replaced by a national cemetery, which is today still used as a burial ground for American veterans.

Anderson, Robert

1805–1871

A West Point graduate who was severely wounded while serving with General Winfield Scott in the Mexican War, Anderson commanded Federal troops at Fort Sumter when asked to surrender the garrison to Confederate soldiers on April 14, 1861, marking the official beginning of the Civil War. Although sympathetic to slavery, Anderson was deeply loyal to the Union. For his brave actions at Fort Sumter, Abraham Lincoln promoted him to the rank of brigadier general on May 15, 1861. He took command of the Department of Kentucky and later of the Department of the Cumberland.

He retired in 1863, but returned to Fort Sumter in 1865 after it was recaptured to raise the Union flag before a respectful crowd. Anderson died in Charleston, South Carolina, in 1871.

Andrews' Raid

APRIL 12, 1862

Also known as "The Great Locomotive Chase," one of the legendary escapades of the war. Union spy John J. Andrews, a shadowy figure believed to have formerly been a Russian army officer, led a band of 21 Ohio soldiers into Georgia on the night of April 12, 1862, to sabotage and cut the Western and Atlantic railroad, a vital supply line between Atlanta and Chattanooga.

Disguised as civilian passengers, the raiders boarded a northbound train at Marietta, Georgia. During the breakfast stop, they disconnected the passenger cars and made off with the train's locomotive, *The General*, driving it toward Tennessee, stopping along the way to cut telegraph wires, burn tracks, destroy bridges, and blow up tunnels. The train's extremely perturbed conductor, W.A. Fuller, went in pursuit of his stolen train. He started on foot, then commandeered a handcar and finally another locomotive, collecting armed volunteers to join the chase.

Andrews' gang had little time for their mayhem, and *The General* ran out of fuel after 90 miles. The saboteurs fled into the woods just across the state border but were soon captured. Andrews and seven of his men were hung in Atlanta as spies, but the execution of their comrades was postponed due to an unexpected Union advance. Eight of the surviving raiders escaped in October 1862, and the remainder were released a year later in a prisoner exchange arranged by U.S. Secretary of War Stanton; all became the first soldiers awarded the Medal of Honor.

Antietam, Campaign and Battle of

SEPTEMBER 17, 1862

Determined to build upon the Confederate victory at Second Bull Run, General Robert E. Lee invaded the North through western Maryland, only to lose a decisive battle during the single bloodiest day of the Civil War. Combined Confederate and Union losses totaled more than 27,000 in just 12 hours of battle.

A major turning point in the war, the Union victory gave Abraham Lincoln the confidence to enact the Emancipation Proclamation, thereby changing the war's aims from sustaining the Union to pursuing the more lofty goal of human freedom and increasing Union troops by including black soldiers. In addition to consolidating a series of Confederate wins during the spring and summer (including a victory in Kentucky by Braxton Bragg, which allowed Lee to open a second front in the eastern theater), Lee had many reasons for invading the North at this time: to relieve an exhausted Virginia from further ravages of war, at least temporarily; to attract support and recruits from Maryland, a border state with strong pro-Confederate sentiments; and, perhaps, to win a decisive victory that could force a Union surrender.

Lee's ultimate goal was the capture of the Federal rail center at Harrisburg, Pennsylvania. To reach it, he devised a campaign which he outlined in Special Order No. 191. The campaign called for the division of his Army of Northern Virginia. While Lee moved his troops into Pennsylvania, Major General Thomas J. "Stonewall" Jackson would capture the Union garrison at Harpers Ferry, then join Major General James Longstreet's three divisions, and together they would move forward until they met up with Lee near Harrisburg. Although Union troops far outnumbered the Confederates, Lee's bold plan may have succeeded because Union commander George McClellan, uncertain of both the strength and the whereabouts of Lee's forces, hesitated to move against them.

By a cruel twist of fate, however, a Union corporal made a discovery that changed the course of the campaign and, hence, the course of the entire war. On September 13, he found a copy of Special Order No. 191 wrapped around three cigars in a meadow near a former Confederate camp, which he immediately forwarded to McClellan. Although the general now had his enemy's strategy in his hand, McClellan continued to display his customary caution. Afraid that the document was a trap and that the 40,000 Confederates actually outnumbered his more than 95,000 troops, McClellan refused to take action for over 16 hours.

In the meantime, Lee, who learned within 24 hours that his plans had been conveyed to the enemy, did his best to shore up his three vulnerable flanks: his lone division at South Mountain; two divisions that were with Longstreet a few miles north at Hagerstown; and Jackson's troops, more than 30 miles south heading toward Harpers Ferry. Fighting soon

Felled Confederate soldiers at Antietam.

broke out in several locations, including Fox's Gap, Turner's Gap, and Crampton's Gap, resulting in heavy Confederate losses. On the morning of September 15, Lee was preparing a retreat to Virginia when he learned that Jackson had captured Harpers Ferry, garnering valuable supplies. Instead of retreating, he ordered all of his divisions to converge at the town of Sharpesburg.

Once again hesitating when action was necessary, McClellan allowed this to occur, waiting until the morning of September 17 to attack. The long day of battle began at 6 A.M., with 75,000 Union troops facing Lee's diminished force of just 40,000. Lee's left flank, located in the woods around a 40-acre field, was hit first and hardest. In places with serenely pastoral names such as Dunker Church, the Cornfield and the West Woods, Confederate troops were decimated by wave after wave of Union troops led by Joseph Hooker, Joseph Mansfield, and Edwin V. Sumner. Only when two fresh Confederate divisions joined Jackson's troops was the Federal attack on the left flank halted—in just 20 minutes, more than 2,200 Yankees were wounded or killed in the West Woods—and Sumner forced to retreat. By the middle of the day, the Union turned its attention to crushing the Confederate center, led by Major General Daniel H. Hill, which converged along a sunken lane.

Sumner's remaining two divisions stormed Hill's line for three hours; the battle resulted in so much mayhem the narrow street was forever after known as Bloody Lane. The Confederate center was now broken. Union forces under Ambrose Burnside crossed Antietam Creek to attack Lee's right flank in mid-afternoon. The Confederate army might have been completely destroyed then and there had not A.P. Hill's division arrived from its 30-mile march from Harpers Ferry in time to deliver a crushing counterattack.

Despite heavy Confederate losses, Lee did not retreat immediately, nor did McClellan take the upper hand and crush his enemy. Instead, the two leaders, who watched almost equal numbers of their men fall during the day, allowed their troops to rest for 24 hours. On the evening of September 18, Lee withdrew into Virginia, about a quarter of his troops having been killed or wounded in the action at Antietam.

Appomattox Court House

APRIL 1865

The Virginia site of formal Confederate surrender on April 12, 1865, after General Robert E. Lee's final two-week campaign to win a Southern victory. Confederate troops, numbering just 35,000 and exhausted after trying to break the Union's grip on Petersburg for more than nine months, attacked Union Fort Stedman. This last ditch effort failed, and when the Federals attacked at Five Forks from April 1–2, they forced the Rebels to retreat from the Confederate capital of Richmond, as well as from Petersburg.

Still hoping to make a final stand, Lee attempted to join up with General Joseph E. Johnston's troops at the terminus of the still operational Richmond & Danville Railroad, where they would also receive supplies. Ulysses S. Grant, however, was able to disable the railroad and to converge with the Union army led by Major General William T. Sherman. Lee, now desperate, led his troops toward Lynchburg and much needed rations, but was stopped by Federal troops, who trapped nearly a third of his army at Sayler's Creek. Lee led his remaining troops across Appomattox River before he was stopped by Grant and Major General Philip H. Sheridan's cavalry and infantry.

Overwhelmed, he chose to meet with Grant at the home of Wilmer McLean on April 9, 1865, to discuss terms of surrender. Ironically, McLean had moved his family from Manassas Junction after First Bull Run to escape the conflict.

The site of formal Confederate surrender.

Appomattox Station, Cavalry Fight at

APRIL 8, 1865

In the ongoing attempt to bleed dry the Army of Northern Virginia in the Appomattox Campaign, in the closing days of the war in Virginia, Union General Philip Sheridan sent General G. A. Custer to try and take advantage of unguarded openings in Robert E. Lee's lines, left as a result of fighting the previous day at Farmville, Virginia, a few miles up the Appomattox River. It was Custer's job to keep Lee from reuniting his scattered forces, by moving west and then north of Lee's position and attempting to block him into the neighborhood of the county courthouse. In a wire to Abraham Lincoln, Sheridan said "if the thing is pressed, I think that Lee will surrender." Lincoln then wired Ulysses S. Grant, quoting the cavalryman and adding the injunction: "Let the 'thing' be pressed." As Custer moved in and captured Lee's vitally needed supply trains at Appomattox Station, the Second, Fifth and Sixth Corps of the Union Army maneuvered, with support from the Army of the James, to surround Lee's men. The way to Lynchburg, the only escape route Lee had been able to see, was now blocked; Lee sent a courier to Grant asking to discuss not necessarily surrender terms per se, but simply to ask "the terms of your proposition." That night, with Grant's response in hand, Lee held his final council of war with his commanders, deciding they would attempt one last assault the next morning, which was Palm Sunday—April 9, 1865. That attack was never launched, however, as Lee realized the futility of such a tactic; he instead arranged to surrender his army to Grant at Appomattox Court House.

Arlington National Cemetery

Seized by the Union government after his resignation from the Union army, the family home of Confederate commander Robert E. Lee was later made the site of the United States' most famous cemetery. George Washington Parke Custis, adopted son of the nation's first president, once owned the Virginia property, located across the Potomac from Washington, D.C., and began building an august Greek Revival mansion there in 1802. It became Lee's home in 1831, when the future general married Custis' daughter Mary, who inherited the estate. Taking leave thirty years later when Lee began his military service with the Confederacy, the family never returned.

The Union army quickly seized and occupied the estate, making the mansion headquarters for officers supervising the defense of Washington and the fields campgrounds for their troops. Shortly after the Battle of Gettysburg, the U.S. government officially confiscated the land on the grounds that its owners had not appeared personally to pay a property tax bill of $92.02. A more permanent use for the land was soon conceived.

In the spring of 1864, Union Secretary of War Edwin Stanton assigned quartermaster general Montgomery Meigs to select a location for a new military cemetery, as there was little room left in other Washington-area graveyards. Meigs chose the Custis-Lee estate, finding it altogether fitting that the home of the Confederacy's military leader be made the final resting place for Union soldiers who were killed fighting against him. Ironically, the first soldier buried at Arlington that May was a Confederate—a prisoner who had died in a local hospital—and more than 200 other Southerners would later join the thousands of Northerners interred there. Most of the early plots were situated in Mary Custis Lee's rose garden, including a mass grave for 2,111 unidentified Union dead. Filing suit for their seized home, the Lee family later won a ruling in the U.S. Supreme Court, which declared that the federal government had not legally obtained the property.

In 1883, the U.S. government formally purchased the Arlington estate, paying Lee's son, George Washington Custis Lee, $150,000. Although Arlington is not the country's largest cemetery, more than 200,000 men and women are buried there, including soldiers from every American war as well as various notables, from Justice Oliver Wendell Holmes and boxer Joe Louis to John and Robert Kennedy. It is projected to be completely filled by the year 2020.

Army, Confederate

Because there was so much confusion and destruction in the South during the waning days of the Confederacy and the months following the surrender of the various armies of the South, facts and figures concerning the makeup of the Confederate military organization are often hard to come by. Records showing interesting minute details of the average Confederate soldier either do not exist any longer, or have yet to come to light. We know that by the war's end many of the survivors had enlisted at comparatively younger ages than their Union opponents, or comparatively older ages; the population of the South was considerably smaller than that of the North, and there were fewer men of appropriate battlefield age available to fill in the ranks when death, disease, and wounds thinned out the lines of battle. But we do not have their averages of height, weight, occupation, or level of education. Some fragmentary records show that the officers were generally elected from among middle-class and upper-class men with prior military experience, either from the Old Army of before the war, or from attending the numerous military schools that were always popular in the South. The Confederate soldier was slightly more rural in background than the Yankee; many more of them had been farmers, and fewer of them lived in cities. New Orleans and Baltimore were the only cities in the Old South that even approached the sprawling size of Northern cities like Boston, New York, Philadelphia, and

Cincinnati. On the average, it can be presumed the Confederate soldier in the ranks was slightly less well educated than the Union boys; in the balance, however, there were better riders and marksmen in the ranks of the South than in the North, for these were soldiers who hunted to live, and who rode from an early age.

There were fewer recent immigrants in the Southern army, as well. Most of these men were of Scots/Irish, English, Welsh, African-American, Cherokee, or Hispanic descent, and could point to ancestors who had been in their region since the colonial days and earlier. They had the advantage, right from the start, of familiarity with the ground on which they fought; their cause, too, was perhaps more clearly cut. They were not necessarily fighting to preserve slavery; the majority of Confederate soldiers had never owned a slave in their lives. They were fighting to save their homes and families, fighting for the right of their states to self-government. They were suspicious of the invading Yankees, and truly believed, at least at first, that the Northern folks were evil people who wished to destroy them. They soon learned that there was very little difference between themselves and the average Northerner, however, and there was a great deal of visiting, trading, and chatting between the two armies when they were not shooting at one another. Perhaps the most telling argument concerning the reason a Confederate lad entered the army was uttered when a Northern soldier asked a captured Southerner why he was fighting, only to be told: "Because you're down here!"

The Confederate army had more to lose than the armies of the Union, and over the course of the four-year war most of their fears in that regard were true. Robert E. Lee, in particular, had strict rules and regulations forbidding his soldiers to prey on civilians when in Union territory. Union soldiers in battle and sometimes while merely encamped, did great damage to the South. They burned private homes, destroyed fields and forests, and set fire to courthouses with their irreplaceable records—all in

Robert E. Lee's soldiers in Virginia, 1864.

The Ninth Mississippi before Shiloh.

the name of punishing Southerners, who they believed to be traitors. When the war was over, many a Confederate came home to find his family destitute, their home gone, their farms all but unusable. It was hard to claim one's land anew when the records of tax surveys were gone, and the Confederate currency had been so devalued by inflation during the war that the majority of Confederate citizens were hard-pressed to rebuild.

Confederate soldiers, often outnumbered by their Union counterparts, fought with great determination. They were very often barefoot, wearing threadbare uniforms and subsisting on hardtack, unbolted cornmeal, and water. The Army of Tennessee, the Army of the Carolinas, the Army of Georgia all made valiant contributions to the Confederate cause, but, perhaps because of the fame of their commander, the peerless Robert E. Lee, the Confederate army most people remember best is the Army of Northern Virginia. More books and articles have been written about this army than about perhaps anything else in Confederate history.

Army, Union

The Union Army, according to the best estimates based on careful review of figures from

1861 to 1865, consisted of approximately two million, two hundred thousand men, ranging in age from roughly 18 to 46, the average age being in the mid-twenties. Statistics have been compiled which give an interesting picture of the common Union soldier. The majority of them had never been in military service before, and most of them had been farmers before the war broke out. Their average height was around five foot eight; the average weight was just under 145 pounds. Slightly over three-quarters of the boys in blue had been born in America, and were mostly volunteers; the drafts held at various times during the war only added about six percent to the total force in the field.

Their reasons for fighting were almost as varied as the soldiers themselves. Some enlisted to free the slaves, while others joined up because their friends went, or in pursuit of excitement. Many of them became soldiers because they felt the Union had to be preserved, and that it was their duty to bring that about. And some, in common with young men of all times and places, went because it was the right thing to do—or out of fear of being labeled a coward for staying home.

Meticulously equipped and poorly trained, they were at first at a great disadvantage on the field of battle. They were, after all, the invaders; they did not know the territory into which they were marching. They headed south believing in their cause, but knowing that the rumor mill gave most of the points to the Confederates: it was widely believed that the South had better commanders at all levels, better cavalry, and better training. Some of this was actually true, and when battlefield experience backed up rumors, the game of war lost a great deal of its glamour.

Their leaders eventually figured out what they were doing, or were dismissed for lack of results; after a virtual parade of failures or might-have-beens in command of their armies, the remaining generals were some of the best soldiers the North had left: Philip Sheridan, John Buford, Winfield Scott Hancock, George Henry Thomas, William Tecumseh Sherman, and Ulysses S. Grant. Under these men and numerous talented others, backed by a seemingly endless supply line and a greater population from which to draw more soldiers when death thinned the ranks, the men of the Union army finally prevailed over the ill-equipped and depleted Southern armies.

In campaigns such as Gettysburg, Fredericksburg, Atlanta, Vicksburg, the Seven Days, the Peninsula, and many more, the Union soldier learned his lessons and sought every weak point he could in Confederate defenses. The many armies under the banner of the Union were named after major rivers in their area of operation: the Army of the James, which fought in southern Virginia and North Carolina; the Army of the Tennessee, not to be confused with the Confederate Army of Tennessee (the state), which besieged Vicksburg and fought Albert Johnston in Tennessee and Kentucky; the Army of the Mississippi, the Ohio, and of the Cumberland. Perhaps the best known of the Union Armies, however, was the Army of the Potomac,

The New York 7th Regiment, leaving for the front.

Federal troops waiting for battle.

led by several prominent generals, of whom Grant was ultimately the most effective. A less well known fact is that army names, or nomenclature, could be decidedly confusing; the Army of the Potomac began the war as the Army of Virginia, which was exactly the same name as the army the Federals met when they invaded the South! The Union changed its army to Potomac—and the Confederates changed theirs to the Army of Northern Virginia.

Artillery

All firearms larger than small arms are known as artillery or cannon. Although there were dozens of different types of cannon used during the Civil War, they all fell into one of two categories: smoothbore or rifled cannon. They were further designated by the weight of their projectile (12-pounder, 24-pounder, 32-pounder, etc.), the caliber or size of their bore diameter (3-inch, 8-inch, 10-inch), method of loading (breech or muzzle), and often their inventor or the factory in which they were made (i.e., Columbiad, Dahlgren, Napoleon, Rodman, Parrott, Whitworth). A further distinction involved the path of their trajectories: guns had a flat trajectory, mortars a high, arching path, and a howitzer a trajectory between the other two. Civil War artillery was also classified according to its tactical deployment, including field, seacoast, and siege artillery. Cannon were made of steel, bronze, or iron, depending on the availability of material.

The basic artillery piece in both the Union

and the Confederacy was the Napoleon, a smoothbore, muzzle-loading, 12-pounder howitzer. Developed under the auspices of Louis Napoleon of France, it first appeared in the United States in 1856. Relatively light and portable, the Napoleon was used as both an offensive and defensive weapon by both armies. Initially made of bronze, Napoleons were cast from iron when the South ran short of the other metal. Its maximum range was between 800 and 1,000 yards, but it was most effective at about 250 yards or less. The Napoleon shot both grape shot and canister (see below), and probably inflicted more casualties than all other artillery pieces combined.

The second most popular artillery were the 3-inch ordnance and Parrott guns. These rifled cannon were more accurate and had a longer range—up to about 2,500 yards—than their smoothbore counterparts. During most battles, however, the longer range was unnecessary and ineffective: during this period, a gunner had to see his target in order to shoot with any accuracy, and the shorter range Napoleons were adequate for that purpose.

However, rifled cannon were particularly effective in knocking down fortifications and played decisive roles at Vicksburg and Atlanta. Almost all Civil War cannon were muzzle-loading; breech-loading models, such as the British 12-pounder rifled Armstrong and Whitworth cannon, were generally unreliable and awkward. The 6- and 12-pound mountain howitzers were among the smallest and most portable artillery; they were essential for battles fought in the mountainous regions of the

A Confederate gun emplacement in James River, Virginia.

Western theater. Naval and siege cannons, including Dahlgrens and Rodman Smoothbores, were among the heaviest and most powerful. The 8- and 10-inch siege howitzers had ranges of over 2,000 yards and could fire 45- and 90-pound shells. Artillery ammunition included solid shot, grape, canister, shell, and chain shot, each of which came in any of the nine common artillery calibers. Solid shot and shell were used against long-range, fixed targets such as fortifications; chain shot, consisting of two balls connected by a chain, was used primarily against masts and rigging of ships.

The most often used field ammunition were grape shot and canister, both of which were scattershot projectiles consisting of several iron balls contained within an iron casement. When fired, the casement disintegrated, releasing the shot in a spray. In effect, then, a gun loaded with grape shot or canister acted like a large, sawed-off shotgun; it was particularly lethal when fired at a range of 250 yards or less. Thanks to its superior industrial strength, the North had an overall advantage over the South in all types of artillery, as well as a higher percentage of rifled cannon to smoothbore cannon.

Atlanta, Campaign and Siege

MAY 1–SEPTEMBER 2, 1864

For four months in the summer of 1864, outnumbered and out-supplied Confederate troops fought hard—but finally failed—to keep their supply lines open and the Union from capturing Atlanta, Georgia. Ultimately a decisive Union victory, the Atlanta campaign resulted in an equal number of casualties—about 30,000—on each side.

Driven from Tennessee during the Chattanooga Campaign, 62,000 Confederates now under Joseph E. Johnston amassed at Dalton, Georgia. Facing them were approximately 100,000 Federal troops, led by Major General William T. Sherman. While Ulysses S. Grant's drive for Richmond and Petersburg continued

in the east, Sherman's objective in the west was clear: to cut all rail lines leading to and from Atlanta and, finally, to take the city itself. Known as the "Gate City of the South," Atlanta was the Confederacy's second most important manufacturing and communications center. Johnston, knowing that his forces were not strong enough to defeat Sherman outright, tried instead to keep him from reaching Atlanta for as long as possible—hopefully until after the November election. Without a convincing victory at either Richmond or Atlanta, the war-weary North might deny Abraham Lincoln's reelection, thereby giving the Confederacy a chance to negotiate with a more sympathetic Union president. Unfortunately for the Confederate cause, Johnston's plan was ultimately rejected.

At the beginning of May, however, Johnston remained in command of forces securely entrenched along Rocky Face Ridge, a sheer rock wall surrounding a canyon through which both the highway and the railroad to Chattanooga passed. The ridge's lower six miles formed the east wall of the Snake Creek Gap, where one of the first skirmishes between Union Major General James B. McPherson's division and Johnston's troops fought. McPherson was forced to fall back, allowing the Confederates to retreat further south. Sherman pursued and another battle occurred at Resaca from May 14–15. For more than five weeks of often vicious fighting at places such as New Hope Church, Mount Zion Church, Picketts' Mill, and Pine Mountain (where Confederate Lieutenant General Leonidas Polk was killed), Johnston was forced to drop down to Kennesaw Mountain. Setting up defensive positions along the mountain's steep, rocky slopes, he was able to repulse Sherman's frontal assault on June 27. Confederate rifle and cannon fire felled more than 2,000 Union men, compared with just 500 Confederate losses.

Nevertheless, by July 4, Johnston had been pushed down to within seven miles of Atlanta. When he withdrew south of the Chattahoochee River, removing the last natural barrier between Sherman and Atlanta, Confederate president Jefferson Davis—anxious for more decisive and aggressive action—replaced Johnston with Major General John B. Hood. Hood quickly delivered the action Davis wanted. Using a plan devised by Johnston, Hood saw an opportunity to strike Sherman's army, which had been divided at Peachtree Creek, on July 20. Although the Confederate infantry troops fought valiantly, the attack ultimately failed, 4,800 Rebels were lost, and Hood retreated to Atlanta.

Thinking that Hood was abandoning the city altogether, Sherman sent McPherson to the south and east of Atlanta in pursuit. Hoping to surprise McPherson, William Hardee's infantry division launched the ill-fated Battle of Atlanta on July 22, losing more than 8,500 men. At 3,700 casualties, the Union experienced a lighter loss, but the respected and able James

McPherson was killed there. Sherman continued his advance by sending McPherson's replacement, Major General Oliver Howard, around the western side of Atlanta to cut off Hood's communications line to the south. Hood launched a third attack at Ezra Church on July 28. Able to protect the railroad, Hood nonetheless lost another 2,500 men. The Confederate army, depleted to less than 45,000, fell back behind Atlanta's formidable defensive lines and waited for Sherman to attack. Sherman instead laid seige. Bringing up heavy Federal artillery, he began a bombardment that would last for more than a month while, at the same time, he attempted to completely seal off the city's supply lines. Thanks in large part to

Ripping tracks in preparation for the evacuation of Atlanta.

the skill of Confederate cavalry commander Joseph E. Wheeler, the Rebels were able to keep the Union from crushing their supply route until the end of August.

On August 28, however, Sherman struck at the Montgomery & Atlanta Railroad south of the city; desperate to keep this vital rail line open, Hood attacked the Union flank at Jonesborough. His loss there decided the outcome of the long siege of Atlanta. The Confederates evacuated the city on September 2; the next day Federal troops marched in. Once a grand manufacturing city, Atlanta lay in ruins, decimated not only by Union shelling, but by the retreating Confederates, who set tremendous fires and looted the city's remaining stores and supplies, preferring to destroy Atlanta's resources rather than see them fall into enemy hands.

B

Baltimore Riot

APRIL 19, 1861

A clash between pro-South civilians and Union troops in Maryland's largest city resulted in what is commonly accepted to be the first bloodshed of the Civil War. Secessionist sympathy was strong in Baltimore, a border state metropolis.

Before his inauguration, rumors in the city of an assassination plot against Abraham Lincoln, who was on his way to Washington, D.C., forced the president-elect to sneak through Baltimore in the middle of the night. Anti-Union sentiments there only increased once the hostilities commenced at Fort Sumter on April 12. A week later, one of the first regiments to respond to Lincoln's call for troops arrived in Baltimore by train, en route to the capital. Because the rail line did not pass through the city, horse-drawn cars had to take the Massachusetts infantrymen from one end of Baltimore to the other. An angry crowd of secessionists tried to keep the regiment from reaching Washington, blocking several of the transports, breaking windows, and, finally, forcing the soldiers to get out and march through the streets. The throng followed in close pursuit. What had now become a mob surrounded and jeered the regiment, then started throwing bricks and stones.

Panicking, several soldiers fired randomly into the crowd, and mayhem ensued as the regiment scrambled to the railroad station. The police managed to hold the crowd back at the terminal, allowing the infantrymen to board their train and escape, leaving behind much of their equipment as well as their marching band. Four soldiers and twelve civilians were killed, and scores were injured. Maryland officials demanded that no more Federal troops be sent through the state, while Baltimore's mayor and police chief authorized the destruction of key rail bridges to prevent Union troops from entering the city. Secessionist groups, meanwhile, tore down telegraph wires to Washington, temporarily cutting the capital off from the rest of the nation. The North was outraged; *New York Tribune* editor Horace Greeley even called for Baltimore to be burned to the ground.

On May 13, Federal troops, including members of the Massachusetts regiment attacked in the previous month's riot, occupied the city and martial law was declared, squelching most subsequent pro-Confederate activities. The police chief, several commissioners, and a number of citizens were arrested for their alleged participation in the riot, and suspected secessionists, including Francis Scott Key's grandson and a number of state legislators, were held without charges. Federal forces continued to maintain an occupying presence in Baltimore for the remainder of the war.

Union troops under attack by angry citizens of Baltimore.

Banks, Nathaniel Sarttle Prentiss

1816–1894

It seemed to have been the fate of Major-General Nathaniel S. P. Banks to step into the shoes of other men whose fame has overshadowed his own. Born into a middle-class mill-town family in Waltham, Massachusetts, Banks was required to leave school at a young age and work in his father's cotton mill; not deterred by this, Banks became a self-educated man, teaching himself Latin and sharpening a talent for public speaking. He also taught himself Spanish, and is probably the first American to state that such a skill would someday be important, given the proximity of the United States to countries whose people spoke that language. By the time he was approaching his fortieth year, Banks had been a member of the Massachusetts state legislature for five years under five different party affiliations. He was an ardent Free-Soiler who opposed the repeal of the Missouri Compromise and proclaimed to be a firm opponent of slavery. On the strength of this stand he moved into the Congress of the United States, and in 1856 declined nomination to the office of president. The following year, he successfully ran for governor of his home state—one of the first candidates in the Commonwealth's history to actually travel through the state campaigning on his own, a strategy which enobled him to defeat a long-term incumbent.

By the outbreak of the war, Banks had retired from his gubernatorial term. He was living in Chicago, where he had succeeded George B. McClellan as president of the Illinois Central Railroad. He immediately volunteered for service himself and was commissioned a Major-General of volunteers. Assigned to the department of Annapolis, Banks played a crucial role in preventing the Maryland legislature from voting in favor of secession; he was then transferred to the Shenandoah Valley in the aftermath of the disastrous defeat of Union forces at Manassas (First Bull Run) on July 21, 1861, where he replaced the incompetent General Robert Patterson as commander of that department. Banks did not fare much better there, however, as a haphazard approach to reassignment of troops left him with an inadequate number of men to defend the pivotal valley town of Front Royal. Outnumbered two to one and facing the seemingly indomitable Stonewall Jackson, Banks lost Front Royal to the Confederates on May 23, 1862, and could see but one course open to him: immediate withdrawal and retreat. He fled before Jackson's superior forces in a running battle all the way to Winchester, Virginia, and with the Confederates on his heels Banks forced a crossing of the Potomac at Harpers Ferry. Upwards of three thousand of his men were taken prisoner, and he lost more than two hundred more in casualties, depleting his undermanned force to under seven thousand soldiers.

Smarting under the embarrassing defeat, Banks got a chance to avenge his honor less than three months later when, assigned to Union General John Pope in the Army of Virginia, he was ordered to attack the enemy at Cedar Mountain the moment the Confederates made any move whatsoever. On August 9, 1862, the Confederates moved—and Banks' men attacked with such violence that two divisions of Stonewall Jackson's left flank were driven from their superior position before the reserve under A.P. Hill could be brought up. Unfortunately two of Banks' commanders were wounded in action, leaving their regiments leaderless. Banks' personal command of the art of tactics was somewhat lacking; he was unable to make good on the initial success of his attack, and when the Federals were forced to retreat during Hill's counter-attack, Pope denied he had ever ordered Banks to attack in the first place. The Joint Committee on the Conduct of

the War looked into the matter and exonerated Banks, passing the blame back where it belonged, as the report said, "Of course, the order should not have been given."

Banks was briefly transferred to command of the defenses of Washington, D.C., before being detailed to succeed General Benjamin Butler as commander of the Department of New Orleans, where Butler had proven disastrously unpopular. Making do with the little he had—less than twenty thousand men effectively ready for offensive maneuvers—Banks gained creditable success in aiding General U.S. Grant in the task of reopening the Mississippi River. In late May 1863, during the attempt to take Port Hudson, Banks put black troops into the action by virtue of what he called their "utmost daring and determination." Laying seige to Port Hudson, Banks and his men endured a month and more of bombardment and a gallant but unsuccessful attempt to storm the garrison on June 13. Less than a week after Grant's victory at Vicksburg, on July 9, 1863, Banks forced the unconditional surrender of Port Hudson at last, removing "the last obstruction to the free navigation of the Mississippi River."

The remainder of 1863 was not good to Banks. Slow and difficult military advances, coupled with problems with the civilian population of his department, gave him all manner of trials; possibly in part due to the unpopularity of the previous commander, there was even an attempt on Banks' life. He tried instituting voting reforms in Louisiana and set up an alternative government for the state. Then early in 1864, Banks was called upon to assist General Grant in his Red River Expedition—which proved to be an unmitigated disaster, for which Grant attempted to blame Banks. With the government in Washington eager to see some substantive advances in Texas and Louisiana, Grant, Banks, and Admiral David Dixon Porter were ordered to make assaults upon Shreveport. Nearing his objective, Banks encountered stiff Confederate resistance at Sabine Crossroads on April 8, 1864, and was routed. The next day there was a vicious fight at Pleasant Hill, which ended in a bloody draw. With no supplies of food, water, or ammunition forthcoming,

Banks was forced to withdraw; in addition, Admiral Porter's fleet was almost left marooned when the Red River suddenly and uncharacteristically receded from its usual April floodstage. They were barely rescued in time by an inspired piece of engineering, in which a swiftly constructed series of dams enabled the ships to float free of the shallows. Grant suddenly withdrew nearly half of Banks' effective fighting force for service elsewhere in the campaign, and on May 13, Banks was forced to give up Alexandria, Louisiana. Peremptorily replaced by the arrival of General E. S. Canby, Banks would later be blamed for the failure of the expedition by a majority opinion of the Joint Committee, with only one member attempting to point out Banks could not possibly have foreseen the Red River's natural, if disastrously timed, behavior. Subsequent appraisal of the situation, however, is more likely to blame the fact that none of the commanders involved in the expedition "had the right to give an order to another," thus making communication between them difficult and pointless.

Banks was honorably mustered out of service several months after the final surrender of the Confederate armies, and resumed a life of political service. He was elected to complete the unexpired term of Republican Congressman D. W. Gooch—the member of the Joint Committee who had sought to defend him—when Gooch passed away, and Banks remained in the House of Representatives from the Thirty-ninth through Forty-second Congresses. Before the end of his final congressional term Banks became seriously ill, and returned to Waltham, Massachusetts, where he died in 1894.

Barton, Clara

1821–1912

This nurse's romanticized reputation as the "Angel of the Battlefield" did not altogether fit the diminutive but dogged future founder of the American Red Cross or her grueling, decidedly unglamorous Civil War service. A former Massachusetts schoolteacher with no formal nursing training, Barton was working in Washington D.C. as a U.S. Patent Office clerk at the outbreak of the conflict. In Washington, she saw some of the war's earliest casualties and observed first-hand the poor medical treatment they received and their lack of proper food and clothing. Beginning an independent effort to procure medicine and other necessary items for Union troops and to lobby her friends in Congress for improved military health standards, Barton remained unaffiliated with either the army or other soldier's relief organizations, such as the Sanitary Commission.

She began taking her one-woman campaign directly to the troops in July 1862, after she obtained approval from the U.S. Surgeon General to travel with her wagonloads of supplies to the

Clara Barton

front lines and field hospitals. Barton appeared in time for—or in the immediate aftermath of—such battles as Cedar Creek, Second Bull Run, Antietam, and Fredericksburg, preparing meals, distributing goods, nursing the wounded and dying, assisting army surgeons, and occasionally performing emergency medical procedures herself.

At Chantilly, she was almost captured when she stayed behind ministering to the casualties, and at Antietam, she was so close to the actual fighting that a Confederate bullet pierced her sleeve and killed the soldier she was tending. Barton also served in the Carolinas, where she possibly had an affair with a married army officer, and returned to Virginia during Ulysses S. Grant's 1864 offensives, receiving an official position with Benjamin Butler's Army of the James.

Near the end of the war, Abraham Lincoln assigned her the monumental task of overseeing the search for missing and captured Union soldiers, compiling lists of the sick and wounded, and identifying those buried in mass graves at sites such as Andersonville Prison. The project took Barton four years to complete, after which she traveled to Europe for an extended vacation. Resting little, she instead became active in the International Red Cross, and upon her return to the United States overcame the reluctance of isolationist politicians to establish the American branch, serving as its first president from 1882 to 1904.

Beauregard, Pierre Gustave Toutant

1818–1893

A poor relationship with Jefferson Davis kept P.G.T. Beauregard, one of the Confederacy's first war heroes, from receiving the top commands his talents and victories merited. The natty Creole general from Louisiana, an exuberant man with a hot temper, graduated second in his class at West Point, supervised dredging the mouth of the Mississippi River as the army's

chief engineer in New Orleans, and ran unsuccessfully for mayor of the city. Appointed superintendent of the U.S. Military Academy in January 1861, Beauregard was dismissed within five days for his vocal pro-secessionist stance.

He soon entered the Confederate army and was assigned to demand the surrender of Fort Sumter in Charleston Harbor from his former West Point artillery instructor, Robert Anderson. Igniting the Civil War with his bombardment and almost bloodless capture of the Union-held citadel in April, Beauregard was idolized throughout the South. Three months later, he commanded infantry forces in Virginia, and though technically outranked by Joseph Johnston, devised much of the Confederate strategy for the First Battle of Bull Run. An elaborate offensive he modeled on Napoleon's Austerlitz campaign did not come off, but a far simpler counterassault routed the Federals and won the South a stunning victory in the war's first major engagement.

Clashing with Jefferson Davis for not proceeding on to attack Washington, he was dispatched from Virginia to serve under Albert Sidney Johnston in the Western theater. In April 1862, Beauregard, despite some misgivings, coordinated the advance on Union forces stationed at Pittsburgh Landing, Tennessee, and took over command in the ensuing Battle of Shiloh when Johnston was killed during the first day's fighting. Prematurely telegraphing Richmond of his imminent victory, he was forced to retreat to Corinth, Mississippi, the following day. One month later, Beauregard evacuated Corinth, strategically avoiding a disastrous confrontation with a far larger oncoming Union force. Davis, however, saw it as a grave setback and, when Beauregard went on sick leave, replaced him with Braxton Bragg. Returning to Charleston to head the defense of the Atlantic coast, Beauregard successfully repulsed numerous Union land and sea assaults on the port city for the next year and a half.

He was sent back to Virginia in the spring of 1864, where he stymied two critical Federal offensives: he halted a Union advance on Richmond in May when he cornered Benjamin Butler's army on the Bermuda Hundred penin-

Beauregard, before the Battle of Pittsburgh Landing: "I will water my horse in the Tennessee River or in Hell before night."

sula; and held off Northern attacks on Petersburg the following month with a minuscule 2,500-man force until Robert E. Lee arrived to reinforce the vital rail center. His contributions still not properly recognized, Beauregard was assigned a vague administrative post in the West that fall, but was again called on to serve as Joe Johnston's second-in-command in the hopeless attempt to halt William T. Sherman's 1865 march through the Carolinas.

After the war, Beauregard, who had also designed the Confederacy's famed "Southern Cross" battle flag, declined military commissions from Romania and Egypt, and returned to New Orleans, where he took up the railroad business and ran the Louisiana state lottery.

Benjamin, Judah Philip

1811–1884

Member of the Confederate cabinet, Benjamin was one of the most prominent Jewish-American statesmen of the nineteenth century. Born in St. Croix to British parents and raised in South Carolina, he went to Yale at age 14. He became a successful New Orleans attorney and slaveholding plantation owner before being elected to the U.S. Senate in 1852.

During the secession crisis of 1860–61, Benjamin was a conservative "cooperationist," believing the South should resort to leaving the Union only if the Lincoln administration attempted a direct assault on Southern rights. Nevertheless, when Louisiana seceded, he resigned from the Senate and became a loyal Confederate, especially devoted to his good friend Jefferson Davis, who appointed him attorney general of the provisional government.

That position gave Benjamin little to do, since the Confederacy had few federal courts, and Davis soon named him secretary of war. The Confederate president, who himself had been a superb war secretary during the Polk administration, made many of the important decisions for the department, leaving Benjamin largely to execute Davis' policies and defend the president's actions. Nevertheless, Benjamin became a controversial figure, mistrusted by many Southerners because of his religion and disliked because of his summary treatment of Confederate war heroes.

In one incident, Benjamin breached military protocol by issuing orders that Stonewall Jackson considered intrusive and disrespectful. It nearly caused the resignation of one of the South's most capable and beloved generals. Finally, blamed for the fall of key ports in North Carolina, the war secretary was forced to resign in March 1862. Davis, however, in a politically risky move, promptly appointed him secretary of state, a position he held until the South's surrender. Despite Benjamin's unpopularity, Davis supported his brilliant cabinet officer. Acknowledged even by his enemies as "the brains of the Confederacy," Benjamin was a tireless worker and effective administrator. As head of the State Department, he secured much-needed foreign loans, although he remained unable to obtain formal recognition of the Confederate nation by European governments.

In December, 1864, with the South's military fortunes waning, he tried to sound out England and France, through his fellow Louisianan, Congressman Duncan Kenner, as to whether a Confederate program of gradual emancipation of the slaves might change their minds. Failing in that, Benjamin became involved in futile peace negotiations with the Union.

Although Benjamin was perhaps the only high government official besides Davis who remained unconvinced even after the fall of Richmond that the Confederacy was doomed, he still managed to escape the country before arrest. He fled to the Bahamas in May 1865 and finally settled in England, where he resumed his law practice, becoming a distinguished member of the British bar and publishing several classic legal treatises.

Judah Benjamin

Bickerdyke, Mary Ann "Mother"

1817–1901

The beloved Sanitary Commission field agent served in 19 battles, often right on the front, throughout the entire four years of the Civil War. In 1861, the 44-year-old Illinois Quaker widow, a large, strong, unrefined yet nurturing and resourceful woman, was selected by her neighbors to deliver their donated food and medical supplies to the filthy and disease-plagued Union army hospital in Cairo, Illinois. She stayed to work at the hospital, then traveled with troops in the Western theater, assisting in amputations and medical procedures, running the kitchens, supervising the laundry, and executing legendary cleanups of squalid camps, habitually seeing first to the needs of the enlisted men, who affectionately called her "Mother" Bickerdyke.

Assigned first to the field hospital at Fort Donelson, Tennessee, she went on to work on Mississippi River warships and with Ulysses S. Grant's army during his Vicksburg campaign. Though she frequently defied regulations and vexed bureaucratic officers, she apparently was as admired by Union commanding generals as

Mary Ann "Mother" Bickerdyke

she was by the soldiers. William Tecumseh Sherman specifically requested Bickerdyke's services, which she performed throughout his Atlanta Campaign; she was the only woman the general allowed in his battlefield hospitals.

In recognition of her contribution to Sherman's army, Mother Bickerdyke was asked to ride at the head of her corps in Washington, D.C.'s, celebratory May 1865 Grand Review of the Armies. After the war, she continued to aid enlisted men, working as a pension attorney to help them obtain their veterans benefits, while she herself did not begin receiving a pension until 1886.

Black Codes

1865–1866

These laws, passed by Democratic Southern state governments during the first year of Reconstruction were designed to control and regulate the political, social, and economic lives of newly freed slaves in the South. The type and severity of the codes varied from state to state, but they generally restricted blacks' rights to buy, own, and sell property; to make legally binding contracts, including marriages; to serve on juries; to own weapons; and to vote or run for political office. Special employment regulations were also enacted that restricted blacks from certain professions, enforced apprenticeship prerequisites, and demanded that blacks prove steady employment.

The black codes also required blacks to carry travel passes and proof of residence, and denied them the right to free assembly. From 1866 to 1877, Radical Republicans instituted a broader Reconstruction plan than the one attempted by Johnson. For nearly 10 years, Southern state governments were run by Republican governors, appointed by the Republican-led Northern Congress, who immediately struck down the black codes. During this period, Southern blacks enjoyed suffrage and other legal rights for the first time.

Black Soldiers, Confederate

In desperate need of fresh troops to bolster its severely depleted army, the Confederate Congress reluctantly passed an act to enlist blacks as soldiers on March 14, 1865. By the time Southern states organized recruitment, however, the war was over. During the war, the Confederate army used slaves as servants and laborers, but never enlisted them as combat troops. Jefferson Davis, an early advocate of using black soldiers, met with fierce resistance from most of his fellow Confederates.

Opponents believed that arming slaves was the first step toward emancipation, a concept they felt was anathema to the Southern cause, one that destroyed the basis for the war and for the Confederacy itself. Only when faced with almost certain defeat during the fall of 1864 and the winter of 1865 did Southerners agree, and then only after the urging of General Robert E. Lee. Although most blacks supported the Union and escaped to the North whenever possible, some were willing to fight with the Rebels. Because the war ended on April 9, 1865, however, no blacks ever officially fought with the Confederate army.

Punishment for breaking laws designed to restrict the rights of newly freed slaves.

Soon after Reconstruction ended and Southerners were once again allowed to assume power, racist laws and customs similar to the black codes, known as "Jim Crow" laws after a popular minstrel song, were enacted and carried out, making segregation a way of life in the South. It was not until the 1954 Supreme Court decision of *Brown* v. *Board of Education*, Topeka, Kansas, that any legal action to address systematic discrimination against blacks was taken.

Black Soldiers, Union

By war's end, nearly 180,000 blacks had served in the Union army. Of that number, about 37,300 lost their lives for the Union cause. Although not officially allowed to enlist until the Emancipation Proclamation of 1863, blacks aided the Union cause almost from the very beginning of the war. The first black troop in United States history—Benjamin I. Butler's 1861 Louisiana Native Guards—consisted largely of fugitive slaves who worked as laborers. Before enlistment was allowed, blacks were considered "contraband" by the conquering Federal troops—property to be looted like other supplies and material. Contrabands were used to help build roads and forts, harvest crops, and

Northern depiction of a plantation owner sending his son off to war, rather than a slave who knows how to work the fields.

perform other camp chores, but were not allowed to carry weapons. Urged by some to use blacks in combat, Lincoln resisted, fearing that the border states would rebel because eventual emancipation was implicit in such an action. It was not until the Union victory at Antietam that Lincoln felt he could risk including blacks in the armed services.

Following the issuance of the Emancipation Proclamation, large numbers of black soldiers were recruited, largely from occupied areas of the South. Although some states organized a few black regiments of their own, the organization of blacks in the military was largely undertaken by the Bureau for Colored Troops, an agency of the Federal government. Blacks served in segregated units commanded by white officers. For more than a year, they were paid only about half of what white soldiers earned: the Militia Act of 1863 provided that blacks would be paid $10 per month, out of which $3 would be deducted for clothing. White privates, on the other hand, received $13 per month plus a clothing allowance of $3.50.

Many black troops demonstrated against such discrimination; some, like the 54th Massachusetts Regiment, refusing to accept any pay at all rather than submit to this indignity, and others, such as the 55th and the 3rd Carolina Volunteeers, threatened to mutiny. One black soldier in the 55th who refused to obey orders if he was not paid his due was courtmartialed and executed. More than 20 men of the 14th Rhode Island Heavy Artillery were thrown in jail.

Pressured by public opinion and encouraged by many white officers of these black troops, Congress enacted equal pay legislation in June

Union recruitment poster.

1864. Black troops suffered about 35 percent more losses than their white counterparts partly because some Confederate commanders refused to take black prisoners. Because they were refused the same clothing allowance as whites, they suffered from a disease rate more than double that of whites.

Black troops were involved in several important battles, the first being at Island Mounds, Missouri, in October 1862. Black troops were used for the first time in a general engagement during the assault on Port Hudson, Louisiana, in May 1863. The bravery displayed by black troops who fought hand-to-hand combat at Milliken's Bend, Louisiana, on June 7, 1863, impressed even the most stubborn segregationists. Nevertheless, few blacks were made officers—fewer than 100 out of 180,000 enlisted men—and no black attained a rank higher than captain. Of all the soldiers who bravely fought for the Union cause, just 23 soldiers and four sailors received Congressional Medals of Honor, though they were forced to wait almost 40 years to receive them. The most famous black regiment was the 54th Massachusetts, led by white Colonel Robert Gould Shaw.

A group of teamsters in Virginia, 1864.

Blockade

More than the brutal war of attrition fought on land, it may have been the Union blockade of Southern ports that won the war for the North. Before the war began, more than 6,000 ships traded through Southern ports; in the first year of the war, only 800 vessels were able to evade the Federal blockade, a number that only decreased during the course of the conflict. The resulting profound lack of supplies—everything from coffee, salt, and other essential foodstuffs to steel, copper, and small arms—demoralized the Confederate citizenry and weakened its armed forces. The loss of income from the cot-

ton trade was also devastating: in 1861, Southern cotton exports exceeded $190 million; by 1862, cotton earned the South just $4 million.

The USS *Sabine* was the first Union ship to blockade a Southern port when it closed off Pensacola, Florida, on April 13, 1861, the same day Fort Sumter fell. Four days later, President Abraham Lincoln officially established the blockade—the largest ever attempted by any nation—by announcing that any vessel leaving or entering Southern ports would be captured or confiscated. At first, the Confederacy welcomed the blockade, believing that Europe would intervene in order to protect its supply of Southern cotton.

Even before the blockade had a chance to be-

A blockade endangered the work of supply boats, which shipped crucial resources to both sides.

come effective, the South refused to export cotton in hopes of provoking a pro-Confederate response from Great Britain and France. What the South failed to consider, however, was the current surplus of cotton on the world market; Europe had no need to upset its diplomatic neutrality for a plentiful commodity. In essence, the South's ploy did nothing but give the Union a chance to organize the blockade. When Lincoln first announced the blockade, the size of the Federal navy was very small: it had just three ships in port and ready to sail.

After repairing and refurbishing damaged ships and purchasing others from Europe, the navy had expanded its fleet to include 140 ships within about six months. The Northern fleet comprised almost anything seaworthy that was large enough to carry a gun, including whalers, excursion steamers, and even tugs. After the first year of war, the only ports left in Southern hands were at Wilmington, North Carolina, Mobile, Alabama, New Orleans, Louisiana, and Galveston, Texas.

One by one, those were also taken in the months that followed; their most important port, New Orleans, was captured in April 1862 by Captain David G. Farragut. The last port to fall was Fort Fisher, near Wilmington, North Carolina, in January 1865. By the end of the war, more than 600 Union ships, including two dozen 500-ton steam-powered gun boats designed specifically to run down the numerous

Chase of a blockade runner, 1864.

blockade runners, effectively guarded the more than 3,500 miles of coastline. More than 1,500 vessels bound for the Confederacy were captured.

Blockade Runners

Violators of the Union blockade of Confederate ports operated throughout the war, earning enormous profits by carrying valuable commodities to and from the South. Some were Southerners eager both to support the Confederate cause and to make a profit at the same time. Other blockade runners bore no allegiance to either side, but were simply mercenaries from both the United States and abroad out for money and adventure. An estimated 8,250 ships, loaded with supplies worth more than $200 million, successfully evaded the 600 Federal vessels guarding ports along the Atlantic.

As the blockade became more effective, runners developed more sophisticated transportation routes and methods to evade patrolling Union vessels. Special boats with long, sleek hulls were designed with speed in mind; they were painted gray for camouflage and used anthracite coal as fuel because it did not emit smoke. Instead of coming directly to Confederate ports, they went to intermediary points, such as Nassau and Bermuda, and there transferred their cargoes to smaller craft that could be sneaked into points along the coast. With names like the *Banshee*, the *Jeff Davis*, and *Let Her Rip*, these ships and their cargoes allowed the Confederacy to survive far longer than would have otherwise been possible. Blockade running was a highly risky venture, however. Nearly 20 percent of the ships were seized, burned, or sunk by Federal vessels.

Booth, John Wilkes

1838–1865

Booth had been enjoying a successful career as a rising young actor before his despondency over the fall of the Confederacy and his obsessive hatred of Abraham Lincoln led him to become America's first presidential assassin.

Born in Maryland into the country's preeminent stage family, he was the son of famed tragedian Junius Brutus Booth and younger brother of Edwin Booth, the most acclaimed Shakespearian actor of the era. Booth began his own acting career at age 17 and toured throughout the country before the Civil War. As a private in a Virginia militia regiment, he was also present at the 1859 hanging of radical abolitionist John Brown, a man whose beliefs he abhorred but whose daring he admired.

Although he never joined the Rebel army and although his Maryland family remained largely pro-Union, Booth fanatically supported the Confederate cause. Detained at one point during the war for making threatening anti-Union remarks, he continued to prosper on the stage, becoming one of Washington D.C.'s favorite actors, noted for his striking good looks and melodious voice. One highlight performance was a November 1863 Ford's Theater appearance in *The Marble Heart*, before an audience that included President Abraham Lincoln, who would be delivering his Gettysburg Address the following week. Booth also attended Lincoln's second inauguration as an invited guest, pictured in photographs of the event standing by a railing directly above the president's podium. There, Booth was reminded of his on-and-off thoughts about a spectacular act against Lincoln to save the South.

Gathering a woeful gang of followers, he first concocted a scheme in early 1865 to kidnap the president and ransom him for Confederate prisoners of war. One attempt misfired when Lincoln failed to appear at the location where the abduction was to take place, and Booth abandoned the whole plot once Lee surrendered at Appomattox Court House on April 9. On the morning of the fourteenth, however, when during a routine visit to Ford's Theater he learned that Lincoln was to attend the play *Our American Cousin* that evening, Booth quickly devised a new plan with his co-conspirators to assassinate the top members of the administration; only Booth was successful. Sneaking into the president's box during the third act, the actor shot Lincoln in the head and jumped theatrically down onto the stage, breaking his leg. Booth shouted to the audience—many of whom recognized him immediately and thought the

John Wilkes Booth

whole episode was somehow a part of the play—"Sic semper tyrannis" ("Thus be it ever to tyrants"), Virginia's state motto, according to most witnesses, though others believed he yelled, "the South is avenged!" Escaping by horseback, Booth fled to Virginia.

A massive manhunt ensued, with a cavalry unit cornering him and an accomplice on the twenty-sixth near Front Royal in the tobacco shed of farmer Richard Garrett. Booth refused to surrender, and troops began to set fire to the barn to smoke him out when an overeager soldier shot and mortally wounded Booth, allowing the actor a dramatic death scene. "Tell my mother I died for my country," he began, ending with a mumbled, "Useless, useless."

Border States

Lying in a long line stretching from the Potomac River to the Nebraska frontier, Delaware, Maryland, Kentucky, and Missouri posed a dilemma for Abraham Lincoln as he plotted war strategy. Each was a slave state, had strong pro-Union factions, and was geographically vital to the Union. If one or all of them fell to the Confederacy, not only would the North be more vulnerable to attack, but valuable inroads to the heart of the South would be lost to the Union. Convinced the border states were the key to Union victory, Lincoln struggled to keep them on his side, even delaying the Emancipation Proclamation until he was sure they were securely in the Union camp. Ultimately, all four border states officially remained in the Union, but thousands of their citizens chose to fight for the Confederacy, making the Civil War one in which brother truly fought against brother, neighbor against neighbor.

In many border states, the war was fought with all the ruthlessness of an internal guerrilla conflict. Of the border states, Delaware was the most loyal Union supporter. Slavery had never been very important to the states' economy; at the start of the war, Delaware had just 1,800 slaves. Rejecting both secession and a proposal to receive Federal compensation in exchange for emancipating the slaves, the Delaware legislature did vote strongly for the Union, and the state provided the North with more than 12,000 soldiers and millions of dollars worth of war matériel, including gun powder and ironclads.

Maryland, on the other hand, had a much larger and more aggressive pro-Confederate contingent. It was in Maryland's capital that the first bloodshed of the war occurred during the Baltimore Riots. Federal troops sent in to quell the disturbance remained in the state for the duration of the war, especially in eastern Maryland, where secessionist sentiment ran highest. This effort kept the state from slipping to the Confederacy. Hoping to recruit troops, Robert E. Lee chose to invade Maryland during his campaign at Antietam.

Unfortunately, he entered the pro-Union western part of the state, where he met George McClellan's forces to fight during the single bloodiest battle of the war. In the west, both Kentucky and Missouri attempted to stay neutral in the war; each had a pro-Confederate governor and a pro-Union legislature, as well as both Union and Confederate recruiters operating throughout the region. Kentucky, the native state of both Union President Abraham Lincoln and Confederate President Jefferson Davis, was unable to retain its neutrality for long.

In September 1861, Confederate Major General Leonidas Polk led his forces from Tennessee into Kentucky, seizing Hickman and Columbus. He was pursued by Brigadier General U.S. Grant, who occupied Paducah. For about a year, fighting between the two sides took place in Kentucky until the state fell under firm Union control in 1862 for the duration of the war. More than 30 percent of Kentuckians who served during the war—about 75,000 for the Union and 25,000 for the Confederacy—were killed by wounds or disease. Missouri's wavering loyalty to the Union was tested by the May 1861 seizure of former Confederate state militia garrison at Camp Jackson by Union Captain Nathaniel Lyon. When a riot ensued, pro-Confederate Governor Claiborn Fox Jackson called out 50,000 troops to repel what he

Martial law in the border counties of Missouri, 1863.

called "the invasion" of his state. He then moved the capital from Jefferson City to Neosho and created his own government, declaring Missouri to be a member of the Confederacy.

The Federals, however, quickly set up their own government at Jefferson City. For the remainder of the war, the Union cause was dominant largely by virtue of the presence of Federal troops and Union control of the Mississippi River. Troops from Missouri fought in both sides of the war; more than 100,000 for the Union and about 40,000 for the Confederacy.

Bounties

The offer of substantial monetary incentives to Union army volunteers may have boosted enlistment and limited the need for conscription in the North, but it also developed into a highly corrupt, mercenary practice that did little to bring good men into the military. Both the U.S. and Confederate governments offered modest bounties to recruits early in the war, usually paid upon their honorable discharge. Local communities in the North would often chip in as well to reward the enlistees and compensate their families for the financial hardship that lengthy military service would bring. It was not until the passage of the Union's first

12th MASS. BATTERY

FOR MAJ. GEN. BANKS' EXPEDITION

👉 $138 👈

Before You Leave the State!

👉 75 👈

AT THE END OF THE WAR!

Good Men are wanted for this, the most popular arm of the service. Tried officers will command.

OFFICE IN BOSTON, 11 COURT SQUARE

J. MILLER, E. M. CHAMBERLIN, C. W. WEEBER.

F. A. SEARLE, PRINTER, 118 WASHINGTON STREET, BOSTON.

Cash was a motive for enlistment.

conscription act in March 1863, however, that the bounty system truly began to flourish.

Districts could avoid the hugely unpopular draft only if they enlisted enough soldiers to meet the quotas set by the War Department. Patriotism and adventure were no longer sufficient incentives to potential volunteers as the savage war dragged on; those who had the keen desire to join the fight had signed up long before. Cash, on the other hand—as long as it was enough—could provide the necessary motivation. With considerable help from the state and federal governments, towns and counties raised funds to furnish bounties that sometimes totaled more than $1,000. Sparsely populated areas frequently had to pay even more if they hoped to fill their quotas. When Abraham Lincoln called for an additional 500,000 recruits in 1864, the result was inevitable: unsavory bidding contests between communities to get the much-in-demand volunteers to enlist in their district.

Also competing for able bodies and driving the price still higher were well-off draftees allowed by law to hire a substitute soldier. With plenty of lucrative options from which to choose, there were ample numbers of new volunteers, many using bounty brokers to get them the best deals. The most unscrupulous of the new recruits never even intended to serve. They would just collect their fees, promptly desert, then travel to a different locale under a new name and repeat the process. Some of these bounty jumpers, hard to catch in a big country with poor communications, were said to have enlisted thirty times or more over the course of the war. Other bounty volunteers, bribing recruiters, waited until after they received their fees to reveal disabilities that rendered them unfit for service.

Paying the bounties in installments, a new tactic, may have brought more of the enlistees actually to the front, but it hardly ensured a decent battlefield performance. Their fellow soldiers considered them incompetent, greedy hirelings, a fairly accurate appraisal, and resented missing out on the windfall. But veteran Union troops would not remain excluded from the bounty system.

In 1864, the Federal government offered $400 to soldiers who reenlisted—supplemented by further payments from their home towns and a 30-day furlough—and more than 135,000 accepted. These old hands, not surprisingly, proved to be the hardiest fighters that the North ever acquired through its spending between $500 and $750 million on bounties during the Civil War.

Boyd, Belle

1843–1900

One of the most celebrated espionage agents of the Civil War, the Confederate spy relished

Belle Boyd

Boyd's habitual lack of discretion, however, also brought her to the attention of Federal authorities, who arrested her half a dozen times. Held in custody in Washington, D.C., in June 1862 after being betrayed by a lover, she continued her espionage work from her jail cell, flinging rubber balls containing detailed notes through the window to an operative waiting outside. After four weeks, Boyd was freed in a prisoner exchange, but imprisoned a second time the following year for five months. Released again in December 1863 when she developed typhoid, Boyd traveled to England, ostensibly to recuperate, though she was actually delivering dispatches to the British government from Jefferson Davis.

She attempted to return to the South aboard a blockade runner, which was captured by a Union vessel, whose captain, Samuel Hardringe, fell in love with Boyd and allowed her to escape to Canada. The two later married in England; Hardringe abandoned his commission but died soon after. After the war, Boyd published her memoirs and enjoyed a successful, decades-long stage career recounting her experiences as an agent. Popular in the North as well as the South, she died while on tour.

every bit of her notoriety. Boyd decided to enter espionage work at age 17, it is said, after Federal raiders ransacked her family's Virginia home in 1861. Operating from a Front Royal hotel owned by her father, she performed particularly valuable services during Stonewall Jackson's spring 1862 Shenandoah Valley Campaign, supplying vital information on Union troop movements and other military secrets she solicited from Yankee officers. Jackson named her an honorary aide-de-camp, and her exploits, including daring nighttime horseback rides through enemy territory to deliver reports, quickly won her fame throughout the South and the admiring nickname "La Belle Rebelle." Her countrypeople may have been shocked by her unladylike behavior but were thrilled by her success and daring.

Brady, Mathew

1823?–1896

Although he personally shot few of the pictures credited to him, Brady became by far the most celebrated photographer of the Civil War and a pioneer of photojournalism. He had started out as a painting student and jewelry box craftsman, then became enamored of the fledgling daguerreotype process. Setting up a portrait studio in New York in 1844 that catered to the rich and famous, Brady soon emerged as one of America's most sought-after photographers and opened a second gallery in Washington, D.C., in 1858.

At the outbreak of the Civil War, Brady recognized the huge potential for documenting the conflict with the new wet-plate photographic process, which allowed a certain amount of mobility. He received authorization to follow Union troops, beginning with the First Battle of Bull Run in July 1861. His eyesight failing, Brady hired a corps of field photographers who took most of the actual pictures but were rarely given credit for their work. Some of his best operatives, including Alexander Gardner and Timothy O'Sullivan, left Brady's employ later in the war, joining nearly 2,000 other photographers covering the conflict and achieving fame in their own right.

Despite Brady's disability, he often joined his photographers in the field, a frequently risky and always arduous assignment. The early technology required unwieldy equipment and chemicals, packed in a horse-drawn wagon that doubled as a makeshift darkroom. Camera lens speeds were too slow for action shots during battle, but Brady and his crew produced over 3,500 photographs covering many facets of the war, from views of army camp life to portraits of generals, privates, politicians, and civilians—Union and Confederate alike—and pictures of dead and wounded troops lying on the battlefield.

Willing to enhance these images, Brady encouraged his photographers to pose live soldiers in battle-ready positions and rearrange corpses for more dramatic compositions. Despite the artifice, the photos nevertheless captured the stark and bloody reality of the war. Still haunting today, they were altogether shocking to a nineteenth-century public that had never been exposed to such explicit documentation.

Images like those from Brady's famous September 1862 New York exhibition "The Dead

Matthew Brady under fire at Petersburg.

of Antietam" even influenced the national debate about the wisdom and importance of the war effort. Suffering severe financial setbacks in the 1870s, Brady sold his entire portfolio of wartime photographs to the U.S. government for $25,000—now one of the Library of Congress' priceless collections—but died in relative poverty.

Bragg, Braxton

1817–1876

Personally disliked by practically everyone in the Confederacy, General Braxton Bragg displayed both tactical genius and fatal indecision on the battlefield. His Civil War career, highlighted by the brash but failed invasion of Kentucky, was marked by brilliantly planned campaigns that nearly all ended in disaster with thousands of troops slaughtered needlessly.

Born in Warren County, North Carolina, on March 22, 1817, Bragg graduated fifth in his West Point Class of 1837. Appointed lieutenant of the artillery, he served in Florida during the war with the Seminoles until 1843, then served on the frontier until the Mexican War. His gallant conduct at the battle of Monterery earned him a brevet to major; at Buena Vista, where he fought with Zachary Taylor, he was breveted twice for meritorious conduct. Bragg was commissioned colonel and then major general in the militia in early 1861.

During the first summer of the Civil War, Bragg commanded the coast between Pensacola and Mobile and was promoted to major general of the Regular army in September. Ordered to join the Army of the Tennessee, Bragg served under Albert Sidney Johnston as chief of staff and led the Confederate right flank at the battle of Shiloh. Both Confederate and Union troops displayed an enormous lack of discipline during this early and bloody battle; Bragg developed a low opinion of volunteer soldiers after his experience here. His abuse of troops in order to instill discipline was legendary. One private

wrote home that "He loved to crush the spirit of his men. . . . The more hangdog look they had about them the better." The fact that he suffered from severe migraines and other illnesses on the battlefield may help explain his disposition.

Nevertheless, his attributes as an able strategist and organizer outweighed—at least temporarily—his personal shortcomings. In June 1862, he earned a promotion to commander of the Confederate Army of the Mississippi, replacing Pierre T. Beauregard. Bragg immediately began to plan his Kentucky campaign—the first invasion of the North by the Confederacy—involving a two-prong attack by his troops and those of Major General E. Kirby Smith. Surprising the Union by taking the initiative, Bragg moved into Kentucky in late August from posts in Tennessee, capturing two important garrisons (Kirby Smith taking the Union garrison at Richmond on August 30; Bragg's troops capturing Munfordville on September 17).

Just as suddenly, however, Bragg seemed to lose his nerve. Instead of consolidating his gains with military action, Bragg lost time by going to Kentucky's capital, Frankfort, to install a secessionist government and set up a recruitment effort. These actions allowed a now alarmed Union to send troops to stop the invasion of this important border state. Within three weeks, Major General Don Carlos Buell's Army of the Ohio had raced northward with nearly 50,000 men.

On October 7, 1862, the Federals moved against the Confederates at Perryville. Bragg, who had miscalculated Buell's intentions, had sent a division to Frankfort, leaving him with just 16,000 men, who were further decimated during the long day of battle that ended in a virtual stalemate with heavy losses on both sides. Realizing that he was outnumbered by the full force of Buell's Army of the Ohio, Bragg decided to retreat. Luckily, his opponent shared his indecision and lack of will; Buell missed his opportunity to pursue the Confederates and crush Bragg's forces once and for all.

Just five months after the start of his bold campaign, Bragg was back in Tennessee in front of Union forces at Nashville, with the bulk of his army in camp at Murfreesboro. On December 31, he attacked the forces of Union Major General William S. Rosecrans at Murfreesboro; two battles which ended, at the great cost of 10,000 men, in another stalemate. Convinced that his enemy outnumbered him and exhausted after months of fighting, Bragg lost the will to fight another battle at this time. After a summer of relative inactivity, Bragg fought to regain Chattanooga, which had fallen into Union hands, from a regrouped Rosecrans.

At the resulting Battle of Chickamauga—a two-day fight that resulted in more than 34,000 Confederate and Union losses—Bragg once again gained the upper hand and hoped to crush the whole Union army. He almost succeeded, but allowed the Union to fall back behind fortified Chattanooga. Once again, too, he failed to follow up and consolidate his win by attacking the retreating Federal forces. His failure to follow through at Chickamauga caused most of Davis' generals to urge the Confederate president to relieve Bragg of command. Davis resisted, granting his general another chance to redeem himself.

By late November, however, Bragg was routed out of Tennessee altogether by the stubborn and wily Rosecrans who, unlike his Confederate counterpart, was adored by his troops and trusted by his commanders. On November 25, Bragg's 40,000 troops met with devastating defeat at the battle of Missionary Ridge. Although Bragg's forces had the upper hand in terms of position, morale was low and leadership poor. As the Federal columns moved up, the Confederate center gave way, and what could have been a decisive Confederate victory turned into a rout.

General Bragg, blaming others for his defeat, then resigned his commission in disgust. Davis made him chief of staff, and Bragg was not seen again on the battlefield until 1865, when he commanded a division at the second defense of Wilmington. His lackluster performance there did nothing to reverse the opinion of him held by both his peers and his subordinates. His military career may be said to end here. He died in Galveston, Texas, on September 27, 1876.

General Braxton Bragg

Brandy Station, Battle of

JUNE 9, 1863

The biggest cavalry engagement of the Civil War, this battle proved that the Union's mounted troops could be a match to the seemingly invincible horsemen of the South. Army of the Potomac commander Joseph Hooker, suspecting that Robert E. Lee's Army of Northern Virginia was planning a major offensive, ordered Alfred Pleasonton, his new cavalry leader, to conduct a reconnaissance mission across the Rappahannock River. In fact, Lee was preparing for an invasion of Pennsylvania, with Jeb Stuart, commander of the cavalry corps that was the army's eyes and ears, concentrating his force of 10,000 by the river at Brandy Station to cover the Confederate advance.

Stuart took time out, however, to present a grand review of his brigades before a thrilled audience of civilians, highlighted by a flashy simulated cavalry charge. Reprising the show when Lee arrived on June 7, Stuart delayed his preparations for the imminent offensive. Meanwhile, Pleasonton's forces, more than 11,000 strong, commenced their mission on June 8. At dawn the following day, hidden by heavy morning fog, the Union cavalry crossed the Rappahannock and took Stuart's forces completely by surprise.

Over the next hours, more than 21,000 troops from the two sides engaged in a mammoth, classic hand-to-hand cavalry battle—the largest that would ever be fought on the North American continent—with headlong charges by saber-, pistol-, and rifle-wielding horsemen accompanied by the sound of artillery fire and bugle calls. The initially scattered Confederate force rallied and mounted a strong counterassault that pushed the Union cavalry back. Near sundown, when Pleasonton spotted Rebel infantry reinforcements marching toward the field, he ordered a calm withdrawal back across the river. The Union force suffered 936 casualties, 486 of whom were captured, while Stuart's troops lost 523. Because he held the field, the Confederate cavalry leader claimed a victory.

But Pleasonton accomplished his goal, reporting back to Hooker that Lee's army was indeed massed and ready to move north. As

The 114th Pennsylvania Infantry at Brandy Station.

importantly, the aggressive Union general demonstrated that his cavalry was no longer the maligned, appearance-obsessed body far inferior to the Confederacy's splendid mounted troops; indeed, it was now a powerfully effective scouting and fighting force. Acknowledging that fact, the Southern press and public ridiculed Stuart for being caught off-guard at Brandy Station and focusing more on showing itself off than supporting Lee. "If he is to be the 'eyes and ears of the army,' " a Richmond newspaper criticized, "we would advise him to see more and be seen less."

Humiliated by the episode and anxious to redeem his reputation, Stuart embarked with his best brigades on attention-getting raids later in the month. While the forays won his renewed acclaim, they did Stuart's commanding general as much harm as good. Out of touch with his scouting force at this critical juncture, Lee would have little idea of the strength or whereabouts of the enemy as he launched his fateful invasion of the North.

Breckinridge, John Cabell

1821–1875

Joining the Confederacy while his home state of Kentucky remained in the Union, the former U.S. vice president and 1860 presidential candidate abandoned politics to serve in the Southern army. Breckinridge had had a stellar career as a state legislator and U.S. congressman, quickly emerging as one of the Democratic party's notable figures. Chosen as James Buchanan's running mate in the 1856 election, Breckinridge, at 35, became the youngest vice president in the country's history.

Although he was a proponent of compromise over the increasingly divisive issues straining the nation, he remained popular with those favoring secession from the Union. When the Democrats split in 1860 over the choice of a presidential nominee, Breckinridge was se-lected in a special convention as the candidate of the party's Southern faction. With Stephen Douglas heading the ticket for the Northern contingent, the election went to Lincoln, while Breckinridge came in second in the electoral college—winning most of the South—and third in the popular vote.

Remaining in public office, however, Breckinridge began a term in the U.S. Senate in 1861. There, he defended Kentucky's initial position of neutrality in the Civil War, and was accused of secretly being a Confederate. Learning in October that he was about to be expelled from Congress and arrested, Breckinridge headed south and joined the Confederate army. Although his military experience was limited to service during the Mexican War, he was named division commander and placed in charge of the

John C. Breckinridge

famous Orphan Brigade of fellow Kentucky confederates. Going on to head an army corps, Breckinridge participated in many of the Civil War's major battles, including Shiloh, Chickamauga, and Missionary Ridge, as well as the siege of Vicksburg and the 1864 Shenandoah Valley Campaign. At the December 1862 to January 1863 Battle of Murfreesboro, Breckinridge came into conflict with his commander, Braxton Bragg, nearly threatening the superior officer to a duel when Bragg blamed him for the Confederate army's defeat. Scraping together a force of fewer than 5,000, which included 250 teenage cadets from the Virginia Military Institute, he stopped a Union drive up the Shenandoah Valley on May 15, 1864, in the Battle of New Market, certainly his most notable military victory.

Jefferson Davis named Breckinridge secretary of war in 1865. Running the department in the Confederacy's waning days, he supervised the evacuation of Richmond before its fall to Grant's army and served as an advisor to Joseph E. Johnston during the Southern general's April surrender negotiations with William Tecumseh Sherman. Breckinridge then fled to Cuba, and lived in Europe and Canada before returning to Kentucky in 1869 to practice law.

Brown, John

1800–1859

"The crimes of this guilty land will never be purged away but with blood," declared John Brown in his last written statement, and the radical abolitionist's own violent actions against slavery brought the nation that much closer to the savage conflict he foresaw. A visionary and martyr to many in the North, a madman and murderer to most (whites) in the South, Brown may have failed in almost every enterprise he attempted, but he remained convinced that he was an agent of God. He came from an old New England family with aboli-

tionist leanings and a history of mental illness. Married twice and the father of twenty, Brown moved about the Midwest, drifting from farming to tanning to land speculation and sundry other businesses, often keeping only a few steps ahead of his creditors. The one calling to which he remained unfailingly committed was the antislavery movement.

Participating in the Underground Railroad and various abolitionist organizations was not enough, however, as Brown aspired to more provocative actions. In 1855, he joined five of his sons in the Kansas Territory to participate in the bloody partisan fighting between pro- and antislavery forces. Retaliating against a raid on the free-soil settlement of Lawrence, Brown, four sons, and two others hacked five innocent proslavery settlers to death near Pottawatomie Creek on the night of May 24, 1856. The massacre brought Brown instant notoriety, and though his homestead was burned, he escaped arrest.

Another raid in Missouri two years later liberated eleven blacks who were smuggled to Canada and left one slaveholder dead. Yet, although the mainstream antislavery movement rejected violence, several prominent abolitionists clandestinely supported Brown and his new scheme to lead a massive slave insurrection in the South and set up an Appalachian republic of free blacks that he himself would govern. An undeniably charismatic personality, Brown traveled to New England several times, trying to round up volunteers and money for the outlandish venture (a request for $100,000 from the Massachusetts legislature was denied). Short of funds and followers and lacking a cohesive plan, Brown launched his holy war against slavery by seizing the Federal arsenal and armory at Harpers Ferry, Virginia, on October 16, 1859, slaying several in the process. Less than three days later, it was all over—ten of the cornered raiders were killed and Brown, knocked unconscious, was captured by U.S. marines.

During his hasty trial for treason and murder, Brown displayed a surprising dignity and eloquence that impressed many who had written

John Brown

regularly marched into battle inspired by the tune "John Brown's Body."

Brownlow, William

1805–1877

Tennessee newspaper editor and ex-minister William Brownlow was a flagrant Unionist, such a thorn in the side of Jefferson Davis' government that he was expelled from the Confederacy. An orphan with little formal education, he traveled the state as an itinerant Methodist preacher before entering journalism, keeping the nickname "Parson" Brownlow for life.

In 1849, he founded the *Knoxville Whig*, through which he espoused his ardent and odd blend of pro-Union, yet also proslavery sentiments. Swearing to "fight the Secession leaders until Hell freezes over, and then fight them on the ice," Brownlow continued to publish his paper during the early part of the Civil War, complete with its virulently anti-Confederate editorial policy. Brownlow, expanding his already considerable gift for rhetoric, ceaselessly hectored the Davis government and celebrated Union battle victories. Thriving in the controversy, the *Whig* was the largest newspaper in east Tennessee, where pro-Union sentiments were strong.

Brownlow became a leader of the State's Unionist movement, whose more radical members organized guerrilla raids against the Confederacy. For one such episode, involving the burning of several bridges, Brownlow himself was arrested in December 1861 along with dozens of others. Expecting to be hanged for treason—though innocent of the specific charges—he prepared a dramatic speech to deliver on the scaffold, but wound up only being subjected to house arrest. His printing presses, however, were destroyed, and his offices converted into an arms factory. Held for several months, Brownlow was turning into a *cause célèbre* and an acute embarrassment to the Confederacy, and was released into Union territory the fol-

him off as a lunatic. To the disgust of white Southerners, the condemned militant was championed by some of the North's most illustrious figures, from Henry David Thoreau, who called him "an angel of light," to Ralph Waldo Emerson, who said his hanging would "make the gallows as glorious as the cross." Others, recognizing how this glorification was exacerbating sectional tensions, conducted anti-Brown rallies, while the Democrats tried linking him to the Republican Party.

On December 2, 1859, the day that a tranquil Brown was executed in Charles Town, Virginia (now West Virginia), church bells tolled and gun salutes were fired throughout the North in honor of the fanatic-turned-martyr. He was not forgotten, and after the war that he hastened began a little more than a year later, Union troops

William Brownlow

Buchanan, James

1791–1868

With the misfortune of being a mediocre leader at a time when even greatness might not have sufficed, Buchanan, the country's final antebellum president, ended his unsuccessful term watching helplessly as seven Southern states seceded from the Union. For over 35 years prior to his election, the rather colorless and stern Pennsylvanian held a wide assortment of elected offices and government positions as a steadfast Jacksonian Democrat. Buchanan served for a decade each in the House and Senate, becoming an influential congressional leader, noted for his adeptness in straddling sectional conflicts between the North and South.

As secretary of state under James Polk, he settled the Oregon boundary dispute with Britain and handled negotiations for the annex-

lowing March. The defiant editor was greeted as a hero in the North; a book of his sketches became a best-seller and Brownlow was a favorite on the lecture circuit.

Returning to Knoxville when the Union army took the city in December 1863, he resumed publishing the *Whig*, calling for total war against the South and harsh punishment of Rebel leaders and supporters. Brownlow succeeded Andrew Johnson—to whom he once lost a congressional election—as governor of Tennessee in 1865, serving in that position until his election to the U.S. Senate in 1869.

James Buchanan

ation of Texas and the treaty that ended the Mexican War. He was also minister to Russia in the early 1830s and to Britain in the early 1850s. During his London appointment, he helped to draft the Ostend Manifesto, which advocated America's annexation of Cuba as a slave state. That position endeared him to the South, while his expedient absence from the national political scene during the wrenching debate over the Kansas-Nebraska Act won him no enemies. Both factors aided Buchanan, an unsuccessful candidate for the Democratic presidential nomination in 1848 and 1852, when he tried again in 1856, receiving his party's nod on the seventeenth ballot. Running on a platform that endorsed states' rights and a limited federal government and condemned the Republicans as a troublemaking, race-mixing party, he won the election with 45 percent of the popular vote.

But from the time he took office as fifteenth president, Buchanan was in trouble. Though years ago he had denounced slavery, Buchanan supported admitting Kansas as a slave state and pressured the Supreme Court to uphold the "peculiar institution" in the Dred Scott Case. These and other actions proved catastrophically divisive. Northerners thought Buchanan was in league with the South; Southerners thought he was too inept to be counted on to protect their rights. Republican fortunes were boosted, and the Democrats were wrenched apart. Plagued in addition by an economic depression in 1857, Buchanan's administration was riddled with corruption and scandal as well, particularly the war and justice departments, but even the post office.

Buchanan, to no one's surprise, was not renominated by the Democrats in 1860, and his repudiation of Stephen Douglas' candidacy helped guarantee the splintering of the party. Although the Union began dissolving while Buchanan was still in office, it was Abraham Lincoln's election that prompted the secession crisis. In one of his final addresses to Congress, the lame duck president blamed the Republicans—indeed the entire North—for causing the predicament by harping on the slavery issue. Buchanan did steadfastly insist that the South-

ern states had no legal right to secede; nevertheless, he claimed he had no authority to stop them, and did not want to start a war before Lincoln took office. Instead, he advocated a national referendum on whether force should be used to preserve the Union.

While many saw Buchanan's failure to take action as final proof of his spinelessness, it was probably a prudent—and preferable—move to leave the mess in the hands of the incoming president. Showing some resolve, however, Buchanan refused to relinquish Charleston Harbor's Fort Sumter to South Carolina, although his attempt to reinforce the isolated citadel was botched and he left its commander without clear orders. On March 4, 1861, a relieved Buchanan stepped down from office. Quietly supporting the Union cause during the Civil War, Buchanan, who remained unmarried for life, retired to his Pennsylvania home.

Bull Run (First), Campaign and Battle of

JULY 16–21, 1861

The first battle of the Civil War, fought on both sides by inexperienced and ill-prepared troops, ended in a surprising victory for the South.

The Civil War began on this summer day not because of any military imperative, but because of several political and popular considerations. Convinced of a quick and easy win for their side, both Confederate and Union civilians were eager for the war to begin. In the South, people claimed that one Confederate could easily whip five Yankees; Northerners believed that their superior moral resolve, combined with formidable industrial resources, would win the day. Another source of pressure was the Confederate intention to have its Congress meet in the new capital of Richmond, Virginia, at the end of July; Northern politicians insisted that action be taken to prevent such treason, coining the slogan "Forward to Richmond!" The North had another especially compelling reason to begin battle at this time: the majority of its troops had signed up for three months of service just after the fall of Fort Sumter in April, and their enlistment terms were about to expire.

Military commanders on both sides, however, agreed on one point: their armies were not prepared for battle. Winfield Scott, the Union general-in-chief, proposed a plan involving a minimum of military action but a maximum amount of time. This plan was reluctantly overruled by Abraham Lincoln, who bowed to public pressure. Ordered by their commanders-in-chief, Union General Irvin McDowell and

Confederate General Pierre T. Beauregard began to map their war strategies in early July. McDowell's goal was to invade Virginia, crush the Confederate forces, and move "forward to Richmond" to reclaim the capital. It was up to Beauregard to stop him and, with any luck, so impress the Union with Confederate strength that a truce would be called and the Confederacy allowed to exist. The Union forces in Virginia consisted of about 49,000 men; the Confederates numbered about 35,000.

Each side was divided into three armies: McDowell's 30,600 troops along the Potomac faced Beauregard's 20,000 Confederates, who amassed behind a creek called Bull Run near the vital rail line at Manassas Junction; near Harpers

New Union volunteers just prior to First Bull Run.

Ferry, Union General Robert Patterson's 18,000 men faced 12,000 Confederates under Joseph E. Johnston; and Yankee Benjamin Butler, who commanded about 10,000 men, occupied Fort Monroe at the tip of the Virginia peninsula and was guarded by a small contingent of Confederates led by John B. Magruder. (Neither Butler nor Magruder would play a part at Bull Run.) McDowell's immediate objective involved attacking Beauregard and driving him from Manassas. He proposed to do this by first feigning an attack on the Confederate center then coming down hard on the Confederate left.

Coincidently, Beauregard had a similar flank movement in mind. Attacking McDowell's troops when they least expected it, he would then swing his right flank and strike the Union left. Crucial to McDowell's plan, however, was his advantage in numbers. For this to hold, he needed to keep Johnston from joining the battle. Ordering Patterson to keep Johnston occupied at Harpers Ferry, McDowell left Washington on July 16, heading for Manassas Junction. Patterson, however, was not up to the task, and the wily Johnston was able to slip away. McDowell's army moved very slowly—too slowly, it might be said—and did not make contact with the enemy until July 18, when Union soldiers on a reconnaissance mission were driven back by Confederates at Blackburn's Ford—a preliminary victory that greatly encouraged the Southerners.

Finally, on July 21, the battle began in earnest. Beauregard's plan, based on Napoleon's strategy at Austerlitz, failed almost immediately, due to his troops' inexperience. McDowell's men were equally green, but because they outnumbered their enemy, they gained an early upper hand. A number of Confederate units were overpowered as Union infantry advanced on a small plateau called Henry House Hill. It was here that Brigadier General Thomas J. Jackson, who commanded a Virginia division, was given his now famous nickname. Standing resolutely before the Union onslaught, he inspired one of his colleagues, Brigadier General Barnard Bee, to exclaim, "There is Jackson standing like a wall." This was just the first of many battles

advanced by Stonewall Jackson's skill and bravery.

Just when it seemed as if the optimistic "Forward to Richmond" might be possible, Johnston's troops arrived from Harpers Ferry. Attacking with vigor, they forced the Union line to fall. When the retreat was called, the men who just days ago set out from Washington with such high hopes were now made to rush to the rear under fire. To add insult to injury, their retreat was hampered by the presence of hundreds of sightseers from Washington who had arrived in carriages and buggies to watch the action from a grassy slope a few miles away. Expecting to see an easy win for the Union, they received first-hand knowledge of the bitter bloodshed to come. In many ways, the First Battle of Bull Run foreshadowed the course of the entire war: the South, outnumbered and lacking supplies, fought bravely and cleverly, despite the odds; the Northern command moved slowly and with considerable indecision, giving precious time to the enemy. The victory—this time for the South—was won at too high a cost in human lives, even for the victor. The Federal losses at First Bull Run numbered 2,968 men killed, wounded, and missing; Confederate losses amounted to 1,982.

Bull Run (Second), Campaign and Battle of

AUGUST 26–SEPTEMBER 1, 1862

Fought over approximately the same territory as First Bull Run just over a year before, Second Bull Run came to roughly the same end as well. Although vastly outnumbered, the South pulled off an extraordinary victory, largely due to its superior leadership and organization. After experiencing the exhausting and draining battle of the Seven Days campaign of the month before, both armies in the East spent the month of July resting, reorganizing, and planning their next offenses. Although the Confederates had protected Richmond during George B. McClellan's Peninsula campaign and during the Seven Days battles, they had gained no new ground. Major General Robert E. Lee, urged by some of his most able and respected generals—including Thomas "Stonewall" Jackson—was planning a bold offensive northward, hoping at least to move the action from the James River to north of the Rappahannock.

The North, still reeling from its failure, fundamentally reorganized its eastern forces. Major General George McClellan's army remained at Harrison's Landing, Virginia, and refused to forge another assault unless given substantial new recruitments. His continued stubborn resistance to action forced Abraham Lincoln to look for other leaders who would advance the Union's position. He summoned Major General Henry W. Halleck from the West in mid-July to become the general-in-chief of all Federal forces. In addition, he ordered Major General John Pope from the Western theater, where he had distinguished himself at Corinth, to command the newly formed Army of Virginia, giving him primary responsibility for launching another attack on Richmond as soon as possible.

Attempting to instill discipline in his troops, Pope made a mistake all too common in the North's high command: he insulted the integrity of the volunteer army and disparaged the entire army's previous performance, thus engendering resentment from his troops and of-

A view of the desolate battlefield.

fending his commanders. Pope's forces were divided at the beginning of August: 75,000 men were located on the north side of the Rappahannock River, while McClellan's 90,000 lay to the east on the Peninsula.

Lee's goal was to keep Pope and McClellan's forces from uniting and overwhelming his own 55,000 men. He developed a bold plan, which involved dividing his troops in two, sending Thomas "Stonewall" Jackson with 24,000 to capture the high Union supply depot at Manassas Junction. He and Major General James Longstreet would follow the next day with 30,000 men to meet Jackson at Manassas. After learning of Jackson's capture of Manassas, he sent his troops to find and destroy the wily general, but could not locate him or his troops for more than a day; Jackson had quietly left the garrison and amassed his troops on the battlefield of First Bull Run.

In the meantime, Pope, partly due to his poor relationship with his field commanders, lost track of Lee and Longstreet's division, who were rapidly approaching. Pope and Jackson clashed in a brutal two-day battle from August 28 to 30. The Southerners repulsed attack after attack by the right half of the Union army. Exhausted at the end of the day, Jackson pulled back some of his troops.

Pope mistook this retrenchment for retreat, sending word to Washington that the enemy was about to retreat and that he was prepared to pursue. Unknown to Pope, however, Lee and Longstreet had reunited with Jackson on August 29, bringing 30,000 fresh troops into the fray. When Pope set out to cut off the supposed retreat, the Confederate forces were ready for him. The entire Union line crumbled under the assault and retreated. Although troops from McClellan's Army of the Potomac arrived on August 31, it was too late. Pope was forced to withdraw into Washington. The Southern victory at Second Bull Run was a costly one for both sides: the casualties from August 16 to September 2 totaled about 14,500 men.

Burnside, Ambrose Everett

1824–1881

Insisting that he was unfit for the position, the modest, congenial Union general quickly proved himself correct when he was appointed commander of the Army of the Potomac in late 1862.

Burnside, so renowned for his muttonchop whiskers that the term "sideburns" was coined from his name, served in the Southwest after graduating from West Point. Resigning from the army in 1853 to go into business manufacturing the innovative breech-loading rifle he invented, he went bankrupt and lost his patent, although the "Burnside carbine" became one of the most widely used small arms of the Civil War. He reentered the military in 1861, raising a brigade that performed capably in the First Battle of Bull Run. The following winter, Burnside led an 80-ship, 13,000-troop offensive force in the sounds of North Carolina, battling gale-force storms as well as the Confederate army and navy to capture such vital Southern coastal positions as Roanoke Island, New Berne, Fort Macon, and Beaufort. Promoted to major general, he twice refused offers to take over the Army of the Potomac from his friend George McClellan.

Despite a hesitant performance in the Battle of Antietam, where Burnside's delayed attack on the Confederate right blew the Union's chances for a more conclusive victory, Abraham Lincoln gave him the position in November 1862. The reluctant general accepted on the urging of colleagues who feared that the distrusted and disliked Joseph Hooker would be appointed otherwise. Knowing well that McClellan was fired for failing to take the offensive, Burnside quickly proceeded with plans for an advance on Richmond. That led to one of the North's worst defeats the following month in the Battle of Fredericksburg, where a series of foolhardy frontal assaults did not even come close to dislodging Robert E. Lee's Army of Northern Virginia from its impregnable defenses in the hills behind the town.

Burnside's request to resign in the wake of

his demoralizing loss was initially declined, but after his equally ill-considered attempt to get around Lee's forces—the embarrassing "Mud March"—literally bogged down, he was relieved in January 1863, a mere three months after he took command. Reassigned to head the Department of the Ohio, he caused a huge civil liberties controversy by ordering a crackdown on Southern sympathizers, including the arrest of the prominent Copperhead politician Clement Vallandigham for making an antiwar speech. Burnside won acclaim, however, for capturing the notorious Confederate raider, John Hunt Morgan, and for occupying Knoxville in September 1863, and he solidified the Union's control of eastern Tennessee further when he held off a poorly mounted Southern attempt to retake the city.

His performance was far less impressive when he returned to Virginia in 1864 as a corps commander, capped by his spectacular failure to break the Siege of Petersburg in the Battle of the Crater. Sent on an extended leave after the botched attempt to blast through the Confederate line with a huge mine explosion, he was never recalled to duty. After the war, Burnside returned to business, served three terms as governor of Rhode Island before being elected to the U.S. Senate, and became the first president of the National Rifle Association.

Butler, Benjamin Franklin

1818–1893

Loathed in the South and controversial in the North, the near-sighted Union general had the political power to continue receiving important appointments throughout the Civil War, despite a string of battlefield losses and contentious policies.

Butler, a successful Boston criminal attorney, was a prominent Democrat and a staunch supporter of the North's war effort, though he had favored Jefferson Davis for the 1860 presidential nomination. Using his influence to win a

military appointment, he achieved an early success in April 1861 quelling pro-secession riots in Baltimore and breaking a blockade on Washington.

The following month, in command at Fortress Monroe, Virginia, Butler earned the South's lasting enmity by declaring that fugitive slaves were a "contraband of war" to be emancipated and employed by the Federal army—and then pressing the Union government to adopt that position officially. In July, he suffered a humiliating loss at Big Bethel in one of the war's first engagements, botching his attempt to advance toward Richmond, but did win a victory two months later at Hatteras Inlet, North Carolina. Leading the ground forces in David Farragut's spring 1862 assault on New

General Benjamin Franklin Butler

Orleans, Butler was named military governor when the city fell.

Although he instituted some civic improvements, Butler's tenure was more noted for his offenses against the populace. Ordering the confiscation of Confederate property, he was accused of filching silverware from homes and churches and acquired the derisive nickname "Spoons." Southerners also called him "Beast Butler" after he issued his infamous "Woman Order," dictating that any woman who insulted a Union soldier be treated like a common prostitute. By December 1862, as corruption and bribery by Northern speculators flourished in his domain, Butler was recalled. He returned to field command back in Virginia late the following year.

In spring 1864, Ulysses Grant gave Butler a chance at glory by ordering him to cut the vital railroad lines between Richmond and Petersburg and attack the Confederate capital. Instead, his force was easily bottled up in May on the tiny Bermuda Hundred peninsula. Butler's mishaps continued as he served under Grant during the Siege of Petersburg, and he was dispatched to New York City in November to prevent election-day rioting by Copperheads. Eager to prove he could do more than quash civilian unrest, Butler obtained command of the land forces in the December 1864 attempt to capture Fort Fisher in Wilmington, North Carolina, one of the Confederacy's last open ports. But he called off his ground assault midway, a fiasco that gave Grant an eagerly awaited excuse to relieve him. Butler went back into politics after the war and was elected to Congress in 1866.

By this time a Radical Republican, he became a leader in the efforts to impeach Andrew Johnson and to impose a harsh Reconstruction policy on the South. Butler later served as governor of Massachusetts and, changing political affiliations yet again, ran for president on the Greenback party ticket in 1884.

C

Calhoun, John Caldwell

1782–1850

As the prime architect of the argument used by Southerners to justify severing the Union, this fiery orator probably did more to pave the way for war than any other single individual. A firm believer in states' rights and in the institution of slavery, Calhoun used his prominent position in state and national politics to expound upon his views.

Calhoun, born near Abbeville District in South Carolina, went north to receive his education at Yale and his law degree in Litchfield, Connecticut. He entered politics at the age of 26, serving for two years as a member of the South Carolina state legislature. In 1810, he was elected to the U.S. House of Representatives as a War Democrat, making a name for himself as an ardent advocate for U.S. participation in the War of 1812. During his nearly seven years in the House, he actively supported the government's post-war program, which included a protective tariff, a national bank, and an enlarged national army and navy.

In 1817, James Monroe appointed Calhoun his secretary of war, and in 1825, he became vice president under John Quincy Adams, all the while following a rigorous nationalistic course. By the time he was in his second term

as vice president, this time under Andrew Jackson, his feelings toward the federal government and its increasing power began to change. The

John C. Calhoun

first break with Jackson and other federalists concerned the protective tariff. Calhoun felt that industry-poor South Carolina, and the South in general, was being exploited by the high tax on imported goods. In fighting against the tariff, Calhoun developed his "doctrine of nullification": Because state conventions had originally ratified the U.S. Constitution, such conventions could also nullify any national law by declaring it unconstitutional. After Congress adopted another protective tariff in 1832, South Carolina acted on Calhoun's radical theory and nullified the new tariff. This action caused a constitutional crisis, culminating in a threat to secede by South Carolina, countered by President Jackson's threat of military action to prevent secession.

Although South Carolina backed down, the issue of states' rights began to smolder, and along with it, the question of slavery. Calhoun, who had resigned the vice presidency to return to the Senate during the nullification crisis, became the chief spokesman for states' rights as a way to protect the South from the increasingly larger and more powerful North. A slaveowner himself, he was fiercely proslavery, calling the institution "instead of an evil, a good—the perfect good." From his seat in the Senate, he warned the North that the South would never tolerate interference with slavery and forewarned of the day when armed conflict would be the only option available to settle the issue.

Except for a one-year stint as secretary of state under President John Tyler, Calhoun remained a powerful voice in the Senate until 1850. At his last appearance before his colleagues, a speech was read—he was too ill himself to give it—that argued against the proposed Compromise of 1850. In it, he stated that if the North threatened the South's right to hold slaves, Southern states would never remain in the Union. He died just a few weeks later, on May 31, 1850, more than ten years before the Civil War began.

Camp Life

"If there is any place on God's fair earth where wickedness 'stalketh abroad in daylight' it is in the army," wrote a Confederate soldier in a letter to his family back home. Indeed, life in the army camps of the Civil War was fraught with boredom, mischief, fear, disease, and death.

Army regulations called for the camps to be laid out in a fixed grid pattern, with officers' quarters at the front end of each street and enlisted men's quarters aligned to the rear. The camp was set up roughly along the lines the unit would draw up in a line of battle and each company displayed its colors on the outside of its tents. Regulations also defined where the mess tents, medical cabins, and baggage trains should be located. Often, however, lack of time or a particularly hilly or narrow terrain made it impossible to meet army regulations. The campgrounds themselves were often abysmal, especially in the South where wet weather produced thick mud for extended periods in the spring and summer; in the winter and fall, the mud turned to dust.

In summer, troops slept in canvas tents. At the beginning of the war, both sides used the Sibley tent, named for its inventor, Henry H. Sibley, who later became a Confederate brigadier general. A large cone of canvas, 18 feet in diameter, 12 feet tall, and supported by a center pole, the tent had a circular opening at the top for ventilation, and a cone-shaped stove for heat. Although designed to fit a dozen men comfortably, army regulations assigned about 20 men to each tent, leading to cramped, uncomfortable quarters. When ventilation flaps were closed on cold or rainy days, the air inside the tent became fetid with the odors of men who had scarce access to clean water in which to bathe.

As the war dragged on, the Sibley was replaced with smaller tents. The Federal armies favored the wedge tent, a six-foot length of canvas draped over a horizontal ridgepole and staked to the ground at the sides with flaps that closed off one end. When canvas became scarce

Passing away the time in Virginia.

in the South, many Confederates were forced to rig open-air beds by heaping straw or leaves between two logs. In autumn and winter, those units that were able to find wood built crude huts, laying split logs on the earth floor and fashioning bunks with mattresses of pine needles.

When not in battle, which was at least three-quarters of the time, the average soldier's day began at 5 A.M. in the summer and 6 A.M. in the winter, when he was awakened by reveille. After the first sergeant took the roll call, the men ate breakfast then prepared for their first of as many as five drill sessions during the day. Here the men would learn how to shoot their weapons and perform various maneuvers. Drill

sessions lasted approximately two hours each and, for most men, were exceptional exercises in tedium. One soldier described his days in the army like this: "The first thing in the morning is drill. Then drill, then drill again. Then drill, drill, a little more drill. Then drill, and lastly drill."

In the few intervals between drill, soldiers cleaned the camp, built roads, dug trenches for latrines, and gathered wood for cooking and heating. Finding clean water was a constant goal: the lack of potable water was a problem that led to widespread disease in both armies. At the outset of the war, the soldiers on both sides were relatively well-fed: the mandated daily ration for a Federal soldier in 1861 included at least 20 ounces of fresh or salt beef, or 12 ounces of salt pork; more than a pound of flour, and a vegetable, usually beans. Coffee, salt, vinegar, and sugar were provided as well. Supplies became limited when armies were moving fast and supply trains could not reach them in the field.

When in the field, soldiers saw little beef and few vegetables; they subsisted for the most part on salt pork, dried beans, corn bread, and hard-tack—a flour-and-water biscuit often infested with maggots and weevils after storage. Outbreaks of scurvy were common due to a frequent lack of fresh fruits and vegetables.

By far, the most important staple in the minds of the soldiers was coffee. Men pounded the beans between rocks or crushed them with the butts of their rifles to obtain grounds with which to brew the strong drink. Although most Federals were well-supplied with coffee, the

Confederates were often forced to make do with substitutes made from peanuts, potatoes, peas, and chicory.

Most armies were forced at some point to live off the land. The Confederates, who fought mostly on home ground, tried harder to curb pillaging, preferring to request donations from townspeople rather than steal supplies or take them by force. Attached to most armies was the sutler, a purveyor of all goods not issued by the army, including tobacco, candy, tinned meats, shoelaces, patent medicines, fried pies, and newspapers. Sutlers were known for their steep prices and shoddy goods, but soldiers desperate for cigarettes, sweets, and news from home were willing to use their pay for these treats.

Boredom stalked both armies almost as often as did hunger. When not faced with the sheer terror of battle, the days in camp tended to drag endlessly. The sheer tedium of camp life led the

Soldiers rested when possible.

men to find recreational outlets. "There is some of the onerest men here that I ever saw," wrote a new recruit, "and the most swearing and card playing and fitin [fighting] and drunkenness that I ever saw at any place."

When not drilling or standing guard, the troops read, wrote letters to their loved ones, and played any game they could devise, including baseball, cards, boxing matches, and cockfights. One competition involved racing lice or cockroaches across a strip of canvas. As hard as most commanders attempted to control vice in camp, both gambling and drinking were rampant, especially after payday. Confederate General Braxton Bragg concurred: "We have lost more valuable lives at the hands of whiskey sellers than by the balls of our enemies."

Army regulations prohibited the purchase of alcohol by enlisted men, and soldiers who violated the rule were punished, but men on both sides found ways around it. Members of a Mississippi company got a half a gallon of whisky past the camp guards by concealing it in a hollowed-out watermelon; they then buried the melon beneath the floor of their tent and drank from it with a long straw. If they could not buy liquor, they made it. One Union recipe called for "bark juice, tar-water, turpentine, brown sugar, lamp oil, and alcohol."

When not drinking or gambling, some men escaped the tedium of daily army life by enjoying "horizontal refreshments," as visiting prostitutes became known. Thousands of prostitutes thronged the cities in the war zones and clustered about the camps. By 1862, for instance, Washington, D.C., had 450 bordellos and at least 7,500 full-time prostitutes; Richmond, as the center of prostitution in the Confederacy, had about an equal number. Venereal disease among soldiers was prevalent and largely uncontrolled. About eight percent of the soldiers in the Union army were treated for venereal disease during the war and a great many cases were unreported; figures for the Confederacy are unavailable, but assumed to be about equal in proportion. With the invention of penicillin more than 70 years away, treating venereal disease with herbs and minerals such as poke-weed, elderberries, mercury, and zinc sulfate may have eased symptoms but did nothing to cure the disease.

Even more pervasive than boredom, gambling, or venereal disease was homesickness. Men spent more time writing letters and hoping to receive them than any other leisure activity. Furloughs were rarely granted, and most soldiers had few opportunities to spend extended periods of time away from the army. Federal troops were often stationed too far from home to have time to get home, while Southern armies, short of manpower, needed every available soldier to fight. For better or worse, Civil War soldiers were forced to call camp home for the duration of their terms of service.

Carolinas Campaign

1865

Undeterred by miserable weather and nearly impassable terrain, William Tecumseh Sherman's grueling and ruthless winter 1865 advance through South and North Carolina was a far greater logistical triumph—and an even more destructive enterprise—than his notorious "march to the sea". Shortly before Christmas, the Union force arrived in Savannah, Georgia, after completing its devastating trek through the state. Sherman was then ordered to turn north and bring his troops up to Virginia, where he would join Ulysses S. Grant to wipe out Robert E. Lee's forces and finish the war. Slicing through the Carolinas, a region left largely unscathed by the conflict, the Northerners would cut the Confederate army off from the Southern heartland and ravage anything in their path that the enemy could use to continue fighting. Due to the worst winter rains in two decades and other problems, the campaign did not commence until February 1.

Once underway, however, Sherman's 60,000-man army could not be stopped. With little military opposition to offer, the Confederates

Columbia, the captured capital of South Carolina.

assumed that the elements would scuttle—or at least bog down—the Union troops' advance. The swampy tidewater region that Sherman's army traversed was arduous terrain in even the best conditions, with dozens of rivers and tributaries fraught with alligators and snakes. The rains so flooded the area that Sherman's advance patrols often had to scout by canoe. But the Union army included experienced backwoodsmen and thousands of veterans who had become accustomed to difficult marches in their years of Civil War combat.

From the thick forests around them, they fashioned miles of log pathways called "corduroy roads" along the swamped route, built bridges and causeways, and, when necessary, waded up to their shoulders through the icy streams. Nursing hatred toward South Carolina—the birthplace of the secession movement—the Federal troops took special delight

in their invasion of the state, and as they reached populated areas many engaged in indiscriminate looting and burning of civilian property, worse than their pillaging in Georgia. Sherman cut through the center of the state toward the capital of Columbia.

Left weakly defended, the town was occupied on February 17, and, within a day, almost completely destroyed by fire. Southerners claimed Sherman's drunken soldiers purposely set the blaze, but the Union general claimed that retreating Confederate forces tried to burn bales of cotton and other supplies in their hasty departure. As Columbia smoldered, Union troops proceeded to Charleston—the home of Fort Sumter—which was ransacked but left standing.

Four days later, on February 22, Federal forces under John Schofield captured Wilmington, North Carolina, the South's last open Atlantic seaport. The same day, deciding that the Union army had to be confronted, Robert E. Lee returned Joseph E. Johnston to command. Having faced Sherman before during the Atlanta campaign, the Confederate general did what he could to prepare for another showdown, gathering a force of 20,000 with help from stalwart cavalryman Wade Hampton, whom Lee had sent down from Virginia.

But Johnston was certain little could stop the Union army, the likes of which, he said, the world had not seen "since the days of Julius Caesar." Entering North Carolina on March 7, Sherman's troops curtailed their plundering but continued to move north, occupying Fayetteville on March 11. Five days later, Johnston was ready to challenge them, fighting a vigorous delaying action at Averasboro, then sending his whole force to attack the Union left wing under Major General Henry W. Slocum near Bentonville on the nineteenth. By the third day of what would be one of the final Civil War battles in the East, the entire Federal army, outnumbering the Confederates three-to-one, poised for assault, and Johnston was forced to withdraw. Having covered an extraordinary 425 miles in 50 days, Sherman's men arrived in Goldsboro on March 23, joining with John Schofield's forces and bringing the total number of Union troops marching northward to over 80,000. By the time the Federals reached Raleigh on April 13, Johnston had received word that Robert E. Lee had surrendered, and though Jefferson Davis ordered him to continue fighting, he knew it was pointless.

The next day, Johnston called for a truce, and an armistice agreement was signed on April 18. After some squabbling among the Union high command over Sherman's authority to choose the terms, Johnston formally surrendered on April 26, essentially ending, aside for some lingering resistance in the West, the Civil War.

Carpetbaggers

So called because they arrived carrying luggage called "carpetbags," Northerners who moved to the South after the war were both feared and despised by most former Confederate citizens. During Reconstruction, many Northerners took advantage of the reigning political and social chaos by securing many local and state political posts, mobilizing a politically unsophisticated and easily manipulated black vote, and earning a reputation for graft, wasteful spending, and influence-peddling. Nevertheless, not all Northerners came to pillage. Some came as teachers, merchants, clergy, or agents of the Freedman's Bureau. Many Union soldiers who had seen the South during the war decided to settle there simply because of its beauty and abundance of arable land. Unfortunately, to many Southerners, black and white, all Northerners were suspect and would remain "carpetbaggers" for generations to come.

Cartes de visite

Few keepsakes were more precious to soldiers and their families than the black and white photographs called *cartes de visite*. Named for the European custom of pasting one's photo on the back of visiting cards, these 2½ by 4-inch snapshots were produced by the millions during the Civil War. Those created in the studio frequently involved elaborate backdrops, soldiers dressed in full battle regalia, and families wearing their finest clothes. On the other hand, those shot in the field—even ones obviously posed—poignantly capture the loneliness and fear of a soldier far from home. At about five cents a piece, *cartes de visite* were relatively inexpensive; when the federal government became desperate for funds as the war dragged on, it levied a tax of about two or three cents on each image. After that, and with the introduction of the larger cabinet photograph in

Cartoon depicting carpetbaggers, originally appearing in Puck, *May 1880.*

1870, the popularity of the *cartes de visite* waned.

Casualties of War, Union and Confederate

Perhaps the most telling compilation of casualty statistics—numbers showing the human toll of the war in terms of the dead, wounded, and missing from both sides of the Civil War—are those arrived at by E.B. Long, after exhaustive research into the question. Just over 350,000 men in the Federal army died from various causes—the majority of them being death from disease, by a margin of two to one over battlefield death or death from mortal wounds. Nearly another 25,000 died from a variety of other causes: suicide, execution, sunstroke, or accident, to name but a few. The Federal navy lost nearly 5,000 men between disease, accidents and battle injuries.

In the Confederate forces, disease was also the major cause of death among Southern soldiers, though it is difficult to be statistically positive about the exact number, owing to destruction of records by accident in the confusion following a battlefield defeat, or by the accidental burning of a courthouse or archive; many records pertaining to the war, as well as to the lives of ordinary Virginians, were lost to fire when Richmond, the Confederate capital, surrendered in April 1865 with most of the city in flames. But those records which did survive point to an approximate Confederate loss of al-

Mass graves sprung up alongside battlefields and prison camps.

most 95,000 killed or mortally wounded, and a little over 150,000 dead of disease. Records pertaining to the losses of the Confederate navy apparently no longer exist.

The reason for so many deaths due to disease can be traced to a number of factors, including a simple ignorance of hygiene, and the fact that there were no inoculations for diseases now considered fairly trivial. Young men with no immunity were called into service to aid their countries and lived together in camps that were rarely clean, very often filthy. The only means of disposal of human waste was in a latrine, a long, deep pit where the men would either relieve themselves directly, or dump out buckets and chamber pots. When the latrine, or sink as it was sometimes called, became sufficiently full as to create an odor, it would be filled in and a new one excavated nearby. These latrines were breeding houses for germs, and attracted large numbers of flies; the flies would then carry the filth to the food and water used by the soldiers. Mass outbreaks of diarrhea were often the result, as well as epidemics of cholera. Diseases such as whooping cough, measles, scarlet fever, smallpox, and dysentery were also of great concern. Sunstroke and tetanus were also ever-present, as were tuberculosis and pneumonia. Unprepared for the ravages of such disease, young soldiers died in great numbers.

Putting all the figures together, the staggering fact emerges that slightly over one million

Rebel soldier killed on May 19, 1864.

Americans spanning four races and several ethnic groupings either had their lives taken from them in death, or saw their lives permanently changed owing to wounds ranging from inconvenient to crippling, in just about 40 months of fighting between April 1861 and April 1865.

Cavalry, Confederate and Union

Although cavalrymen theoretically fight from the saddle, almost all cavalry corps in the Civil War were "dragoons" or mounted infantrymen: they rode to battles on horseback, but dismounted to fight. The Confederate army had two major cavalry corps which, at least for the first two years of the war, were better equipped and better trained than their Northern counterparts. Confederate Major General Joseph Wheeler's cavalry corps was part of the Army of Tennessee. Comprising Wheeler's corps were 4,200 horsemen, who distinguished themselves in several battles in the western theater, including Murfreesboro and the extraordinary maneuvering at Chattanooga known as Wheeler's Raids.

In the east, the Army of Northern Virginia's cavalrymen, famous both North and South for their abilities and showmanship, were led by Jeb Stuart. Stuart was promoted to brigadier general and given command of all the army's cavalry after his victory at First Bull Run. His cavalry corps grew steadily and performed well during the first two years of the war, generally

The Third Pennsylvania Cavalry, March 1864.

out-riding and out-fighting their Union counterparts, particularly during the Seven Days campaign. At the beginning of the war, the Union had just one cavalry corps attached to its Army of the Potomac.

Early in the war, a number of volunteer cavalry regiments were called in to supplement the infantry, but until the spring of 1863, when Joseph E. Hooker took command of the corps, mounted soldiers were poorly trained and used. Once organized and trained, however, the Union cavalry distinguished itself in battles such as Brandy Station (the first and only true cavalry battle of the Civil War) and Gettysburg.

In April 1864, Philip H. Sheriden took command of the cavalry corps, which now numbered nearly 12,500 men. Sheriden was able to lead his corps to victory at Five Forks on April 1, 1865, a battle which broke open the defenses of Petersburg and led to Lee's surrender at Appomattox Court House. The cavalry in the Union's western theater was not organized into a corps until the end of November, 1864, but then played a decisive role in the Battle of Nashville and in Sherman's March to the Sea.

Chamberlain, Joshua Lawrence

1828–1914

Fighting in many of the Civil War's major battles, the Maine college professor quite possibly saved the Union army from defeat at Gettysburg with his legendary defense of Little Round Top. Chamberlain, a former minister, taught rhetoric, oratory, and modern languages at Bowdoin College. When he was denied a leave of absence to enlist in the military, he took a sabbatical in 1862, ostensibly to perform research in Europe, then headed instead to the army recruiter's office. Appointed lieutenant colonel of the 20th Maine, Chamberlain had been offered a higher rank, which he rejected, asking to "start a little lower and learn the business first." He learned the business quickly enough, serving at Antietam, Fredericksburg, where he was wounded, and Chancellorsville, where he was wounded again.

At Gettysburg on July 2, 1863, the battle's second day, Chamberlain and his 350-man regiment—mostly lumberjacks, trappers, and seamen—was immersed in desperate, fierce fighting to protect the Union's left line. After three previous units had tried and failed, Cham-

berlain's regiment was ordered to ascend Little Round Top—a rocky, wooded hill critical to the protection of the army's flank—and hold it "at all hazards." An Alabama regiment under Colonel William C. Oakes was poised for attack before Chamberlain's men had finished scrambling up the southern slope. Over a ferocious two-hour period, the Union soldiers managed to beat back a total of five assaults that at times turned into virtual hand-to-hand combat.

But having lost a third of their men and exhausted their ammunition, their situation was desperate as the Confederates readied for another attack. Rather than retreat, however, Chamberlain, remaining remarkably calm under the circumstances, opted for a final, gallant effort to hold the hill. Ordering his men to fix bayonets, he led a sudden charge down the slope that caught the Confederate troops by complete surprise. Dozens surrendered before they even realized that the enemy was unable to return fire, others turned and ran, and Little Round Top, against all odds, remained in Union hands. Wounded a third time during the day's fighting, Chamberlain would later receive the Medal of Honor. Twelve days after he returned to combat duty in May 1864, following a months-long bout with malaria, Chamberlain was wounded yet again at Petersburg, this time so severely that he was expected to die.

An impressed Ulysses Grant, thinking there was little time left, promoted him brigadier general right on the field. But that wound would not kill Chamberlain for another fifty years; he was not even out of the war. Reaching the rank of major general, Chamberlain was named to accept the Army of Northern Virginia's formal surrender at Appomattox on April 12, 1865.

He declined to remain in the military after the war and returned to Maine. Serving four terms as the state's governor, Chamberlain then became the president of Bowdoin College before dying of his old wartime injury well into the twentieth century.

General Joshua L. Chamberlain

Chancellorsville, Battle of

APRIL–MAY 1863

Called "Lee's masterpiece," this Confederate victory allowed the South to take the initiative in the eastern theater in the spring of 1863. Facing a force more than double his own, Robert E. Lee skillfully, and with nerves of steel, outmaneuvered his less decisive opponent, Joseph E. Hooker, and drove him north of the Rappahannock River.

After a discouraging winter of defeats in Fredericksburg and during Ambrose E. Burnside's "Mud March," Abraham Lincoln replaced the inept Burnside with "Fighting Joe" Hooker. The cocky Hooker had distinguished himself in the Peninsula Campaign and at Antietam and was a vocal critic of Burnside. When he took control of the Army of the Potomac, he did so with vigor, inspiring the troops with an energy and confidence his predecessor lacked—and an arrogance that would prove his downfall. "May God have mercy on General Lee, for *I* will have none," he wrote to Lincoln on the eve of a planned offensive against Robert E. Lee's troops centered around Fredericksburg. Leaving a third of his 115,000 troops near Fredericksburg to keep Lee occupied, he led the other 75,000 men on a long swing up and across the Rappahannock and Rapidan to strike at Lee's unprotected left flank and rear.

On April 27, Hooker arrived at Chancellorsville, a house in the midst of a clearing ten miles west of Fredericksburg, and set up camp, certain that he would destroy Lee's army within 48 hours. His plan may have worked had he not faced a man far more clever and audacious than he. With just 60,000 troops, Lee used the same plan that had met with such success at Second Bull Run a year before: he divided his troops. Leaving just 10,000 men at Fredericksburg, he rushed the rest west to shore up his flank. The first clash occurred on May 1 when Hooker's men headed south toward Confederate lines.

Trudging through woods so dense they were called the wilderness, the men were surprised by an attack led by Thomas "Stonewall" Jackson. Hooker, who later admitted that he simply lost his nerve, ignored the advice of his corp commanders and ordered a sudden withdrawal back into the Wilderness. When Lee's cavalry commander, Major General Jeb Stuart, reported that Hooker's right flank was vulnerable, Lee took another huge risk and further divided his forces to take the offensive. He ordered Jackson to march with 26,000 men beyond Hooker's vulnerable flank and attack while he remained with troops at Chancellorsville.

Although alerted to Jackson's movements by his scouts, Hooker was not convinced Jackson posed any real danger. Troops under General Oliver O. Howard were relaxing in camp when Jackson swooped down upon them at twilight on May 2, forcing them to withdraw some two miles to the rear before Union artillery stopped the Confederate sweep short of the Chancellorsville house.

In the midst of this great victory, the Confederates sustained a deadly blow when Jackson was shot inadvertently by his own men in the growing darkness. Stuart took command of the infantry, and at daylight on May 3 launched another assault on Hooker's lines, pushing them back to the Rappahannock and Rapidan. Meanwhile, Lee's rear was threatened by Union troops advancing under the command of Major General John Sedgwick.

On May 4, a detachment from Lee's forces at Fredericksburg swarmed the Union contingent at Salem Church, fighting a vicious day-long battle, until Sedgwick finally withdrew across the Rappahannock at nightfall. The next day, Hooker's army joined the retreat in what was—considering its overwhelming advantage in manpower—one of the most needless and humiliating Union defeats of the war. His boasts of a great victory ended in more than 17,000 Union casualties.

Hooker was removed from command of the Army of the Potomac about a month later. Lee's victory, however, was in many ways a Pyrrhic one. Not only did he lose almost 13,000 soldiers—a greater percentage than did the Federals—he also lost Stonewall Jackson, one of the South's greatest and most irreplaceable assets.

Chase, Salmon Portland

1808–1873

Perhaps the most radical member of Lincoln's cabinet, the treasury secretary served skillfully for three years before conflict with the president compelled his resignation. Chase, tall, portly, and thrice-widowed, began his career as an abolitionist Ohio lawyer, becoming so renowned for defending fugitive slaves that

Salmon P. Chase

he was called "the attorney general for runaway negroes." A leader of the antislavery Liberty party and founder of its offshoot, the Free-Soil party, he entered the U.S. Senate in 1848, where he was a principal opponent of the Compromise of and the Kansas-Nebraska Act.

Beginning in 1855, he served two terms as governor of Ohio, now as a prominent member of the new Republican party. Chase's staunch abolitionist position and unwillingness to negotiate with the South lost him the Republican presidential nomination in 1860 to the more conservative Abraham Lincoln. Appreciating his rival's political power as much as his talents, the president-elect nevertheless invited Chase to join his cabinet.

The treasury secretary was instantly confronted with the country's plummeting credit rating, a mounting budget deficit that was already the highest in four decades, and the promise of a monstrously expensive war to deplete the treasury still further. Despite his lack of experience in finance, Chase moved quickly and effectively to fund the conflict. With the aid of financier Jay Cooke, he secured revenues through bank loans and the unprecedented sale of several billion dollars of government bonds in small denominations to everyday investors.

To strengthen the Union's financial position further, Chase also successfully advocated restructuring the U.S. banking system, urged passage of the Legal Tender Act of 1862, which introduced a national paper currency known as "Greenbacks," and supported Congress' vote for higher tariffs and the country's first federal income tax. The treasury secretary concerned himself with nonmonetary matters as well. Determined to offer military advice, Chase entreated Lincoln to remove George McClellan from command, favoring generals such as Joseph Hooker who were hardly more able. Moreover, he continued to cultivate his political fortunes throughout his cabinet tenure, engaging in a bitter rivalry with Secretary of State William Seward and berating Lincoln's reluctance to advocate emancipation.

Becoming a favorite of the Republicans' radical wing, Chase quietly began maneuvering for the party's 1864 presidential nomination. However, the February release of a Kansas senator's endorsement of the surreptitious bid, known as the "Pomeroy Circular," became a huge embarrassment to Chase, who offered Lincoln his resignation. By early summer, the president finally took him up on the offer, somewhat to Chase's surprise. Equally surprising, though politically prudent, was Lincoln's decision to nominate his adversary as Supreme Court chief justice in December 1864.

In Chase's early decisions from the bench, he proved a strong supporter of some of Lincoln's more legally questionable policies like the suspension of the writ of habeus corpus, and later annoyed his Radical Republican allies by his impartial performance in President Andrew Johnson's impeachment trial of 1868. That year, he again unsuccessfully sought the presidential nomination, this time as a Democrat, then continued to serve on the Supreme Court until his death.

Chattanooga, Campaign and Battle of

OCTOBER–NOVEMBER, 1863

The battle over the gateway to the eastern Confederacy and the rebel war industries in Georgia was long and fierce, but it ended with Tennessee firmly in the Union's hands. Under siege by Major General Braxton Bragg since their humiliating defeat at Chickamauga the month before, Union troops in Chattanooga were cold, hungry, and discouraged.

At the beginning of October, Bragg sent his cavalry corps commander, Joseph Wheeler, out on a series of raids that effectively cut off all Union supply lines. The arrival of Major General Ulysses S. Grant, just appointed commander of the newly formed Military Division of the Mississippi, signaled the start of a new Union offensive. Replacing William S. Rosecrans with Major General George H. Thomas as commander of the Army of the Cumberland,

Grant and his chief engineer, William F. Smith, devised a bold plan to break the siege. The first order of business involved opening a supply line by assaulting the Confederates on the east bank of the Tennessee River, then setting up a bridgehead at Brown's Ferry. Supplies shipped by water to Brown's Ferry could then be hauled across Moccasin Point to the hungry troops in Chattanooga.

After driving the Confederates off Raccoon Mountain, the Union put its "Cracker Line Operation" into effect on October 26. Although the Confederates assaulted the new line at Wauhatchie from October 28 to 29, the first steamboat laden with Union supplies arrived safely on November 1. While waiting for reinforcements to come from Memphis and Vicksburg with Major General William T. Sherman Grant planned the next phase of his offensive: to drive the Confederates off their perch on Missionary Ridge, along the north- and southeastern side of Chattanooga and from Lookout Mountain on the southwest.

Meanwhile, the Confederates underwent profound—and unwise—organizational changes. Braxton Bragg, a man disliked and disrespected by virtually everyone who knew him, experienced a quasi-mutiny of his corps commanders. Lieutenant General Leonidas Polk, Daniel H. Hill, and Thomas C. Hindman asked for and were granted transfers by the War Department after they complained about Bragg's indecisive and slow actions at Chattanooga. Bragg also ordered several divisions and 35 cannon under Lieutenant General James Longstreet eastward to aid West Virginia troops in their actions against Ambrose Burnside, weakening his lines on Missionary Ridge just as the Federals were planning to attack.

On November 23, news of Sherman's arrival with fresh troops allowed Grant to proceed. His first objective was to take Orchard Knob, the Confederate's forward position in the center of their line on Missionary Ridge. The battle began when divisions dressed as if for a military parade marched below the hill. When bored and curious Confederates on the knob came down for a closer look, Union troops rushed them and, after a pitched battle, took the hill. Making

Orchard Hill his headquarters for the fight, Grant then ordered Sherman's divisions, located north and west of Chattanooga, to cross the Tennessee River and attack the Confederate right on the north end of Missionary Ridge.

In the meantime, Hooker's goal was to take Lookout Mountain on the Confederate left. Moving forward at 4 A.M. on November 24, Hooker found himself embroiled in a blind battle with the enemy. Sheets of rain and dense fog hid most of the battle from the troops below, earning the fight for Lookout Mountain the nickname "Battle above the Clouds." When the fog cleared, however, the Union flag flew from the crest. While Hooker had been enveloping the Confederate left, Sherman had been slogging his way through the rain to Bragg's right, not arriving until the afternoon of November 24.

Bragg then made a fatal mistake. He split his forces, putting half on the bottom of the hill with orders to fire a volley when the enemy got within 200 yards, then withdraw up the slopes. Hampered by his usual lack of communication skills, Bragg failed to fully inform all the men of this plan. The next morning, the Battle of Missionary Ridge began.

Sherman's troops and artillery battered Confederates along the north end, but were repulsed several times. To draw Rebels away from Sherman's front, Grant ordered Thomas to attack the Confederate line at the base of the ridge. Although some of Bragg's men knew enough to withdraw immediately, most stayed and fought—and died, overwhelmed by Union troops. After taking the line, the men—without orders from either Grant or Thomas—decided to pay back the Rebels for their humiliating loss at Chickamauga. They went straight up the steep mountain slope and drove the Confederate army off in complete retreat.

The defeat at Chattanooga was a severe blow to an already weakening Confederate cause. The loss of the vital communication and supply lines that ran through the city made Sherman's Atlanta Campaign possible.

Chesnut, Mary

1823–1886

Through her diary, this remarkably observant and keenly compassionate woman provided future generations with detailed and clever insights into the South during the Civil War. The wife of James Chesnut, Jr., the first United States senator to resign his post and join the fledgling Confederate government, Mary Chesnut was privy to the inner workings of the Confederacy, especially as she became friends with Varina Davis, wife of the Confederate president.

As the daughter of prominent lawyer and congressman, Stephen Decatur Miller, Chesnut was born into the life of wealthy Southern planters. Well-educated and with exceptional writing skills, she used her diary well, noting every important event and evaluating every major personality of the day from her unique perspective. At the beginning of the war, she wrote of the struggle that faced the South: "The Southern Confederacy must be supported now by calm determination and cool brains. We have risked all and we must play our best, for the stake is life or death." She described Confederate general Robert E. Lee, by writing, "Can *anybody* know the General? I doubt it, he looks so cold, so quiet, so grand."

After William T. Sherman swept through Atlanta, she summed up well what most Confederates must have felt on that day at the end of August 1864: "Atlanta is gone. That agony is over. There is no hope but we will try to have no fear." For the duration of the war, James and Mary Chesnut lived in Richmond. When they returned home to South Carolina in 1866, they found that their home and plantation had been sacked by Union soldiers. Ever resourceful, Chesnut brought income into the household by selling butter and eggs while her husband attempted to revive the plantation. Putting away her diary for a time, Chesnut nevertheless continued to write, earning money by selling stories to local newspapers. About 20 years after the end of the war, she turned her attention once again to her voluminous war journal, hoping to turn it into a book worthy of publishing.

In this endeavor, she was encouraged by Varina Davis, former first lady of the Confederacy, who told her old friend, "I think your diaries would sell better than any Confederate history of a grave character." Mary faced an enormous task: her diary consisted of more than 400,000 words and the entries lacked consistency and direction; some important events had not been recounted at all, while minor occurrences and matters of a personal nature of no interest to general readers received much attention.

By the time she died, on November 22, 1886, Chesnut had managed to transform the unorganized mound of material into a cogent, fascinating diary by both adding insight and details and deleting extraneous text. In her will, she left the diary to a friend, Isabella Martin. Martin later agreed to collaborate with an editor, Myrta Lockett Avary, to further pare down the manuscript to suit the needs of D. Apple and Company of New York. Poorly edited and footnoted, this version of Chesnut's diary was published in 1905 under the title, *Diary From Dixie*; this version was revised and republished in 1949 by a Boston publisher. In 1981, Civil War historian C. Van Woodward edited what is considered the most reliable version, titled *Mary Chesnut's Civil War*.

Chickamauga, Battle of

SEPTEMBER 19–21, 1863

The Confederate army came close to delivering a knockout blow to Federal forces in the West in this horrific two-day September 1863 battle, the region's deadliest Civil War confrontation. After a nearly bloodless campaign ending earlier in the month, Union commander William Rosecrans' Army of the Cumberland occupied Chattanooga, Tennessee, strategic gateway to the southeastern Confederacy.

Eager to continue pressing Braxton Bragg's Army of Tennessee, Rosecrans listened to false rumors fostered by Bragg that the Southern troops were retreating and launched his forces in pursuit. Actually, the Confederate general was gathering reinforcements in northern Georgia to mount an attempt to retake Chattanooga. With the arrival of James Longstreet's corps, his force now outnumbered Rosecrans', 60,000 to 50,000.

Moreover, the Union army had to separate into three columns during its advance through the hilly terrain below the city. Delays and poor coordination kept Bragg's subordinates from successfully attacking the scattered Federals, however, and the clashes alerted Rosecrans to Bragg's ruse. On September 13, the Union general was able to start regrouping his troops, assembling by the west bank of Chickamauga Creek, a small stream just across the Georgia border. Union and Confederate patrols skirmished near the creek on September 18, and the battle began in earnest the following morning.

Bragg's new goal was to attack Rosecrans' left flank and destroy the whole Union army by forcing it into a dead-end valley to cut off any possible retreat back to Chattanooga. Onslaughts by entire divisions of Southern troops were met by counterassaults from George Henry Thomas' corps in a day of brutal, hand-to-hand combat amid dense woods that concluded with only minimal Confederate gains and heavy losses on both sides. After Leonidas Polk delayed a sideways echelon attack against Thomas early on September 20, Bragg ordered Longstreet to launch an all-out frontal assault. The Confederate commander's timing could not have been better. Rosecrans, unable to spot a large section of his troops obscured by the thick forest, mistakenly believed there was a breach in his line and sent a whole division to fill it, creating a real gap on the Union right in the process. Longstreet's forces smashed straight through, overrunning the Union commander's headquarters and sweeping nearly one half of his army from the field. With Rosecrans himself among the troops sent reeling back to Chattanooga, George Henry Thomas was left in command of what remained of the Federal force. Refusing to retreat, he rallied the troops to form a stalwart, if tattered, line on the ridge

The battle lines at Chickamauga, Georgia

of Snodgrass Hill. Relentless assaults by Longstreet and Polk's men throughout the rest of the day failed to dislodge the forces under Thomas, who would earn himself a celebrated nickname, "The Rock of Chickamauga."

Finally, at dusk, he ordered a withdrawal. The Confederates won a huge victory, although Thomas' legendary stand saved the Union army from annihilation. Both sides suffered devastating casualties: 16,000 for the Union and 18,500 for the Confederacy—nearly 30 percent of the troops involved in the battle. Among the dead were a teenaged girl who had disguised herself as a soldier to fight for the Union, and Confederate Brigadier General Ben Hardin Helm, brother-in-law of Mary Lincoln and a close friend of the president. Ten of Bragg's generals

had been either killed or wounded, and his despondency over the heavy cost of victory kept him from following up the next day with an attack on the Federal forces still in retreat. Bragg's surviving subordinates were furious that he let the Union army return unchallenged to their solid Chattanooga fortifications. Longstreet and Polk wanted Bragg to be dismissed and Nathan Bedford Forrest refused to serve under him any longer, while the Confederate commander suspended Polk and two other generals for what he claimed were inferior battlefield performances.

Despite the bickering and the lack of a conclusive blow against the Union army, the victory at Chickamauga raised spirits throughout the South, which had been demoralized by two big losses earlier that summer at Gettysburg and Vicksburg. With the Army of the Cumberland pinned at Chattanooga and about to be besieged by Confederate forces, the North's hopes of holding onto eastern Tennessee were now tenuous.

Clem, John

1851–1937

Only one of many young boys who served in the Civil War before their teen years, Clem became a favorite of the Northern press, which ascribed two popular legends—probably exaggerated—to him. The nine-year-old ran away from home in early 1861 to join up with an army regiment that rode through his Ohio town. Turned away, he tagged along after another unit and became its self-appointed drummer boy, also performing miscellaneous camp chores for the soldiers. His drumming was not much, but Clem, who gave himself a new middle name—Lincoln—was allowed to stay on unofficially, the officers chipping in to pay him a full soldier's wages of $13 a month.

Clem's first brush with fame came in the aftermath of the April 1862 Battle of Shiloh. Giving him the nickname "Johnny Shiloh," Union papers identified Clem as the subject of an instant-hit song and play about a drummer boy whose instrument was punctured during the fighting by a round of artillery fire. Now officially enrolled in the army, complete with a miniature musket fashioned by his comrades, he received even more extensive press as "The Drummer Boy of Chickamauga" after the September 1863 battle, in which he allegedly shot and apprehended a Confederate soldier who tried to take him prisoner during a Union retreat.

Captured once and wounded twice, Clem continued to serve in the army for the remainder of the war, rising to the rank of lance sergeant though he was not 14 by the war's end. When he reached college age, Clem attempted to get into West Point, but was rejected for lacking a formal primary education. After a direct appeal to President Grant, he was given a commission as second lieutenant of a unit of black soldiers. Clem made the military his career, retiring as a major general shortly before World War I.

John Clem

Cold Harbor, Battle of

JUNE 3, 1864

Culminating the awful one-month campaign in Virginia that had already seen the Battles of the Wilderness and Spotsylvania, this contest was Robert E. Lee's last major field victory and, by his own admission, probably the worst mis-

Part of General Grant's army crossed this pontoon bridge during the Battle of Cold Harbor.

take of Ulysses S. Grant's Civil War career. After the fighting at Spotsylvania concluded, the two commanders followed what was becoming a familiar routine, the Union Army of the Potomac advancing further south toward Richmond to try to get around Lee's Army of Northern Virginia and provoke a clash, and the Southern forces dashing ahead to entrench themselves and await the coming onslaught.

There were few lulls in the fighting: in late May, the opponents battled along the North Anna River and Totopotomoy Creek. Both armies then lurched toward Cold Harbor, a crossroads hamlet near the Chickahominy River that was little more than a single tavern, only eight miles from the Confederate capital. Again, the Southerners got there first, a cavalry unit under Lee's nephew Fitzhugh approaching on May 31 and confronting Philip H. Sheridan's mounted troops.

The Union managed to seize the crossroads and held on during a seesaw battle among arriving infantry forces the following day. Replenished with fresh troops, the Union and

Confederate armies alike, despite their grievous losses during the month's fighting, were as large as they had been at the start of the campaign: 110,000 and 60,000 strong, respectively. Although the North had a far greater supply of manpower, most of those sent to Cold Harbor had seen little action, while the Southern reinforcements were experienced battle veterans.

Still, believing the enemy was thoroughly exhausted and dispirited, Grant began to see his chance for the knockout blow against the Confederates that he had been waiting to deliver. "Lee's army is really whipped," the Union commander was convinced, suspecting that a successful assault at Cold Harbor could destroy the Southern force altogether and might win the war right there. Grant ordered Winfield Scott Hancock's corps, which performed so well at Spotsylvania but was not yet on the field, to lead a massive attack he scheduled for the morning of June 2. Marching all night, they were delayed by heat and fatigue, and Grant had to postpone the assault until dawn the next day. The holdup allowed Lee's army to dig in and form a virtually impregnable seven-mile line, protected on both ends by two rising rivers, as the Confederate commander nursed an illness.

With Grant planning an all-out attack against the forbidding Southern defenses, it was his troops, not Lee's, who were demoralized that evening, many pinning pieces of paper with their name and address to their uniforms so that their bodies could later be identified. At 4:30 A.M. on June 3, the Federal assault began, a force of more than 50,000 rushing straight toward the enemy. The entrenched Confederates, hidden by the terrain, waited until the hapless foe got close, then, with a thunderous sound, let loose devastating barrages of gunfire. Unit by unit, the advancing Union men were simply mowed down. Nearly 7,000 fell in the first minutes of the charge. "It was not war," Confederate general Evander Law would later remember. "It was murder."

Although some in Hancock's corps had been able to breach a section of Lee's line, they were quickly repulsed. Within 30 minutes, it was all over—a total failure. Grant called off the attack, ordered his troops to begin digging trenches for a prolonged stay, and assessed the damage. The entire battle had cost him over 12,500 casualties, while Lee's losses were under 4,000. "I have always regretted that the last assault on Cold Harbor was ever made," the Union commander wrote later.

Unwilling to admit defeat to his enemy, it would be days before he would ask for a truce to collect the wounded men still left on the field. By the time a ceasefire was arranged, almost all of them had died. The two forces remained entrenched at Cold Harbor until the evening of June 12, when Grant ordered a withdrawal in the darkness. The war in Virginia then took a new turn as the Union troops headed south yet again—to begin an assault on Petersburg.

Colonization Movement

The idea of establishing foreign settlements for emancipated slaves was considered by a number of Northern abolitionists, who may have supported emancipation but did not care to live among free blacks, and by Southern plantation owners, who preferred that no former slaves be around to give those currently in bondage any ideas above their station. In 1816, an organization of the movement's supporters, the American Colonization Society, was founded. Buying a portion of land on Africa's western coast in what is now Liberia, the organization established a colony for emancipated slaves in 1822.

Most American blacks, however, strongly opposed the movement, and by the early 1830s fewer than 1,500 had settled in Liberia. Failing to receive funding from Congress and divided by tensions between abolitionist and slaveholding members, the society faded, though it did not disband for another two decades. The concept, however, still thrived, with some foreign support (France established another African colony in Libreville, Gabon, for emancipated slaves in 1849).

As tensions between the North and South mounted in the 1850s, some Northern politi-

Joseph J. Roberts, first president of Liberia.

Mrs. Joseph Roberts

cians, including ex-Illinois Congressman Abraham Lincoln, favored an emancipation policy compensating slaveowners for their lost property and then returning the freed slaves to Africa. Though the wishful plan really amounted to deporting an entire race, Lincoln tried putting a better spin on it, calling the idea the return of "a captive people to their long-lost homeland." He had not abandoned the philosophy once he became president and the Civil War began.

In the summer of 1862, to soothe the widespread hostility that was certain to greet his upcoming announcement of the Emancipation Proclamation, Lincoln again started speaking publicly about a colonization policy. In August, the president asked a delegation of black leaders to recruit volunteers for an experimental settlement in Central America that could be expanded to accommodate thousands of free blacks if successful. Assuring them the effort would be entirely voluntary and trying to convince them that it was the best way to ensure blacks freedom from prejudice, better opportunities, and public acceptance of emancipation, he received a scathing response.

Frederick Douglass accused Lincoln of hypocrisy and of having contempt for black Americans, saying that such a policy, which broadly insinuated that former slaves were not able or worthy to live as citizens in the United States, would encourage violence against black people. A black newspaper sarcastically suggested that the slaveowners be shipped abroad instead. Most white abolitionists and Radical Republicans considered the scheme downright immoral. Nevertheless, there was sufficient support in Congress—whose rather skeptical members were certain the enterprise was politically expedient in a midterm election year—to pass a $600,000 appropriation. After Central

America was quickly ruled out as a location for the colony when the governments of Honduras and Nicaragua balked, a group of investors offered in October 1862 to manage a settlement on Ile de Vache, a small island off the coast of Haiti.

More than 450 free blacks were recruited, and in April 1863, the government-sponsored group left for the new colony. The project was doomed from the start. The private backers did not provide the promised buildings or equipment and soon stopped funding the enterprise altogether.

With disease and starvation decimating the settlers, a naval vessel was dispatched in March 1864 to return the 368 survivors to the United States. Congress refused any additional allocations, and there were no more colonization efforts by the Lincoln administration. In any event, by that time black Americans were proving to be far too vital to the Union war effort, in the military as well as in civilian work, to be summarily sent away.

Compromise of 1850

The acquisition of vast new territory following the Mexican War brought the issues of slavery and states' rights—which had been festering for decades—to the forefront of American politics. Spearheaded by Virginia Senator Henry Clay and Daniel Webster of Massachusetts, the bill was an attempt to forge a spirit of cooperation and union in an increasingly disputatious Congress and American public.

Four years earlier, Pennsylvania Congressman David Wilmot introduced legislation stipulating that slavery not be allowed in any new territory or state accepted into the Union. Passed by the Northern-dominated House but failing in the more heavily Southern, pro-slavery Senate, the Wilmot Proviso literally divided the country in two. The threat of secession hung heavily as Congress weighed the future of the newly acquired territory. Although both Clay and Webster opposed slavery, neither believed that the issue should be allowed to destroy the country. It was in that spirit that they ironed out the Compromise of 1850. After ten weeks of debate in the House, the bill reached the Senate floor.

The Compromise allowed slavery to continue but prohibited the slave trade in Washington, D.C. It admitted California to the Union as a free state, but gave newly acquired territories the right to decide for themselves whether to permit slavery. The Compromise also included a strict fugitive slave law that required Northerners to return escaped slaves to their owners. As delicately balanced as it was, the bill was opposed by both anti- and proslavery factions. John C. Calhoun, a passionate states' rights and proslavery advocate, claimed that the Compromise did not go far enough to secure the future of slavery. Without that security, according to Calhoun, the South would eventually secede. Northerners, on the other hand, were appalled by the provisions of the Fugitive Slave Act. Instead of fostering a spirit of compromise, these harsh measures spurred the already active abolition movement.

In the end, however, the Compromise of 1850 was enacted into law, and for ten years, it was enough to stave off the conflict known as the Civil War, a conflict that John Calhoun foresaw ten years before it began, describing it as "irrepressible."

Confederate States of America (CSA)

Its ideology far more conservative than revolutionary, the nation of seceded Southern states faced a paradox in maintaining a centralized government comprised of entities whose very motivation for departing the Union was their objection to federal authority. On February 4, 1861, representatives from the seven states—Alabama, Florida, Georgia, Louisiana, Mississippi, South Carolina, and Texas—that had already seceded from the United States met in Montgomery, Alabama, to form a new republic. On February 8, the convention announced the

Henry Clay addresses the Senate in support of the Compromise of 1850.

establishment of the Confederate States of America and declared itself the provisional Congress.

The following day, Jefferson Davis and Alexander Stephens were unanimously chosen provisional president and vice president, two men moderate enough, it was hoped, to convince the eight other reluctant slave states to join the Confederacy. A committee spent the next five weeks composing a national constitution, which was approved on March 11. The document closely followed the U.S. Constitution—including its Bill of Rights—with a few notable differences. Language promoting "the general welfare" was omitted, while the right to own slaves was explicitly guaranteed (although foreign slave trade was forbidden).

The president, serving a single six-year term, was given line-item veto power over the budget, and his cabinet awarded nonvoting seats in Congress. To guarantee Southerners their much-desired states' rights, the federal government had no authority to levy protective tariffs, make internal improvements, or overrule state court decisions, while states had the right to sustain their own armies and enter into sepa-

The cabinet of the Confederacy.

rate agreements with one another, and were given greater power in amending the constitution. Although there was a provision for a federal Supreme Court, Southern legislators could never agree on its configuration or even the wisdom of its establishment, and so the Confederacy lacked a high court throughout its existence. The provisional Congress sent three envoys to Washington to try to negotiate a final, peaceful split from the United States, although at the same time preparing for combat by establishing an army.

Hopes for a nonviolent settlement died after the April 12 attack on Fort Sumter, and four more Southern states—Virginia, North Carolina, Arkansas, and Tennessee—joined the Confederacy once the war started. Secessionist governments were established in Missouri and Kentucky, two border states that officially remained in the Union, while the western counties of Virginia rejoined the North. The Confederacy's capital was moved from Montgomery to Richmond, Virginia, in May 1861, and regular presidential and congressional elections were held in November.

Running unopposed, Davis and Stephens were formally reinaugurated, quite pointedly, on George Washington's birthday, February 22, 1862. Although there were no established parties, Confederate politics soon divided along pro- and anti-administration lines, and the lack of designated factions only caused confusion and disorganization. Among the opposition, some merely objected to Davis' policies—or his personality—while supporting the war effort; others urged negotiations for peace with the North. Still others, the most ardent states' rights proponents, claimed that the president sought dictatorial powers and denied Davis had anything but the most cursory executive authority.

Some even advocated that their states secede from the Confederacy and form separate countries. After the next congressional elections, held over a nearly six-month period in 1863 due to the logistical problems of the Union military presence across the South, nearly two-fifths of the Confederate House and one half of the Senate were openly anti-administration. Besides the actual waging of the war and futile attempts to win formal recognition from European nations, the Confederate government's main con-

Confederate notes issued in Virginia.

cern was raising money for the costly military effort.

Hampered by constitutional limitations, its attempts included issuing paper currency, which brought rampant inflation, seeking loans and selling government bonds, which did not produce sufficient revenue, and passing tax and tax-in-kind legislation, which was hugely unpopular. As the South suffered continued military setbacks, the government's daily operations were sorely impeded, with congressional members from Union-occupied territories unable to serve in the capital and much of the country essentially out of the Confederacy's jurisdiction.

When Richmond fell to Union forces on April 2, 1865, the Confederate government effectively collapsed. Davis and most of his cabinet, taking the remnants of the country's treasury, fled south by train. Against the advice of most, the president intended to reestablish a seat of government west of the Mississippi River and continue the struggle. But Davis' capture outside Irwinville, Georgia, on May 10 ended the pretense, and there was no longer any

question that the Confederate nation—established little more than four years earlier—had ceased to exist.

Confiscation Acts

1861–1862

Two bills passed by the U.S. Congress in 1861 and 1862 concerning the status of slaves in Union-occupied territory were instrumental in linking emancipation to the North's war effort. From the opening days of the conflict, it was obvious how the forced labor of blacks—building fortifications and transporting supplies, growing cotton for foreign trade and growing food for Southern armies—hugely aided the Confederate cause. Northern military leaders argued that slaves should be confiscated just like any Rebel property used in the waging of their rebellion.

When three fugitive slaves sought asylum at

Union-held Fortress Monroe, Virginia, in May 1861, Commander Benjamin Butler declared that they and others would be considered a "contraband of war," a term that was soon commonly accepted. By that summer, nearly 1,000 contrabands had flocked to the fort, and blacks seeking freedom made their way to Union lines throughout the South. In addition, a massive effort was underway on South Carolina's Sea Islands by the Treasury Department and numerous freedmen's aid societies to establish a contraband colony of over 10,000.

Abolitionists in the military pressed the slavery issue further. In August 1861, John C. Freémont, commander of the Department of the West, issued a decree freeing all slaves belonging to Missouri secessionists, and the following May, David Hunter proclaimed the abolition of slavery throughout his entire department—encompassing South Carolina, Georgia, and Florida. Abraham Lincoln, afraid that emancipation would kill Union support in the border states and the Midwest, revoked both unauthorized orders. By passing its first Confiscation Act in August 1861, however, a badly divided Congress gave Northern commanders limited authority to seize slaves in occupied territory, but only those who had specifically performed war-related work for the Confederacy. While these contrabands could be used by the Union armies, it was left unclear whether they were, in fact, emancipated.

The military's obligations to them were also vague. Some commanders established camps for hundreds of black families, others leased them to local pro-Union planters, and still others sent them back to slaveholders. In March, Congress clarified the army's responsibility, threatening court martial for any officer who returned fugitive slaves. Four months later, the legislature issued a second, more comprehensive Confiscation Act, authorizing the seizure of property—slaves included—belonging to Confederate supporters from seceding states and holding that those slaves "shall be declared and made free."

Initially planning to veto the July 1862 bill, a hesitant Lincoln signed it into law. Because the legislation exempted slaveholders loyal to the North, the president even hoped that it might encourage some vacillating Confederate states to rejoin the Union. Still, the Confiscation Act showed that the North was becoming resolute. With Congress approving the military enlistment of blacks that same month and with Abraham Lincoln himself two months away from issuing the Emancipation Proclamation, abolition was clearly emerging as a Union war goal.

Conscription

Greeted with widespread hostility in both the North and South, the first military drafts in American history were introduced during the Civil War. To many, the very notion of compulsory service went against the nation's precepts of liberty (for white men) and the freedom from federal authority that the seceding states had left the Union to ensure.

At first, it had not been necessary. The war fever that swept through North and South alike in early 1861 brought both armies ample numbers of volunteers. Within a year, however, the Confederacy began to face severe manpower shortages. The hordes of soldiers who had enlisted for 12 months would end their service in spring 1862, and most were not expected to sign up for another hitch. That March, Jefferson Davis, with the endorsement of Robert E. Lee, asked the Confederate Congress to authorize the conscription of new troops. After acrimonious debate, America's first draft law was passed by the Southern legislature on April 16. Current enlistees were required to continue serving for an additional two years, while other able-bodied white males between 18 and 35 (raised to 45 later in the year, and to between 17 and 50 by 1864) were subject to a three-year term.

Workers necessary to the war effort were exempted, from teachers and civil officials to railroad employees and miners. In policies benefiting the rich, draftees were allowed to hire substitutes to serve in their place, and owners and overseers of large plantations were added to the exemption list in the notorious "20 Negro Laws" of October 1862. The following year, to correct the inequities of the draft legislation, substitution was forbidden and the exempted slaveowners were required to pay a $500 "commutation fee." But that did not stop the outcry in the Confederacy against conscription and its chief proponent, Jefferson Davis. His own vice president, Alexander Stephens, was a vocal opponent of the policy, siding with such ardent states' rights advocates as Georgia governor Joseph Brown, who considered it a despotic act and balked at participating in its administration. Thousands of Southern conscripts refused to participate as well, some even forming armed resistance bands in the hills.

The law was difficult to enforce, and army officers like Nathan Bedford Forrest took matters into their own hands, rounding up every able-bodied man in a district and taking them off to service at gunpoint. Up North, meanwhile, the Union faced declining enlistments too. In July 1862, Abraham Lincoln received the legally questionable authorization to order state militias into war service, forcing several states to call drafts of their own to meet the demand and leading to the imprisonment without trial of hundreds of resisters.

On March 3, 1863, U.S. Congress passed the Enrollment Act, a national conscription bill for men between 20 and 45. Instead of granting occupational exemptions, and in addition to permitting the hiring of substitutes, the legislation

Conscription in New York.

excused draftees who paid a $300 commutation fee each time their name was drawn. It was an amount meant to be affordable to the working class, but Democrats and Radical Republicans alike condemned the government's conscription policy, "a rich man's bill" in the words of Congressman Thaddeus Stevens.

When the first call for three-year conscripts came in the summer of 1863, army provost marshals conducted warrantless house searches to locate evaders as antidraft riots erupted throughout the North, from New York City and Boston to the Ohio Valley and the coal mining region of eastern Pennsylvania. Lincoln issued three more calls in 1864, removing the commutation fee option in July but retaining substitution and exempting religious pacifists. Because districts that filled their recruitment quotas with volunteers were excused from the despised draft, local communities paid substantial bounties to draw enlistees.

Stimulating volunteer enlistment was precisely the intention of the conscription laws in both the North and South, for grudging soldiers were thought to make poor fighters. Indeed, despite the uproar, few draftees in the North actually wound up in the military—only 46,000 over the course of the Civil War, about two percent of the Union force. Avoiding service, 87,000 men paid the commutation fee, 118,000 hired substitutes, 310,000 were exempted due to real or feigned disabilities or family hardship, and over 150,000 simply never showed up at their draft boards. The Confederacy was more dependent on conscripts, who comprised almost 20 percent of the total military.

By the fall of 1864, the South even began drafting slaves to build fortifications and perform other manual labor, freeing more white soldiers for front-line duty. Going still further, the Confederate Congress approved the conscription of black men for armed field service in the desperate days of March 1865, but the war ended before slaves were given the dubious opportunity to fight for the South.

Contraband, Black

General Benjamin Butler, the Federal commander at Fortress Monroe, Virginia, added a new term to the American lexicon on May 24, 1861, barely a month into the Civil War. Upon receiving a demand that he turn over to their owner three slaves who had entered Butler's lines in search of freedom, the Union general was faced with a dilemma: to placate the locals by abetting something he abhorred, namely slavery, and return the men; or to find some way to finesse the situation and still stick to his principles. Butler, a Massachusetts politician of some skill, chose the latter option. He declared that the three slaves were "contraband of war," property confiscated for military reasons, and therefore they could not be returned to the putative owner. For the next several months, Butler tried to get the Secretary of War, Simon Cameron, to formulate a standard policy concerning the "contrabands"; Butler was employing them to help strengthen fortifications at Fortress Monroe, and since they were willing workers, he wanted to keep them on the job. There were some 900 newly freed blacks at Monroe, and Butler was determined not to have them turned back into slaves.

He had his difficulties with Confederate officials in the area. In August 1861, Butler found himself opposing the forces of John B. Magruder near the town of Hampton; Butler forced the evacuation of the town for military reasons, but somehow a rumor began to circulate that Butler intended to confiscate the entire town for the "contrabands" at Monroe. Butler got into a heated exchange of ill-considered words with Magruder, arguing over the use of the term "runaway slaves" versus "contraband," but finally Butler managed to convince his opponent that he had evacuated Hampton in a perfectly reasonable manner—and had never intended to give the town away to anyone. This was a distinct embarrassment to Magruder—who had ordered the town burned to the ground. The very next day, August 8, Secretary Cameron gave Butler an interesting solution to his difficulties: the fugitive slave laws, which required the re-

Black contrabands in Culpeper, Virginia.

turn of runaways, were only to be respected in states loyal to the Union. Virginia was in a state of officially recognized "insurrection"; therefore, the laws did not hold in such a territory—or presumably in any similar place.

Cooke, Jay

1821–1905

Selling government bonds to both the public and private sectors, the wealthy financier raised hundreds of millions of dollars for the Union war effort. As a young man, he became a partner at a prominent Philadelphia bank after only eight years in the business, soon heading the firm. Cooke, not yet 40, was enjoying a luxurious semi-retirement when the Civil War brought him back to full-time work. Through his politically influential family's friendship with Salmon P. Chase, he became a close financial adviser to the Union treasury secretary.

First, Cooke used his considerable connections to help the government, plagued by an $80 million deficit, secure much-needed loans from the nation's top banks at a time when gambling on the Union's economic stability seemed a risky investment. Then, turning to the public, he instituted a massive sale of government bonds, fulfilling Chase's novel idea of letting millions of small investors help finance the war. Appealing to the patriotism of the American people, Cooke ran the nation's first war bond drives—so successful that, at some points, nearly $10 million worth of bonds were being sold a day.

The pace hardly slackened as the war continued; in the first six months of 1865, over $850 million in government bonds were purchased. Although the money he raised contributed vastly to the Union's success on the battlefield, Cooke was not without his critics. Receiving commissions for the bond sales, he was accused in some circles to be a profiteer, and a distrustful U.S. Congress once temporarily rescinded his commission to operate as a government agent.

In reality, the commissions Cooke and his firm earned amounted to less than one half of one percent, and the expense of the elaborate bond drives ate up nearly four-fifths of his profits. Moreover, near the end of the war, Cooke used a large portion of his own money to stabilize a rickety market brought to the verge of a financial panic by rampant speculation. Cooke continued in banking after the war, investing in railroads and losing—but later regaining—much of his fortune during a depression in the 1870s.

Copperheads

The antiwar Peace Democrats, also known as Copperheads, posed a nagging political challenge to Abraham Lincoln throughout the war. Although they received the nickname from their opponents, who likened them to venomous snakes, the Copperheads apparently enjoyed the sobriquet and took to wearing copper Indian Head pennies on their lapels. They emerged after the secession crisis of 1860 when the Democratic party split into two factions: the War Democrats—who backed the war effort if not Lincoln's politics—and the Peace Democ-

rats, who would accept an independent Confederacy and were fiercely anti-Republican.

Copperheads asserted that Republican Party policy directly caused the Civil War by purposefully provoking the South to secede, and that they did so to consolidate their own power and to impose "racial equality," a race-baiting phrase sure to alarm the many racists who might otherwise support the fight for union. Copperheads lived in every state in the North, but were most numerous in the Midwest, where anti-Republicanism ran the highest and fears about emancipation the deepest.

As was true for the entire Democratic Party, the popularity of the Copperheads rose as the fortunes of the Union army fell. Their antiwar policies were most appealing as the war dragged on, casualties mounted, and no end appeared in sight. During the winter and spring before the election of 1864, when the Union seemed to be losing ground daily to the persistent Confederate army, the Peace Democrats launched a candidate of their own: none other than Union General George B. McClellan would run on a ticket with a Copperhead vice president.

With a series of stunning Union victories, the threat to Lincoln dissipated. Frequent targets for charges of disloyalty and even treason, some Copperheads formed semi-secret societies with names like Knights of the Golden Circle, Order of the American Knights, and Sons of Liberty.

Lincoln dealt with the most radical groups and individuals forcefully, shutting down antiwar newspapers, arresting suspects and suspending habeas corpus, and censorship. The most prominent Copperhead leader, Clement L. Vallandigham, was convicted of treason and banished forever to the Confederacy.

Cotton, "King"

Overestimating the importance of its cotton exports to the world market, the Confederacy attempted an embargo as a cornerstone of its diplomatic efforts to gain foreign recognition, and wound up seriously undermining its own war effort. The South's confidence was not entirely unwarranted; by 1860, it was producing nearly three-quarters of the world's raw cotton, about one billion pounds a year. England's huge textile industry—indeed its entire economy—seemed dependent on the crop; France's almost as much. "Cotton is King," South Carolina Senator James Hammond proclaimed in a famous 1858 speech. Without it, he concluded, "England would topple headlong and carry the whole civilized world with her." Thus, when the Civil War began, many in the Confederacy expected that England and France would throw their support to the South.

To compel that support—possibly leading to military aid as well as formal recognition—Jefferson Davis and other Confederate leaders ad-

vocated an embargo that would bring a "cotton famine" to Europe. Never formally legislated or mandated, the embargo was still voluntarily observed throughout the South. Within months, cotton exports to England fell to less than five percent of their 1860 level, as Southern planters concentrated on growing food for the Southern armies. Waiving a primary source of income when money was desperately needed to finance its struggle for independence, the Confederacy took a great risk on King Cotton's ability to influence the European powers. The strategy failed badly.

With vast cotton surpluses from the South's bumper crops of 1857 to 1860 on hand, and with India and Egypt emerging as significant new sources of the crop, England and France

This 1863 cartoon depicts members of the Copperhead Party as dangerous snakes.

were not hit by the anticipated shortage for more than a year. Several British textile manufacturers even had enough extra raw cotton to sell bales back to New England mills, also cut off by the South. By late 1862, the British and French economies did begin to feel the effects of the embargo. Rather than the politically influential textile magnates, however, it was the thousands of unemployed mill hands who were hardest hit, and though some urged concessions to the South to resume the cotton trade, the sympathies of the English working class were hardly with the slaveholding Confederates.

Meanwhile, other British industries—from iron to shipbuilding—flourished, as the country's neutral position guaranteed that large orders for war-related goods would continue from both the North and South. Crop failures in Western Europe during the early 1860s, moreover, meant that England and France needed corn and wheat from the North far more than cotton from the South. And once the Emancipation Proclamation brought a moral ingredient to the Union's fight and a string of Northern military victories put the viability of the Confederacy in doubt, the South's attempt to gain European support through what was essentially economic blackmail seemed all the more hopeless.

No longer able to afford wasting its chief asset, the South abandoned its embargo. But by that time, the Union naval blockade was tightly in place, choking off the Confederacy's gravely belated efforts to trade cotton for weapons and supplies.

Crater, Battle of the

JULY 30, 1864

With the potential of being a spectacular success, this mine assault against the Confederate defenses at Petersburg, Virginia, instead became one of the Union army's most tragic fiascos. By June 1864, Grant and his generals were looking for a way to break the entrenched Confederate line protecting the strategically vital Virginia town. Members of a regiment of Pennsylvania coal miners stationed at the front had an idea of their own. By running a mine shaft, packed with explosives, underneath a temporary Confederate stronghold built on high ground 150 yards away, they could simply blow up the fort and watch as a few divisions moved right through the Rebels' center and into Petersburg.

A colonel in the regiment, Henry Pleasants, a mining engineer himself, thought the idea was an excellent one, and brought it to the attention of his corps commander, Ambrose Burnside. Recognizing the chance to salvage his blemished war record in a single, sensational act, Burnside approved the plan, despite the skepticism of his superiors George Meade and Ulysses S. Grant. The Pennsylvania regiment began digging the tunnel on June 25 under Pleasants' supervision, receiving no help from sneering army engineers. Resorting to makeshift tools and using Pleasants' improvised ventilation system, they spent the next month successfully constructing—undetected, contrary to most expectations—a shaft 511 feet long, ending 20 feet directly under the Confederate line.

Up top, Burnside began planning the assault. He assigned his one fresh division to lead the attack, black soldiers who received special training and were eager to prove themselves capable of front-line assignments. Whether he doubted their abilities or feared negative public reaction, Meade overruled Burnside, ordering him to choose a white division to lead the chancy assault instead. Shortly before 5 A.M. on July 30, a charge of four tons of gunpowder packed in the mine shaft exploded in a phenomenal blast, making a crater 170 feet long, 70 feet wide, and 30 feet deep.

Several Confederate units were flung into the sky, one entire regiment and an artillery battery were instantly buried, and Southern soldiers for hundreds of yards around ran in terror.

But the federal assault did not begin for one hour. The commander of the ill-prepared division now leading the attack, James H. Ledlie,

The aftermath of the explosions on July 30, 1864.

was busy drinking rum in a shelter while his troops advanced. Moving forward with two other divisions, many of the soldiers jumped down into the hole rather than going around it. By this time, the Confederates had regrouped and surrounded the rim of the crater, shooting down on the Union troops trapped inside who made gruesomely easy targets. Avoiding the crater, the black division, meanwhile, met a strong Confederate counterattack.

As was all-too-frequent, scores of the black soldiers were shot by infuriated Southern troops while trying to surrender. The total casualties for the Union were 3,798, while the Confederates lost approximately 1,500. Calling the failure "the saddest affair I have ever wit- nessed in the war," Grant dismissed James Led- lie and gave an extended leave to Burnside.

Crittenden, John Jordan

1783–1863

Crittenden, George Bibb

1812–1880

Crittenden, Thomas Leonidas

1819–1893

The abstract concept of the Civil War as one that set "brother against brother" was realized in a very concrete way in this prominent Kentucky family. A father who had toiled for decades to prevent the Civil War watched his two sons take up arms on opposite sides, one as a Union general, the other as a Confederate. John Jordan Crittenden devoted his life to public service in Kentucky and on the national stage, serving in a variety of positions, including U.S. district attorney, U.S. attorney general (under William H. Harrison, from March to September 1841 and again under Millard Fillmore, from July 1850 to March 1853), and governor of Kentucky (1848 to 1850). Apart from these positions, Crittenden spent the majority of his political life in the U.S. Senate, where he was a forceful voice against secession and where he worked tirelessly to forge a compromise that would save the Union from civil war.

As a Democrat, he opposed the Kansas-Nebraska Act of 1854 because it repealed the Missouri Compromise of 1820 and allowed the prospect of slavery to extend below previously

John J. Crittenden

George B. Crittenden

set boundaries, a state of affairs he felt sure would collapse the Union. When Abraham Lincoln was elected president in 1860, Crittenden became the center of the compromise movement in the Senate.

In December 1860, he placed before his congressional colleagues a set of proposals known as the Crittenden Compromise, which attempted to satisfy both sides of the slavery question. When his bill failed to pass and with the country that much closer to war, Crittenden returned home to try to prevent Kentucky from seceding. In that, at least, he was successful, and for the next several months he worked to convince those states that had seceded to re-

consider their positions. Crittenden was not an abolitionist, by any means; his fight was not against slavery, but rather for union. To that end, he supported the North until its aims became more involved in the moral issue of slavery itself. Increasingly discouraged, the elderly statesman—he was 74 years old when the war began—watched his two sons fight in a war he had worked so hard to avoid.

His younger son, Thomas Leonidas, followed most closely in his footsteps, becoming a lawyer and serving as a state attorney in the early 1840s. After fighting in the Mexican War, Thomas returned to Kentucky to practice law. Like his father, he was a firm defender of the Union and joined the Northern army at the start of the war. Serving with distinction at Shiloh, Murfreesboro, and in the Tullahoma Campaign, his career was blighted by his actions at Chickamauga, when he was removed from command after his corps was overrun.

Although he was acquitted of all charges, he was demoted and transferred to the Army of the Potomac; he resigned from the army in December 1864. Thomas' older brother, George Bibb, had an altogether different Civil War experience. Unlike his father and brother, George's staunch proslavery views compelled him to join the Confederacy after graduating from West Point and serving in the Mexican War. Made a major general by Jefferson Davis, George accepted an assignment to lead an invasion of his home state of Kentucky. He fought just one major battle, at Mill Springs, and lost badly when his forces were outflanked by Union Brigadier General George H. Thomas. Accused of being drunk during the attack, George was almost courtmartialed then and there, but remained in the army for another several months, serving under Albert Sidney Johnston to regain Tennessee.

His military career survived just another few months, until he was found drunk and his corps in disarray on April 1, 1862. After being arrested, courtmartialed, and resigning his command, George served out the remainder of the war in various subordinate positions in western Virginia.

Thomas L. Crittenden

Custer (right), with a Confederate prisoner and former West Point classmate.

Custer, George Armstrong

1839–1876

Custer's 1876 last stand at the Little Bighorn was a suitably flashy end to a military career that began so promisingly during the Civil War. His student days were far from illustrious; Custer graduated last in his 1861 class at West Point. In less than a week he was on the battle-field—and in his element—at First Bull Run, and went on to participate as a cavalry officer in all but one of the major engagements fought by the Army of the Potomac. Custer's audacious and fearless charges—some called them reckless—along with his long, curly golden hair and flamboyant dress, gained him notice quickly.

By June 1863, Custer, only 23, became the Union army's youngest general. Soon after, "the Boy General" distinguished himself on the second day of battle at Gettysburg with a series of headlong attacks that held back Jeb Stuart's advance on Culp's Hill. Custer faced Stuart again in May 1864 at the Battle of Yellow Tavern, leading his brigade in the charge that killed the Confederate general.

The following month, Custer and his men were responsible for the hardest fighting at Trevilian Station, the war's bloodiest cavalry engagement. But the golden-haired officer's most notable Civil War contribution was in besting Jubal Early's forces in such battles as Winchester and Cedar's Creek during the 1864 Shenandoah Valley campaign. These feats made Custer, who relished fame and glory, a national hero, although the Confederate cavalry by that time had already been severely weakened. Not that the wartime action Custer saw was effortless; his brigade suffered more casualties than any other Union cavalry unit, and over the course of the conflict 11 horses were killed underneath him, though Custer himself was wounded only once. His valuable service continued through the end of the war. He captured four trainloads of supplies at Appomattox Station on April 8, 1865, one of the final death blows to Robert E. Lee's Army of Northern Virginia, which surrendered the following day.

Custer was nearby when the meeting between Grant and Lee took place in Wilmer McLean's house, and he later grabbed a parlor table as a souvenir. After a court-martial for an 1867 incident, he was reinstated in the army, beginning his Indian-fighting career, which brought Custer more of the fame and glory he so loved. His reputation has been considerably diminished by the historic reappraisal of the U.S. government's treatment of Native Americans.

Custer, Thomas Ward

1845–1876

The younger brother of General George Armstrong Custer, Brevet Colonel Thomas W. Custer has the distinction of being the only person in any branch of the U.S. Army who received two Congressional Medals of Honor during the Civil War.

Enlisting in the Union army at the tender age of 17, he began his military career as an infantryman in Sherman's march to the sea. He was transferred to the cavalry and made an aide to his famous brother upon the elder Custer's promotion to brigadier general in late 1863. His tremendous courage and apparent lack of concern for his own safety earned young Custer a great compliment from the older brother he very much admired: General Custer once told a group of friends, "to show you how much I esteem my brother as a soldier, I believe it is he who should be the general, and I the captain."

As an officer in the 6th Michigan Cavalry, Custer captured Confederate battle flags at great personal risk at Five Forks (April 1, 1865), while leading what proved to be a crucial charge. In that charge he was shot at point-blank range in the face by a Confederate color bearer; the pistol ball entered Custer's left cheek and exited just behind the left ear. He survived the wound, however, and went on to a career as a line officer in the 7th U.S. Cavalry; he died at the head of his troop at the Battle of the Little Bighorn in June 1876, and is buried on the battlefield alongside his men.

D

Davis, Jefferson Finis

1809–1889

Jefferson Davis—cantankerous, in frail health, and reluctant to take on the job—became the provisional president of the Confederate States of America on February 18, 1861. Davis faced challenges so great that most likely even a brilliant military strategist and master politician could not have met them—and Davis was neither. His wide experience in public affairs and the military, as well as his deep, sincere devotion to the Southern cause, made him the most eligible presidential candidate in a field populated by either radical firebrands or inexperienced politicians when the new nation was born. But he was ill-suited to the position.

Obsessed with details, easily distracted by political infighting, physically frail, and with an aloof, abrasive manner, Davis seemed able to accept the enormity of the undertaking before him. In many ways the perfect prototype of a Southern aristocrat, Davis was in fact only a second-generation Southerner. His grandfather was a Pennsylvanian who moved to Georgia, where Davis' father was born.

Davis himself was born in Christian County, Kentucky, the youngest of ten children. A few years after his birth, his family moved to Wilkinson County, a prosperous cotton-growing region of Mississippi. After studying at Transylvania College in Kentucky, he accepted an appointment to West Point. His record there was far from sterling—he graduated twenty-third in a class of 33—but he was not unintelligent. He had a passion for literature, philosophy, and history that lasted throughout his life. After graduation, Davis served as lieutenant on the northwestern frontier, where he gained some military experience during the Black Hawk War. Marrying the daughter of Colonel Zachary Taylor in 1835, he resigned his post and returned to Mississippi, where he settled on a 1,000-acre cotton plantation on the delta. Just three months later, his new bride died of malaria; for the next ten years he lived the life of a solitary gentleman farmer, becoming wealthy by developing his cotton plantation called Brierfield.

In 1845, Davis married Varina Howell of Natchez, whose influence on him and his political life was enormous. The same year he remarried, he entered politics for the first time and was elected to Congress as a Democrat. Except for a short stint in the Mexican War, he worked in the public service throughout his life.

From the start, he was a champion of states' rights and the Southern cause, advocating sound currency, a low tariff, and territorial expansion. His first term in Congress was cut short by the Mexican War. In 1846, he took command of the Mississippi Rifles and fought well the Battle of Monterrey, and then at Buena Vista, where he was wounded when his regiment stopped an enemy cavalry charge. This experience, which accorded him a hero's welcome upon his return, gave Davis confidence in his own military skills, a confidence some say was exaggerated.

With the war over, he was appointed to represent Mississippi in the Senate, then resigned to make an unsuccessful bid for the governorship in 1851. In 1853, President Franklin Pierce appointed him secretary of war, a post he served with distinction. Some of Davis' actions as secretary were not those of a typical anti-federalist: he took steps to improve the national army, to offer protection to the far-flung territories, and to explore routes for a transcontinental railroad. Nevertheless, the interests of his home region always came first, and Davis found time to push for passage of the controversial 1854 Kansas-Nebraska Act.

When Davis returned to the Senate in 1857, he was recognized as the spokesman of the South, openly proclaiming slavery as an economic and moral good and openly supporting its extension. He championed what he considered to be the constitutional right of a state to choose and maintain its own institutions—including slavery. At the same time, however, Davis was not an adamant secessionist. He worked tirelessly to find common ground between the radicals on both sides of the Mason-Dixon line, supporting John Breckenridge—who, like Davis, was a Southerner first, but loved the Union nonetheless—for president in the election of 1860.

Once Abraham Lincoln was elected, Davis knew there was no longer any room for compromise. On January 5, 1861, he joined other Southern senators in urging each state to secede as soon as possible and to provide the means of organizing a Southern Confederacy. After Mississippi seceded, Davis resigned to accept the rank of major general and the command of his state's military forces. Expecting a top military command from the new Confederacy, he was both shocked and dismayed at learning the provisional Confederate Congress had selected him as president. As the country prepared for war, Davis organized his cabinet and reviewed the South's military and economic resources.

The challenge he faced from the North was, perhaps, insurmountable. Behind him he had fewer than nine million people, more than a third of whom were slaves, and an economy largely based on agriculture. His opponent, on the other hand, consisted of 22 million people and an extensive industrial base. Davis immediately ordered the construction of factories to produce war matériel, sent agents abroad to secure arms and ammunition, and set about choosing his cabinet.

Of the more than 15 men who served in Davis' cabinet, only three remained his loyal supporters: Judah Benjamin, first attorney general, then secretary of war; Stephen R. Mallory, secretary of the navy; John H. Reagan, postmaster general. In addition, his two secretaries of

Jefferson Davis

the treasury, Christopher G. Memminger and George A. Trenholm also served him well. Together, Davis and Benjamin attempted to raise foreign support for the Confederate cause, but to no avail. Britain, perhaps because of its critical need for Northern wheat, refused to recognize the Confederacy, and France feared to act alone. Apart from his efforts in foreign affairs, Davis spent most of his time and effort conducting the war. His interference in military matters was so great that five secretaries of war quit the post during the course of the war.

For the most part, however, Davis' military instincts were good, especially when it came time to choose generals to lead his army. At least at first, he had far more luck in finding willing and able commanders than was Abraham Lincoln in the North: unlike Union generals George B. McClellan and John Pope, Joseph E. Johnston and Robert E. Lee were tenacious fighters willing to take risks from the very start of the war. With Johnston at the head of the Confederate army (then called the Army of the Potomac), the Confederacy won the first major battle of the war at First Bull Run. When Johnston was wounded at the Battle of Seven Pines, Davis made one of his best military decisions of the war when he replaced him with Robert E. Lee, and the renamed Army of Northern Virginia. This appointment, made on June 1, 1862, was a controversial one, for Lee was neither well-known or well-respected. Davis instinctively trusted Lee, however, and stood by him throughout the war.

The president's trust was rewarded almost immediately when Lee chased McClellan away from Richmond and back toward Washington during the Seven Days campaign in the summer of 1862. Davis wholeheartedly supported Lee's decision to invade the North during the fall; only because Lee's battle plans fell into McClellan's hands did the South lose the battle at Antietam on September 17, 1862. By the spring of the following year, Davis, faced by an increasing shortage of men to fill his army's ranks and the prospect of at least another year of war, was forced to raise troops by conscription, an act adamantly opposed by a Confederate Congress largely made up of staunch states'

rights advocates. The conscript law raised an opposition to Davis in Congress and throughout the South that lasted to the war's end, as did his decision to suspension of habeus corpus on at least three occasions in 1862 and 1864. His efforts to raise funds through taxation were also denounced. In fact, the longer the war dragged on, the more resistance Davis faced from his cabinet and Congress.

The need for a powerful, centralized government—especially in times of war—went against the very concept of the Confederacy as a group of independent states, and Davis was often called a dictator when taking action required of a commander-in-chief. As the war progressed and Davis assumed more power, his cabinet and Congress fought him every step of the way. With no formal political parties in the South, the internal politics of the Confederacy quickly divided into pro- and anti-Davis factions. His tendency toward cronyism did not help matters, especially when he supported people in positions they were clearly unsuited to, such as Braxton Bragg, whose ineptness as a commanding officer was evident for years before Davis finally removed him. Although it is unlikely that his interference in military matters significantly altered the outcome of the war, Davis became a convenient scapegoat for those in the South who wanted someone to blame for their mounting losses.

With the fall of Richmond in April 1865, Davis and his cabinet fled to Georgia to escape arrest. Davis was captured about a month later near Irwinsville, Georgia, and held for two years at Fort Monroe. Never brought to trial, he was finally released on bail and a decision not to prosecute was made by the Federal government. After traveling for a number of years, Davis returned to Mississippi, where he spent his last years writing *The Rise and Fall of the Confederate Government*, a book every bit as self-righteous as its author, who remained a proud, unrepentant Confederate warrior until his dying day, December 9, 1889.

Davis, Varina Howell

1826–1905

The Confederacy's only first lady was a woman of wit and intelligence. Like her Union counterpart, Mary Lincoln, she was frequently the object of public criticism.

Born in Mississippi to a family with Northern roots, she was the granddaughter of an eight-term governor of New Jersey. Her education, extensive for a young woman of her era, included several years at a Philadelphia finishing school. At 17, Varina Howell met Jefferson Davis, a widower more than twice her age, whose first wife was a daughter of Zachary Taylor. The couple married in 1845, and as her husband rose in the Democratic party, Mrs. Davis became a prominent Washington hostess while managing the affairs of their Mississippi plantation.

Varina Howell Davis

Keenly interested in politics herself, she silenced her Whig beliefs for the sake of Davis' political career. She joined her husband in Montgomery, Alabama, shortly after his inauguration as Confederate president in February 1861, and the family moved to the new capital, Richmond, that spring. There, Davis gave birth to two of her six children. Another child, Joe, died at age five in a fall from the rear balcony of the Southern "White House" in 1864.

Despite personal tragedy and the challenges posed by the South's armed struggle, she performed well the disparate duties of first lady, though there were those who found reason to complain. Some criticized her for entertaining too lavishly in wartime; others criticized her for not entertaining enough to raise the beleaguered nation's spirits. She was suspected of Union loyalties because of her family's Northern background, accused of interfering in the South's political affairs because she voiced her opinions to her husband, and chastised for supposedly hiring a white nanny.

Less noticed was her subtler work as her burdened husband's companion, confidante, staunch defender, and—during his frequent illnesses—nurse. They were together when Davis was captured by Union forces near Irwinville, Georgia, in May 1865, and she spent the next two years lobbying for his release from prison, her efforts including a personal meeting with a sympathetic President Johnson.

The couple subsequently settled at "Beauvoir," an estate near Biloxi bequeathed by a benefactor, which Varina Davis converted into a home for Confederate veterans following her husband's death in 1889. Publishing her memoirs the following year, she then moved to New York City, where she lived with her one surviving daughter and continued to write for magazines until her death in 1905.

Desertion

Although totals are difficult to calculate, both the Union and Confederate armies were plagued by desertions during the Civil War. Neither side needed precise statistics to recognize that military strength was sapped and morale damaged by troops abandoning their posts.

Desertions were especially rife after long campaigns and bloody battles. Army of the Potomac officers, for instance, reported well over a hundred new absentees a day in early 1863 after the Union's disastrous defeat at Fredericksburg. At times, perhaps as much as one third of the North's fighting force was absent without leave, and over 260,000 desertions (and 75,000 arrests for the crime) were recorded by the end of the war. The proportion was even greater in the South, occasionally between one third to one half of the troops.

As the Confederacy faced collapse in 1865, almost 200,000 Rebel soldiers had left their units—some heading for home, others seeking food and shelter from the enemy—and Robert E. Lee was losing nearly an additional ten percent of his men each month. Throughout most of the conflict, however, army deserters were as likely to be absent only temporarily as to abandon the military altogether. Those who had been farmers returned to their fields for planting season, and other soldiers, especially those from the war-ravaged South, went to their families' aid when they received word of desperate circumstances at home.

The wholesale attack on civilian property during William T. Sherman's march through Georgia and the Carolinas, in particular, drove thousands of Confederates home to help their loved ones. Others deserted—temporarily or permanently—out of sheer frustration with military life: the homesickness and tedium, the poor food, clothing, and shelter, the strict discipline and infrequent furloughs, the arduous daytime marches and all-night trench-digging sessions, and the possibility of death on the battlefield or from epidemics that swept through the camps.

Hundreds of proslavery Northern troops—encouraged by antiwar Copperheads, who would sometimes furnish train tickets and civilian clothes for their flight—abandoned the fight when emancipation became a Union war

policy in 1862. Some Southerners who would defend their homeland did object to invading the North and left their units during the Antietam and Gettysburg campaigns. And with conscription laws offering men of wealth and prominence plenty of loopholes, Union and Confederate soldiers alike came to view the whole conflict as a "rich man's battle/poor man's fight" and decided they were no longer willing to risk their lives for those who could easily buy their way out of the service. On occasion, deserters even switched sides, including hardscrabble Southerners who left the army to join Unionist guerrilla bands in the backwoods of lower Appalachia.

The most frequently committed military infraction, desertion was usually treated lightly in the Civil War's early days. When the magnitude of the problem became clear, commanders on both sides were not certain whether harsh discipline or leniency was a more effective response. Subject to arrest, flogging, branding with an ignominious "D," and imprisonment, deserters received harsher punishment as the war progressed, but the Union and Confederate armies rarely resorted to the firing squad. Although he approved several executions earlier, Abraham Lincoln commuted the death sentences of deserters in a February 1864 clemency act, and the previous March issued the first general amnesty for returning military absentees, with up to 15,000 rejoining their units.

That August, on the urging of Robert E. Lee, Jefferson Davis pardoned deserters as well, but far fewer Southerners took up the offer. Because it could not afford to waste the dwindling number of able-bodied men in stockades, the Confederacy, to a great extent, relied on patriotic appeals to discourage absenteeism. By the final months of the war, however, the tide of desertion could not be stemmed. The thousands of Southern soldiers abandoning the field were not forsaking their patriotism as much as merely acknowledging earlier than their commanders that the cause was lost.

Dix, Dorothea

1802–1887

A noted social reformer, Dix became the Union's Superintendent of Female Nurses during the Civil War.

The soft-spoken yet autocratic crusader had spent more than 20 years working for improved treatment of mentally ill patients and for better prison conditions. A week after the attack on Fort Sumter, Dix, at age 59, volunteered her services to the Union and received the appointment in June 1861 placing her in charge of all women nurses working in army hospitals. Serving in that position without pay through the entire war, Dix quickly molded her vaguely defined duties.

Dorothea Dix

She convinced skeptical military officials, unaccustomed to female nurses, that women could perform the work acceptably, and then recruited women. Battling the prevailing stereotypes—and accepting many of the common prejudices herself—Dix sought to ensure that her ranks not be inundated with flighty and marriage-minded young women by only accepting applicants who were plain-looking and older than 30. In addition, Dix authorized a dress code of modest black or brown skirts and forbade hoops or jewelry.

Even with these strict and arbitrary requirements, relaxed somewhat as the war persisted, a total of over 3,000 women served as Union army nurses. Called "Dragon Dix" by some, the superintendent was stern and brusque, clashing frequently with the military bureaucracy and occasionally ignoring administrative details. Yet, army nursing care was markedly improved under her leadership.

Dix looked after the welfare of both the nurses, who labored in an often brutal environment, and the soldiers to whom they ministered, obtaining medical supplies from private sources when they were not forthcoming from the government. At the war's conclusion, Dix returned to her work on behalf of the mentally ill.

"Dixie"

A simple song composed by noted minstrel performer David Decatur Emmett became the unofficial anthem of the Confederacy after it was played at Jefferson Davis' inauguration in 1861. First titled "I Wish I was in Dixie's Land" when it was copyrighted in 1860, its melody and lyrics inspired many a Rebel soldier during the war and still evokes images of the antebellum South today. The origin of the name that has become synonymous with the South remains uncertain. Some believe that Dixie comes from Louisiana, where the French word for ten, *dix*, was printed on the ten-dollar bill. A more likely theory holds that it derives from the Mason-Dixon Line, the unofficial political dividing line between North and South.

Douglas, Stephen Arnold

1813–1861

In his desire to expand the size and power of the United States, this Illinois senator instead divided the country down the middle. Of the legislation passed in the decade preceding the Civil War, none so completely undermined the chances of compromise between the North and South as the Kansas-Nebraska Act introduced by Douglas in 1854. A Democrat, friendly to the South but hardly an avid proslavery advocate, Douglas' interest lay in putting an end to the long argument by pleasing both sides of the slavery issue, an apparently impossible task.

Douglas won election to the U.S. Senate in 1847, after spending several years in the House of Representatives and working as a lawyer in Jacksonville, Illinois. A short man with a large head and broad shoulders, Douglas earned the nickname the "Little Giant," both for his appearance and for his energy and integrity. As chairman of the Senate committee on the territories, Douglas found himself at the center of the slavery controversy over whether new states should be free or slaveholding.

Douglas' main goal was to settle the issue as quickly as possible and get on with the business at hand which was, as he saw it, to expand the country's territory through to California and build a transcontinental railroad across it. To solve the deadlock, Douglas proposed the Kansas-Nebraska Act, which embodied the concept of "popular sovereignty": the people who lived in each frontier region should themselves decide if slavery should exist in their territory. By doing so, the act would repeal the Missouri Compromise, which specified that slavery was restricted to land below latitude 36° 30'.

After much debate, the Kansas-Nebraska Act passed, with disastrous results. "Bleeding

Kansas" became embroiled in near civil war as proslavery and abolitionists fought it out, often with violence. Taking responsibility for the fiasco, Douglas continued to work within Congress to solve the festering problem.

When Douglas ran for reelection to the Senate in 1858, his opponent was Abraham Lincoln, a man then almost unknown outside Illinois. During the campaign, Douglas publicly challenged Lincoln's antislavery stance in a series of seven debates. With Lincoln claiming that "a house divided against itself cannot stand" and Douglas clinging to the concept of popular sovereignty, the debates drew national attention. Douglas made enemies among radical Southerners during the debates with his

Stephen Douglas

"Freeport doctrine," in which he described his theory of popular sovereignty: slavery could not exist without friendly local legislation, which the people could withhold if they chose.

Douglas won the election, but by a close margin, on November 2, 1858. However, his stance on the sovereignty issue lost him the Democratic presidential nomination in 1860 and forced a split within the party. This split assured Lincoln's election. Once war was declared, Douglas put aside his differences with his former opponent and vigorously supported the Union cause. "There can be no neutrals in this war," he declared, "only patriots—or traitors." Douglas died a few months later, before he could witness the brutality of the war he had done his best to avoid but, ironically, had helped to set in motion.

Douglass, Frederick

1817–1895

This son of a slave and a white man became the chief spokesman for the abolition movement and for the rights of African-Americans before, during, and after the Civil War.

Born Frederick August Washington Bailey to a slave, Harriet Bailey, and an unknown white man, Frederick was sent to Baltimore to work as a house slave when he was eight years old. Educated by the mistress of the house, he learned to read and write and later was trained in ship repair. After making one failed attempt at escape, he finally made it north to New Bedford, Massachusetts, where he found work as a ship caulker and changed his name to Douglass to avoid capture.

In 1841, at the age of 24, he attended a meeting of the Massachusetts Anti-slavery Society, an abolitionist group headed by William Lloyd Garrison. There he spoke for the first time in public about his experiences as a slave—and as a free black man in a North full of prejudice. His eloquence impressed Garrison enough for him to hire Douglass as a full-time lecturer,

bringing him from meeting hall to meeting hall across the country to stir up support for the abolitionist cause.

In 1845, Douglass published his autobiography, *Narrative of the Life of Frederick Douglass*, which brought him to national prominence. Fearing that his notoriety would lead to his arrest and return to the South, Douglass moved to England for two years, where he was able to raise enough money to buy his freedom. Upon his return, he broke with Garrison and the more radical abolitionists.

Douglass was, in essence, a conservative man who believed in the principles embodied in the U.S. Constitution. He did not want to change the fundamental structure of the Constitution or of the nation itself, but rather wanted to effect peaceful, legal solutions to the problems the country faced. Altough he struck up friendship with John Brown, Douglass was shocked at the violence displayed by abolitionists at Harpers Ferry and elsewhere.

On one point he was adamant, however: the institution of slavery was an abomination not to be tolerated; black men—and women, for Douglass also worked for women's rights—must be considered and treated as equals. To that end, he founded the antislavery newspaper, the *North Star*. For more than 16 years, the *North Star* and it successor, *Douglass's Monthly*, were voices for the abolition movement in the United States.

As the country drew closer to civil war, Douglass tried his best to make slavery—not states' rights or protective tariffs—the main issue. After the fall of Fort Sumter, he wrote in *Douglass's Monthly*, "Fire must be met with water, darkness with light, and war for the destruction of liberty must be met with war for the destruction of slavery . . . This war with the slaveholders can never be brought to a desirable termination until slavery, the guilty cause of all our national troubles, has been totally and forever abolished."

When appeals to consider the immoral nature of slavery went unmet, Douglass took a different tack: Northerners should support abolition if only to rid the South of their most important economic resource. Douglass also argued, persistently and eloquently, for allowing African-Americans to serve as soldiers. On both of these points, he found himself at odds with the commander-in-chief of the North, Abraham Lincoln.

While he personally found slavery offensive, Lincoln was willing to make its abolition an issue only when it would help the North win the war. That time came in the fall of 1862; Lincoln needed the moral and economic support Europe would give him when he clearly linked emancipation to the Union cause; he hoped thousands of blacks in the south would rush north, disrupting if not crippling the Confederacy; and he also looked forward to adding black soldiers to his own dwindling forces.

On January 1, 1863, Douglass rejoiced at news of the Emancipation Proclamation. Although he knew it did not go nearly far enough to assure blacks equal rights, he worked with new energy to support Lincoln's war effort. Throughout the late winter and spring of 1863, Douglass devoted himself to black recruitment. He urged blacks to "fly to arms, and smite with death the power that would bury the government and your liberty in the same hopeless grave."

Black recruitment was extremely important to Douglass; only with their participation in the war would abolition and full citizenship be granted to them. "Once let the black man get upon his person the brass letters *U.S.*; let him get an eagle on his button, and musket on his shoulders and bullets in his pocket, and there is no power on earth which can deny that he has earned the right to citizenship in the United States." Nevertheless, when he realized how badly African-Americans were being treated in the Union armies, he appealed directly to President Lincoln. The two men met in July 1863. Although disappointed in the president's response—Lincoln claimed that giving black soldiers equal pay ran counter to popular feeling and would provoke opposition he couldn't risk at that time—Douglass left impressed with his honesty and candor.

After the war, Douglass continued to work for the civil rights cause, claiming that the work of abolitionists would not be over "until the black men of the South, and the black men of the North, shall have been admitted, fully and completely, into the body politic of America." He fought with Andrew Johnson over his reconstruction policies, pressuring the Republican-dominated Congress to provide some measure of relief to the beleaguered black man in the South.

After the election of Ulysses S. Grant to the presidency, Douglass' last years were spent in honor and comfort. He held a number of government positions, including marshal of the District of Columbia and consul general to Haiti. He died at the age of 78 at his home in Cedar Hills, Washington, D.C.

Dred Scott Decision

MARCH 1857

By declaring the Missouri Compromise unconstitutional and denying slaves the right to U.S. citizenship, this Supreme Court decision solidified antislavery sentiment in the North and deepened the rift between North and South.

From 1834 to 1838, Scott, a slave, accompanied his master, army surgeon Dr. John Emerson, to posts in Illinois and the Minnesota territory, where slavery was illegal. In 1838, Scott returned to Missouri with his master. After Emerson's death in 1843, Scott sought freedom for himself and his family through the Missouri courts. Scott's lawyers argued unsuccessfully that his stay in a free state and free territory had released him from slavery.

After losing the initial trial, Scott won a retrial, but the latter reversal was overruled by the state supreme court in 1852. Undaunted, Scott's lawyers succeeded in shifting the case into the federal district court in 1853 through a rather tricky maneuver: In 1852, Scott became the property of John Sanford, Emerson's widow's brother, when the former Mrs. Emerson remarried. Scott then sued Sanford for assault in the federal court. Whether or not the charge was true or not has never been documented, but the case soon became a cause célèbre across the country. Sanford's lawyers challenged the federal court's jurisdiction on the basis that Scott could not be a citizen because he was a slave. The jury returned with a mixed verdict: it found Sanford not guilty and Scott still Sanford's slave.

Scott's lawyers appealed the case to the Supreme Court in 1854; due to a backlog, the case was not heard until February 1856. Scott's case as presented to the Supreme Court boiled down to three major issues. First, was Scott, as a black man and as a slave, entitled to sue in the federal courts? Second, did his temporary stay in a free state and territory give him freedom upon return to the slave state of Missouri? Third, did Congress have the constitutional power in the Missouri Compromise or any other legislature to prohibit slavery in the federal territories?

At the time the case was brought forward, the Supreme Court was made up of five proslavery judges from the South and four Northerners with various opinions on the matter. At first, the proslavery contingent intended to avoid all

The Dred Scott decision left the country further divided over the question of slavery.

three issues by simply claiming that the state law of Missouri was binding in the case. However, at least two of the Northerners on the Court were not prepared to drop the matter, but instead threatened to write dissenting opinions declaring the Missouri Compromise legal and Scott a free man.

To avoid giving the abolitionists the chance for a propaganda victory, the five Southerners came out in favor of issuing a far broader decision. Before they could do so, however, they felt they needed to have the support of at least one Northern judge. They urged President James Buchanan to convince his friend on the Court, Justice Robert Grier of Pennsylvania, to join them; perhaps out of loyalty to his friend and perhaps because he was himself in favor of slavery, Grier agreed.

In the end, *Dred Scott* v. *Sandford* (Sanford's name was misspelled in the official court document) was a 6–2 decision against Scott. Although each of the judges wrote separate opinions, Chief Justice Roger Taney spoke for the majority. In the opinion of the Court, slaves and their dependents were neither citizens of the United States nor of the state of Missouri and hence not entitled to sue in the courts. Further, despite Scott's temporary residence in a free state, his status as a slave was determined by his residence at the time the case was brought before the Court. Third, the Supreme Court ruled that the Missouri Compromise was unconstitutional under the Fifth Amendment, which states that Congress may not deprive persons of property without the due process of law.

The two dissenters on the Court, John McLean and Benjamin R. Curtis, refuted Taney's opinion, stressing Scott's stay in Minnesota and Illinois, as well as the authority of Congress to prohibit slavery in the territories. The first decision since *Marbury* v. *Madison* in 1803 to declare an act of Congress unconstitutional, Dred Scott added another log to the growing fire of sectional animosity.

E

Early, Jubal Anderson

1816–1894

Hunched with arthritis, unkempt, feisty, abrasive, and sacrilegious, with a stinging wit and a taste for liquor, "Old Jube," as he was affectionately called by his troops, was an unforgettable character and one of the South's favorite and ablest generals.

A member of an aristocratic Virginia family, Early graduated eighteenth in his 1833 West Point class and fought in the Seminole War and Mexican War. He retired from the army and became a lawyer and legislator, attending his state's 1861 secession convention, where he voted for remaining in the Union.

Once the war began and Virginia joined the Confederacy, however, he returned to the military for the South. After an impressive performance at First Bull Run, Early was promoted to brigadier general. He led a brigade in the spring 1862 Peninsula campaign in Virginia, until he was wounded in the shoulder at the Battle of Williamsburg in May. Recovering quickly, Early led a division in such major battles as Antietam, Fredericksburg, Chancellorsville, Gettysburg, and the Wilderness.

Although he was often perilously impetuous in battle, he proved to be a superb commander and was rapidly promoted. As lieutenant general heading a corps of 14,000, he led his most daring attack—a raid on Washington, D.C., in June and July 1864—that was a shocking setback for the Union. Heading up from the Shenandoah Valley, his troops seized or destroyed property throughout the Maryland countryside. Threatening to burn the villages, Early wrested $20,000 in ransom from Hagerstown and $200,000 from Frederick.

Early's corps crushed a small Federal force near the Monocacy River on July 9 and in two days came within five miles of the Union capital. Its fortifications lightly manned, Washington seemed in serious jeopardy. But Early's advance had been stalled at Monocacy, giving a Union corps time to reinforce the capital, and Early withdrew back into the Shenandoah Valley.

Later that month, Early's troops raided even deeper into the North and burned Chambersburg, Pennsylvania, on July 30 when the town refused to turn over $500,000. Sending Philip Sheridan's forces into the Shenandoah Valley, Ulysses Grant ordered the general to pursue Early "to the death."

A subsequent series of defeats in the valley decimated Early's army. After an old-fashioned yet lethally effective saber charge by Union forces at the Battle of Winchester on September 19, Early lost a quarter of his men. Sheridan's army routed the survivors three days later at Fisher's Hill, forcing Early into a 60-mile retreat.

In a final attempt to hold the valley, the Confederate general led a surprise attack at Cedar Creek at dawn on October 19. What first appeared to be a smashing triumph for Early soon turned into one of the Union army's most decisive victories, when Sheridan's men successfully counterattacked, shattering the Confederate forces and driving them from the region. The following March, Early's small remaining army was badly beaten again by Sheridan in Waynesborough, and Early, relieved of command by a reluctant Robert E. Lee, headed to Texas to join the fighting out West.

The war ended before he arrived, however, so Early went to Mexico, then Cuba and Canada, where he wrote his memoirs. Returning to Virginia in 1869, he resumed practicing law and later worked for the Louisiana state lottery. For the rest of his life, Early defiantly remained an unreconstructed Confederate and became the first president of the Southern Historical Society.

Election of 1860

Pre-war tension between North and South—mounting for decades—reached its peak in the spring of 1860. A bitter presidential nomination process, a hard-fought campaign, and a decisive Republican and Northern victory ultimately pushed the nation into civil war.

Perhaps more than any other single event, John Brown's Harpers Ferry raid polarized the country and set the political stage for the election of 1860. Southern whites, already fearful of an increasingly powerful North, were badly shaken by this brutal attack on slavery; the reaction of many Northern whites, who almost immediately elevated Brown to martyr status, only exacerbated these Southern fears. Even Northern conservatives, who by and large condemned the violence of the raid itself, were appalled by the hasty trial and execution of its leader.

The deep divisions within the U.S. Congress reflected the tension and hostility of the general public: with the Democrats controlling the Senate but no party comprising an absolute majority in the House, legislative matters stood at a standstill as the two parties prepared for their nominating conventions.

The Democrats held their convention first, meeting in April at Charleston, South Carolina. The leading Democratic contender up to this point had been Stephen Douglas, but his willingness to compromise on the issue of slavery in the territories alienated most white Southerners. A minority of Democrats, mostly from the lower South and led by Alabama senator William Lowndes Yancey, demanded that the party endorse a federal slave code in its national platform. Based on Jefferson Davis' theory that Congress had a positive duty to pass legislation protecting the rights of slavery in the territories whenever those rights were threatened or denied, the controversial slave code proposal split the Democratic party. Douglas refused to endorse it, convinced that such a platform would lose him votes in the North. In response, the minority Democrats refused to participate and stormed out of the meeting hall. The fractured Democratic party planned another convention for June 19, hoping to mend itself in time to form a united front.

In the meantime, the Constitutional Union party was formed in May by Democrats desperate for compromise. Led by John Bell of Tennessee and Edward Everett of Massachusetts, the party's platform consisted largely of a declaration of support for the Union, a love of the Constitution, and an attitude of compromise on the issue of slavery. It appealed largely to proslavery Democrats in the border states who wanted to avoid a war that would surely be fought most fiercely in their territory.

In May, the almost equally divided Republican party was nevertheless able to effect a compromise by nominating Abraham Lincoln. Party members considered preconvention front-runner Senator William Henry Seward of New York too radical on the slavery issue—he was an ardent abolitionist unable to compromise—to win support from conservative Republicans, particularly in the border states. Although Lincoln and his running mate, Hannibal Hamlin of Maine, were fairly moderate on the slavery question—they insisted that Congress could prohibit slavery in the territories, but also felt that the Constitution protected slavery in those states where it already existed—the South had a great deal to fear from his election. A Republican administration would no doubt support Northern economic interests over Southern ones, including the institution of high tariffs, promotion of homesteading in the West, and the granting of government subsidies to build a Pacific railroad.

When the Democratic party regrouped in Baltimore, it was unable to mend the split between the Northern and Southern factions. A predominately Northern group nominated Douglas, while Southern Democrats nominated John C. Breckinridge, whose platform called for a federal slave code. During the campaign that followed, Lincoln succeeded in his main objective—to "hedge against divisions in the Republic ranks"—but the Democratic party appeared hopelessly divided.

The results of the November election reflected the sectional appeal of its candidates. Lincoln carried the North with a sweeping majority of 180 electoral votes. Democrats gave Breckinridge 72 electoral votes and Bell 39. Douglas, whom the Northern Democrats hoped would appeal to moderates on both sides, took

The Republican ticket in the Election of 1860.

only the 12 electoral votes from Missouri and New Jersey. The popular vote, however, was much closer. Lincoln polled 1,866,452 votes, but Douglas came in a close second with 1,376,957. Breckinridge trailed with 849,781 and Bell with 588,879.

After Lincoln's election, disunion quickly followed. South Carolina was the first to secede in a state convention held on December 20. Within weeks, four other states—Georgia, Alabama, Florida, and Mississippi—had followed suit by calling for state conventions in January. By February 1861, a month after Lincoln's inauguration, seven states had left the Union. Two months later, the American Civil War began when Fort Sumter fell to the newly born Confederate army.

Election of 1864

The first time any nation held a free election in the middle of a civil war, this presidential campaign, almost a referendum on continuing the armed struggle, would determine the conflict's outcome.

Although Abraham Lincoln wound up winning with a solid, if not overwhelming, majority, his reelection was by no means assured. For a time, it seemed questionable that he would even receive his own party's nomination for a second term—no president had even been renominated, let alone reelected, since 1840—and it took some timely military victories to reverse the president's fortunes. The stagnation of the war effort, highlighted by such discouraging defeats as Grant's disastrous loss at Cold Harbor in June, plunged the North into a sour mood.

Fed up with the conflict, many voters, especially Democrats, were willing to seek a negotiated settlement with the Confederacy. Many Radical Republicans, on the other hand, believed Lincoln's policies were not aggressive enough and quietly looked for another candidate to run. A surreptitious bid by Secretary of Treasury Salmon P. Chase, however, was scuttled with the "Pomeroy Circular," an endorsement of Chase's intention to run by a Kansas senator that proved deeply embarrassing to the cabinet member when it was released publicly.

The Republican mainstream, nevertheless, continued to support Lincoln—nervously—hoping to improve their chances by forming a coalition with pro-administration War Democrats, under a National Union ticket that ignored the divisive Reconstruction issue. To strengthen the alliance, Lincoln allowed, and perhaps encouraged, his vice president, Hannibal Hamlin, to be dropped as his running mate at the June nominating convention, in favor of Democrat Andrew Johnson, military governor of Tennessee.

The Democratic party, meanwhile, nominated ex-Army of the Potomac Commanding General George McClellan in August, expecting to benefit from his vast popularity with his former troops. McClellan, however, was saddled with a contentious pro-peace platform—pushed through by Copperheads, who wielded great power at the August party convention—that he would not endorse, and a running mate, Ohio's George H. Pendleton, who was an outspoken ally of the most notorious Copperhead, Clement Vallandigham. There was also the splinter candidacy of General John C. Frémont, supported by an odd alliance of abolitionists and German-Americans, that was abandoned shortly before election day.

Radical Republicans, who were quietly helping Frémont's efforts, finally agreed to unite behind Lincoln after the president removed Postmaster General Montgomery Blair, a constant thorn in the Radicals' side, from the cabinet.

The campaign was an ugly one, with Republicans equating support of the Democrats to treason and Democrats using race-baiting tactics to alienate the public from the pro-emancipation administration. As late as August, Lincoln was relatively certain he would lose, "and unless some great change takes place, badly beaten." To better his chances, he even considered abandoning emancipation as a war goal.

That "great change," however, did, in fact, occur. The fall of Atlanta on September 2 to

Union soldiers vote.

William Tecumseh Sherman, coming shortly after David Farragut's victory in Mobile Bay the previous month, and followed by Philip Sheridan's string of battlefield successes in the Shenandoah Valley throughout the fall, validated Lincoln's efforts and suggested that ultimate victory was near.

Southerners began praying for McClellan's election as the only way they could avoid total defeat.

On election day, November 8, Lincoln received 2.2 million votes to McClellan's 1.8 million, a ten percent margin. The Electoral College results were more impressive: Lincoln, 212; McClellan, 21; with the president losing only two slave states, Delaware and Kentucky, plus New Jersey. The troops, predicted by some

to support McClellan, turned out to vote for Lincoln by a greater than 70-30 margin, resenting the Democrats' peace platform. And with the president's reelection, there would, indeed, be no turning back from a war policy that demanded the capitulation of the Confederacy.

Emancipation Proclamation

JANUARY 1, 1863

Considered by Abraham Lincoln "the central act of my administration," the Emancipation Proclamation may not have actually freed any slaves, but it changed the entire character of the Civil War.

At the beginning of the conflict, the Union president was all too willing to put aside any personal distaste for slavery, believing that calling for emancipation would divide the North, and maintaining he did not have the authority to do so in any event.

It soon become apparent, however, that the North could not win unless it fought against slavery as well as disunion. Growing food and performing manual labor for the Southern forces—indeed, sustaining the entire Southern economic system—slaves were proving crucial to the Confederate war effort. Congress tried to address the problem with laws permitting the confiscation of slaves used by the enemy armies, but abolition sentiment continued to mount in the North, and Republican leaders pressured Lincoln for a more comprehensive policy.

Not waiting for the president to act, thousands of Southern slaves, meanwhile, were already emancipating themselves, escaping to Union lines or to the camps of the invading Northern troops. By summer 1862, Lincoln finally found the resolve to make a dramatic gesture against slavery, in spite of the questionable legal grounds for taking such an action, and an exemption to keep the Union's own four slave states from seceding.

In a July 22, 1862, cabinet meeting, the president announced that he had decided to declare the emancipation of Southern slaves. As the Union's commander-in-chief, he claimed the constitutional power to issue such a directive during wartime, as long as it was limited to territories in armed rebellion against the nation. That meant, not coincidentally, slaveholders in states remaining loyal to the Union could keep their slaves. Though the measure was essentially unenforceable in the South, the explicit linking of the Union cause to the cause of emancipation was in itself a momentous act.

With the North suffering a recent series of battlefield defeats, Secretary of State William Seward convinced Lincoln to wait for a military success before announcing his decision, so that he would be acting from a position of strength and confidence. Antietam, though hardly a convincing Union victory, would suffice. Five days after the battle, on September 22, 1862, the president issued his preliminary Emancipation Proclamation, which stated that unless the seceded states returned to the Union by January 1, their slaves "shall be then, thenceforward, and forever free."

Northern response to the stunning announcement was mixed. Abolitionists and Radical Republicans, though disappointed at the proclamation's limited scope, hailed Lincoln's decree as a sure sign that slavery was doomed. Others, concerned that the freeing of millions of enslaved African-Americans would cause mass unemployment and unrest, objected just as strongly.

The proclamation brought an undeniable new vitality to the Union's fight by giving it the quality of a moral crusade, but overall support for the war and the Lincoln administration actually declined in the North. Opposing the edict—calling it dictatorial and unconstitutional—the Democratic party made significant gains in that November's midterm elections. Union soldiers, mostly indifferent to emancipation as a moral issue, saw firsthand how the Southern war machine benefited from the use of slaves, and so largely approved of the measure.

In the South, of course, the proclamation was furiously denounced, considered nothing more than a Northern attempt to foment slave insurrections. Perhaps the most significant reaction, however, occurred in Europe, where the Union's announcement that its war with the South was now a struggle to end slavery ensured that the British and French governments would never support the Confederacy.

Despite the diplomatic coup, there was some belief that Lincoln would delay or rescind the edict. But as scheduled, the president issued the final Emancipation Proclamation on New Year's Day, 1863, which also reaffirmed the government's new policy favoring the recruitment of black soldiers. Calling the proclamation "an act of justice" and "a fit and necessary war measure," he thus designated the eradication of slavery as both a Union military goal and a means for victory.

The document displayed Lincoln's politically expedient understanding of his executive powers, exempting the border states and those parts of the Confederacy already under Union control—the entire state of Tennessee plus regions in Louisiana and Virginia. Slaves elsewhere in the South may have been *declared* free, but only those who fled North actually enjoyed that official status. The others—nearly four million—would have to wait until the ratification of the 13th Amendment abolished slavery throughout the United States eight months after the end of the Civil War.

Enlistment

During the first few months of the war, neither Abraham Lincoln nor Jefferson Davis had trouble raising troops, each presiding over a population that believed its side would win—quickly, easily, and gloriously. As the war dragged on, however, both men found it increasingly difficult to replenish their dwindling forces.

At the start, the South was better organized to raise manpower; each state as it seceded established its own military forces, including traditional militia and volunteer organizations. After putting Davis in charge of Confederate military operations, the Congress authorized him to call out the militia for six months' service and to accept 100,000 volunteers for one year. At the same time, they created a regular army of about 10,000 men.

Although the population was optimistic after First Bull Run, the government appeared to have a more realistic perspective on the duration of the war, calling for another 400,000 volunteers before the summer was over. As military fortunes began to run against the South, especially after the discouraging spring of 1862, recruiting diminished and the 12-month enlisted men prepared to go home. Ignoring public sentiment against the measure, the Confederate Congress authorized Davis to draft white men between the ages of 18 and 35 for three years' service; later, the age limits were widened to 17 to 45. By the end of the war, the use of slaves was authorized in labor units (February 1864) and as soldiers (1865).

Unlike the South, the North, perhaps having more hope that war could be averted, waited until after the fall of Fort Sumter to prepare for enlistments. Its regular army of about 16,000 men would clearly be unable to handle the rebellion without a massive influx of volunteers. The Militia Act of 1792, which gave the president the power to use the militia to suppress insurrection, allowed Lincoln to call for 75,000 troops after Fort Sumter surrendered.

From the start, quotas were assigned for each state based on its estimated adult male population. Even before Congress met to extend Lincoln's powers, the president increased the size of the regular army by almost 23,000 men, calling for 42,000 volunteers for three years, and asking for 18,000 seamen for the navy. Still, Lincoln realized he would need many more soldiers to fight the long, bitter war he feared lay ahead. On July 4, he called for another 500,000 volunteers to serve from six months to three years, at his discretion.

As the war progressed, more volunteers were called from the states and, frequently, regiments were raised by private individuals. As in the South, the strength of the volunteer system diminished as the war raged on. By the end of the war, only six percent of the total Union army had been raised by conscription.

Apart from the difficulty of raising troops, the biggest problem faced by both military organizations was the confusion caused by the large numbers of short-term enlistees. In neither army was there any consistency; men could enlist for 90-day, 6-month, 1-year, 2-year, or 3-year terms. As the war progressed, both governments attempted to tighten control over enlistment terms, but the constant need for new soldiers caused them to offer a number of compromises and exceptions as well.

Young boys often served in combat. This boy served as a "powder monkey" by helping load the cannon.

Ethnic Composition of Civil War Fighting Forces, C.S. & U.S.

The soldiers who fought for the Confederacy did not come from diverse ethnic backgrounds.

The majority of them had ancestors from Scotland, England, Wales, and Ireland; many others, however, could point to roots in France, Southern Europe, and North America itself. The Hispanic soldiers of such regiments as the 33rd Texas Cavalry, C.S., also served, and could

African-Americans enlisting in New York.

count forebears farther back than their Eastern brothers, who boasted ancestors that had founded their states or commonwealths. The Easterners chose their officers from among the descendants of men who had led the revolution: George Washington's grandnephew, John Augustine Washington, died fighting for Virginia. Robert E. Lee's father, "Light-Horse Harry" Lee, had been a trusted friend of Washington's, and one of his most skilled cavalrymen. Joseph and Albert S. Johnston could name Revolutionary forebears. Jeb Stuart was a relative of Virginia patriots who had helped frame the Constitution. The Texans chose leaders from among the patriots who had formed the old Texas Republic, or who were descended from the lines of the Spanish Conquistadors. And in parts of the deep South, the Cherokee Nation allied itself as

an equal with the Confederacy, contributing many brave regiments of Native Americans and giving the South one of its most colorful generals, the Cherokee chief General Stand Watie.

The sense of honor that so often hampered as well as aided Confederate efforts to obtain independence could be legitimately traced back to the staunch patriotism of more distant Celtic ancestors, who had in their turn fought bravely against tremendous odds in hopes of attaining their goals, or to the unbending pride of the old Spanish nobility with their rigid moral codes, or to the quiet pride of the ancestral Cherokee. There was a kind of paternalism, a cavalier sense of nobility and a dogged belief in the rightness of their cause which hallmarked the Confederate forces—and in the end, according to many historians, may have been one of the

The war brought people of many backgrounds into close contant with one another.

major causes of their defeat. If so, then it was also the stuff of which their survival and rebirth as a region was made, for such qualities generally allow a people to come back strongly from a devastating defeat.

The Union forces were a more disparate lot. Because the North was not ringed about by a blockade, immigration continued unabated, and was in fact enhanced, by the war; some of the newcomers, grateful to be in the land of the free, joined up within months of their arrival in hopes of somehow becoming more worthy of their new land. But the forces that marched off

at the beginning of the war to subdue the secessionists were made up of just as many old Revolutionary families as the South could boast; descendants of Paul Revere, of Ethan Allen, and of other colonial Americans were among them. Whole regiments from the privileged families of the East Coast marched off to war; their commanding officers were very often their professors from the university, a fact of life in the South, as well. German immigrants from Pennsylvania and western New York; Swedes and Norwegians from the upper Midwest; Irish and Italians from Boston, Philadelphia, and New

York; and the North, too, had its Texan contingents, such as the Second Texas Cavalry (Union).

On both sides, the men brought along with them to war their own ethnic and racial stereotypes. The industrious drive of some of the Northerners made them look down on the Southerners as a slothful lot. Some of the fastidious Germans and Scandinavians were appalled at what they termed "squalor" and laziness—until they experienced their first deep South summer, and learned why life takes a slower pace in other climates. The Southerners, on the other hand, were by turns annoyed or amused at the incessant busyness of their Northern brethren, believing that gentlemen did not need to always "have something to do." The Southerners who went off to war were almost unilaterally horse-oriented, be they Virginians, Kentuckians or Texans; Northern boys, many of them raised in cities, had to be taught how to ride at all before they could begin more basic training as cavalrymen. And all of them were men convinced they were right, and that God was on their side.

F

Family Life in the Civil War

The first and perhaps most obvious impact of the Civil War on family life in America was felt when beloved fathers, sons, and brothers enlisted in the army of their choice, be it South or North. The loss of a principle breadwinner was a difficult burden to bear, especially for the middle class, where the women of the household might not have had the experience of having to provide for the family as their working-class sisters had been doing for many a year. In what could arguably be seen as the beginning of feminist consciousness in America, women started to see just what they were capable of when everyday life was turned upside-down by the onset of war. In this era before widespread industrialization and expansion of metropolitan centers, having the menfolk off in the army meant increased difficulties at planting and harvest time. In families where the women were extremely sheltered, the adjustment to doing nearly everything for themselves was a sincere trauma, in addition to the emotional burden of worrying over the absent loved one.

As a result of the absence of men, women began to gain a new understanding of personal independence only glimpsed before, not only in terms of getting a job and running households at the same time, but also in earning their own wages, and choosing how to use their income.

Many families on both sides experienced severe personal loss. The return of a severely wounded loved one was a source of a different upset; psychology was a very young science, and there was little outlet to understand what we now recognize as post-traumatic stress brought on by the harsh rigors of combat and the dual suffering from wounds and well-meaning but comparatively crude surgery techniques. The wives, sisters and offspring of severely depressed, permanently handicapped men had little knowledge of how to help their loved ones, and were told to rely upon vigilant prayer and unwavering patience. Self-sacrifice was not only asked of the soldiers themselves but of their families as well; all too often, that sacrifice meant giving up any hope of a normal life in pursuit of forever nursing a man. The tension between natural, instinctive love and the need for freedom and normalcy often resulted in family strife during and for many years after the war.

In order to preserve a sense of home, soldiers in the field very often bonded together in the same way as their families did, through shared experience and common trials. Many senior officers referred to their staff personnel as their "little family," and in some cases it was literally true; nepotism, the practice of appointing a person to a position because of one's familial relationship to that person, was widely and unblinkingly practiced, with it being not at all

The Carrolls, a Northern family living in Washington, D.C., circa 1862.

uncommon for a general officer to have his sons, nephews, or brothers on his staff. During winter encampments, especially, women and children came to live with their husbands and fathers, making the occasional visit during more active seasons.

Back home again, women participated in activities geared toward relief and assistance of the army; sewing bees and starvation parties provided soldiers with comforting goods and useful extras from home that the men could not get through their quartermaster. Families separated from one another communicated through

rich, detailed letters, many of which still exist and provide us with invaluable insight into the war era.

In the Confederacy, a much broader cross-section of the male population entered the war, subjecting Southern families to even more stress. As the Northern states only realized during the Gettysburg and Sharpsburg Campaigns, having the war on your doorstep was a far greater problem for the average family than simply watching a loved one march off to fight elsewhere. The blockade of Southern ports by the Federal navy kept basic supplies out of the grasp of Southern families. Currency became increasingly worthless, and, on top of all else, Southern families worried that their homes could be attacked at any moment.

A family that chose to remain when the enemy army marched through was subject to all manner of indignity, from the annoying—losing all their livestock or produce to the invaders—to the harrowing, up to but certainly not excluding rape, thievery, or bodily harm. Many families were forced to become refugees, wandering from place to place often a step ahead of the incoming army, taking along only what they could carry. Many times, families might return only a day or two after an attack only to find all trace of their home or harvest completely gone.

Whenever possible, soldiers in both armies did what they could to alleviate the suffering of the civilian population. In this very Victorian war, almost the last "gentleman's war," the examples of acts of kindness by officers to civilians seem quaint, like something out of a fairy tale. Religion was a great comfort, and the spur which led people to rise above the horror of the war, to maintain their humanity in the face of overwhelming tragedy and difficulty.

As the war dragged on, families throughout both nations encountered a range of difficulties and problems they had not necessarily been prepared for. Throughout the North and the South, families learned to make do with what they had, practiced charity even when they had little for themselves, and remained steadfastly loyal to loved ones and each other, awaiting the day when their soldier would come home, hopefully to peace.

The Remberts, a Southern family living on a plantation in Bishopville, South Carolina, 1857.

Farragut, David Glasgow

1801–1870

In his early 60s and after an already distinguished career at sea, Farragut became the Union's favorite Civil War naval hero.

If not born to the sea, he was certainly adopted to it, taken in as a young boy by Commodore David Porter, America's leading early nineteenth-century naval commander. Farragut entered the navy at age nine, and saw action in the War of 1812 as a midshipman. After acquiring a formal education, he returned to the navy, sailing in the Mediterranean, West Indies, and South Atlantic, serving in the Mexican War, and becoming a captain in 1855.

Farragut's home was in Norfolk, Virginia, but at the start of the Civil War he hastily moved North as an ardent supporter of the Union. Although his loyalty was questioned at first by some, and his first Civil War assignment was a modest one—serving on a board that issued officer retirements—Farragut was soon given an important command.

In December 1861, he was made head of the Union's West Gulf Blockading Squadron, and ordered to capture New Orleans, the Confederacy's largest city and major port. Farragut's fleet commenced its attack on the forts guarding the city in early April. Six days of intense shelling, led by Farragut's foster brother David D. Porter, had little effect, so Farragut made a bold nighttime run on April 24 past the forts, with all but four of his boats smashing through barricades the Confederates had erected in the water. Sinking or running ashore most of the defense squadron in a spectacular fight, Farragut continued on to New Orleans itself, which surrendered the next day.

He followed up that critical victory with the capture of other important lower Mississippi River strongholds, including Baton Rouge and Natchez in the summer of 1862 and Port Hudson in July 1863, although he was unable to take Vicksburg, by far the most strategic. Attempting to tighten the blockade on the Gulf Coast, Farragut captured Galveston in October 1862, which Union forces only held for less than three months, as well as other Texas ports.

In 1864, he turned his sights to an even more important Gulf port still open to blockade runners: Mobile, Alabama. Preparing the assault for nearly seven months, Farragut made his attack on the fortresses and gunboats guarding the heavily mined entrance to Mobile Bay on August 5. In the middle of the three-hour fight, Farragut climbed the mast of his flagship, the *Hartford*, to see above the smoke of battle. Tied to the tall pole because he had vertigo, he made a legendary sight that inspired the entire Union fleet, which abruptly halted when one ship, the ironclad *Tecumseh*, struck a mine and exploded. Farragut shouted what would become an immortal phrase, "Damn the torpedoes! Full

Rear Admiral David G. Farragut

speed ahead," and led his squadron through the minefield and by the forts, forcing the surrender of the Confederate flotilla and effectively closing the harbor.

It was his biggest triumph; during a hero's welcome in New York City later that month, Farragut received a gift of $50,000 from grateful civilians, and in December he was promoted to vice admiral, a rank created especially for him. After the war, Farragut became the first U.S. naval officer to be named full admiral and, commanding the navy's European Squadron, led a good-will tour of major foreign ports.

54th Massachusetts Regiment

Composed of African-Americans from Massachusetts and other Northern states, the Massachusetts 54th was the most famous and distinguished black regiment to fight in the Civil War.

Immediately following the Emancipation Proclamation, the abolitionist governor of Massachusetts, John Andrew, took the lead in organizing the 54th, which would be the first black regiment to be raised in the free states. With a relatively small black population living in Massachusetts, Andrew recruited throughout the Northern states to find the 650 black volunteers comprising the 54th who assembled for duty in February 1863.

Realizing the racist resistance the troops would face from their white counterparts, Andrew chose his officers carefully from among those he knew were sympathetic to the cause of black civil rights. The regiment's colonel, Robert Gould Shaw, came from a Massachusetts abolitionist family and had previously served as captain in the 2nd Massachusetts Regiment. As Shaw and other white officers trained the raw recruits in a camp near Boston, all eyes were upon them. "Its success or failure will go far to elevate or depress the estimation in which the character of the colored Americans will be held throughout the world," wrote

Governor Andrew to Robert Gould Shaw's father.

In fact, even before they had a chance to prove themselves under fire, the 54th set an example for other black troops—and challenged the way an entire nation treated African-Americans. Insulted and angry over the fact that they received considerably less pay than their white counterparts, the men of the 54th, with support and encouragement from Colonel Shaw, refused to accept any pay at all—and a few decided to refuse to obey orders—until the situation was addressed. Governor Andrew, too, was enraged enough to go to Washington to appeal directly to the secretary of war. Told that the pay scales were set by the Militia Act of 1862, Andrew raised private and state funds to make up the difference, but not before two soldiers were shot and wounded by their reluctant officers for refusing to obey orders.

Despite this dissension, Shaw and his men were anxious to prove their battle mettle. Assigned to the Department of the South and sent to the South Carolina coast in May 1863, the regiment's first and only major battle occurred later that summer. Major General Quincy Gillmore had devised a plan to recover Fort Sumter and capture Charleston from the Confederates. To do so, he first had to capture Battery Wagner on the southern tip of Morris Island, just a mile and a half from Fort Sumter. Although small and isolated on a strip of sandy beach, Battery Wagner was heavily defended by about 1,200 troops and heavy artillery.

Gillmore had made some headway on July 10, when under shelling from navy gunboats, Confederates on the southern end of Morris Island fled toward the fort, allowing Gillmore to establish a beach head. Another offensive proved unsuccessful, however, and Gillmore was growing impatient. After a week of pounding the fort with cannon fire, he launched his second assault. Putting the proud black soldiers of the 54th Massachusetts in the lead, he sent 6,000 infantry forward to overcome the fort's defenses.

At 7:45 P.M., the black volunteers bravely stormed across the beach and climbed to the top of the fort's wall amid a downpour of ar-

The 54th Massachusetts paved the way for other black regiments like this one, shown entering Charleston at the war's end.

tillery and rifle fire. Atop a palmetto parapet, the 54th Regiment fought a vicious hand-to-hand battle before it was beaten back. Colonel Shaw and a full 40 percent of the regiment he had trained so well were killed.

Indeed, the entire campaign became a Union massacre: more than 1,515 Federals fell compared with just 714 Confederate casualties. The garrison remained in Confederate hands for another two months, causing one Federal soldier to refer to Gillmore's plan as "the most fatal and fruitless campaign of the entire war." Shaw and his men were buried together in a mass grave on the South Carolina beach.

Although the battle was lost, respect for black soldiers rose among those who learned of the bravery and tenacity with which the 54th

fought. The *New York* Tribune wrote, "It is not too much to say that if these Massachusetts 54th had faltered when its trial came, two hundred thousand troops for whom it was a pioneer would never have put into the field . . . But it did not falter."

The surviving troops, under Colonel Edward N. Hallowel, remained in South Carolina for another year, until they returned home to a hero's welcome from Governor Andrew in Boston in 1864. Official recognition for their distinguished service, however, did not come for several decades. Sergeant William Carney, a black soldier who seized the regiment's colors from a fallen color bearer and made it back to his lines despite sustaining several bullet wounds, did not receive a Congressional Medal of Honor until 1901. He was the first of 23 African-Americans in the Civil War to win the honor.

Five Forks, Battle of

APRIL 1, 1865

The campaign which would culminate in the surrender of Lee's Army of Northern Virginia began at this confluence of five major roads above Petersburg, Virginia, with a decisive clash between Confederates George Pickett, Fitzhugh Lee, and W.H.F. "Rooney" Lee, versus the cavalry of Union General Philip Sheridan and Gouverneur K. Warren's 5th Corps of Infantry. Pickett had orders from Robert E. Lee to "hold Five Forks at all hazards," since the crossroads was on the far right of Lee's army, and Ulysses S. Grant had begun a systematic process of extenuating Lee's line to the point of desperate thinness by constantly moving left, forcing the Confederates to counter or be flanked. Pickett ordered his men to dig in, and the two younger Lees probed throughout the morning and early afternoon to try and keep constant watch on the progress of Sheridan's pickets.

The situation was tense and difficult on both sides; Warren and Sheridan were busy accusing each other of improper conduct and failure to move fast enough or to support where ordered, and one of Fitz Lee's junior officers, General Thomas Rosser, invited Pickett and Fitz Lee to a shad bake some miles from where their men were busy containing the enemy. With inattention the order of the day on both sides, by late afternoon the situation was ripe for disaster.

Sheridan sent forth dismounted cavalry directly at the Confederate front, while Warren got his infantry into motion and attacked to the left. Rooney Lee, technically in command of the cavalry forces because his cousin was absent from the field, had not been apprised of Fitz Lee's departure—and thus did not know he had twice as many troops of which to make use.

Pickett's second in command was equally unaware of his commander's absence, to similar disastrous effect.

Inexplicably, at the height of the battle with success in full view, Sheridan sent to Grant for permission to relieve Warren of command for being slow, disobeying orders, and lack of cooperation, charges from which Warren was later exonerated—too late to save his reputation or career. The end effect of the fight at Five Forks was that Pickett's men had been quite effectively separated from the main army—crippling Lee's line to a dangerous degree.

Foote, Henry Stuart

1804–1880

A small man with a loud voice and abrasive personality, Foote was a persistent thorn in Jefferson Davis' side for many years. Foote was elected to serve in the Confederate Congress from 1861 to 1865, where he opposed nearly every move Davis made during the war.

A lawyer by trade, Foote was born in Virginia and graduated from Washington College. He migrated to Alabama and then Mississippi, where he practiced criminal law before entering politics. His political—and often personal—feud with Jefferson Davis began when the state legislature elected Foote to join Davis in the U.S. Senate. From the start, the two Mississippi senators battled over the question of states' rights and secession. Foote vacillated before endorsing the Compromise of 1850, while Davis consistently and adamantly opposed it.

In 1853, Foote resigned his senate seat to run for governor; Davis reluctantly decided to run against him. The campaign was a bitter one, with Davis accusing Foote of being a cunning opportunist and Foote denouncing Davis as an uncompromising secessionist. Foote won the election, but faced an uphill battle with the growing ranks of states' rights advocates in his party and throughout the state. In the end, his party denied him renomination.

Five days before his term ended in January 1854, Foote resigned his post and moved to California. After losing a bid for the California senate, Foote returned to the east in 1858 and settled in Nashville, Tennessee. Foote's outspoken support for union appealed to enough people in the more pro-Union eastern part of the state to win him election to the Confederate Congress in 1861.

Foote immediately established himself as an antagonist to Jefferson Davis' administration. He ferociously opposed conscription, the suspension of habeas corpus, and nearly every aspect of Davis' military strategy, including his choice of command. In the Confederate Congress, already known for its raucous behavior, Foote stood out as a particularly aggressive man. He frequently issued challenges to duels and came to blows with colleagues on more than one occasion.

As the war dragged on and Confederate losses mounted, Foote urged the South to negotiate a peace settlement. When the Hampton Roads Conference failed in February 1865, Foote decided to take matters into his own hands by attempting to open his own unofficial peace talks with Abraham Lincoln. About to cross the Potomac en route to Washington, Foote was captured by the Confederacy. Censured by Congress for his actions, Foote just missed being expelled; his critics were only a few votes short of the two-thirds majority required to oust him.

His second attempt to meet with the Northern leader failed for another reason: Lincoln refused to meet him. Rather than face the South's scorn and ridicule, Foote resigned his post and moved to Europe. After the war, he returned to Washington and lent his support to the Reconstruction policies of President Ulysses S. Grant. Grant rewarded him with a government appointment to the New Orleans Mint. Foote held various administrative posts at the mint until he died in 1880.

Forrest, Nathan Bedford

1821–1877

Rising from private to lieutenant general, Forrest became the Confederacy's most feared cavalry commander, and in the estimation of his foe William T. Sherman, "the most remarkable man our Civil War produced on either side."

Forrest was a poorly educated, self-made man from the deep South who made a fortune as a real estate baron, cotton planter, and slave trader. With no military training, he used his own money to raise a cavalry battalion at the

Lieutenant General Nathan B. Forrest

start of the war. Forrest's initial combat fame came after the Union capture of Fort Donelson, Tennessee, in February 1862, when he led his entire unit through enemy lines in a daring escape.

Two months later, his cavalry successfully covered the Confederate army's withdrawal following the Battle of Shiloh, despite Forrest's own serious injury. The fearless horseman then embarked on the first of his notorious lightning raids that terrorized Union forces throughout the war. Destroying railroad and telegraph lines and capturing vital garrisons and arms, Forrest stalled a Federal movement toward Chattanooga in July and halted Ulysses Grant's advance on Vicksburg in December.

A tactical genius with a killer instinct and an invaluable asset on the battlefield as well, he became noted for simple pronouncements that concisely summed up arcane military principles, such as his famous statement, "Get there first with the most men." Led by Braxton Bragg, Forrest fought in the New Year's 1863 Battle of Murfreesboro, but disgusted with his superior's performance at Chickamauga that September, refused to continue serving under him.

Forrest was given an independent command in Mississippi, and soon led the most controversial foray of his military career. During the capture of Union-held Fort Pillow, Tennessee, in April 1864, Forrest's men were accused of slaughtering, with his encouragement, over 200 unarmed troops—primarily black soldiers who had already surrendered.

In June, he followed that ugly episode with one of his greatest victories. Against a force numberng more than twice his own, Forrest delivered a mortifying defeat at Brice's Cross Roads, Mississippi, inflicting over 2,000 casualties and capturing a huge cache of small arms, artillery, and supply wagons in his rout of the Union forces.

Although the battle diverted Forrest from harassing Sherman's army in its advance toward Atlanta, he continued to wreak havoc on the Union general's supply lines, leading Sherman to call for Forrest's death even "if it cost 10,000 lives and breaks the treasury." But Federal forces could not catch the cunning cavalry leader, and he joined John Bell Hood in the Confederate general's desperate late-1864 invasion of Union-occupied eastern Tennessee.

Not much, in fact, could stop Forrest, a rugged man who over the course of the war had 30 horses shot from under him and was himself wounded four times. But unable to halt the Union's sweep through Alabama in the Confederacy's final days, Forrest, to the surprise of some, surrendered magnanimously in May 1865.

After the war, which ruined him financially, he went into the railroad business. Also joining the nascent Ku Klux Klan, Forrest became, according to most accounts, its first Grand Wizard in 1867 before resigning over the organization's terrorist bent.

Fort Donelson

FEBRUARY 13–16, 1862

In order to take control of Kentucky and western Tennessee, Union commander Ulysses S. Grant devised a plan to capture Fort Donelson, a Confederate garrison located 12 miles east of Fort Henry, which had fallen into Union hands a few days before. Grant knew Fort Donelson would not be easy to take; it was manned by a force equal to his own (about 17,000 men). It was, however, commanded by two men for whom the general had little respect: Brigadier General John B. Floyd and Major General Gideon J. Pillow.

Grant planned to take Donelson by using his army to block the fort while Flag Officer Andrew H. Foote's gunboats shelled it into submission. On February 14, in the middle of the afternoon, Foote's ships steamed upriver. When they were just 400 yards from the fort, they began to fire, only to be met with a ferocious counterattack. With the guns on high ground above the river, however, the Confederates had the advantage. Within a few hours, two of six Union vessels were sunk, the rest badly damaged, and Foote himself wounded.

The Battle of Fort Donelson.

After this defeat, Grant assumed that the only way to take the fort would be through a long siege during the cold Tennessee winter. For reasons still unknown, however, Pillow and Floyd apparently believed the fort was indefensible and decided to evacuate on the morning of February 15. Planning to cut their way through the Union lines and open a road to Nashville, Confederate cavalry, under Nathan Bedford Forrest, attacked the Union's right flank in the snow- and ice-covered woods outside the garrison. Fighting bitterly for several hours, Forrest had just carved out an escape route when Pillow inexplicably ordered his men to fall back, leaving only a thin line of defense to hold the position.

Grant's fierce counterattack quickly regained the ground the Union had lost, pushing the Confederates back to the fort. As night fell, the Confederate commanders considered how and when to surrender. General Floyd demurred, claiming that he had sworn an oath never to surrender. Pillow, too, declined, leaving the sorry duty to the third in command, Simon Buckner. During the night, Floyd, Pillow, and some 2,500 men escaped by boat, and Forrest's mounted infantrymen rode across the frozen Cumberland backwater. Buckner, meanwhile, sent a note to Grant, asking surrender terms. He received a reply that set the standard for the war: "No terms except an unconditional and immediate surrender can be accepted." On the morning of February 16, 15,000 men surrendered to the Federals. Both the Tennessee and Cumberland rivers were now in Union hands.

Fort Henry, Capture of

FEBRUARY 6, 1862

A gunboat flotilla commanded by Flag Officer Andrew H. Foote subdued this Confederate fort, located at the crucial juncture of the Tennessee and Cumberland rivers.

Along with Fort Donelson, Fort Henry formed the linchpin of the Southern line of defense from Columbus to Bowling Green, Kentucky, then southward to the Cumberland Gap. Its capture would ensure that both Kentucky and western Tennessee remained within the Union and give the Union armies an invasion route to the South.

Built on low ground near the edge of the Tennessee River, Fort Henry was not easily defensible—in fact, at the time of the attack, some of the fort was submerged under flood-level waters. This fact was not lost on its commander, Brigadier General Lloyd Tilghman, who decided to send most of his men to defend Fort Donelson. He kept just 100 artillerymen to fire the fort's 17 guns.

The Union forces, led by Brigadier General Ulysses S. Grant, numbered approximately 15,000. A naval force commanded by Foote consisted of three unarmed gunboats and four ironclad river gunboats, any one of which was powerful enough to subdue the enemy. Grant's strategy, reluctantly approved by his commander, Major General Henry W. Halleck, included a combined attack between his ground and naval forces. Action commenced on February 6, as Union gunboats came within 600 yards of the fort and fired.

By the time Grant's forces, delayed by muddy roads, arrived at the fort, all but four Confederate guns were destroyed, about 20 Confederates were killed or wounded and 63 were missing, and Tilghman had surrendered. Federal losses amounted to 11 killed, 5 missing, and 31 injured. The first step in the Union plan to invade the South completed, Grant's men regrouped at Fort Henry until the night of February 11, when they started their overland march to Fort Donelson.

Fort Pillow, Battle of

APRIL 12, 1864

"The river was dyed with the blood of the slaughtered for 200 yards," Nathan Bedford Forrest reported after the battle of Fort Pillow. "It is hoped that these facts will demonstrate to the Northern people that negro soldiers cannot cope with Southerners." One of the largest engagements between black soldiers and Confederate troops during the Civil War continues to engender controversy today.

Located in Tennessee about 40 miles north of Memphis on the east bank of the Mississippi, the Union's Fort Pillow was charged with protecting Federal navigation along the river. In April 1864, it was held by 262 black soldiers (the 11th U.S. Colored Troops and Battery and the 4th U.S. Colored Light Artillery) and 295 whites (the 13th Tennessee Calvary). These men were under the command of Major Lionel F. Booth, with Major William Bradford second in command, and were reinforced by Captain James Marshall's ironclad, the *New Era*.

On April 12, 1,500 Confederate troops under Nathan Bedford Forrest arrived at dawn prepared to take the fort. Confederates, perched atop the small hills that dotted the surrounding terrain, fired directly into the fort. One bullet hit and killed Major Booth at 9:00 A.M., leaving Bradford in command. At 11:00, Forrest ordered a general assault to take the fort's south barracks; with this accomplished, the Confederates were able to bombard the fort's interior with more small-arms fire. At 3:30, Forrest sent in a demand for surrender. Bradford demurred, asking for an hour to decide. Forrest, realizing that Federal reinforcements were on their way,

Rebel massacre of Federal troops at Fort Pillow.

gave him just 20 minutes. Bradford's reply was succinct: "I will not surrender."

The Confederates then charged the fort and drove the Union troops down the riverbank, where they encountered another contingent of Confederate troops, under Captain Charles W. Anderson. At the end of the day, 230 Federals had been killed, 100 wounded, 168 whites and 58 blacks captured. How the casualties occurred, however, remains in dispute.

Federal accounts claim that Union troops surrendered as soon as the Confederates entered the fort, but were massacred in cold blood by soldiers shouting racial epithets, including "Kill the damn niggers. Shoot them down!"

Southerners, on the other hand, insist that the losses were incurred because the Federals refused surrender and lost their lives fighting on the banks of the Mississippi.

The Joint Committee on the Conduct of the War conducted an investigation and issued a report of the incident, which included hair-raising accounts by Union troops of Confederate brutality. Whether or not the event amounted to wholesale slaughter, as the Union claimed, it appears likely that the Southern soldiers acted upon their deep animosity toward whites who tolerated black soldiers and, of course, toward the black soldiers themselves.

Fort Sumter

APRIL 12–13, 1861

Commencing on April 12, 1861, the two-day bombardment of the Union garrison at Charleston Harbor, South Carolina, signaled a bloodless start to the Civil War.

With the nascent Confederacy taking control of military installations throughout the South, the very visible Federal presence at the birthplace of secession was considered a particular affront. Despite South Carolina's demands in late 1860 that Union forces leave Charleston, two companies, numbering less than 100, resolutely remained stationed at Fort Moultrie under the command of Robert Anderson, a Kentucky ex-slaveowner with Southern sympathies but resolute Northern loyalties. Still, an indecisive President Buchanan offered no direc-

tives about how to deal with the hundreds of secessionist militia that had amassed in the city.

On December 26, Anderson took up a more secure position in the middle of the harbor at Fort Sumter, a formidable pentagon-shaped brick structure, whose construction, begun in 1829, was still not complete. His situation remained precarious, with a belated reinforcement attempt failing in January, when Confederate gunfire kept the Union's relief ship *Star of the West* from entering the harbor.

By March, Anderson reported to incoming President Abraham Lincoln that, unless he received provisions, Sumter would fall within weeks. Though Union General-in-Chief Winfield Scott and most of Lincoln's cabinet favored abandoning the fort, public sentiment in the North demanded the stalwart garrison not be forsaken. The president, avoiding an overt act of aggression that might lose support for the Union, announced in early April that he would

Confederate flag floats over Fort Sumter after Union forces withdraw, April 1861.

attempt peacefully to supply Sumter. Considering that provocation enough, Confederate President Jefferson Davis ordered Pierre G. T. Beauregard, commander of the 6,700-man force now ringing Charleston Harbor, to take the fort.

Hours before dawn on April 12, a handful of Southern officials rowed out to the fort to order its surrender. Anderson refused, and at 4:30 A.M., the Confederates commenced shelling. Hopelessly outgunned and outnumbered, the tiny Union force managed only sporadic return fire, while civilians lined the waterfront to view the bombardment. After 34 hours under assault, with several buildings ablaze inside the fort, the Federals capitulated and were allowed to return North.

Neither side suffered any casualties until the fighting ceased, when, in the middle of the surrendering garrison's hundred-gun salute to its lowered flag, a freak explosion killed two Union men. Rousing emotions in North and South alike, the events at Charleston Harbor finally sparked the long-coming Civil War.

On April 15, Lincoln called for 75,000 volunteers to quell the "rebellion." Two days later, as the South also began mobilizing, Virginia voted to secede from the Union. The North would not regain Fort Sumter until Charleston was occupied in the conflict's final days. At a huge ceremony on the afternoon of April 14, 1865—five days after Lee's surrender and just hours before Lincoln's assassination—Robert Anderson brought out the battered American flag he had taken down from the beleaguered fortress exactly four years earlier and triumphantly raised it once again.

Franklin, Battle of

NOVEMBER 30, 1864

Hoping to reawaken the Army of Tennessee's fighting spirit with a brash frontal assault against the deeply entrenched enemy, Confederate John Bell Hood lost a quarter of his force in this battle.

The general's actions had been brazen since he took command four months before. Invading Tennessee after Atlanta fell to William T. Sherman's army, Hood had not only hoped to cut off the Union's supply line—halting its devastating march through Georgia—but even to drive all the way through Kentucky and come to Robert E. Lee's rescue in Virginia with a rear attack on Ulysses S. Grant's forces.

The wildly ambitious campaign began in late November, when Hood's army of 40,000 entered Tennessee from Alabama. Sherman sent John Schofield with 30,000 men to reinforce an equal number of George Henry Thomas' troops at Nashville. The combined Union forces would likely be more than enough to thwart Hood, so it was the Confederate general's intention to keep them divided.

At first, he was successful in pursuing and outmaneuvering Schofield. After three days of fighting outside Columbia, Hood had the opportunity on November 29 to trap the Union force at the crossroads of Spring Hill. His poorly coordinated attempt to replicate Stonewall Jackson's brilliant Chancellorsville flanking maneuver failed, however, and the Federal troops were able to continue on their way to Nashville.

Reaching the town of Franklin, 15 miles south of the Tennessee capital, on the morning of November 30, the Union forces were unable to cross the damaged bridges spanning the Harpeth River. Schofield ordered his soldiers to erect fieldworks and dig in while the bridges were being repaired. By the time Hood and most of his army arrived on the scene shortly after noon, the Federals had formed a heavily fortified arched line protected on both ends by the river and an abundance of artillery.

The formidable defenses did not faze the Confederate commander, though. Blaming his failure at Spring Hill on his troops' timidity, Hood decided to force them to more aggressive action: a headlong assault against the Union line. The attack had little strategic purpose—Schofield was clearly planning to withdraw soon anyway—and much of the Confederate force, including its artillery, was too far in the rear to be used.

Recognizing the debacle they faced, Hood's subordinates—including Nathan Bedford Forrest, a man who could hardly be accused of lacking gumption—vehemently opposed the plan, but their commander, more convinced than ever that they and their troops needed a good fight, went ahead. Without artillery cover, the attack began at 3:30 P.M., an extraordinary effort rivaling Pickett's Charge at Gettysburg. Union soldiers held their fire until two of their front-line brigades withdrew to safety, then let loose a furious barrage against the 20,000 advancing Confederates spread across nearly two miles of open ground.

Pressing forward even while they were being shot down by the hundreds, the Southern troops proved Hood had no reason to doubt their mettle. But their situation was hopeless. Sheer momentum carried some over the Union line, only to be trapped in the trenches they had just overrun. The Confederates launched several more desperate charges, and the fight continued in the dark until they finally pulled back at 9 P.M.

Two hours later, Schofield ordered a quick withdrawal as the Federal forces resumed their movement north to Nashville. The futile assault cost Hood's army more than 6,250 casualties, including 12 generals, while Union losses were under 2,400. With his numbers greatly depleted and his troops now seriously doubting the abilities of their commander, Hood's chances for success in Tennessee were dimmer than ever. Yet, the resolute Confederate still advanced his pummeled army toward the state capital, where it would face even larger and more daunting Union forces.

Fredericksburg, Campaign and Battle of

NOVEMBER–DECEMBER, 1862

One of the Union's worst Civil War defeats, the Battle of Fredericksburg was a tragic demonstration that superior numbers could not make up for inferior generalship. Ambrose Burnside, who had reluctantly replaced the hesitant George McClellan as Army of the Potomac commander in November, promptly fell under pressure from both Abraham Lincoln and the Northern public to mount a new offensive against the Confederacy. Since Richmond remained the popular target, the accommodating general planned an immediate movement of his entire force of 120,000 toward the Southern capital by way of Fredericksburg. The initial advance was startlingly swift, as Union troops marched 40 miles east from their encampments near Warrenton Junction.

By November 19, Burnside's army had arrived across the Rappahannock River from Fredericksburg, to find the Virginia town lightly defended and Confederate commander Robert E. Lee unprepared for an assault. Burnside could not attack, however, because he did not yet have the pontoons his huge army needed to bridge the river.

Bureaucratic blunders delayed their arrival six days, and even after receiving them, Burnside waited nearly another three weeks. By that time, Lee had concentrated his forces; Fredericksburg was evacuated and 75,000 solidly entrenched troops of the Army of Northern Virginia lined the hills overlooking the town. Though he had lost the advantage, Burnside refused to call off his planned offensive. To the contrary, he calculated—incredibly—that his best chance was to surprise Lee by a direct assault on the most formidable point of the Confederate line.

At dawn on December 11, Burnside finally ordered army engineers to begin constructing six pontoon bridges across the Rappahannock, their progress hindered by sniper fire. Lee, satisfied with his brilliantly formed defensive position, allowed the Federals to approach. By the next day, Burnside's troops had finished crossing the river and occupied Fredericksburg, spending the hours before battle on an unseemly looting spree.

The Union onslaught began at 9 A.M. on December 13, as William B. Franklin's corps advanced against the Confederate right, commanded by Stonewall Jackson. Leading two cannon out to the middle of the field, Southern

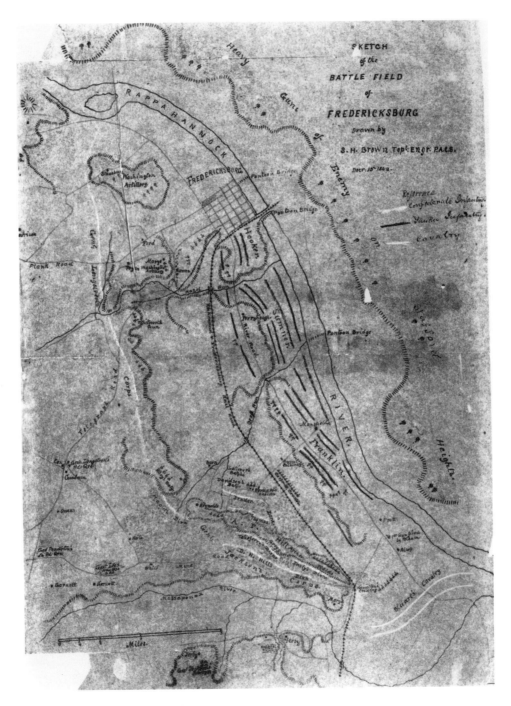

Map of the Battle of Fredericksburg.

horse artillery officer John Pelham faced down the entire attacking force, startling Lee and the Federals alike with his audacity. George Meade's division managed to breach the Confederate line, but had to fall back when they received no reserves. A Southern counterassault, in turn, was repelled by Union artillery fire, and the two sides continued to skirmish inconclusively as Franklin declined to resume his advance. "It is well that war is so terrible," Lee remarked, watching the battle. "We should grow too fond of it."

Meanwhile, Burnside launched his main thrust against James Longstreet's impregnable position at Marye's Heights. Atop the ridge, hundreds of Confederate guns aimed down on the sloping open field that the Federals were about to traverse, while four ranks of infantrymen waited along the sunken road at the base, protected by a 4-foot-high stone wall that ran more than half a mile. "A chicken could not live in that field once we open on it," a Confederate predicted, and that was hardly an exaggeration.

The charging Federals could not get near the stone wall before being annihilated by the almost nonstop fire pouring forth from behind it. Brigade after brigade streamed out of Fredericksburg in their valiant but hopeless attempts to storm Marye's Heights, as a seemingly oblivious Burnside continued ordering assaults through nightfall.

That evening, as the aurora borealis—rarely seen so far south—lit the winter sky, the distraught Union commander discussed renewing the offensive the following morning, planning to lead the charge himself. Talked out of the suicidal plan by his officers, Burnside withdrew the Northern army back across the Rappahannock during a heavy storm on the night of December 15.

Union casualties at the Battle of Fredericksburg exceeded 12,500, most cut down on the frozen fields approaching Marye's Heights, while the Confederate lost fewer than half that number—about 5,000. As well as destroying the Army of the Potomac's morale, the appalling defeat sobered spirits throughout the entire North during the bleak Christmas season of 1862.

Freedmen's Bureau

EST. MARCH 4, 1865

"It is not . . . in your power to fulfill one-tenth of the expectations of those who framed the Bureau," General William T. Sherman told the bureau's director. "I fear you have Hercules' task."

On March 4, 1865, the U.S. Congress established the Bureau of Refugees, Freedmen, and Abandoned Lands. Despite its title, its main purpose was to help the more than four million former slaves, most without any resources or education, populating the South after the Civil War. Officially existing for just one year, plagued by corruption, and lacking enough funding and manpower to complete what was indeed a Herculean task, the bureau nonetheless made great strides in providing newly emancipated African-Americans with access to equal justice, fair labor practices, land, and education.

Commonly called the Freedmen's Bureau, the agency was born of the American Freedmen's Inquiry Commission, which was created by the War Department in 1863 to suggest methods for dealing with emancipated slaves. The commission's key conclusion was that no bureau or agency set up to help the ex-slaves should become a permanent institution but should instead encourage African-Americans to become self-reliant as quickly as possible.

In 1865, after many months of negotiation, Congress created the Freedman's Bureau—with a lifespan of just one year—to distribute clothing, food, and fuel to destitute freedmen and to oversee "all subjects relating to their condition" in the South. The bureau was not granted a separate budget for its work, but instead drew funds from the Department of War. Heading the bureau was General Oliver O. Howard, a graduate of Bowdoin and West Point and a distinguished Civil War veteran. Howard, a devout churchgoer and fervent civil rights advocate, helped manage the bureau's approximately 900 agents.

One of the most difficult challenges was instituting a judicial system that would be fair to both blacks and whites. At first, the bureau established its own judicial authority, with local agents setting up temporary three-man courts to hear individual disputes. Many cases concerned disputes between white employees who were dealing for the first time with black employees demanding fair wages.

Without adequate manpower or financial resources for such an enormous undertaking, however, the bureau instead worked to persuade the Southern states to recognize racial equality in their own judicial proceedings. Bureau agents monitored state and local legal affairs and often intervened on behalf of blacks.

Introducing a system of free labor economy was another of the bureau's responsibilities. The bureau's goal in this respect was to return the ex-slaves to plantation labor, which was still essential to the Southern economy, but to do so under conditions that would allow blacks to work their way up and out of the labor class. One way to accomplish this was to distribute lands confiscated or abandoned during the war—some 850,000 acres in 1865—to newly freed slaves. "Forty acres and a mule" was the slogan for the Reconstruction land-grant plan, but in the end only about 2,000 South Carolina

An office of the Freedmen's Bureau.

and 1,500 Georgia freedmen actually received the land they had been promised—less than one percent of the four million ex-slaves populating the South.

Another challenge facing African-Americans in the South was the abysmal lack of health care services. The bureau attempted to strengthen existing medical care facilities as well as expand services into rural areas through newly established clinics.

Perhaps the most important contribution the bureau made to Reconstruction efforts involved expanding educational opportunities to emancipated African-Americans. Lacking adequate resources, the bureau did not establish new schools itself, but instead acted as a catalyst between Northern relief societies and local governments and individuals. By 1869, about 3,000 new schools serving more than 150,000 pupils, as well as dozens of evening and private schools, had been established. Working with the American Missionary Association and the American Freedman's Union Commission, the bureau also founded and staffed the first black colleges in the South, all of which were initially designed to train black teachers who would teach black students.

Also, despite inadequate funding and a shortage of facilities, the bureau enabled an estimated 500,000 freedmen to receive medical attention in more than 100 hospitals.

Despite its accomplishments, the Freedmen's Bureau was also known to be a corrupt and often inefficient organization. Although Howard himself was above reproach, the agents in the field, usually left completely to their own devices, used their positions to exact money and power from the very people they were meant to serve.

In December 1865, the Radical Republicans in Congress managed to pass a strengthened Freedman's Bureau Act, but were disappointed when President Andrew Johnson vetoed it. The Freedmen's Bureau was eventually discontinued, but much of the groundwork it had laid for civil rights in the South remained in place.

Frémont, John Charles

1813–1890

As a Union general, Frémont's major Civil War contribution was more political than military when he focused Union attention on the role emancipation should play in the North's war policy.

The magnetic and legendary "Pathfinder" became a national hero early in life for his trail-blazing exploits in the Far West. A leader in wresting California from Mexico, he served as one of the state's first senators and got rich in the Gold Rush. Frémont's popularity and his antislavery position were equally instrumental in his being chosen the Republican Party's first

General John C. Frémont

presidential nominee in 1856, the youngest man yet to run for the office. With Southern states threatening secession if he were elected, Frémont's loss to James Buchanan forestalled disunion for another four years.

In Europe at the outbreak of the Civil War, he purchased a cache of arms in England for the North on his own initiative and returned to America. Abraham Lincoln, mostly for political reasons, appointed him major general in May 1861, placing him in command of the precarious Department of the West. Based in St. Louis, Frémont spent more energy fortifying the city and developing flashy guard units than equipping the troops in the field. His forces suffered several losses, particularly a major defeat at Wilson's Creek that August.

Attempting to gain a political advantage in the absence of a military one, Frémont, in an unprecedented and unauthorized move, issued a startling proclamation at the end of the month declaring martial law in Missouri and ordering that secessionists' property be confiscated and their slaves emancipated. The action was cheered by antislavery Republicans, but Lincoln, concerned that linking abolition to the war effort would destroy Union support throughout the slave-holding border states, asked Frémont at the very least to modify the order.

The Pathfinder refused, sending his wife, the politically influential daughter of former Senate leader Thomas Hart Benton, to Washington to talk to the president. Displeased with Frémont's effrontery, Lincoln revoked the proclamation altogether and removed him from command. Pressure from his fellow Republicans forced Lincoln to give the popular Frémont another appointment, and in March 1862 he was named head of the army's new Mountain Department, serving in Western Virginia.

Over the following two months, he endured several crushing losses against Thomas "Stonewall" Jackson during the Confederate general's brilliantly successful Shenandoah Valley Campaign. After a military reorganization placed him under the command of former subordinate John Pope, Frémont angrily resigned his post, never to receive a new Civil War appointment.

In 1864, however, he began another presidential bid with the backing of a cadre of Radical Republicans, but withdrew from the race in September and threw his support to Lincoln after a rapprochement in the party. When he lost most of his fortune by the end of the war, Frémont tried the railroad industry. His reputation damaged by an 1873 conviction for his role in a swindle, he nevertheless resumed his political career, and later in the decade began serving as territorial governor of Arizona.

French-Americans in the Civil War

There have been settlers of French extraction in North America since the beginning of white colonization. Lured by the promise of life in the New World, however, French immigrants continued to arrive in America over many years; between the census of 1850 and that of 1860, the number of French arriving doubled to just over 100,000. Other than Canada, where the majority of French settlers had gone to live in the early days, it is difficult to pinpoint any one area of the United States where the newcomers headed—with the dramatic exception of Louisiana. So many French settled there that today the culture is indelibly marked by the presence of their language and other ethnic preferences.

The French left quite a presence on the Civil War, too. The colorful, seemingly bizarre uniforms of Zouave units, in both the Confederate and Union armies, can be traced directly back to the garb of French soldiers in Algiers, adapted to that hot climate. Striped or red baggy trousers, bright waistcoats, cropped jackets with braided trim, fez-style hats, and sashes tied dramatically about the waist were, to say the least, unusual sights on Civil War battlefields—but woe be to the soldier who made fun of a Zouave comrade, for they were numbered among some of the fiercest fighting units. The Louisiana Tigers of the Confederate Army and the New York Fire Zouaves of the Union are but two of those fabled regiments, and their fame is spread across the history of the war.

Famous French Confederates included Pierre Gustave Toutant Beauregard. Born in St. Bernard Parish, Louisiana, on May 28, 1818, he was the number two graduate of the West Point Class of 1838, and was a staff officer for Winfield Scott during the Mexican War, where he was a comrade of Robert E. Lee and George Meade. In January 1861, Beauregard was appointed superintendent of West Point—only to be relieved a mere few days later because of his Confederate sympathies. Beauregard can be said to have served as the Confederacy's midwife, bringing the infant nation into the world: he commanded the attack on Fort Sumter in April 1861, then helped Joseph E. Johnston defeat the Federals in the Battle of First Manassas (First Bull Run). There is no theater of the war in which Beauregard did not fight; in addition to Virginia, he was also prominent in the West, taking command of the Army of Tennessee when Albert Sidney Johnston was killed at the Battle of Shiloh in April 1862. He assisted in the defense of Richmond in May 1864, and was again at Joe Johnston's side at the end in North Carolina. His fiery Creole temperament made him occasionally difficult to get along with, and he was in almost constant disagreement with President Jefferson Davis. But few others can be said to have had as much effect on the Confederacy's military legend, with the possible exception of Robert E. Lee.

Camille Armand Jules Marie, Prince de Polignac, was another colorful Confederate Frenchman—this time a true native of the old soil. Born in Seine-et-Oise, France, in 1832, Polignac had served gallantly in the French army in the Crimean War; in Central America at the outbreak of the war in America, Polignac offered his sword to the Confederate cause and served it well. He was a staff officer for Beauregard, and later saw service in Louisiana with General Richard Taylor; near the end of the war he became involved in a Confederate bid to win French support for their flagging cause.

Polignac ran the blockade in March 1865; he was in Spain, trying to secure passage to France, when news of Lee's surrender reached him. He was the last man holding the rank of Confederate major general to die, passing on in November 1913.

The Union, too, had their colorful Frenchmen. Prince Jerome Bonaparte served as an officer in the Federal forces, volunteering his services; one of the most important and gentlemanly services he rendered, in addition to his bravery and sense of honor, was to leave behind a record in watercolors of the places and people with whom he served. It was considered a gentleman's pastime and hobby to be able to paint amusing little pictures for one's friends; Bonaparte's pictures give an accurate and discriminating view of life in the Union army from the brush of a royal admirer.

Fugitive Slave Act

An integral part of the Compromise of 1850, meant to quell regional tensions over the slavery issue, this controversial piece of legislation had precisely the opposite effect, inflaming passions in both the North and South, which contributed enormously to the country's ominous movement toward disunion.

A federal fugitive slave law had been on the books since 1793, mandating the return of runaways to slaveholders, but by the 1840s it was no longer effective. As the abolitionist movement grew, individual Northern states passed "personal liberty" laws securing expanded rights for accused fugitives to contest their recapture, while members of the burgeoning Underground Railroad and sundry "vigilance committees" assisted escaping slaves outright.

Considering these actions insulting and unlawful violations of their property rights, Southerners demanded a stronger federal statute. Congress, busy rancorously resolving other slave-related matters, passed a new, much tougher Fugitive Slave law in 1850 with surprisingly little debate.

Ironically, the fervent states' rights advocates of the South were supporting legislation that

Abolitionist depiction of the Fugitive Slave Act.

greatly expanded federal jurisdiction. Under the terms of the new law, U.S. marshals and their deputies were required to participate in the capture and return of escaped slaves, the cost to be borne by the government. Persons helping or protecting runaways were subject to a six-month prison term and a fine of $1,000 plus the market value of the slave. Accused fugitives did not get a trial; they could not even testify in their own defense.

Specially appointed commissioners administered the cases, accepting affidavits from Southern courts or the statements of white witnesses as sufficient proof of a slaveholder's ownership. The commissioners received payment for their services—$10 for each fugitive sent back south, $5 when the accused was exonerated—which critics of the law observed was a bribe-like encouragement to rule in favor of the slaveowner.

Greeted with outrage throughout the North, the Fugitive Slave Act ignited antislavery and anti-Southern sentiment to an unprecedented degree, as moderates joined militant abolitionists in their opposition. New personal liberty laws were passed in eight Northern states to try to nullify the legislation. The Underground Railroad grew busier still, slavehunters were harassed in the streets of Boston, and on a few occasions mobs even broke captured fugitives out of jail and smuggled them to Canada.

Although the Federal government enforced the law zealously, the widespread resistance convinced many Southerners that antislavery forces in the North would go to any extreme to continue interfering with their "peculiar institution." Still, over 300 runaways were returned to bondage under the Fugitive Slave Act. Because there was no statute of limitations, blacks who had lived in free states for 20 years or more were being arrested, causing thousands of African-Americans to move to Canada in the 1850s.

Upheld by the Supreme Court in 1859, the law remained technically in force during much of the Civil War—even after the Emancipation Proclamation—and was not officially repealed until June 1864.

G

Garrison, William Lloyd

1805–1879

Regarded as the conscience of the American abolition movement, Garrison started a moral crusade against the "peculiar institution of slavery" as early as 1831 and continued it throughout the war. Although personally mild in temperament, he took a strident, often radical tone in the hundreds of speeches he made with his New England Anti-Slavery Society and in the pages of his abolitionist newspaper, the *Liberator*.

Born into a pious but poor family in Newburyport, Massachusetts, Garrison attended school until the age of 13, then began learning the newspaper trade as an apprentice at the Newburyport *Herald*. By the age of 17, he was a contributor to its editorial page.

In 1827, after a failed attempt to start his own journal, Garrison moved to Boston to work on a temperance journal called the *National Philanthropist*. It was there that he met a local abolitionist named Benjamin Lundy, who inspired him to join the antislavery cause. Within a short time, Garrison broke with Lundy and others who supported the colonization of freed blacks; believing in equal rights for all within the United States, he established his own wing of the abolition movement.

William Lloyd Garrison

For Garrison and his followers, emancipation was nothing less than a moral crusade to be pursued with an uncompromising urgency. In 1831, Garrison began publishing the *Liberator* in Boston. Supported mainly by free African-Americans and never holding more than 3,000 subscribers, the newspaper nevertheless had enormous influence throughout New England. Although a proclaimed pacifist, Garrison's urging of "immediate" abolition and his likening of slaveholding to a criminal act was seen by many as the spark that set the radical movement aflame.

When the Nat Turner Rebellion occurred in August, 1831, several Southern states banned distribution of the newspaper and threatened Garrison with prosecution. Garrison formed the New England Anti-Slavery Society the following year, which attracted a number of free blacks as well as several prominent members of Boston aristocracy. A second branch of the society opened in Philadelphia in 1833. As the antislavery movement began to pick up momentum through the 1830s and 1840s, Garrison's radical call for immediate emancipation began to attract more and more of the radical fringe, while at the same time alienating those abolitionists attempting to work within the system.

By the time the Compromise of and the Kansas-Nebraska Act were passed in the early 1850s, Garrison's urgency gained new respect as the antislavery movement had become inexorably tied with the economic and political interests of the North. The refusal of Garrison and his followers to compromise on the issue of slavery added to the tension building between North and South as the country drew closer and closer toward war.

At first, Garrison opposed the war, claiming that the U.S. Constitution itself was a racist document and therefore not worth defending. Once Abraham Lincoln signed the Emancipation Proclamation, however, support for the Union cause was evident in the *Liberator*'s pages. After the war, Garrison discontinued his newspaper but never lost his spirit for change and reform, supporting the women's suffrage movement, civil rights for African-Americans, and prohibition.

German-Americans in the Civil War

The majority of German personalities in the Civil War can be found wearing the uniform of the United States. Immigrants from Germany itself, as well as Austria and the Netherlands, came to the United States in the decades before the war; between 1850 and 1860 alone, the number of immigrants from what was then known as the German Empire more than doubled, from a little over half a million to well over a million just before the war broke out. Hardworking, organized people, the Germans settled, as did most newcomers to America, in places that reminded them of home; the Appalachians and the Blue Ridge were not as dramatic as the Alps, but they were mountains, and they had as near neighbors the rolling hills and meadows of the Piedmont and the coastal regions. Concentrated around Pennsylvania, Delaware, parts of Maryland and Virginia, and on up into New York, the Germans and their Dutch cousins settled and left their mark upon those regions, and came forth to serve their adopted land when hostilities erupted between North and South in 1861.

There are many worthy Germans in the annals of the war to whom one could point with pride. Among them was Carl Schurz, who lost a promising academic career at the University of Bonn after becoming involved in the German revolutionary movement of 1848. One of many young Germans who admired the democratic ideals of the United States, Schurz joined the revolutionary army and was one of the defenders of the key Fortress of Rastatt in 1849. When the fortress fell, Schurz escaped almost certain execution and slipped across the Rhine River to freedom in Switzerland. He was later involved in a daring rescue of his teacher, Professor Gott-

German-American Generals August v. Kautz and Godfrey Weitzel.

fried Kinkel, who had led the revolution, only to be imprisoned and sentenced to life behind bars; the rescue is one of the best-known incidents of the revolution. After marriage and

many more adventures, he ended up in America, where he became a confidante of Abraham Lincoln; he served his president as minister to Spain, and later as an officer of the line in the

11th Corps, which boasted a number of German regiments. The men he commanded served gallantly, though not uncontroversially, at Chancellorsville and Gettysburg. Schurz was later promoted to major general and saw action at Chattanooga and Nashville; at the end of the war, he was chief of staff to General William Tecumseh Sherman. Schurz remained in public life until his death in 1906, serving the government in many capacities, including a term as secretary of the interior.

On the Southern side, surely one of the most interesting German figures was Jeb Stuart's aide, Major Johann August Heinrich Heros Von Borcke. A tall, handsome blond young man in the German ideal, Von Borcke came from an old Prussian military family of the titled nobility. Serving in the Second Brandenburg Regiment of Dragoons at the time the Civil War began, either from boredom with garrison duty or due to an argument with his father, young Heros departed for the Confederacy, landing in Charleston, South Carolina, in May 1862. Introduced to Jeb Stuart by Confederate Secretary of War George Randolph, Von Borcke quickly became a dear friend of the equally young Confederate cavalier, and from then on the Prussian was rarely far from Stuart's side. Despite a regrettable tendency to ascribe to himself a number of exploits which were actually the actions of others, Von Borcke's writings about his year on Stuart's staff and subsequent adventures in Virginia following his near-fatal wounding in June 1863 are entertaining and fill in a number of historical gaps. He was beloved and admired by his Confederate comrades.

Von Borcke returned to Prussia and served his native land in a war with Austria in 1866; to his amusement and pleasure, the famous Austrian military genius Helmuth von Moltke greeted him with the words, "Are you not the American?" Forced to an early retirement in 1867 due to a Yankee bullet he still carried in his lung, Von Borcke married and had three sons. When he inherited a castle and estate at Giesenbrugge, it was his delight to fly the Confederate flag from its battlements. He died in 1895, reminiscing fondly about his days as a Confederate right up to the end.

Gettysburg Address

NOVEMBER 19, 1863

Invited as an afterthought to the dedication of a national military cemetery at one of the Civil War's great battlefields, Abraham Lincoln delivered what became American history's best-remembered speech.

Plans to provide a fitting burial ground for the Union dead of Gettysburg began soon after the July 1863 battle concluded. Although work on the cemetery had yet to be completed, a dedication ceremony was scheduled for November 19. It was to be an important event. Edward Everett, former governor of Massachusetts, 1860 vice-presidential nominee of the congressional Union party, and the most celebrated orator of his day, was asked to be the main speaker. Top government and military officials were invited to attend, including Abraham Lincoln, who was expected to decline.

When the president surprised the ceremony's planning committee by accepting, it felt obliged, belatedly, to ask him to prepare "a few appropriate remarks" for the event. Contrary to legend, Lincoln did not hastily compose the address on the back of an envelope as he rode a train to the ceremony. He worked on a first draft at the White House, probably writing a revision following his arrival in Gettysburg the day before the dedication.

A crowd of 15,000 had gathered on the brisk and hazy morning of November 19. After a short parade to the speaker's platform, followed by a 20-minute restroom delay by keynote speaker Everett, the ceremony began. A clergyman gave an invocation, which was followed by the reading of messages from dignitaries who could not attend, among them George Gordon Meade, the battle's victorious Union commander. Edwards came next, delivering a crowd-pleasing speech, even though he went on for nearly two hours.

After he concluded, at around 2 P.M., a short dirge was played, and then it was the president's turn to speak. In his high-pitched, raspy voice, seasoned with a Western accent, Lincoln

Lincoln (in the crowd to the left) at Gettysburg, November 19, 1863.

delivered the ten-line, 270-word address, adding a few impromptu words to the draft before him. Within two minutes, he was finished. Photographers, requiring a lengthy exposure, were unable to get a picture until the president had returned to his seat. The audience—many caught off guard by the brevity of the speech, some distracted by watching the photographers, and others feeling applause was inappropriate to the occasion—remained largely silent, although there was scattered clapping.

Lincoln may have been disappointed by his performance, but there were those in attendance who felt otherwise. Edward Everett wrote the president the following day, "I should be glad if I could flatter myself that I came as near the central idea of the occasion, in two hours, as you did in two minutes." Newspaper comments were mixed, dividing largely on party lines. The Democratic press chastised the president—as always—and his speech.

Republican papers, however, lauded it: "It will live among the annals of the war," one wrote. That was more out of loyalty than prescience. While these pro-administration journalists would have heaped praise on a far less worthy effort, their automatic endorsement, in this case, was justified. And their prediction of the speech's import was more accurate than Lincoln's own, offered in sentence eight of the address itself: "The world will little note, nor long remember, what we say here. . . ."

Gettysburg, Battle of

JULY 1–3, 1863

This three-day victory for the North remains the epitome of the bloody tragedy that was the

Civil War. The battle of Gettysburg, Pennsylvania, effectively ended the second, and final, Confederate invasion of the North.

Undertaken after Robert E. Lee's stunning victory at Chancellorsville, the risky invasion encompassed several Confederate priorities. First, Lee did not want another battle to take place in Virginia, where supplies were scarce and communities already savaged by months of war. Second, a battle won on Northern soil possibly could win the Confederacy some much-needed foreign support. Strangled by the Union blockade, overwhelmed by the North's superior manpower and matériel, the South desperately needed a stunning victory.

Believing that a best defense is a strong offense, Lee advanced the first of his 70,000 troops from Fredericksburg northwestward on June 3, 1863. Just four days later, the Battle of Brandy Station was fought between Union and Confederate cavalry near Culpeper, Virginia. Although the Rebels were able to push back their opponents, the Northern horsemen surprised them with their skill; for the first time since the war began, Federal cavalry were able to almost match their Southern counterparts on the battlefield.

During the next two weeks, the Northern army regrouped, waiting while Abraham Lincoln prepared to replace its disliked and largely ineffective commander, Joseph Hooker. All the while, the 100,000-man Army of the Potomac tracked Confederate troop movement and guarded the Union capital of Washington, D.C. In order for Lee to attain the Confederate objective—to win a military victory over a superior enemy—it was essential for him to choose the most propitious conditions under which to fight.

Lee entrusted cavalry commander Major General Jeb Stuart to discern the exact location, size, and intent of the Union army. Stuart, however, miserably failed his commander. Instead of performing quick forays and returning to camp, he embarked on a raid similar to the one that gained him much fame during the Peninsula campaign. In this case, however, his largely unsuccessful efforts took him out of

Lee's range as he rode around the Union's seemingly endless rear.

For more than two crucial weeks, Lee had no idea of the Union army's location or strength; he did not learn that his enemy had crossed the Potomac heading northwest until June 28. As it marched toward the Pennsylvania city of Harrisburg, northeast of Gettysburg, the Army of the Potomac moved with a new enthusiasm sparked by its new commander, the well-respected Major General George Meade.

In the meantime, Lee, whose hopes of surprising the enemy had been dashed, ordered his troops to stop their advance and converge west of Gettysburg until word from Stuart arrived. On July 1, a group of Confederates under Major General Henry Heth, innocently hoping to find a supply of new shoes in town, headed into Gettysburg. Encamped on a hill to the southwest of town, the Union cavalry commander, Brigadier General John Buford spotted the enemy troops, deployed his men, and called for reinforcements. After the Confederate soldiers reported the Union troop movements back to camp, a Confederate attack upon the newly formed Union cavalry line was ordered, thus beginning the Battle of Gettysburg.

The Union force was ready with new troops from the 1st Corps, led by Major General John F. Reynolds. Heth's division then stormed into Reynolds' line on McPherson's Ridge, killing Reynolds and devastating one of his best-fighting units, the Iron Brigade of the West. The Confederates seized the ridge, pushing the Federals back to Seminary Ridge. In the meantime, the battle had attracted troops from both sides in great numbers. The Union troops were converging from the south and east, while the Confederates came from the north and west.

On this first day, the Confederates outnumbered the Federals three to two, another rare occurrence. In the afternoon, the Confederates used their greater numbers to good advantage, driving Northern troops led by Major General Winfield Scott Hancock through the town of Gettysburg to Cemetery Ridge, just south of town. An immediate and vigorous Confederate attack on the hills might have succeeded, but

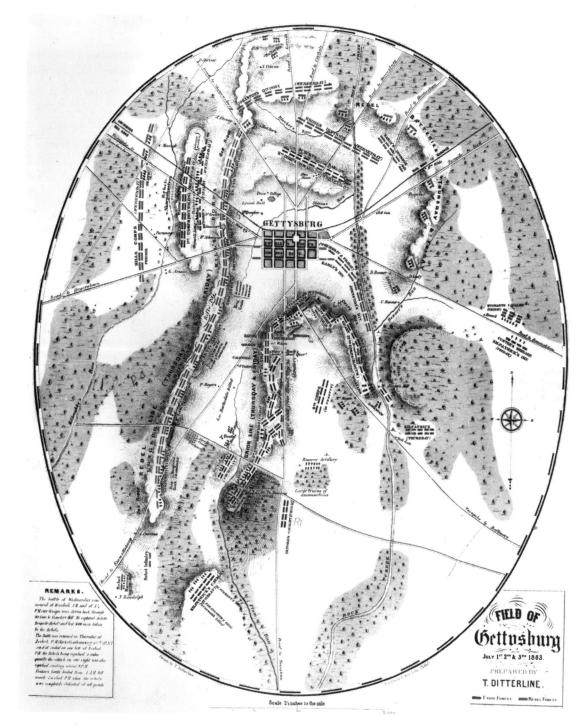

Map of the Battle of Gettysburg.

General Richard Ewell, under orders from Lee to attack "if possible," decided not to attempt such a risky venture in the waning hours of daylight.

During the night, both Union and Confederate troops regrouped. The Union position on the morning of July 2 resembled a huge fishhook, the shank of it located at Cemetery

Ridge, a long low ridge running north-south and dominated at each end by hills; the bent part of the hook curved around the ridge and ended with its barb on Cemetery Hill and Culp's Hill to the east. The high hills (Little Round Top and Round Top) to the south were unoccupied.

The Confederates were divided on how to attack the Union position. Lieutenant General James Longstreet argued for a flanking movement beyond the Union left which might force the Union to attack, while Lee pushed for a more offensive approach. One aim was to secure one or both of the high hills upon which the Confederates could mount artillery. Early in the afternoon, Union Major General Daniel E. Sickles, on his own initiative, moved his corps about one mile forward of the main line of defense to occupy a peach orchard and wheat field, thus weakening the Union left just as the Confederates planned to attack. Longstreet, however, delayed deployment of troops, then delivered a half-hearted thrust at the hills at about 4 P.M. In the meantime, Meade had become aware of the Confederate plans for the Round Tops and diverted troops to reinforce Sickles.

In the early evening hours, both sides fought raging battles in the peach orchard, wheat field, and a mass of boulders that earned the nickname "Devil's Den" after the carnage that took place there that day. Meade's quick maneuvers saved Little Round Top and secured the Union position. Later, Confederate troops made valiant efforts to take Cemetery Hill and Culp's Hill, but only made slight headway before being overwhelmed by the Union.

Union soldiers killed at Gettysburg.

Exhausted and severely depleted, both armies faced another day of heavy fighting on July 3. It began at daylight on the north end of the line, when Union General Henry W. Slocum's troops managed to retake its positions near Culp's Hill. As the armies prepared for the major coordinated assault that was sure to come, Longstreet again urged a flanking maneuver to force the Union to assume the offensive. Lee vetoed him once again, feeling he had no choice but to either admit defeat or try one more assault.

His strikes at the Union flanks having failed, Lee issued orders for an attack directed at the center of the Union line at Culp's Hill. Spearheaded by Major General George E. Pickett's fresh division, the offensive would involve 15,000 Confederate men. At the same time, Lee ordered the newly arrived Jeb Stuart to attack the Union rear from the east with his cavalry.

The last battle of the engagement began at 1:00 p.m. with a tremendous Artillery duel, which continued until both armies were almost out of ammunition. Pickett's Charge, an ill-fated and desperate attempt by the Confederates to storm Cemetery Ridge, began at about 3:30 P.M. A full contingent of soldiers marched across an open field while Union artillery fire mowed them down. A few men managed to reach the Union position and capture a short stretch of the line, but finally could not hold it. Jeb Stuart's three-hour assault on the Confederate rear flank was equally devastating to the Confederate position. At the end of the day, Lee admitted defeat to his battered men, saying to them, "It's all my fault. My fault."

The losses at Gettysburg were horrifying, even in a war known for its carnage. Of the 85,000 Union forces at Gettysburg, more than 23,000 were killed, wounded, captured or missing; the Confederates lost 20,000 of their 70,000 troops. On the evening of July 4, just as word reached Richmond that the Confederates at Vicksburg had capitulated, Robert E. Lee began his retreat to Virginia. Had the Union army pursued and attacked, the war may have ended then and there. Exhausted and aware of the South's tenacity, Meade decided to let Lee fall back. The war would rage on for nearly two more years.

Gorgas, Josiah

1818–1883

Overcoming woefully limited resources, the Confederacy's chief of ordnance did a masterful job of arming the South during the war.

Gorgas, who came from a poor Pennsylvania background, attended West Point and served in several federal arsenals in his early career. Married to the daughter of a former Alabama governor, he resigned from the U.S. Army in April 1861 and accepted the Confederacy's offer to head its ordnance department. His responsibility was to keep the Southern army supplied with the vast amount of weapons and ammuni-

Josiah Gorgas

tion it would need to fight the war, as well as to obtain the raw materials required to produce them. With the alarming lack of manufacturing and mining development in the South, it was an overwhelming assignment.

At the beginning of the war, the Confederacy possessed just one foundry able to produce heavy artillery and only a few small rifle works. Employing an equal amount of organizational skill and improvisation, Gorgas managed to get new arsenals, rolling mills, and factories built across the South. He also established a corps of agents who purchased arms from manufacturers in the North and in Europe, operating his own fleet of blockade runners to smuggle the goods past Federal ships guarding Southern harbors.

Neglecting few means of obtaining weapons, Gorgas urged the Confederate armies to make the seizure of small arms and artillery a battlefield priority. That proved surprisingly effective; in a one-year period, more than 100,000 Union rifles were confiscated. He inaugurated a mining bureau to extract iron, sulfur, and saltpeter from the hills of the South, and sent field representatives throughout the Confederacy in search of items—from liquor stills to church bells—to melt down for their metal. In addition, Gorgas appealed to the citizenry to bestow their jewelry and silver for the cause, and to save manure and human waste for leeching into niter.

The chief of ordnance's varied efforts paid off well. Though the Confederate military suffered chronic shortages of food, clothing, and manpower, its troops did not often lack adequate arms supplies. Yet Gorgas' considerable achievement was not fully appreciated at the time. Finally promoted to brigadier general in November 1864, he worked briefly in the iron industry after the war, then turned to a career in education highlighted by serving as president of the University of Alabama.

Grand Review of the Armies

MAY 23–24, 1865

Over a two-day period in Washington, D.C., May 23–24, 1865, the immense, exultant victory parade of the Union's main fighting forces in many ways brought the Civil War to its conclusion. With the nation's new president, Andrew Johnson, declaring on May 10 that all armed resistance was "virtually at an end," plans commenced for the review. It would far eclipse the two victory celebrations held before the assassination of Abraham Lincoln and bring Washington out of its formal mourning period for the slain president.

William Tecumseh Sherman's Army of Georgia, just finishing its 2,000-mile march through the heart of the Confederacy, arrived from North Carolina and bivouacked around the capital near George Gordon Meade's Army of the Potomac. Though the two armies camped on opposite sides of the river, the troops met up with one another in the taverns and brothels of Washington, D.C., where the customary rivalries led to numerous fistfights.

Sherman, concerned that Meade's army would outshine his own in the upcoming parade, was not immune from the rivalry either. Ordering some last-minute drilling and spit-and-polish sessions to whip his ragged troops into marching shape, Sherman knew they could not match the close-order discipline that the Army of the Potomac perfected.

The parade's first day was devoted to Meade's force, which, as the capital's defending army, was a crowd favorite. May 23 was a clear, brilliantly sunny day. Starting from Capitol Hill, the Army of the Potomac marched down Pennsylvania Avenue before virtually the entire population of Washington, a throng of thousands cheering and singing favorite Union marching songs. At the reviewing stand in front of the White House were President Johnson, General-in-Chief Ulysses S. Grant, and top government officials. Leading the day's march, General Meade dismounted in front of the stand and joined the dignitaries to watch the parade. His

Triumphant Union troops marching up Pennsylvania Avenue

army made an awesome sight: a force of 80,000 infantrymen marching 12 across with impeccable precision, along with hundreds of pieces of artillery and a seven-mile line of cavalrymen that alone took an hour to pass. One already famous cavalry officer, George Armstrong Custer, gained the most attention that day—either by design or because his horse was spooked— when he temporarily lost control of his mount, causing much excitement as he rode by the reviewing stand twice.

The next day was Sherman's turn. Beginning its final march at 9 A.M. on another beautiful day, his 65,000-man army passed in review for six hours, with less precision, certainly, than Meade's forces, but with a bravado that thrilled the crowd. Along with the lean, tattered, and sunburnt troops was the huge entourage that had followed Sherman's on his march to the sea: medical workers, laborers, black families who fled from slavery, the famous "bummers" who scavenged for the army's supplies, and a menagerie of livestock gleaned from the Carolina and Georgia farms. Riding in front of his conquering force, Sherman later called the experience "the happiest and most satisfactory moment of my life."

For the thousands of soldiers participating in both days of the parade, it was one of their final military duties. Within a week of the Grand Review, the Union's two main armies were both disbanded.

Grant, Ulysses Simpson

1822–1885

As a Civil War commander, Grant ranked second to none, winning the first major Union victories, earning promotion to general-in-chief of the Union army, and finally receiving General Robert E. Lee's Surrender at Appomattox Court House shortly after his own brilliant months-long Siege of Petersburg had broken the enemy.

That Grant became a true military hero—a cunning strategist with courage, tenacity, and the ability to lead—may have come as a surprise to those who knew him as a young man; indeed, it may have surprised Grant himself. The son of a hardworking, ambitious tanner, Grant was baptized Hiram Ulysses Grant and grew up in the small town of Georgetown, Ohio. A mediocre, rather lazy student, his only love was of horses; he became an accomplished rider at a young age. Despite his poor grades, Grant's father managed to secure him an appointment to West Point through his local congressman, who mistakenly referred to his young constituent as "Ulysses Simpson Grant" in his recommendation to the academy. The name stuck.

Grant's West Point record was far from spectacular. He graduated twenty-first in his class of 39 cadets and was commissioned brevet second lieutenant. Stationed at Jefferson Barracks, near St. Louis, Missouri, he not only began to learn the art of soldiering, but also met the woman who would become his wife, Julia Dent.

A year later, Grant was sent to the Southwest frontier; he served there until the Mexican War, in which he served under "Old Rough and Ready" Zachary Taylor, whose lack of pretense on the battlefield he would later emulate, and Winfield Scott. Grant took part in the Battles of Palo Alto, Monterey, Molino del Rey, where he was made first lieutenant for bravery, and Chapultepec, where he was brevetted captain.

After the Mexicans surrendered, Grant served in various garrisons across the country. His four years at Sackets Harbor, New York, and Detroit, Michigan, were relatively happy ones, largely because Julia Dent, whom he had married in 1848, kept him company. The years that followed in Fort Vancouver and on the West Coast, however, were among the most miserable in his life. Bored and lonely, Grant for the first time, but not the last, took to drinking whiskey. An argument with his commander caused him to resign his commission on April 11, 1854.

Returning to Missouri, Grant tried for several years to support his family. He moved his family to Galena, Illinois, where he worked in his father's leather shop. Barely able to survive during this period, Grant was, in many ways, saved when the Civil War started because it gave him both a job and a sense of purpose. After the fall of Fort Sumter, Grant helped organize the first company of Union volunteers in Galena.

In June 1861, Grant became colonel of the 21st Illinois Infantry and helped to whip the green troops into an effective fighting force. On August 7, 1861, President Abraham Lincoln appointed Grant brigadier general of volunteers and sent him to occupy Paducah, Kentucky, at the strategic junction of the Ohio and Tennessee rivers.

After a promising start, Grant's first offensive against the Confederates near Belmont, Missouri, ended when Rebel reinforcements arrived in time to drive Grant's troops back. In

General Grant with his wife, Julia, and son, Jesse, 1864.

February 1862, he had a chance to recoup his lost honor when General Henry W. Halleck, his commanding officer, authorized him to move against Forts Henry and Donelson. With 17,000 men and a flotilla of gunboats under the command of Andrew Hull Foote, Grant captured both forts in just over two weeks. At the fall of Fort Donelson, his unyielding statement, "No terms except unconditional and immediate surrender can be accepted," earned him the nickname "Unconditional Surrender" Grant.

His next important battle, at Shiloh, Tennessee, was less than a stunning victory for the Union. It appeared that Grant was surprised by General Albert Sidney Johnston's army when it burst through unfortified Union lines and threatened to drive Grant's men back into the river. Grant was able to regain lost ground through a long battle the following day, but rumors of his incompetence raged for months afterward. His tenacity at Shiloh impressed Abraham Lincoln, however, who is quoted as saying, "I can't spare this man—he fights."

After several months occupying an ambiguous position under Henry Halleck, who took pleasure in spreading rumors about Grant's drinking, Grant was made commander of the Department of Tennessee and charged with the taking of Vicksburg. Although the first few months of the campaign went badly when his supply bases were destroyed by Confederate raiders, Grant turned the situation around by early spring. Claiming "there is nothing left to be done but to go forward to a decisive victory," Grant devised an unexpected, clever plan and executed it brilliantly. He combined an amphibious movement down the Mississippi past Vicksburg with an overland march through the countryside and back across the river to set up camp behind Confederate lines. Although he had cut himself off from any supply lines, he was able to wait out his enemy during the almost three-month siege that followed.

The Confederate capitulation at Vicksburg on July 4, 1863, marked a turning point in the war and in Grant's own career. Promoted to major general, he next saw action in East Tennessee where, with customary perseverence, he managed to raise the siege of Chattanooga. He then consolidated Union control of the region with victories at Lookout Mountain and Missionary Ridge. Grant's stunning maneuvers brought him both public accolades and professional rewards.

In March 1864, Lincoln promoted him to general-in-chief commanding all the armies of the United States. Grant prepared to launch a coordinated offensive against the Confederacy that spring. For the first time, the four Union armies would work together to hit the Confederates hard enough to force a surrender. Grant planned to maneuver around the Confederate armies and destroy their supply lines behind them. Unfortunately, his well-planned venture became a costly campaign of attrition. The terrible losses of Union as well as Confederate troops earned Grant the ignominious nickname of "Grant the Butcher" in the Northern press.

Lee's army took relentless pounding at the Battles of the Wilderness, Spotsylvania, and Cold Harbor, but remained strong enough to fight on. In June 1864, Grant and Lee faced each other at Richmond. When Grant failed to make headway there, he adroitly withdrew, crossed the James River, and headed for Petersburg, where he settled down for a siege. For more than nine months the Army of the Potomac worked at cutting Lee's transportation lines and performing indirect assaults on his flanks. In the meantime, Major General William T. Sherman slashed through Georgia and Philip H. Sheridan devastated the Shenandoah Valley.

In April, 1865, the Confederate cause was lost forever when Grant's maneuvers finally stretched the Confederate line to the breaking point. Lee abandoned Richmond and Petersburg on April 2. Marching west, he hoped to join the army of General Joseph E. Johnston and make a final stand. Grant cut him off with a series of battles that finally convinced his worthy opposing general to capitulate. On April 9, 1865, at Appomattox Court House, Virginia, Grant offered Lee generous terms of surrender, which Lee immediately accepted.

After the war, Grant was given the grade of full general in 1866. For a time, he supported President Andrew Johnson's administration, serving as secretary of war after Edwin M. Stanton resigned. Disillusioned with Democrats, he slowly drifted into the Radical Republican camp. With his spectacular war record, he became the natural Republican candidate for president in 1868, an election he won easily.

As president, however, Grant displayed the lack of leadership and discipline his critics had accused him of at the beginning of the war. Although not personally corrupt, his two-term administration became notorious for its scandals and laissez-faire attitude at a time when the country faced an economic depression and struggled with Reconstruction. Grant left office in 1877.

Never an adroit businessman, he lived his last years in poverty, forced to sell his war mementoes and write his memoirs in order to support his family. His *Personal Memoirs* eventually earned the Grant family almost a half million dollars, but Grant died of throat cancer before reaping the book's rewards. He is buried in the mausoleum dedicated to him in 1897 in New York City.

Grant's General Orders No. 11

DECEMBER 17, 1862

Often referred to as Grant's "Jew Order," or more accurately his "Anti-Jew Order," this short-lived edict was one of the Union general's more regrettable wartime actions, and among the most notorious antisemitic regulations in United States history.

Early in the war, the treasury department guardedly favored reestablishing cotton trade in Union-occupied territories between selected Northern civilian merchants and Southern planters. However, the speculating soon got out of hand and the process became riddled with corruption. Bribery was widespread, the planters often used their proceeds to buy supplies for Confederate troops, and the attention of Federal soldiers was diverted as they participated in the profiteering themselves.

In southwestern Tennessee, the rampant speculation began to interfere seriously with the Union war effort. Regional commander Ulysses S. Grant, already perturbed because his advance on Vicksburg had stalled, blamed the merchants for the trouble, first directing his officers in November 1862 to refuse permits to certain unsavory traders, particularly, he added, voicing a common prejudice, the "Israelites."

Unsatisfied with the result, he issued a more sweeping order on December 17 through his assistant adjunct General John A. Rawlins, which stated in part, "The Jews, as a class violating every regulation of trade established by the Treasury Department and also Department orders, are hereby expelled from the department." In fact, several, though hardly all or even a majority of the speculators who were drawn to the region, did happen to be Jewish—including three sponsored by Grant's own father.

Nevertheless, the entire Jewish population of the department was affected by the order, and families were forced to leave such towns as Holly Springs and Oxford, Mississippi, and Paducah, Kentucky. News of the events in Grant's department was greeted with revulsion by both Jews and gentiles throughout the North, including several members of Congress, creating a controversy and tarnishing Grant's reputation.

In the meantime, representatives from the region's Jewish community hurried to Washington, protesting directly to Lincoln. On January 1, 1863, the president instructed Grant's superior, Henry Halleck, to rescind the order, agreeing that crooked trading should not be tolerated, but pointing out that "a whole class, some of whom are fighting in our ranks," could hardly be blamed.

Greeley, Horace

1811–1872

Despite his often eccentric and inconsistent views, the editor of the *New York Tribune* was an influential opinion-maker throughout the Civil War era. Greeley was born in poverty in New England and moved to New York after learning the printing trade. In 1841, he founded the *Tribune,* which after its Whig origins became an early Republican standardbearer. Thanks to its expert staff and Greeley's provocative editorials, in less than a decade the *Tribune* became the nation's most powerful and widely read newspaper.

With his paper as his platform, Greeley supported protective tariffs, organized labor, temperance, and westward expansion—his editorial appeal, "Go West, Young Man!" became the pioneers' rallying cry. Greeley also was a vocal abolitionist, and during the secession crisis of 1860, he scorned the idea of either compromise or going to war, voicing the conviction of many opponents of slavery that the country was well rid of the South.

His opinions, however, were often hard to predict and erratic. In early 1861, Greeley first advised Abraham Lincoln to surrender Fort Sumter, then commended the president when he did not. When pro-Confederate rioters in Baltimore attacked a regiment of Federal soldiers that May, he demanded the city be burned

Horace Greeley

matter in his own hands, Greeley traveled to Canada with Lincoln's private secretary, John Hay, for negotiations with two Confederate agents. The peace conference came to nothing, and he received much criticism for his efforts.

Shortly after the war, Greeley committed an even more unpopular act. Despite his opposition to Andrew Johnson's lenient Reconstruction policies, he posted bail for the imprisoned Jefferson Davis and supported a general amnesty for former Confederates. His readers were appalled; the *Tribune* lost thousands of subscriptions.

Yet Greeley retained enough public support to be nominated by a coalition of Liberal Republicans and the Democratic party to run against incumbent Ulysses S. Grant for the presidency in 1872. In a particularly ugly campaign, Greeley, a frail, peculiar-looking man with a high-pitched voice, was ruthlessly ridiculed by an electorate tired of his eccentricities. Greeley suffered more heartbreak when his wife died a few days before the election. Badly beaten by Grant, Greeley himself passed away less than a month after his defeat.

to the ground. Blazing the "Forward to Richmond!" war cry on the front pages of the *Tribune*, Greeley wanted to abandon the entire war effort after the Union's disastrous July defeat in the Battle of First Bull Run.

One opinion that did not waver, however, was his insistence on immediate emancipation. In Greeley's famous July 1862 editorial, "The Prayer of the Twenty Millions," he decried Lincoln's hesitation in acting on the matter. "Whatever strengthens or fortifies Slavery," Greeley wrote, "drives home the wedge intended to divide the Union." That viewpoint brought him trouble in July 1863, when a lynching party of antidraft, antiblack rioters in New York attacked the *Tribune*'s offices.

Greeley's resolve wavered once again during the late spring 1864 stalemate at Petersburg. "Our bleeding, bankrupt almost dying nation," he proclaimed, "longs for peace." Taking the

Greenbacks

The green ink used to print the nation's first national currency gave this paper money its nickname. Decreed to be legal tender, but not backed by any explicit promise of redemption in gold or silver, greenbacks were first issued by the Federal Congress through the Legal Tender Act of February 1862.

Other attempts to establish a national currency in 1781 and 1791 had failed: up until this time, money in the United States consisted largely of various bank notes and coins issued by each individual state. By the second year of the Civil War, the crisis facing the North spurred the creation of a new system to meet its financial needs.

In late December 1861, banks across the country had suspended payment of specie—gold coin—as backing for their notes. Neverthe-

A Federal Greenback.

less, Democrats and fiscal conservatives of both parties denounced the Legal Tender Act, claiming that it represented an unconstitutional—and dangerous—extension of federal authority. The Republicans managed to push through the legislation only because of the pressing need to support the skyrocketing costs of war; by the end of 1862, the Federal government would be spending about $2.5 million a day on the war.

About $150 million in these noninterest-bearing treasury notes were issued during the spring, and a second Legal Tender Act, passed in July, released about $250 million more into circulation. Eventually used to pay more than 13 percent of the war's cost in the North, greenbacks were also used by Northerners to purchase government bonds. More than one million Northerners used greenbacks to buy a stake in the Union.

However, because greenbacks could not be exchanged for gold and silver, their value depended on people's confidence in the government. When the fortunes of the Union army fell, so did the value of greenbacks, at one point dropping to a value of less than 40 cents in gold. To help alleviate this problem, Congress passed the National Banking Act in February 1863, which created a system of national banks authorized to issue bank notes of uniform value.

By the end of the war, the Republicans had consolidated control of the nation's finances in the hands of northeastern bankers. At the same time, however, the country found itself in financial chaos. The federal debt had risen from just $2 per capita in 1860 to more than $75 in 1865. Moreover, the amount of currency had doubled with the addition of greenbacks and national bank notes, adding to inflation. Although greenbacks were eventually taken out of circulation, the concept of "easy" money implicit in paper currency remained in the hearts and pocketbooks of Americans.

H

Habeas Corpus, Suspension of

By suspending the "great writ" that prevents governments from improperly imprisoning their citizens, Abraham Lincoln exercised unprecedented and questionable presidential power during the Civil War by detaining political opponents and imposing martial law even in regions far from the fighting.

The right of individuals under arrest to petition a court for a writ of habeas corpus—a judgment releasing them for being held without just cause—is among the most fundamental of civil liberties, although Article I of the U.S. Constitution does allow this right to be suppressed "when in cases of rebellion or invasion the public safety may require it." Lincoln, maintaining that the unfolding Civil War was precisely that kind of national emergency, proclaimed the suspension of habeas corpus in April 1861 in order to apprehend the ringleaders of secessionist uprisings near Washington.

Issuing a writ nevertheless for one of the arrested officials, Supreme Court Chief Justice Roger Taney ruled that only Congress, not the president alone, could authorize the suspension. Lincoln, with the initial support of Republicans and several prominent constitutional scholars, simply ignored the ruling. Moreover, he reserved the right to have the military jail anyone throughout the North who demon-

strated "substantial and unmistakable complicity with those in armed rebellion."

Southern sympathies as well as actual acts of treason were considered sufficient proof of that complicity; excessive, arbitrary roundup commenced over the objections of Democrats and Republicans alike. Responding to the criticism, Lincoln released nearly 200 political prisoners in the spring of 1862. Hundreds more were arrested later in the year, however, when he suspended habeas corpus again to curb opposition to the militia drafts begun by several states.

The following March, Congress officially endorsed Lincoln's authority to take such actions in its Habeas Corpus Act of 1863. Peace activists, draft resisters, anti-administration newspaper editors, Copperhead judges and politicians—anywhere from 13,000 to 18,000 Northern citizens may have been held without trial over the course of the war. This was perhaps the most controversial aspect of Lincoln's presidency, becoming a key Democratic campaign issue in the 1864 election.

At his February 1862 inauguration, Jefferson Davis ridiculed these Northern abuses of civil liberties. Within five days, however, the Confederate president, with the reluctant approval of the Southern Congress, temporarily suspended the writ of habeas corpus himself, declaring martial law in Richmond and other areas in the war's direct path.

Davis was given similar restricted authoriza-

dent gave him an advance look at the Emancipation Proclamation and changed some of the wording at Hamlin's suggestion. Nevertheless, he ignored Hamlin's advice to issue the proclamation immediately, and the vice president later acknowledged that Lincoln's decision to wait until the Union victory at Antietam was a sound one.

Tired of his lack of meaningful work, Hamlin enlisted in the Maine coast guard while in office. Nevertheless, he intended to remain on the ticket in 1864. Republicans seeking to form a coalition with pro-administration Democrats and concerned about his association with the Radical wing of the party, however, rejected him. At the convention, Lincoln claimed to be neutral, but he likely worked behind the scenes to ensure the choice of Democrat Andrew Johnson. Thus, when Lincoln was reelected, then assassinated, it was Johnson, not Hamlin who succeeded to the presidency.

Returning to the Senate in 1869, Hamlin served in Congress for another 12 years, then left to become the U.S. minister to Spain.

Hampton Roads Conference

FEBRUARY 3, 1865

In a last-ditch effort to negotiate an end to the war, President Abraham Lincoln and his Secretary of State William Seward agreed to meet with agents of the Confederate government on a steamboat in Hampton Roads, Virginia, at the mouth of the James River.

The idea of a peace conference originated with newspaper editor Francis P. Blair, Sr., an early and ardent Republican, who hoped that the two sides could be convinced to join forces—and thus end the conflict—in order to secure American interests in Mexico, now under the rule of Austrian archduke and emperor Maximillian. Blair held an unofficial meeting with Confederate President Jefferson Davis and, with permission from Lincoln, arranged the Hampton Roads conference.

Both sides had reasons to agree to meet. Davis, knowing the chances for a successful conference were limited, hoped that by standing up to the North he could steel his weary nation for another year of war. For his part, Lincoln wanted to avoid the harsh Reconstruction that would certainly come after a decisive Union military victory.

Lincoln and Seward spent several hours negotiating with Confederate Vice President Alexander Hamilton Stephens, ex-Supreme Court Justice John A. Campbell, and former secretary of state Senator Robert M. T. Hunter. The conference ended when Lincoln refused to accept anything less than a complete restoration of the Union and the abolition of slavery, terms which the Confederates refused to consider.

Davis had the Union demands printed and distributed throughout the South, thereby provoking a much-needed resurgence of Confederate patriotism. In the meantime, Radical Republicans were shocked by Lincoln's plans for a mild Reconstruction and at once began to plan a far more humiliating retribution on the South.

Hampton, Wade

1818–1902

With no formal military education, one of the South's richest planters rose to become commander of the Confederate cavalry after the death of Jeb Stuart.

Hampton's experience running his family's vast South Carolina cotton plantations led him to doubt the economic wisdom of slavery, though he did not oppose the institution in principle. Also skeptical about secession, Hampton nevertheless used his own money at the outbreak of the Civil War to raise a unit of infantry, cavalry, and artillery for the Confederate army.

As its colonel, he led his unit, known as "Hampton's Legion," into battle at First Bull

Negotiations on the James River at Hampton Roads.

Run in July 1861, where he was slightly wounded. Participating in the Peninsula campaign of spring 1862, Hampton was wounded again at the Battle of Seven Pines. After recovering, he was assigned to the Army of Northern Virginia's cavalry as a brigadier general. Hampton fought at Antietam and, as second-in-command, joined Jeb Stuart in his celebrated October ride around George McClellan's army in Maryland.

Wounded a third time at Gettysburg, the legendarily robust and athletic Hampton returned to duty later in 1863. With the new rank of major general, he led a cavalry division in the Bat-

tle of the Wilderness in May 1864. Although Hampton was the ranking officer, he was not immediately appointed Jeb Stuart's successor when the commander of Robert E. Lee's cavalry corps was killed four days later at Yellow Tavern. Hampton was ultimately given the position in August and, the following month, proved his merit in a daring raid that nabbed nearly 2,500 head of cattle for ravenous Confederate troops entrenched at Petersburg.

When the South started suffering a shortage of horses as well as food, he began training his cavalry to fight on foot. In January 1865, Hampton returned to South Carolina, where he tried to raise military equipment and civilian morale. There, he also commanded Joseph E. Johnston's cavalry corps during the Confederate general's struggle against the invading Union army of William Tecumseh Sherman. Hampton avoided surrendering with Johnston in April and considered making a final stand for the Confederacy in the West. Instead, he returned to his home and worked to rebuild his ravaged plantations.

After the Reconstruction era, Hampton became a major force in South Carolina politics for a generation, serving as both governor and U.S. senator.

Hancock, Winfield Scott

1824–1886

"My politics are of a practical kind—the integrity of the country, the supremacy of the Federal government, an honorable peace or none at all." This clever, tenacious general who fought in many of the war's major battles, including Gettysburg, earned the admiration of his troops and the respect of his commanders. His integrity, lack of political ambition, and his concentration on the matter at hand—namely the discipline and training of his men—made him one of the Union's most valuable soldiers.

Born in Pennsylvania, Hancock graduated from West Point in 1844. Breveted second lieutenant, he served first at Fort Towson on the frontier before being stationed in Mexico as that country headed toward war. In the Mexican War, under the command of General Winfield Scott, Hancock fought in four principal battles for which he was awarded a brevet to first lieutenant. Between the Mexican War and the Civil War, Hancock continued to improve his skills as a soldier against the Seminoles in Florida (1855), in Kansas under General Harney (1857–58), and during the Mormon uprising in Utah (1859).

Fort Sumter fell while Hancock was serving as chief quartermaster of the Southern District of California; he immediately requested a transfer to active duty in the East. He was then appointed brigadier general of volunteers and assisted in organizing the Army of the Potomac. Under General George B. McClellan, he played an important role in the Battles of Williamsburg and Frazier's Farm during the Peninsula campaign, at Antietam where he commanded the first division of the 2nd Army Corps, and during the Battle of Fredericksburg.

After the Battle of Chancellorsville, as Union forces attempted to stop Robert E. Lee's invasion of the North at Pennsylvania, President Lincoln appointed Hancock commander of the entire 2nd Army Corps. At the same time, Lincoln made another change in command by replacing General Joseph Hooker with General George Gordon Meade just as the Confederate army faced its foe in the tiny town of Gettysburg, Pennsylvania.

Hancock helped Meade to choose an excellent position for the Union army on the first day of battle. On the second day, his army was able to push back Lee's attack on the Union left flank. Riding up and down the front lines of battle to inspire and command his men, Hancock was heard to say, "There are times when a corps commander's life does not count." Indeed, Hancock received serious wounds at Gettysburg from which he never fully recovered.

Nevertheless, after recuperating for only six months, Hancock returned to his corps and fought through the Virginia campaigns of 1864. In the Battle of the Wilderness, Hancock pulled off a major reversal after his corps was nearly crushed by a flank maneuver led by James Longstreet. Instead of retreating, Hancock ordered his men to form a new line of battle across a north-south road along which the Confederates were advancing; when the Confederates arrived, they were stopped and driven back.

Hancock showed the same courage and tenacity at Spotsylvania, Cold Harbor, and at Petersburg; in recognition for his service in these battles, he was appointed brigadier general in the Regular army on August 12, 1864. Later that month, the man so devoted to his troops was disheartened and saddened when a surprise Confederate attack at Reams Station

General Winfield S. Hancock (seated).

during the Petersburg campaign devastated his corps.

Shortly after this defeat, Hancock, exhausted after three long years in battle, was reassigned to Washington, D.C. to recruit a corps of veterans. He remained in the capital, except for a brief term as commander of the Middle Military Division of Virginia, until the end of the war.

His career as a soldier was far from over, however. In July 1866, Hancock became major general in the Regular army and fought in the Missouri Indian wars. He then went on to as-

sume a post in the South as part of the North's Reconstruction effort as commander of the 5th Military District covering Texas and Louisiana. Hancock found the military's role in Reconstruction offensive, and angered many Radical Republicans by refusing to carry out certain measures, including replacing civil courts with military ones. He asked for and was granted a transfer to the North, eventually assuming command of the Department of the East.

By this time, Hancock's reputation as an honest, intelligent leader—as well as a bona fide war hero and anti-Reconstructionist—prompted the

Democrats to nominate him for president in 1880. He lost to Republican James Garfield, another war veteran, by a small margin of the popular vote.

On August 8, 1885, Hancock carried out his last official public duty of national importance, which was conducting General Ulysses S. Grant's funeral. This was an appropriate gesture since Grant held his corps commander in the highest esteem, once remarking that "[Hancock's] genial disposition made him friends, and his personal courage and his presence with his command in the thickest of the fight won him the confidence of troops serving under him." Hancock died on Governor's Island, New York, on February 9, 1886.

Hardee, William Joseph

1815–1873

Lieutenant General William J. Hardee, grandson of a Revolutionary War veteran and son of a cavalry major in the War of 1812, was born to military tradition and served it well. Born in Camden County, Georgia, Hardee attended the U.S. Military Academy at West Point and graduated with the class of 1838.

Assigned to the Second Dragoons, a regiment of note, Hardee quickly rose to first lieutenant and later to captain. He was sent to Europe with a military commission to study the operations of continental cavalry regiments, and upon his return was assigned to duty as a tactical officer in Louisiana, at Fort Jesup.

Twice brevetted for gallantry in the Mexican War, Hardee was involved in the seige of Vera Cruz, the Battles of Contreras and Molino del Rey, and the taking of Mexico City. As a result of both his travels in Europe and his experiences in Mexico, Hardee undertook the writing of what he is perhaps best known for: *Rifle and Light Infantry Tactics*, popularly known as "Hardee's Tactics," published in 1855—just in time to become a premier manual of instruc-

tion to both the United States and Confederate States Armies.

Hardee was senior major of the famous 2nd U.S. Cavalry, which boasted among its officer corps Colonel Albert Sidney Johnston, Lieutenant Colonel Robert E. Lee, and Junior Major George H. Thomas, Jr. Later assigned to a position of commandant of cadets at West Point, Hardee was on leave in his home state when Georgia's legislature voted for secession on January 19, 1861. Sources disagree on the date of Hardee's resignation from the U.S. Army; some say as early as January 21, others date it 10 days later. However, by June 17, Hardee was a brigadier general in the Confederate army, and a major general before the end of 1861.

Hardee's first assignment involved the organizing of a brigade of troops from Arkansas, which later was dubbed "Hardee's Brigade" in the general's honor. Transferred in the fall of 1861 to Kentucky, Hardee participated throughout the war in some of the hardest-fought battles of the Western Confederate army, known as the Army of Tennessee. Hardee was at Shiloh in April 1862, and Perryville, in October of the same year.

Promoted to lieutenant general to rank from October 10, Hardee was commander of the left wing of the army during Braxton Bragg's campaigns in Kentucky, and at Murfreesboro he was responsible in large part for Bragg's strong offensive on the Federal right at dawn on December 31, 1862.

In July 1863, Hardee was replaced by D. H. Hill as commander of Bragg's 2nd Corps and ordered to Mississippi, only to be similarly caught up in a government-ordered shakeup of the command structure when he was replaced by General Leonidas K. Polk. Hardee later commanded a corps at Chattanooga and shortly thereafter refused command of the Army of Tennessee, and after the fall of Atlanta in 1864, received command of the military departments of South Carolina, Georgia, and Florida.

He assisted General Joseph E. Johnston in the campaign to contain Union General Sherman's March to the Sea, but found he had insufficient men or supplies to do anything more than harrass and annoy Sherman's seemingly unstoppable progress through the heart of the Confederacy. On December 18, 1864, Hardee was forced to evacuate Savannah and withdrew into South Carolina after refusing Sherman's suggestion that he surrender his army.

A month later Sherman came forth from Savannah and pursued Hardee, who was unable to defend Charleston and had to finally retreat further into North Carolina, meeting up eventually with Joseph Johnston once more. Before anything much could be made of a joint effort between them, Hardee received word of the surrender of Robert E. Lee's army at Appomattox; it was not long after that before Johnston also realized the futility of continuing the fight and surrendered at Durham Station, North Carolina, on April 26, 1865.

Hardee retired to a plantation near Selma, Alabama, after the war, having married in 1863 at the height of his fame. He died while on a trip to Wytheville, Virginia, in 1873, and is buried in Selma. His was a distinguished career of mil-

itary service, which led even opponents and former comrades such as Sherman and Thomas to refer to him as a competent and capable soldier. From his own people he received even more accolades, being described by E. A. Pollard as a man possessed of a "courage . . . of an order which inspires courage in others."

Harpers Ferry, Capture of

SEPTEMBER 15, 1862

A crucial element in General Robert E. Lee's strategy to invade the North during his Antietam campaign concerned the capture of the federal garrison of 11,000 men in Harpers Ferry. While Lee took one division up to Hagarstown, Pennsylvania, and sent another division to guard Boonseboro Gap with Daniel H. Hill, he

Harper's Ferry, before the war.

Ruins of the Bridge at Harper's Ferry, 1862.

ordered Thomas "Stonewall" Jackson to capture the garrison with nearly half of Lee's 36,000-man army. Jackson then divided his own forces into three groups, each approaching from a different direction to effectively seal the town and garrison. Built on low ground surrounded by hills now swarming with Confederates, the Union fort, under the command of Colonel Dixon S. Miles, was in an untenable position, making surrender or utter carnage inevitable.

Remarkably, however, a contingent of 1,300 cavalry, led by Colonel Benjamin F. Davis, managed to fight their way out of the garrison and fled to Union lines. On the way, they captured a Confederate ammunition train of 97 wagons and its escort of 600 men without losing a single man themselves. The rest of the garrison troops, however, were forced to surrender after the first round of artillery fire from Jackson's forces. Jackson's victory netted the Confederates invaluable supplies, including 13,000

small arms and 73 cannon. After securing the garrison, Jackson sped with his troops to join the less-than-successful Confederate offensive at Antietam.

Harpers Ferry Raid

OCTOBER 16–18, 1859

John Brown's deadly assault on a Federal arsenal in 1859 may not have incited the mass slave rebellion that he intended, but it did help bring the entire nation to war. Having already turned to violence in the Kansas territory three years earlier, when he led a massacre of five slaveholders near Pottawatomie, the bearded radical abolitionist sought to ignite an insurrection in the South itself.

Brown's plan was an incredible one: to take a

makeshift army into the Appalachian Mountains, where it would recruit thousands of fugitive slaves, establish a renegade government of free blacks, and wage guerrilla warfare against the slaveholding states. He managed to win the clandestine support of a group of renowned white abolitionists called "the Secret Six," including Samuel Gridley Howe, noted physician/philanthropist and husband of Julia Ward Howe, and Theodore Parker, one of the nation's most prominent clergymen.

With other allies like Frederick Douglass warning that the scheme was suicidal, Brown had difficulty recruiting volunteers for the action. Harriet Tubman was planning to participate, but she had to pull out when she became sick. Ultimately, Brown managed to summon a force of only five blacks and seventeen whites, including three of his own sons. From their base at a Maryland farm across the Potomac, the tiny band slipped into the town of Harpers Ferry, Virginia (now West Virginia), on the evening of October 16, 1859, and seized the arsenal, armory, and gun works there. The insurgents were now in possession of a vast store of arms and ammunition, but they had no escape plan and little way of notifying the slaves on nearby plantations that their liberators had arrived. A patrol was dispatched to spread word of the uprising and returned with a few hostages—including a great-grand nephew of George Washington—but with no blacks willing to join the struggle.

By the following afternoon, armed townspeople and the local militia had cornered Brown and his men in the village's engine house. That evening, a company of 90 U.S. Marines from Washington, D.C. arrived on the scene, led by cavalry officers Robert E. Lee and Jeb Stuart. On October 18 the marines stormed the engine house, using bayonets rather than bullets so the hostages would not be harmed. By the time Brown was captured, two of his sons and eight other raiders were dead or mortally wounded, as were a marine and several Harpers Ferry citizens, including a black railroad baggage master.

Turned over to the state of Virginia, Brown was quickly tried and convicted of treason and murder, and hanged on December 2; four of his

fellow raiders were later executed as well. Most of the Northern press and Republican and Democratic leaders alike condemned Brown and his murderous act, but a number of Northerners, even those who denounced the violence, exalted Brown as a martyr—misguided perhaps—to a just cause.

In the South, where panicked rumors spread of the approach of more gun-wielding slaves and abolitionists, alarm over the raid itself was replaced by fury at the lionization of Brown in the North. Onetime opponents of secession reconsidered the wisdom of remaining in the Union and, with Southern states purchasing arms and hundreds of men signing up for the military reserve, preparations were beginning for the possibility of a major armed conflict.

Haupt, Herman

1817–1905

Serving in the military for one critical year as the Union's railroad expert, he revolutionized the use of trains in warfare.

An 1835 West Point graduate, Haupt soon left the army, becoming a college professor, an authority in bridge construction, and a superintendent for the Pennsylvania Railroad. In the 1850s, he financed, designed, and built a series of rail lines in the Northeast that were extraordinary feats of engineering, highlighted by the five-mile long Hoosac tunnel through the Berkshires.

Haupt was appointed by Union Secretary of War Edwin Stanton in 1862 to manage transportation and construction for military railroads, and served in Virginia under General Irvin McDowell. Resenting army red tape and the interference of Union officers, the no-nonsense engineer ran a hugely efficient operation, safeguarding tracks from Confederate raiders and building and repairing bridges "quicker than the Rebs can burn them down," as one of his men noted.

One noteworthy accomplishment was Haupt's

construction, using inferior wood and unskilled laborers, of a bridge across Potomac Creek, measuring 80 feet high and 400 feet long, in less than two weeks. Marveling that there was "nothing in it but beanpoles and cornstalks," Lincoln called the bridge "the most remarkable structure that human eyes ever rested upon." During Second Bull Run, Haupt had trains running near Manassas Junction within four days after a lengthy stretch of railroad track was cut by Confederate General "Stonewall" Jackson. Haupt also devised prefabricated parts for bridges and tracks, organized the first Union construction corps, and vastly improved the use of rail lines for troop and supply movements. In the midst of fierce fighting, Haupt was able to send trains through to deliver food, weapons, and reinforcements and bring back wounded soldiers.

Named brigadier general in September 1862, he turned down the appointment and resigned from the military a year later for being restricted from accepting private business projects. Haupt continued in railroading for more than 40 years, wrote several important engineering treatises, and invented an innovative pneumatic drill. Fittingly, he died aboard a train of a heart attack.

Heroes of America

The largest and best developed of several peace societies active in the Confederacy, the Heroes of America were also known as the "Red Strings" for the identifying threads they wore on their lapels. Although its exact date and place of origin is unknown, the organization was especially active in North Carolina, parts of Virginia, and eastern Tennessee. Like the Knights of the Golden Circle, its counterpart in the North, the Heroes of America was a highly secretive group of antiwar activists. Although neither as numerous nor active as the Knights, the Heroes had their passwords, their secret signs, and their objectives, which included discouraging enlistment, opposing con-

scription, encouraging desertion, and agitating for a return to the Union.

The Heroes also protected deserters—of which there were more than 100,000 during the course of the war—aided spies and escaped prisoners, and supplied Federal authorities with information about Confederate troop movements and strength in order to bring about a more rapid Union victory. Some members of the organization joined because they had lost heart in the Confederate cause due to its mounting military losses. Others were die-hard Unionists, and still others were pacifists. Most had one thing in common: poverty. Owning few or no slaves and little or no property, a majority of the Heroes wanted no part of what they called "a rich man's war and a poor man's fight." As occurred in the North, the ranks of the South's peace societies swelled after each battlefield defeat. As the war dragged on, and the possibility of a Southern victory diminished, the Heroes of America grew stronger and more powerful, thereby sapping strength from the Confederacy just when it needed it the most.

Hill, A(mbrose) P(owell)

1825–1865

Hill was one of Robert E. Lee's favorite lieutenants, but his best Civil War service actually came before he was promoted to high command. From a prominent Virginia family, Hill attended West Point, where his roommate was future Union commander George McClellan. His courtship of McClellan's fiancée went awry when the woman heard rumors that Hill had gonorrhea, an illness that may explain Hill's frequent sick leaves late in the Civil War. Said to be an opponent of slavery, he still resigned from the Federal army to serve with the Confederacy even before his state seceded.

Hill proved audacious, if impetuous, in battle, gaining early notoriety as the leader of "Hill's Light Division." Celebrated for its nimble and unencumbered advances, the unit per-

Southern antiwar activists faced harsh reprisals from Rebel troops.

formed magnificently in the Peninsula campaign of spring 1862 despite heavy losses. Many of these came in the Seven Days campaign, when Hill, lacking the expected support from Stonewall Jackson, nevertheless led an assault against the solidly entrenched Union line at Mechanicsville on June 26. He and his men were left largely to their own devices again the following day at Gaines' Mill, and again later in the week at White Oak Swamp. Hill and Jackson's efforts would be better coordinated over the next year in such victories as Second Bull Run, Cedar Mountain, Fredericksburg, and Chancellorsville.

Although they made a splendid team, the two men clashed occasionally, with Jackson

even arresting Hill for insubordination shortly before the Battle of Antietam. His punishment suspended by Lee for the campaign, Hill's timely arrival on the field—in his characteristic red battle shirt—knocked the attacking Union left flank back across Antietam Creek and saved the Confederate army from a catastrophic defeat. When Jackson was shot at Chancellorsville, Hill temporarily took his command until he was wounded himself, then was promoted to lieutenant general by Lee following Jackson's death. A month later, one of Hill's divisions kicked off the Battle of Gettysburg as it approached the Pennsylvania town in search of a desperately needed supply of shoes. In a lackluster performance, Hill also commanded a corps in the May 1864 Battle of the Wilderness, but illness kept him from several of the Army of Northern Virginia's later engagements. He was on hand, however, during the Union's final assault on Petersburg in April 1865. Rallying his troops on April 2, Hill was shot through the heart, his death yet another devastating blow for Lee.

Hill, Daniel Harvey

1821–1889

Born in York District, South Carolina, Daniel H. Hill was a member of the West Point class of 1842 from which a dozen young cadets, including James Longstreet, were destined to gain generals' stars in the War Between the States.

Hill participated in the Mexican War, being in most of the crucial battles of that war, receiving brevet ranks for gallantry at Chapultepec and Churubusco. At the close of the conflict he resigned his commission and turned to teaching mathematics at Washington College, Lexington, Virginia (later to become Washington and Lee). He later taught the same subject at Davidson College, and was thus engaged until accepting an appointment as superintendent of the North Carolina Military Institute in 1859.

Hill was responsible for organizing North Carolina's first camp of military instruction upon the secession of his state in 1861, and in July of that year was appointed brigadier general, one month after commanding the First North Carolina Infantry at the battle of Big Bethel. Less than a year later, Hill was promoted to major general, and saw service in Joseph E. Johnston's command at Williamsburg, Yorktown, and Seven Pines.

Robert E. Lee's reports following the Seven Days campaign give a great deal of praise to Hill's handling of his division, and he is cited for excellent conduct at Second Manassas (Second Bull Run) and South Mountain; during the latter engagement he protected the Confederate

supply train by holding off the attacks of a significantly larger Union force with only 5,000 men.

It was widely held for many years that the strayed copy of Lee's famous "Lost Order" had been mislaid by Hill at Sharpsburg (Antietam), a charge which Hill roundly denied in the postwar years. In that same battle, Hill had the dubious distinction of losing a mount in what has to be the most bizarre and embarrassing instance of a horse's death recorded in the tragic annals of war. While engaged in reconnaissance with Robert E. Lee and James Longstreet, both of whom had dismounted lest they draw enemy fire, Hill had no sooner been told he, too, ought to dismount when a Federal shell struck their position, neatly removing the forelegs of Hill's charger. The general was only able to dismount from the animal by clambering over its rump in an ungainly fashion.

Hill was one of those responsible for the protection of Richmond while the Army of Northern Virginia invaded Pennsylvania in July 1863. Shortly after that he was appointed lieutenant general and was transferred to the army of Braxton Bragg in Tennessee. After the Battle of Chickamauga, Hill signed a petition requesting that Bragg be relieved of command for incompetence, a move which did little to ingratiate him to Bragg's chief supporter, President Jefferson Davis. The president refused to ask Congress to confirm Hill's promotion, and relieved him of command of his corps to boot; not until the battle of Bentonville, a three-day inconclusive fight in the closing days of the last stand in the Carolinas, was Hill allowed to command troops in the field.

D. H. Hill was one of the generals who participated in Joseph Johnston's surrender at Durham Station, near Greensboro, North Carolina, on April 26, 1865.

Hill returned to Charlotte, North Carolina, upon his parole, and in 1866 established a popular monthly periodical, *The Land We Love*. Three years later, he also instituted a weekly newspaper called *The Southern Home*. He became deeply interested in education, citing a need to vindicate the "truth of Southern history" and to train young men in agriculture and industrialization. To this end, Hill became president of the University of Arkansas, a post he held until illness required him to take leave of absence in 1884.

In 1886, Hill accepted the presidency of the Middle Georgia Military and Agricultural College, which later became the Georgia Military College, a position he held until his death. He also did a great deal of writing in view of a desire to set the record straight on the Confederacy's behalf, and was a contributor to many historical collections and publications, including the *Battles and Leaders of the Civil War* series. General Hill died in Charlotte, North Carolina, in 1889, and is buried in the Davidson College Cemetery, Davidson, North Carolina.

H.L. Hunley

The first submarine in history to sink an enemy vessel—and the only one to do so in the Civil War—the cigar-shaped, iron *H.L. Hunley* was slow, awkward, and ultimately more dangerous to its crew than to its opponent. The Confederate government looked to the nascent submarine technology as one possible way to break the increasingly tight Union blockade at Charleston and Norfolk. Its first attempt at creating an underwater vessel was the CSS *Pioneer*, built in 1861, which had a few successful test runs in New Orleans' Lake Pontchartrain.

When the Union captured the port city, however, the Confederates scuttled the *Pioneer* rather than let the enemy have it. In the meantime, the Union navy had developed its only submarine, the *Alligator*, a clunky vessel which was propelled underwater by manually operated oars. The *Alligator* had an equally inglorious fate: it sank under tow during a storm off Cape Hatteras before ever being tested in battle.

In 1863, the Confederates finished building the *H.L. Hunley*, designed to hold an eight-man crew and armed with a torpedo loaded with 90 pounds of gunpowder. After more than 20 *Hun-*

ley crewmen were killed during trial runs, General Pierre G. T. Beauregard ordered no further testing.

Finally convinced of its seaworthiness, the commander allowed it to be used against the Union sloop, the *Housatonic*, on February 17, 1864, in the waters off Charleston. Ramming its torpedo into the Union ship's starboard side, the *H.L. Hunley* managed to sink the vessel within minutes. Unfortunately, the submarine was unable to extricate itself from the *Housatonic's* rigging and so preceded the warship to the bottom of the river, taking all eight crewmen to their deaths.

The Confederate navy constructed one other submarine, the *St. Patrick*, which saw battle in Mobile, Alabama, in 1865. When its torpedo failed to fire, it was brought safely back to port, effectively ending the role of the submarine in the Civil War.

Hood, John Bell

1831–1879

Lacking neither courage nor fighting skills, Hood's deficient strategic abilities and ill-suitedness to high command helped cause the destruction of the Confederacy's Army of Tennessee late in the war.

The tall and imposing Kentucky native graduated in the bottom fifth of his class at West Point, and his early military service included a stint in the elite 2nd Cavalry, during which he had already begun to demonstrate bold, if reckless, tendencies.

Leaving the U.S. Army in April 1861 to join the Confederacy, he and his famed brigade of Texans made noteworthy showings in the Seven Days battles, Second Bull Run, and Antietam, where they sustained heavy casualties breaking the Union's initial attack. A gunshot wound at Gettysburg crippled Hood's left arm, and he lost his right leg later in 1863 in the Battle of Chickamauga. Thereafter, he had to be

General John B. Hood

strapped to his horse before each day's fighting, but the injuries did not slow his military advancement.

As Joseph E. Johnston's chief officer in the 1864 defense of Atlanta against William T. Sherman's invading Union army, Hood roundly criticized his superior's cautious strategy. In July, he was given the chance to do better, when Jefferson Davis, eager for a hard fighter, appointed Hood to take over the Army of Tennessee from Johnston in the middle of the campaign. Within two days of gaining command, Hood went on the offensive, playing into Sherman's hands. His three attacks against the Union army—at Peachtree Creek, near Decatur, and at Ezra Church—cost him 15,000 men, and he was forced to retreat back to At-

lanta's strong fortifications. The city was besieged and, a month later, fell to the North. Hood still managed an effective withdrawal of his troops and, with help from Nathan Bedford Forrest, attacked the Union's supply lines in north Georgia and Tennessee.

Hardly halting Sherman's relentless "March to the Sea," though, the impetuous Confederate conceived a bolder—and hopelessly unrealistic—plan: an all-out invasion of Tennessee. Along with forcing Sherman to turn and fight, he hoped to retake the state altogether, and then, advancing further northeast and collecting reinforcements, he could even crush Ulysses S. Grant's forces in Virginia from the rear. Instead, Hood's outnumbered men wound up confronting John Schofield's entrenched troops in Franklin. On November 30, against the furious objections of his lieutenants, he ordered a massive assault on the fortified Union line. After over a dozen valiant but futile charges, Hood lost a quarter of his army. Losing the confidence of the survivors as well, he nevertheless proceeded north to Nashville, this time encountering George Henry Thomas.

With his depleted force camped outside the city, Hood ran out of ideas and waited, first for reinforcements that never arrived, then for Thomas' inevitable attack. When it came, an overpowering two-day onslaught in mid-December, the Army of Tennessee virtually disintegrated. Retreating deeper and deeper South with what was left of his force, a despondent Hood resigned his command in January of 1865. After the war, he went into business in New Orleans, where he, his wife, and one of his eleven children died in a yellow fever epidemic four years later.

Hooker, Joseph

1814–1879

Hooker earned the celebrated nickname he so disliked, "Fighting Joe Hooker," with his aggressive tactics, though he faltered at his most critical juncture, leading the Union army in its devastating defeat at Chancellorsville.

The cocky, once-dashing military man's early service included West Point administrative work, border duty in the Far West, and action in the Seminole War and Mexican War. With a knack for getting on the wrong side of his superiors, he left the army to take up farming in California. Hooker attempted to reenlist at the start of the Civil War but, perhaps because of his troublemaking reputation, was initially denied a commission. After he received his military appointment in May 1861, Hooker directed the defense of Washington, D.C., that summer and distinguished himself in the Peninsula campaign the following spring.

Leading the Union's dawn attack at Antietam in September 1862, he was seriously wounded, but recovered to command a corps in the Battle of Fredericksburg three months later. Hooker freely criticized his commander Ambrose Burnside for the Union's embarrassing loss there, nursing an ambition to head the Army of the Potomac himself. He got his wish on January 26, 1863, when Abraham Lincoln appointed him to succeed Burnside, who had only accepted the position originally because he did not want Hooker to have it. The president, somewhat apprehensive about the choice and annoyed at Hooker's comment to a reporter that the Union needed a good dictator, acerbically wrote his new commander, "What I ask

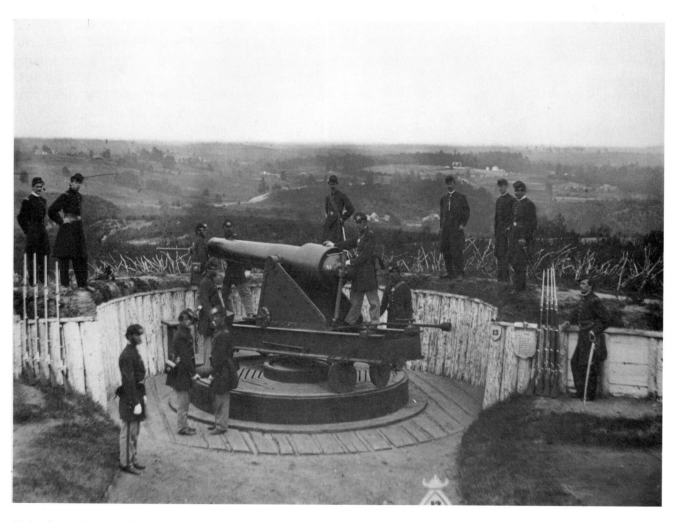

Major General Joseph Hooker led the defense of Washington, D.C., Summer 1861.

Some of Hooker's men, killed in skirmishes leading up to the battle at Antietam.

of you is military success and I will risk the dictatorship."

A popular choice among the dispirited troops, Hooker began by boosting morale, effectively reorganizing the army and cleaning up the camps. He also cleaned up his own behavior, trying to live down his well-earned reputation as a hard drinker and gambler, whose rowdy headquarters were likened to "a combination of barroom and brothel." (Notwithstanding the widespread belief, the slang term "hooker" predates the general.) Remaining sober and on relatively good behavior, what he could not do was deliver the "military success" that Lincoln requested. Hooker planned a bold assault on Robert E. Lee's Army of Northern Virginia, but lost his nerve in the face of a

greatly outnumbered Confederate force at Chancellorsville in early May. Ordering his troops to fall back as the battle commenced, Hooker lost his advantage and, hampered by a concussion from a shell blast, continued to act with uncharacteristic hesitation throughout the engagement. With a humbling defeat that cost him 17,000 men, he was hesitant to confront Lee again, even though the Confederate general was preparing to invade the North. Lincoln removed Hooker from the Army of the Potomac's command on June 28, 1863, three days before the Battle of Gettysburg began.

He was sent west, where he fought with his old resolve at Chattanooga in October, leading the Union's gutsy charge up Lookout Mountain, and during the summer 1864 siege on Atlanta. Miffed when he was not given command of the Army of the Tennessee upon the death of James McPherson, Hooker resigned his post, and spent the rest of the war out of action in the Midwest. He remained with the Regular army until debilitated by a stroke in 1868.

Horse Artillery

Sometimes referred to as "Mountain" or mounted artillery, the horse artillery of the Civil War was a military innovation that truly came into its own between the Crimean War of the 1850s and the Civil War of the 1860s. Simply put, horse artillery consisted of a number of small but powerful cannon, usually howitzers, that could be disassembled, packed onto a number of horses with a special kind of tack arrangement, and be carried along by the cavalry into rough terrain where ordinary artillery could not hope to pass save with great difficulty, if at all. Jeb Stuart and Nathan Bedford Forrest both made use of this innovation to great effect, while utilizing the more customary larger artillery pieces, as well. Horse artillery enabled a cavalry unit to move into a hilly or rocky territory, unpack, assemble and set up their guns, then fire upon an otherwise unsuspecting enemy; then the guns were rapidly taken apart, repacked onto the horses, and off they would ride, to repeat the action elsewhere to the bemusement of enemies who often became convinced they faced a far larger force than they actually did.

Howe, Julia Ward

1819–1910

Author of "Battle Hymn of the Republic," the song perhaps most closely identified with the Union cause during the Civil War, was born to a prominent New York banking family and married to noted physician/reformer Samuel Gridley Howe. Howe joined in her husband's antislavery activities, helping him edit the abolitionist newspaper *The Commonwealth*, while pursuing her own work as a writer and lecturer.

Her first collection of poetry was published in 1854, followed by several other volumes, and numerous essays, biographies, children's songs, and travel pieces. A leader of the American Woman Suffrage Association for over 50 years and a lifelong peace activist who nevertheless supported the Union's war effort, Howe is also credited with originating the idea of Mother's Day in 1872.

But it was the poem she wrote in 1861 set to the tune of "John Brown's Body," that made Howe one of the most celebrated American women of her era. Visiting Washington, D.C., she attended a review of army troops outside the city on November 18. By some accounts,

Julia Ward Howe

hearing the marching song itself provided the inspiration; by others it was merely the sight of the soldiers. Whatever the inspiration, Howe got up in the middle of the following night and wrote the verse before dawn.

Atlantic Monthly bought the poem for four dollars; before the magazine published it in its February 1862 edition, however, the *New York Herald Tribune* obtained a copy and was the first to run "Battle Hymn of the Republic" on January 14. By spring of that year, Howe's verse was eclipsing the "John Brown's Body" version. The song became hugely popular with Union troops and the public alike. Ironically, the tune itself is attributed to a Southerner—Charleston, South Carolina, Sunday school teacher William Steffe, whose 1850s' version was a revival hymn. He, in turn, may have taken it from a Swedish song.

Infantry

The infantry, also known as the "Queen of Battles," has been acknowledged for many centuries as the backbone of the army.

In the ages before mechanized warfare, it was all very well to have artillery, be it catapults or cannon, to shell the battlefield and try to drive the enemy back; and just fine to have cavalry to scout the enemy position, or charge on the flank, or side of the opposing army, to try and break their resistance. But when it came time to actually confront the enemy and attack, the majority of such tactical maneuvering was accomplished by the use of massed infantry attacks.

Especially during the Civil War, when American *esprit de corps* or army spirit reached an all-time high, rivalries between the branches of service was common, and not always amicable. The infantry felt justifiably that they took the brunt of the burden in terms of fighting the war; there were more infantry regiments in both armies than artillery or cavalry. Soldiers in both the Confederate army and the Union army were often chagrined to see the cavalry go forward, gather some information, perhaps exchange a few shots with the enemy pickets, then retire to watch the rest of the fighting—the infantry's part of the battle—from what certainly seemed a safer position.

Confederate General D. H. Hill was famous in both armies for offering a reward to anyone who could bring him the body of a cavalry trooper slain in battle, preferably with the spurs still on his boots; this led to derisive cries of "Whoever saw a dead cavalryman?" and "There they go, off to a nice, safe spot!" that greeted mounted troops, to their great embarrassment and annoyance, whenever they were required to ride past an infantry column or entrenched position.

In reality, most of the soldiers of the Civil War were well aware of the part each segment of the army played in the overall strategy of the fighting. But the infantry did, in all honesty, shoulder the heaviest burden, and their comparatively higher casualty rates show this perhaps more clearly than anything else. In battle after battle, regardless of the competence of an individual commander, the men of the infantry went forward to what became very often a slaughter; Ambrose Burnside's Union boys at Fredericksburg and Pickett's Virginians at Gettysburg are stunning examples of amazing bravery in the face of terrible loss, gaining a collateral reputation for the courage of the infantry regardless of what one might think of the sense of making such attacks.

The Civil War was fought in an era when honor was paramount, a fact of history that must be carefully considered and understood in order that we may comprehend all that these

The 5th New Hampshire Infantry strengthening a bridge over the Chickahominy.

men endured. Men such as James Longstreet of the Confederacy and John Buford of the Union, men of unquestioned bravery, were beginning to formulate notions of defensive warfare, preferring to use their infantry and cavalry in a more sensible fashion.

Rather than having them march in long, open lines across a field in the face of artillery and an entrenched enemy, they wanted to make strategic and tactical use of the terrain on which the battle was being fought, and try to move their men into position to surprise the enemy, rather than let him see all at once exactly how many men are coming to the attack.

Buford preferred to dismount his cavalrymen and place them behind stone walls and trees, fighting infantry-style, the better to pick off their Confederate adversaries with the long-range repeating carbines the Union army was using, but this plan did not always meet with approval from his superiors, although he used it to great effect in several battles.

Longstreet, arguing against men to whom honor was even more important than survival, made absolutely no headway in trying to convince his superiors to let him dig trenches and maneuver obliquely across battlefields, rather than making costly assaults on an enemy's front; knowing what would happen when Pickett made his now-famous charge at Gettysburg, he was either too angry or too grief-stricken to actually give the order to march, but rather gave a single nod that Pickett interpreted as the signal to attack.

For many years after the Civil War—through World War I, in fact—infantry would continue to be used in costly, bloody frontal assaults by generals who considered it dishonorable to fight from behind a safer position or obstruction. Not until tanks and armored weaponry had truly come into its own by World War II would infantry begin to be shaped into what it is today: still the backbone of the army, but diversified, rearmed, and fighting bravely with much better tactics.

Irish-Americans in the Civil War

There is perhaps no other ethnic group so closely identified with the Civil War years and the immediate aftermath of the war as Irish-Americans.

Of those Irish who came over much later than the founding generations, fully 150,000 of them joined the Union army. Unfortunately, statistics for the Confederacy are sketchy at best; still, one has but to listen to the Southern accent, and listen to the sorts of tunes Southern soldiers loved to sing, to realize that a great deal of the South was settled by Irish immigrants. But because the white population of the Confederate states was more native-born than immigrant during the Civil War years, there did not seem as much of a drive in the Southern army to recognize heritage in the names and

uniforms of regiments as there was in the Union forces.

In the Federal army there was the fabled Meagher's Irish brigade, led by the flamboyant Thomas Meagher; they went into battle with an emerald green flag with a large golden harp in its center, celebrating their heritage even in the midst of death.

In the North, centers of Irish settlement were Boston and New York, both of which had sizeable Irish neighborhoods. There were major immigration periods in the 1830s, 1840s, and 1850s; the numbers steadily increased until, according to the 1860 census, well over one and a half million Americans claimed to have been born in Ireland. The majority of these lived in the North. There were periods of severe economic difficulties both before and after the war when the immigrant Irish were singled out for the distrust and hatred of their fellow Americans; "No Irish Need Apply" was a frequently seen placard sign above the doors of factories, shops, warehouses, and farms.

The Irish were chiefly distrusted because they were Catholic, and there was much opposition in the United States to the Church of Rome. The frustration this prejudice caused led indirectly to the boil-over of tempers in July 1863, when the first official draft was held; a mob of mostly immigrant laborers gathered at the site of the draft lottery, and as names were called and those not wealthy enough to purchase a substitute were required to join up, the mob's temper flared. The situation escalated into full-scale rioting; for three days, cities like New York and Boston were caught up in a rampage of looting, burning, and destruction. Many of the rioters were frustrated Irish laborers who could not get jobs, and their targets were draft officials, as well as free blacks living in the North, who seemed able to get jobs that the Irish were denied. It took the return of armed troops from the fighting at Gettysburg to bring the cities back to peace and quiet.

Such events did little to help the image of the Irish in America, until many years after the war. Despite their wartime heroics, many Irish veterans came home to find the same ugly bias they faced before going off to fight for the Union. Many of them chose to go into the post-war army. Still others followed Thomas Meagher into Canada, where they joined up in an attempt to free Canada from British domination. Many simply chose to remain in the Eastern cities, hoping matters would improve as time went by. Eventually things did get better for the Irish, but it was many long years before ugly anti-Irish prejudice faded.

Iron Brigade of the West

Also known as the Black Hat Brigade for the natty black felt toppers they wore, the only all-Western brigade in the Army of the Potomac won the ignominious distinction of having among the highest casualty rates of any brigade in the United States Army.

Tough, apparently fearless, and often irreverent and rowdy—probably because they all came from the backwoods of the Western frontier—the brigade was comprised of three regiments from Wisconsin (the 2nd, 6th, and 7th), and one from Indiana (the 19th). First assembled in Fredericksburg, the troops were assigned Brigadier General John Gibbon as their commander. Gibbon, who had studied at West Point and was used to dealing with professional soldiers, was at first a bit dismayed by the raw recruits, but soon realized that training and discipline would make them into good soldiers.

While camped near Washington in the spring of 1862, the brigade showed a great deal of the humor typical of boys who had not yet witnessed the horror of combat, needling comrades in other regiments (mostly Easterners) and boasting of their own untested merit. Their high spirits were dampened considerably after their first trial by fire at Groveton, on August 28, 1862. After capturing the Union supply depot at Manassas Junction, Confederate Major General Thomas "Stonewall" Jackson set up camp just north of the First Bull Run battlefield in a concealed line.

Meanwhile, Union Major General John Pope,

uncertain of his enemy's whereabouts, ordered a concentration of troops at nearby Centerville. As Gibbon led his brigade to Centerville, the green troops were ambushed by a corps of Jackson's men. They fought bravely for two hours in near hand-to-hand combat conditions until they halted the Confederate assault. The price they paid was high, however. While the bravery they displayed earned them their nickname of the Iron Brigade, they lost more than one-third of their men during the encounter. When it was over, a regimental historian wrote that although the brigade would always be ready for action, "we were never again eager." At South Mountain on September 14, 1862, at Antietam three days later, and later at Fredericksburg and Chancellorsville, the Westerners fought with as much resolve and tenacity, but with equal or higher losses.

Remarkably, and largely thanks to Gibbons' appreciation of his men's unique character, the brigade was able to remain "all-Western" until after the Battle of Gettysburg, even when new recruits were added. Gettysburg, however, effectively destroyed the hard-fighting Black Hats. The regiments sustained heavy losses while defending McPherson's Ridge and Seminary Ridge. The Iron Brigade lost more than 65 percent of its men in the three days of bloody battle. Although the use of its name continued until the end of the war, the entire character of the brigade changed as Eastern soldiers replaced the mighty, but fallen, Black Hats.

Ironclads

Steaming into battle for the first time during the Civil War, iron-armored vessels of both the Union and Confederacy so clearly outmatched wooden ships that naval warfare forever changed.

Ironclad development was in its infancy at the start of the conflict; the British navy had just two such vessels, and the French had one. The logic behind the iron-plating of warships was simple and sound. Since most artillery

An early Federal ironclad, the Monongahela.

shells did not penetrate heavy armor, ironclads were nearly impervious to enemy broadsides, and they could also ram wooden vessels to pieces. Still, the Union navy, confident in the vast superiority of its fleet, initially saw little need to explore this new realm of shipbuilding, concentrating instead on its conventional squadrons of wooden vessels for the blockade of Southern ports.

The Confederacy, on the other hand, its navy all but nonexistent, saw little option but to chance the unproven technology. With the Confederate Congress' June 1861 approval, Navy Secretary Stephen Mallory quickly launched a program to construct ironclad warships. Southern engineers overcame a woeful lack of iron and adequate shipbuilding facilities through ingenuity and improvisation, salvaging the scuttled U.S. frigate *Merrimack* and refashioning it into a formidable, if unwiedly, armored ship. Rumors of the project so unsettled the U.S. Congress that in August 1861 it authorized the development of prototype ironclads for the Union navy.

The *Merrimack*, rechristened the CSS *Virginia*, lived up to the North's worst fears, effortlessly sinking two wooden frigates and threatening the entire Union blockading fleet at Hampton Roads in Chesapeake Bay on March 8, 1862. The following day, the Union's one ironclad, the *Monitor*, arrived for its legendary duel with the Confederate vessel, which ended in a draw. With wooden warships proven obsolete in a single engagement, both sides, fearing the other would gain the naval advantage, stepped up their efforts to construct new ironclads.

By the end of the Civil War, 58 armored warships had been launched or were in the process of being built by the Union; 21 by the Confederacy. Many were modeled after the *Monitor* and *Merrimack*, with refinements that greatly improved on the two imperfect pioneer ships. Still not usually very seaworthy, most of the ironclads that saw Civil War action were limited to river and bay engagements. Several odd-looking, flat-bottomed armored paddle-wheelers, nicknamed "Pook turtles" after their designer Samuel Pook, became the core of the Union's Mississippi fleet.

Also on the river, the CSS *Arkansas*, a *Merrimack* look-alike, tormented Federal gunboats during the Vicksburg campaign before it was destroyed by its crew to prevent its capture. The *Albemarle*, ultimately torpedoed and sunk, was a vital part of the South's 1864 naval operations in the North Carolina sounds, while the *Tennessee*, the Confederacy's largest ironclad, valiantly but unsuccessfully fought David Farragut's entire Federal fleet in the Battle of Mobile Bay. During that same engagement, one of the North's most advanced ironclads, the *Tecumseh*, which had earlier served in the James River squadron, struck a mine and was literally blown out of the water.

The one ocean-going ironclad, a partially ar-

mored Union cruiser named *New Ironsides*, was a South Atlantic Blockading Squadron flagship, and joined the successful early 1865 sea assault on Fort Fisher, North Carolina, the Confederacy's last open East Coast port. While wooden warships still comprised virtually the entire Union and Confederate navies, the success of the ironclads was undeniable. Suitably impressed, the European naval powers began introducing armored vessels in force to their own fleets as the Civil War established that ironclads were the wave of the future.

Italian-Americans in the Civil War

Between the Census of 1850 and the Census of 1860, the number of Italians emigrating to America jumped by 7,000, so that on the eve of the Civil War just over 11,000 Americans listed themselves as having been born in Italy. Many of them came to escape from stifling poverty, only to find it pursued them to the crowded cities of the East Coast of the United States; still others came to find freedom from the oppression of the Roman Catholic Church, which was trying to enforce orthodoxy upon its believers. Most Italians were simply looking for peace, for their homeland was torn by wars of its own.

New York City was the destination of the majority of Italian immigrants. There, they found many of their own people already established; the language was familiar and, despite the opposition of the Catholic Church in America, the old religious practices were still being observed. They had their own schools, when they could afford them, and their own newspapers; Francesco Secchi de Casale, a political activist who escaped from Italian authorities just in time, found refuge in New York and funded the publication of *L'Europee-Americano*, the first periodical to be printed both in English and Italian, the purpose of which was to keep people informed of events in Italy and Europe—and to make written attacks on the Church authorities, which got Casale in trouble. He felt so strongly about keeping his people informed, however, that when the first publication failed, he pawned his watch and some of his wife's jewelry to fund what is said to be the first important Italian language weekly published in the United States, *L'Eco d'Italia*, which remained in circulation until the end of the century.

Italians in New York had to deal with a number of social issues, including poor housing and schools, medical difficulties, and poverty. Again, their hero was Casale; he raised money to start an evening school for Italians in the Five Points slum, seeing to it the children were taught to read, write, do mathematics, and study the history of Italy and America. Casale failed to get widespread backing for a project dear to his heart, however; he very much wanted to find a way to move Italian immigrants out to the farmlands beyond the cities, since farming was what they had done in the Old Country. When he could not get the governments of Italy or the United States to back his plans, he turned to private businesses; finally by the 1880s Italian farmers were back on the land in a sense, when American businessman Charles Landis donated land near Vineland, New Jersey, to start a farming cooperative.

Italian involvement in the Civil War was intense and passionate. Their militant hero back home, Giuseppe Garibaldi, was their inspiration; his republican views led many Italians to back the Union cause, though they were represented in the Southern armies as well. Francesco Casale spearheaded the formation of an Italian Legion, and later the founding of the Italian Garibaldi Guard, and was joined by many like-minded Italians: Luigi Tinelli, a former consul to Portugal and an industrialist, had experience as a militia commander; Francesco Spinola recruited four regiments in New York, and was appointed by President Abraham Lincoln to be their general; and Count Luigi Palma di Cesnola, a veteran of the Crimean War, es-

tablished a military academy in New York City, where many young Italians learned the art of war and later served in the Union army. Their stories are fascinating and colorful. Cesnola, for instance, was left wounded and pinned under his horse after fighting Jeb Stuart's cavalry at Aldie, Virginia, in June 1863; while a prisoner of war, he agitated for better treatment for prisoners, to the point that his captors put him in charge of the prison commissary at Belle Isle. Spinola, finding his men of the Spinola Empire Brigade outnumbered six to one in a battle, ordered them to fix bayonets—and they charged, scattering the amazed Southerners before them in disorder.

Italian Garibaldi Guard, the

The Garibaldi Guard was the nickname of the 39th New York Infantry, a regiment of Italian-Americans recruited mostly from New York City under the auspices of Francesco Casale and other Italian leaders in the North. Most of the members of this regiment were men who had fought under Giuseppe Garibaldi, the freedom fighter and republican agitator; they wore a distinctively styled red shirt as part of their uniform to show their connection to their countryman, whose partisans had worn such a shirt in Italy. Other Italian nationals joined the guard as well, however, out of a feeling that the Union's cause matched their own ideals of freedom and equal justice. They also viewed the Northern ideology as closely allied with the aims of Garibaldi and felt such alliance lent credence to the great patriot's ideas, since they were clearly being adopted by other nations.

The Garibaldi Guard marching on the double quick in New York City.

J

Jackson, Thomas Jonathan "Stonewall"

1824–1863

Remarkable bravery, precise attention to military detail, and the ability to engender loyalty and inspire devoted service from his men combined to make Thomas "Stonewall" Jackson an irreplaceable member of the Confederate army. Known for his deep religious convictions, his exemplary personal habits (he never smoked or drank), and his unrelenting insistence on strict discipline within his ranks, Jackson nevertheless was one of the army's most popular leaders. He also appeared to possess a kind of second sight during battle. Able to disappear from enemy view—sometimes accompanied by more than 15,000 men—he would then turn up just in time to attack his enemy's weakest point.

Orphaned at an early age and brought up by an uncle, Jackson grew up in rural Virginia and barely received even a middle school education. Through sheer will he made it through West Point; ever determined, he managed to graduate in the top third of his 1842 class. Like so many of his Civil War comrades, Jackson first saw action in the Mexican War. Under John B. Magruder, Jackson fought well at Vera Cruz, Contreras, and Chapultepec. After the Mexican War, Jackson served for a time in Florida during the Seminole uprising. He left the army in 1851 to join the faculty of the Virginia Military Institute at Lexington, where he taught philosophy and artillery techniques for almost a decade.

Jackson and a corps of his cadets were present at what some would say was the spark that set the Civil War off: the hanging of John Brown in 1859. Like many of his Confederate compatriots, Jackson would have preferred that the issues dividing the nation be solved with politic compromise that would allow the Union to persist. When his home state of Virginia seceded, however, he felt compelled to defend the South and joined the Confederate army. His first assignment involved bringing a battalion of cadets to Richmond to serve as drillmasters.

In April 1861, Jackson was made a colonel of the infantry and sent to Harpers Ferry. There he organized what would become known as the "Stonewall Brigade," the only brigade to have an officially designated nickname, which it received from the Confederate Congress on May 30, 1863. Composed of five Virginia regiments from the Shenandoah Valley, the brigade of 4,500 raw recruits underwent weeks of Jackson's grueling training program, which managed to turn them into a quite effective military organization.

Their first chance to prove their mettle came in July, during the Battle of First Bull Run. As commander of a brigade under Albert Sidney

Johnston, Jackson ordered his men to bolster the Confederate left flank at a crucial point in the battle. His bravery, and the bravery of his men, earned Jackson the famous nickname; a nearby colleague was so impressed with his stalwart behavior, he remarked, "There is Jackson standing like a stone wall." For his service at Bull Run, he was elevated to major general on October 7, 1861, and was sent to assume command in the Shenandoah Valley.

Jackson's assignment in the valley was, at first, largely a tactical one: to create a diversion that would keep troops under Nathaniel Banks from joining George B. McClellan's forces as they headed toward Richmond. Jackson's total strength was about 10,000 men, while Banks commanded nearly twice that number. Although the first part of his campaign went poorly, Jackson managed to pull off one of the most brilliant maneuvers in military history early in the spring of 1862 during his Shenandoah Valley campaign. For nearly three months, Jackson and his men attacked Union troops where and when they least expected it, defeating three separate Union armies in five battles. With just 17,000 men (reinforcements arrived during the campaign), Jackson played a crucial role in Robert E. Lee's successful attempt to stop McClellan's drive to the Confederate capital.

After their coup in the valley, Jackson and his command were transferred to the Richmond area in time to fight in the Seven Days campaign. Perhaps still exhausted and certainly unfamiliar with the terrain, Jackson seemed to lose his otherwise impeccable sense of battle readiness as well as his automatic obedience to his commanding officer—this lapse caused some of his colleagues to question his sanity. At both Mechanicsville and White Oak Swamp, he failed to deliver his troops as Robert E. Lee commanded, putting the entire Army of Northern Virginia in jeopardy.

Jackson managed to recover his skills, perhaps simply by resting, in time to display his more characteristic genius at Second Bull Run. Jackson and his men undertook a grueling 51-mile march across Virginia to Manassas Junction, a trip they concluded in just two days. Once there, Jackson was able to so thoroughly confuse Union General John Pope as to his whereabouts that the Confederates—once again with less than half the manpower of their opponents—won another victory.

Jackson's unique ability to inspire his troops and to remain prepared to fight was once again on display at Antietam. Lee's plan to invade the North for a second time depended upon the capture of the federal garrison at Harpers Ferry. Jackson accomplished this on September 15, 1862, giving him just enough time to move his troops back to Antietam, possibly saving Lee's

General Thomas "Stonewall" Jackson, two weeks before his death.

army from total destruction. On October 10, 1862, Jackson was promoted to lieutenant general and was given command of the 2nd Corps in the Army of Northern Virginia.

At the battle of Fredericksburg on December 13, he led the right wing of the army to victory. Having fought long and hard, this devoted family man then took time off to visit his wife, who had just given birth to a baby daughter. He was called back almost immediately with the news that almost 135,000 Federal troops were crossing the Rappahannock on both sides of Fredericksburg. Dividing his forces, Jackson headed toward Lee, sending one division to stop Major General John Sedgwick's left flank. Together, Lee and Jackson were able to drive the Federals, led by Hooker, back to Chancellorsville on May 1.

That night, Lee and Jackson devised a remarkable plan: in the face of military logic, they decided to further divide the army. Lee would stay at Chancellorsville to face Hooker's front while Jackson made a sweeping flank movement around Hooker's right to attack from the rear. Jackson's tricky maneuver succeeded and he and his men were able to rout the Federal right flank and win the battle.

Unfortunately, the pinnacle of his military career came during his last few hours of life. In the faint light of dusk, some of Jackson's own men mistakenly fired at their beloved leader. One bullet penetrated the palm of his right hand, a second passed through his left wrist, and a third splintered the bone of his left arm. His injured left arm was amputated, and for a brief time it appeared he would survive. Unfortunately, his condition was complicated by pneumonia, and he died on May 10, 1862.

Jewish-Americans in the Civil War

Most Jews living in the United States in the years preceding the Civil War came from Western Europe, perhaps the bulk of them from Germany. They brought with them a rich heritage in religion, art, folklore, and food. For the first time in their long history, the Jews found themselves in a land where they were not required to live in separate sections of the city (known as ghettos in Europe), or be forced to wear distinctive clothing to mark them as different. They were treated on an equal footing with their fellow immigrants and were some of the first white settlers to arrive in the New World. They founded synagogues for their worship, filling them with the rich religious treasures so carefully brought from their homelands; they built schools, or their children attended local schools and academies as any other children did.

Some of the oldest synagogues in North America were founded in the South, in coastal cities such as Alexandria, Virginia, and Charleston, South Carolina. Whether farmers, businessmen, politicians, or religious leaders, the Jews were determined not to lose the heritage they had maintained over so many difficult centuries. During the Civil War, Jewish men fought in both the armies of the North and of the South, and the women and children they left behind raised money, tended the sick and wounded, and worked for the relief of widows and orphans on both sides.

Perhaps the most prominent Jewish-American in the Civil War period was Judah P. Benjamin. Born on the island of St. Croix while his parents were attempting to get through a British blockade to emigrate to New Orleans in August 1811, Benjamin was a U.S. senator from Louisiana at the beginning of the Civil War; he had the interesting honor of having almost duelled then-Senator Jefferson Davis, later President of the Confederacy, owing to some argument between them. Benjamin believed in the legality of slavery, which led Senator Wade of Ohio to comment that Benjamin was a "Hebrew with Egyptian principles." Upon Louisiana's secession, Benjamin and his fellow senator (who had also been his law partner) James Slidell withdrew from the U.S. Senate on February 4, 1861. Benjamin was named the first attorney general of the provisional government of the Confederate States, and by late summer he had replaced the Secretary of War, Leroy

Walker. Accused of incompetence, Benjamin resigned in anger—and was immediately given the post of Secretary of State, which he held until the collapse of his government in 1865. Known as the "Brains of the Confederacy," Benjamin's tireless intellect led him to absorb the duties left undone by other sections of the administration; Jefferson Davis relied on him heavily.

One of the darkest tales of Jews during the Civil War bespeaks the prejudice this religious and ethnic group has historically faced. On December 17, 1862, General Ulysses S. Grant issued an order from his headquarters in Holly Springs, Mississippi, ordering all Jews out of the area over which he had command. Known as Order No. 11, it read as follows:

> The Jews, as a class violating every regulation of trade established by the Treasury Department and also department orders, are hereby expelled from the department within twenty-four hours from the receipt of this order.

Ordered by General Henry Halleck and President Abraham Lincoln to rescind the order on January 4, 1863, Grant immediately obeyed; but no apologies were forthcoming, and in any case would not have been accepted. Grant was attempting to expel from the area a group of illegal speculators who were trying to take advantage of his soldiers, and he chose to target the local Jews as the cause of that speculation. No Jews were actually sent away, but it was an embarrassing and humiliating moment the Jewish community never forgot, a stain upon their freedom and equality in the New World.

Johnson, Andrew

1808–1875

Appointed a Union war governor and chosen as Abraham Lincoln's 1864 running mate, the Tennessee politician was a staunch anti-Confederate, but after succeeding to the presidency he was nearly removed from office for his opposition to Congress' tough Reconstruction policy against the South.

Johnson was born and raised in North Carolina under conditions even more desperate than Lincoln's legendarily modest upbringing. Destitute, unschooled, fatherless at age three, he worked as a tailor's apprentice and moved to eastern Tennessee in 1826. There, Johnson's wife, Eliza, taught him to read, and once his tailor shop began to prosper, he entered politics. A Jacksonian Democrat whose populist views and antagonism toward the planter aristocracy made him popular with small farmers and the emerging middle class, Johnson soon advanced from local to state and national office. He was elected to Congress in 1847, and after serving as Tennessee governor, entered the Senate in

Andrew Johnson

1857, though he failed in an 1860 presidential nomination bid.

Hardly an advocate of emancipation—owning, in fact, several house servants himself—Johnson, like many in his state, still bitterly opposed the South's secession after the election of Lincoln. He branded the secessionists as traitors, and was alone among the Southern senators in refusing to resign his seat in Congress, even after Tennessee left the Union in June 1861. While wholly backing the North's armed struggle against the Confederacy, the following month Johnson sponsored a resolution disavowing emancipation as a war aim.

In March 1862, Lincoln selected the maverick politician to serve as military governor of his home state, now partly occupied by Federal forces. Supported by Tennessee Unionists and despised by pro-Confederates, clashing with army authorities and laboring to restore a civil government loyal to the North, Johnson held that onerous post for three years. His capable performance and his ticket-balancing expediency earned Johnson the vice presidential nomination in 1864 by a coalition of Republicans and War Democrats. Recovering from typhoid, Johnson saw his reputation soiled, however, at the March 1865 inauguration, when he appeared so unsteady that many assumed he was drunk. Six weeks later, after Lincoln's assassination, he was sworn in as the seventeenth president.

With the war all but concluded, Johnson embarked on the nation's Reconstruction. Essentially following Lincoln's intention to treat the South leniently, he pardoned thousands of ex-Confederates and favored the quick readmittance of seceded states to the Union. The Republican-dominated Congress, resenting the new Democratic president, favored a much harsher reconstruction policy and condemned Johnson's veto of civil rights legislation and opposition to the Fourteenth Amendment guaranteeing black citizenship.

Taking matters into their own hands, the legislature passed its own Reconstruction acts and overrode many of the president's subsequent vetoes. It attempted to inhibit Johnson further with the Tenure of Office Act, requiring congressional approval before the president could dismiss any cabinet member. Considering the law unconstitutional, he fired Radical Republican Secretary of War Edwin Stanton anyway, which the House used as an excuse to bring 11 counts of impeachment against him in February 1868. After a two-month trial, which Johnson refused to attend, the Senate fell one vote short of the two-thirds necessary to remove him. But Johnson, the only U.S. president ever impeached, was rendered powerless in his final year in office, though he did issue a defiant Christmas 1868 amnesty for all unpardoned former Confederates. Remaining in politics, the persevering ex-president was reelected to the Senate in 1874, and served there among his bitter enemies for four months before he died.

Johnston, Albert Sidney

1803–1862

Considered the ablest professional soldier to join the Confederacy, this Texas maverick was killed in action just a year after the Civil War began, striking a devastating blow to the Confederate military.

Eighth in the West Point class of 1826, Johnston saw action in several theaters in the 35 years between graduation and the start of the Civil War. His first post took him to the frontier, where he fought in the Black Hawk War. He resigned from the army in 1834 to care for his ailing wife, who died the following year. A true adventurer, Johnston then settled in the republic of Texas in 1836, enlisting as a private in the Texas army. Named senior brigadier general, he later became the republic's secretary of war. Resigning in 1840 to try his hand at farming in Brazoria County, he soon returned to the battlefield during the Mexican War, where he fought under General Zachary Taylor on the Rio Grande.

He continued to climb the ranks of the military as colonel of the 2nd U.S. Cavalry division in 1849 and commander of the Department of

General Albert S. Johnston

Texas in 1856. Breveted to brigadier general in 1857, Johnston was posted in Utah. When the Civil War began, he was living in California as commander of the Department of the Pacific. Although he supported the idea of union and had hoped for a compromise between North and South, Johnston chose to fight for the Confederacy when the Civil War began.

Federal authorities, loathe to lose such a promising soldier, took steps to block his passage back home from California, but with a firm resolve to stand by his adopted home state of Texas, Johnston managed to safely return to the South.

He arrived in Richmond in mid-September and was at once appointed commander of the Confederate Department of the Mississippi, a huge territory stretching from the Appalachian Mountains in the east to the Indian Territories in the west. Although woefully undermanned and undersupplied, Johnston's army made a

bold first move by invading Kentucky and establishing a bulkhead there to protect Tennessee from a Union offensive. Constantly urging the Confederate government to reinforce his 4,000 troops, Johnston was able to hold the Union in check until January 1862, when General Ulysses S. Grant attacked Tennessee with full force.

Johnston, realizing that Fort Donelson on the Cumberland River was the linchpin of Confederate control of Tennessee, pulled resources from the indefensible Fort Henry to protect it. Indeed, Fort Henry was Grant's first target upon his ascent of the Tennessee River early in February, and he was able to capture it quickly. Led by Brigadier General John B. Floyd and Major General Gideon J. Pillow, Johnston's troops fought hard at Fort Donelson, but were forced to surrender on February 16.

With Fort Donelson lost, Johnston retreated south from his headquarters in Nashville, writing to his superiors that he was leaving behind a "scene of panic and dismay." Amassing a force of 17,000 men at Murfreesboro, Johnston planned to defend the Mississippi Valley from an anticipated Federal thrust. When forces under P. G. T. Beauregard arrived, Johnston's troops numbered more than 44,000. The extra forces allowed Johnston to take the offensive and surprise the enemy with an attack on Grant's 39,000 men situated on the west bank of the Tennessee River—and to do so before Major General Don Carlos Buell's 36,000 troops converged with Grant's.

On Sunday, April 3, he led his men on what was expected to be a simple one-day march. Unfortunately, heavy rains and unfamiliar territory considerably slowed the advance. Fearing that the two days lost in travel meant that Buell's men had arrived—and some of them had—Beauregard urged Johnston to call off the attack and retreat to Corinth. Johnston replied with typical resolve, "I would fight them if they were a million."

At dawn on April 6, he mounted his horse to lead his men to the gruesome two-day Battle of Shiloh, the first engagement of the Civil War with heavy loss of life, and a devastating defeat for the Confederates. On the first day, as Johnston attempted to regroup his critical east flank in thick woodlands near the Peach Orchard, he was struck in the leg by a minié bullet. He bled to death within minutes.

President Davis, upon hearing of his fallen friend and valued commander, offered a special message to Congress in which he said of Johnston, "In his death he has illustrated the character for which through life he was conspicuous—that of singleness of purpose and devotion to duty with his whole energies."

Johnston, Joseph Eggleston

1807–1891

Though in perpetual conflict with Jefferson Davis, who mistook his defensive fighting strategies for a lack of will, Johnston continued to hold top Confederate commands throughout the Civil War in both the eastern and western theaters.

The compact and fiercely intelligent Virginian, a West Point graduate and civil engineer, had earlier fought and been wounded in the Seminole War and Mexican War, and served in "Bleeding Kansas" during the tense 1850s. Appointed the U.S. Army's quartermaster general in 1860, he resigned the following April to join the Confederacy.

Johnston's initial assignment was in the Shenandoah Valley, from there leading his units to Manassas Junction in July to reinforce Pierre G. T. Beauregard's troops at First Bull Run. Officially in command of the combined forces, he deferred to Beauregard's superior knowledge of the field, and the Southerners routed the Union army in a startling victory.

Johnston was named one of the South's five full generals the following month, launching his first disagreement with Davis when he complained about not receiving the proper seniority. Still placed in charge of the Confederacy's Virginia forces, he faced George McClellan's Army of the Potomac in an uncontested standoff near Washington, then con-

fronted the Union commander at the beginning of the North's spring 1862 advance on Richmond. Johnston wanted to take up the solid defenses outside the Confederate capital, but Davis insisted he hold the invading troops east on the Virginia peninsula. Making a series of canny tactical retreats anyway, Johnston then launched an attack at Seven Pines on May 31. He was seriously wounded in the indecisive battle, and was succeeded by Robert E. Lee.

After a six-month recovery, Johnston was given the unwieldy, ambiguous general command of Confederate armies in the West. In spring 1863, he directed John C. Pemberton, whose troops at Vicksburg were facing Ulysses S. Grant's superior numbers, to evacuate and help him consolidate their separated forces,

General Joseph E. Johnston

while Davis issued contrary orders to defend the Mississippi River stronghold at all costs. With Johnston unable to relieve the besieged Confederates, Vicksburg fell to the North on July 4. The commander and the Southern president, seething in mutual dislike, blamed each other for the defeat. But Johnston was revered by his troops and popular with the public, and Davis was compelled to place him in charge of the Army of Tennessee in December 1863.

Opposing William T. Sherman's advance against Atlanta the following spring, Johnston's strategy again was a deft, staged withdrawal that spared his outnumbered army and delayed the Union movement. Davis, though, demanded a more aggressive approach that would stop Sherman altogether and, certain he would never get it from Johnston, relieved the general in June. By the following February, the Union forces had smashed through Georgia and turned on the Carolinas, and Robert E. Lee reappointed Johnston. This time, however, the Confederate commander could barely stall Sherman's advance, despite a valiant assault at Bentonville in March. Though Davis ordered him to continue the fight after Lee's capitulation, Johnston asked for an armistice on April 18 and formally surrendered on April 26, all but concluding the Confederacy's armed struggle.

He went on to enter the insurance business, served a term in the U.S. Congress, became a federal railroad commissioner, and wrote his memoirs. As a pallbearer at William T. Sherman's chilly winter 1891 funeral, Johnston refused to wear a hat out of respect for his former foe and died of pneumonia shortly after.

Joint Committee on the Conduct of the War

1861–1865

First established to investigate the surprising Union losses at the early battles of Ball's Bluff and First Bull Run, this Federal congressional committee soon became a powerful political tool of the Radical Republicans.

A month after it was formed under the leadership of Senator Benjamin Wade of Ohio, a staunch Republican, the committee called before it Brigadier General Charles P. Stone of the Army of the Potomac. Stone had commanded troops at the Battle of Ball's Bluff in Virginia. An early battle with little impact on the Union position in Virginia, it nevertheless resulted in more than 200 Union casualties, including the death of a U.S. senator, Colonel Edward Baker of Oregon, a popular politician and personal friend of Abraham Lincoln.

At the request of George McClellan, Stone had sent Baker with a brigade to distract Confederate forces on the other side of the Pomotac River. By all accounts, Baker performed his mission carelessly and was easily ambushed by Confederate troops. Nevertheless, Stone was blamed for the incident. The Joint Committee suspected that Stone, despite his own friendship with Lincoln and McClellan, was in fact a Confederate sympathizer. That he was also "soft" on slavery—evidenced by the fact that he had recently ordered his men to return all fugitive slaves to their owners—did not help matters at all.

Forced to appear alone and without counsel before the committee, Stone was never presented with formal charges or given the chance to defend himself against them. Considered disloyal to the Union cause, he was then arrested and placed in solitary confinement for 50 days at Fort Lafayette, then transferred to Fort Hamilton, New York, for an additional 189 days.

His military career ruined, Stone was just the first victim of the committee's often vindictive and always politically motivated investigations. Although all Union generals with conservative tendencies eventually came under its scrutiny, the committee's main target was McClellan himself, especially after he penned his now famous Harrison's Landing Letter in late 1862. It may have been at the committee's urging that Lincoln finally decided to replace him.

On the other hand, commanders who supported the Radical Republican agenda, even those who were clearly incompentent, such as Joseph Hooker and Benjamin Butler, were often promoted shamelessly by the committee. Comprised of popular politicians spouting a patriotic message to a public eager for reassurance, the committee was indeed a fearsome political force with which Lincoln was forced to contend; appeasing them without risking military strategy was no easy task.

The committee continued for several months after the war, urging Lincoln and his successor, Andrew Johnson, to pursue a harsh Reconstruction policy. Its findings were published in *Reports of the Joint Committee on the Conduct of the War*, a fascinating, albeit heavily biased, view on the Union effort.

K

Kansas-Nebraska Act

1854

The first decisive step in the perhaps inexorable march toward civil war, this 1854 congressional act upset the long-standing, delicate balance of power and spirit of compromise between proslavery and antislavery political interests.

Written by Senator Stephen Douglas, the bill divided part of land garnered by the Louisiana

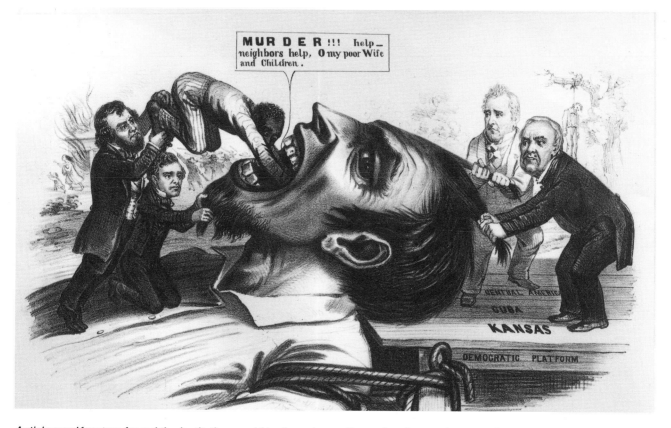

Antislavery Kansans feared the institution would be forced upon them, despite popular sovereignty.

Purchase into two territories—Kansas and Nebraska—along the 40th parallel. The act, in effect nullifying the 1820 Missouri Compromise, also provided that when the people of each territory organized as a state, they could decide by popular vote whether to permit slavery—a concept referred to as *popular sovereignty*. "If the people of Kansas want a slaveholding state, let them have it," urged Douglas, who was eager to settle the question in time to build a transcontinental railroad. "And if they want a free state, they have a right to it, and it is not for the people of Illinois, or Missouri, or New York, or Kentucky, to complain, whatever the decision of the people of Kansas may be."

The first test of popular sovereignty indeed came in Kansas, where a majority of the population voted against becoming a slave state. Proslavery forces, however, refused to accept the decision and the situation quickly erupted into violence. For more than five years, the brutal conflict raged throughout the Kansas wilderness, earning the new territory the nickname "Bleeding Kansas." Perhaps the most notorious of these violent skirmishes was the massacre at Pottawatomie by antislavery fanatic John Brown.

Shortly after Congress passed the act by a bare majority in both houses, antislavery forces massed to form the new Republican Party, thus drawing the line between Northern and Southern interests more clearly than ever before. As a result, the issue of slavery became the focal point of intense, and often violent, debate within Congress and across the nation until 1861, when South Carolina declared secession from the Union and set the stage for the Civil War.

Kearny, Philip

1816–1862

The Union lost one of its most promising commanders when Phil Kearny was killed before the Civil War was even half over. Born into a distinguished New York family, he was steered away from a military career toward law, but when he received a million-dollar inheritance from his grandfather in 1836, he joined the Union cavalry. Kearny was sent to Europe to study the latest cavalry tactics, which the eager young officer put into practice fighting with the French in Algiers.

General Philip Kearny

Returning to America, he served as aide-de-camp to Winfield Scott in the Mexican War, losing his left arm in battle. Kearny left the army after a stint in California but, longing for further military adventure, headed to Europe again in 1859. Joining Napoleon III's Imperial Guard, he was awarded the Legion of Honor for his service during the Italian Wars. With the outbreak of the Civil War, Kearny hurried back to the United States, and he was given command of a brigade whose uniforms he had adorned with a flashy piece of scarlet cloth known as the "Kearny Patch."

Already famous for his earlier military exploits, he won new acclaim during the spring 1862 Peninsula campaign in Virginia—and a promotion to major general—for his showing at Williamsburg, Seven Pines, and in the Seven Days campaign. Kearny also received attention when he vigorously protested George McClellan's decision to retreat at the conclusion of the campaign, claiming that "such an order can only be prompted by cowardice or treason."

Noted for riding into battle holding his reins in his teeth, Kearny cut a glamorous figure, which he matched with gallantry and fine fighting skills. He displayed those talents once again during Second Bull Run in August 1862, leading an aggressive, albeit unsuccessful, charge on Stonewall Jackson's left. Two days later, during heavy fighting around Chantilly mansion (Ox Hill), Kearny accidentally rode into enemy territory. Ordered to surrender, he was shot to death when he attempted to return to the Federal line.

Robert E. Lee, who admired Kearny and regretted the manner of his death, called a truce while his body was brought to Union officials, and personally sent Kearny's sword, horse, and saddle to his widow. As a tribute to its revered late general, the North issued the Kearny Medal and Kearny Cross, two decorations awarded for heroic acts performed by members of his former division.

Kennesaw Mountain, Battle of

JUNE 27, 1864

The battle at Kennesaw Mountain, Georgia, will long be remembered as one of the bloodiest segments of the Atlanta Campaign between William T. Sherman and Joseph E. Johnston. The Union Armies of the Tennessee and the Cumberland, aided by the Army of the Ohio, faced Johnston's Army of Tennessee near Marietta, Georgia; several days of skirmishing and maneuvering in relentlessly rainy weather finally erupted in conflict as the Federals attacked the well-entrenched positions of the Confederates. Charging uphill, the Union forces were able to do little more than gain small footholds. The main line was so strong as to be nearly impregnable, for Johnston had taken excellent advantage of the rock-strewn landscape.

Sherman has been often criticized, then and now, for making three concentrated assaults on Johnston's front to heavy losses. The end result was an expensive embarrassment for Sherman and a moral victory as well as a military one for Johnston; however, the Confederate commander would increasingly from this point adopt a tactic of withdrawing and refusing unless pushed to actively engage the enemy. He would earn for himself first the nickname of "Retreating Joe," and then the disapproval of his president, leading to his being relieved of command in favor of the more aggressive John Bell Hood. Sherman would continue to pick at and maneuver around the Confederate lines until his objective, Atlanta, was reached in September 1864.

Entrenchments at Kennesaw Mountain.

L

Lee, Fitzhugh

1835–1905

Often confused with his first cousin, William Henry Fitzhugh "Rooney" Lee, General Fitzhugh Lee was the son of Sidney Smith Lee, arguably the favorite brother of Confederate General Robert E. Lee. He attended West Point two years behind his cousin Custis Lee and his lifelong friend Jeb Stuart; Fitz graduated forty-fifth in the class of 1856, and was assigned to duty on the frontier with the fabled 2nd U.S. Cavalry. In May 1859, he took an arrow shot in the chest at point-blank range while fighting Native Americans in Texas and was not expected to live. However, he survived with no apparent after-effects, and while recuperating was assigned to the position of assistant instructor of tactics at West Point. Several of his students would figure prominently in the war that was even then brewing; among them, Cadet George A. Custer would win fame as a Union cavalry brigadier, and Cadet John Pelham would die tragically at Kelly's Ford while serving as Jeb Stuart's brilliant artillery chief.

On May 3, 1861, Fitz Lee tendered his resignation following Virginia's secession from the Union; he immediately offered his sword to his native state and was made a first lieutenant in the Confederate Regular army. His first duty was as a staff officer to Joseph E. Johnston, with whom he saw the fighting at the First Battle of Manassas (First Bull Run). In August 1861, Fitz received command of the First Virginia Cavalry and was assigned to the cavalry corps under his friend Stuart. Serving in the same corps was his cousin William H. Fitzhugh Lee—who was saddled yet again with his childhood nickname of "Rooney," so as to lessen the confusion between the two of them.

After participating in the Peninsula campaign of spring 1862, and in the fabled Rides Around George McClellan, Fitz was promoted to brigadier general in July. Censured for not moving quickly enough to contain the advance of Union General John Pope's army in the Second Manassas (Second Bull Run) campaign in August, Fitz nevertheless redeemed himself in later campaigns; he was active at Antietam, and at Occoquan and Dumfries, Virginia. Fitz Lee was also of significant assistance to the Confederacy in the Chancellorsville campaign; it was he who discovered that the Union Army of the Potomac had failed to adequately protect their right wing, and Fitz led his men brilliantly to the assistance of General Stonewall Jackson when the Confederates decisively attacked the Union right to defeat General Joseph Hooker.

Unable to participate in the Battle of Brandy Station in June 1863, owing to a severe flare-up of arthritis to the extent that he could not ride, Fitz Lee was back in the saddle a few weeks later when Stuart's cavalry made their controversial roundabout ride to join the army in the invasion of Pennsylvania. He distinguished himself in the rearguard action on the third day of the Battle of Gettysburg, and in autumn of 1863, he was promoted to major general. Fitz Lee's gallant stand at Spotsylvania Court House on May 8, 1864, enabled the Confederate First Corps to seize what proved to be the key point of the battlefield and hold it against General Ulysses S. Grant's advance.

Grief-stricken at the death of Stuart a few days later, Fitz Lee entered into an unpleasant and perhaps uncalled-for wrangle with Wade Hampton over who should succeed Stuart in command of the cavalry corps. For a while, Robert E. Lee simply allowed his three senior cavalry commanders—Fitz, Hampton, and his own son Rooney Lee—to operate independently; when cooler heads prevailed in the squabble, Hampton received the corps command by virtue of his seniority. During part of that time, Fitz Lee was sent with his division to assist General Jubal Early in the Shenandoah Valley; on September 19, 1864, in the Battle of Winchester, Fitz's men were so heavily engaged against the enemy that their commander had three horses shot out from under him in the course of several hours of fighting, and he received a serious chest wound which incapacitated him until the first of the new year. By then Hampton had been reassigned to the Carolinas, in January 1865. Fitz technically received command of the cavalry, but did not effectively take command until the closing weeks of the war, when he was senior cavalryman in the Petersburg campaign.

Perhaps the least distinguished moment in his career was when he accepted an invitation to General Tom Rosser's shad bake and picnic on the morning of April 1, 1865. The Confederates under command of General George Pickett were spread over Five Forks, Virginia, a critical crossroads near Appomattox, with orders from General Robert E. Lee to "hold . . . against all hazards"; it was a major staging place for any action against the Union forces, and possibly the only line of retreat for the Army of Northern Virginia should disaster strike. Yet Fitz and

Pickett both left the field and joined Rosser on the riverbank for a party, none of them having informed their subordinates that they were leaving, much less where they would be found in case of emergency. The Federals attacked in force under Philip Sheridan; Fitz's cousin Rooney was the senior officer on the Confederate line, but only directed the actions of his own cavalrymen, unaware that he could have called on all the cavalry and the infantry besides. Sheridan's men swept the Confederate position and took a commanding position across Five Forks, effectively cutting off any hope the Confederates could withdraw and regroup.

During the subsequent retreat toward Appomattox Court House, Fitz Lee did what he could to make up for his error by shadowing the Union army's every move, keeping an eye on them and reporting often to his uncle, the commanding general. When it became obvious that the Confederates were surrounded and surrender was likely their only option, Fitz got permission to take as many of his men as he could and make a break for North Carolina, where Joseph Johnston was attempting a last stand. However, Fitz realized before they had gotten very far at all that there was no use in even making the attempt; he turned his men around and surrendered his division at Farmville, Virginia, on April 11, 1865.

Fitz joined his extended family in Richmond, where not only his parents and his four brothers waited, but all of Robert E. Lee's family as well, in the crowded house on Franklin Street. Always a physically active man, Fitz decided the city and the house were too cramped for him to stay, and he headed out to Stafford County to try his hand at farming. Never one to let adversity get him down, he joked with friends that he had been a soldier all his life and was therefore accustomed to going to the army quartermaster to get his corn; now he was finding it hard "to draw it from the obstinate soil, but I did it!" He married in April 1871, and after several years of farming and trying various business ventures he found his true place: in politics. He was a very skilled public speaker, having as he did a cheerful, amusing nature and a natural gift as a storyteller; that and the fact that he was a Lee led in 1885 to election as governor of Virginia, a position once held by his famous grandfather, General "Light-Horse Harry" Lee of Revolutionary War fame.

When his term was over, Fitz then tried for election to the U.S. Senate, but failed to receive nomination from the Democratic party, of which he was a lifelong member. In 1896, Fitz was named consul general to Havana, Cuba, a post he held with great control and dignity in the face of a confusing series of ever more violent political problems, leading to the outbreak of the Spanish-American War in 1898. One of a few former Confederates who returned to Federal blue uniforms in this war (the other most prominent being perhaps Joe Wheeler), Fitz became a major general of volunteers, and received command of the 7th Army Corps, the frontline combat troops in the occupation of Cuba. He set his soldiers up at Camp Columbia near Havana, and took over peace-keeping duties after the capture of Santiago. Upon his return to the United States, Fitz Lee served from April 1899 until March 1901 as a brigadier general; he retired with that rank on March 2, 1901.

Besides his excellent military and political skills, Fitz Lee is also remembered for having written a charming, very readable biography of his famous uncle, Robert E. Lee; though amazingly full of odd inaccuracies for someone who had been so close to his subject, Lee's book is considered today to be one of the standard works on the life of the great general, and contains many family anecdotes that might otherwise have been lost to history.

Lee, Robert Edward

1807–1870

"His name might be 'Audacity,'" remarked a Southern colleague of Robert E. Lee. "He will take more chances and take them quicker, than any other general in this country, North or South." Facing an army larger and better equipped than his own, Lee was able to fashion, through sheer nerve and finesse, as well as dogged determination, several great victories for the Confederacy until forced to surrender at Appomattox. Indeed, his remarkable military skills as commander of the Army of Northern Virginia and as general-in-chief of the Confederate army kept the Confederacy fighting long after it had lost any chance to win the war.

Every ounce the Southern gentleman, Lee was strikingly handsome, charming, and, when not in one of his frequent fits of temper, exuded warmth and good humor. Devoted to his family and to the duty he felt toward his home state, Lee had a reputation for personal integrity that was second to none—a rarity in the heady politics-driven days of the Civil War. Union general Ulysses S. Grant, to whom Lee was finally forced to surrender, said of his battlefield opponent, "There was not a man in the Confederacy whose influence with the whole people was as great as his."

Lee came from a distinguished Virginia family. One ancestor, Thomas Lee, had served as royal governor of the colony; relatives Francis Lightfoot Lee and Henry Lee had been statesmen and soldiers during the Revolutionary War. His own father, Henry Lee, was known as "Light-Horse Harry" for his daring exploits as a cavalry commander during the American Revolution. "Light-Horse Harry," however, was an incompetent businessman who fled to the West Indies after plunging his branch of the family into debt.

Robert Edward Lee was raised by his mother, Anne Carter Lee, to whom he remained devoted until her death in 1829. Armed with a testimonial letter signed by five senators and three representatives—evidence of his powerful family connections—Lee entered the United States Military Academy at West Point in 1825. He graduated four years later, second in his class and without a demerit; his attention to his studies and his quiet demeanor earned him the nickname "the Marble Model." After graduation, he was appointed to the elite Corps of Engineers and spent more than 15 years engaged in several civil and military engineering projects largely involving the fortification of coastal defenses.

Except for the fact that the assignments took him away from his wife, Mary Ann Randolph Custis, and his growing family, Lee appeared to enjoy military life. Mary, a relative of Martha Washington, was a strong-willed, often bitter woman, who became crippled by arthritis. Nevertheless, the Lee marriage produced seven children. In 1836, Lee was promoted to first lieutenant; two years later, he was promoted again to the rank of captain.

At the outbreak of the Mexican War, Lee was stationed at New York Harbor. Although he ob-

General Robert E. Lee

jected to the expansionist aims of the war, he was anxious to prove his mettle as a soldier. First ordered to report to Brigadier General John Wool at San Antonio de Bexar, Texas, Lee was then assigned to General Winfield Scott's personal staff in Veracruz, Mexico. On several occasions during Scott's five-month campaign to secure the Mexican capital, Lee located key flanking routes that enabled Americans to outmaneuver and defeat a larger enemy, displaying strategy and tactics that would serve him well in the Civil War. At the victory celebration at the fall of Mexico City, Scott toasted the captain as the man "without whose help we would not be here." For his service, Lee received a brevet to colonel.

In 1852, he began a three-year term as superintendent of West Point, a position he served with distinction. He oversaw the extension of the academy's course of study from four to five years, increased the curriculum to include the study of strategy, and improved cadet discipline. Accepting the position of lieutenant colonel of the newly formed 2nd Cavalry Regiment in 1855, Lee spent most of the next several years in the wilds of Texas, fighting against Native Americans and Mexican bandits.

Then, in 1859, Lee took part in what many claim to be the opening salvo of the Civil War. Leading four companies of local militia and a handful of U.S. Marines, Lee captured John Brown after his Harpers Ferry Raid. Although opposed to both secession and slavery, Lee found he could not agree to fight against his home state of Virginia when offered command of the Union army in 1861. "I cannot raise my hand against my birthplace, my home, my children. . . ." he wrote. "Whatever may be the result of the contest I foresee that the country will have to pass through a terrible ordeal, a necessary expiation for our national sins."

Resigning from the U.S. Army, he accepted a brigadier general's commission in charge of all Virginia's military and naval forces after his state seceded in April 1861. By June 1861, Lee had supervised deployment of over 40,000 men and received a full general's commission on June 14. Unable to prevent Federal forces from taking western Virginia at the end of July, Lee then set out to put coastal defenses into place along South Carolina and Georgia.

On May 31, after Joseph E. Johnston was wounded in the Battle of Seven Pines, Lee took command of his army, which he renamed the Army of Northern Virginia (previously named the Army of the Potomac, not to be confused with the Union's). From his first day of command, Lee faced what looked like an impossible task. Union General George B. McClellan had approached within seven miles of Richmond with 100,000 men, Union Major General Nathaniel Banks threatened important Confederate supply forces in the Shenandoah Valley, and Union Major General Irvin McDowell was encamped in nearby northern Virginia. In every instance, the Federals far outnumbered the Rebel forces opposing them. Lee believed the only viable solution was to combine his entire force against one of the threats, eliminate it, and thus dislocate the remaining Union forces. This approach formed an important cornerstone of Lee's strategy against the North throughout the war.

In a series of engagements that took place at the end of June, known as the Battle of the Seven Days, Lee forced McClellan back down the peninsula and away from Richmond. Taking the offensive, Lee then turned north to deliver another blow to the Union army in the battle of Second Bull Run at the end of August. At both Seven Days and Second Bull Run, Lee was assisted by the clever general, Thomas "Stonewall" Jackson. Jackson so admired Lee's abilities that he claimed, "I would follow him onto the battlefield blindfolded."

Having won two decisive victories, Lee continued his offense by preparing a northern invasion. His plan involved dividing his army as it advanced, each section then undertaking separate missions against the Union before reuniting in a main attack. Jackson was able to capture Harpers Ferry, but because a copy of Lee's plans fell into Union Major George B. McClellan's hands, Lee was forced to take up a defensive position at Antietam Creek, in Maryland. After fighting through the war's most bloody single day of battle on September 17, 1862, Lee was forced to retreat to Virginia.

Three months later, Lee redeemed himself and his army in a surprising victory at Fredericksburg, Virginia. The Union attack by an army significantly larger than Lee's and led by Ambrose Burnside, took weeks longer than planned, allowing Lee to form strong defensive positions in the hills surrounding the town from which he was able to devastate his opponent. In May 1863, the determined general forced another remarkable victory against a formidable enemy at Chancellorsville; although the battle was a strategic masterpiece expertly executed, it lost him his most precious corps commander, Stonewall Jackson.

Lee decided to attempt another northern invasion that summer, and by late June occupied the entire Cumberland Valley and other parts of Pennsylvania. Concentrating his forces at Gettysburg against new Federal commander George G. Meade, Lee lost his first major battle after three days of bitter fighting and was forced to retreat. The following spring, with just 60,000 men, Lee faced Union General Ulysses S. Grant and his 120,000-man Army of the Potomac for the first time.

During the Wilderness campaign, Lee was pounded by Grant's better-equipped forces in a series of battles. Finally, the Confederates were forced back into defensive positions at Richmond and Petersburg. To protect the capital, Lee had to stretch his already depleted lines to meet Grant's continual encroachments on their right flank. As the Confederacy collapsed on other fronts, Lee's manpower shortage continued; in a one-month period, desertions claimed nearly eight percent of his strength.

In February 1865, although the Confederacy had clearly lost the war, Lee was placed in charge of all its armies. For three more months, he attempted to hold off the inevitable, but was finally forced to abandon Richmond in an effort to join his remaining 28,000 troops with those led by Albert Sidney Johnston in North Carolina. At Appomattox, however, he lost his final battle against Grant, to whom he surrendered on April 9, 1865. As Lee made his last ride down the lines on his famous horse, Traveller, he told his army, "Men, we have fought through the war together. I have done my best for you; my heart is too full to say more."

Although his home at Arlington had been confiscated by the Federals, he appeared to hold no bitterness for his former enemies and urged his fellow Southerners to accept the peace and rebuild their country. Lee chose to spend his last years as president of Washington College in Lexington, Virginia, where he established the nation's first journalism and business schools. Lee died on October 12, 1870, and was buried in the chapel he built on the campus of what was renamed Washington and Lee University after his death.

Lee, William Henry Fitzhugh "Rooney"

1837–1891

This youngest of the six Lee generals boasted by the Confederate army was the second eldest son of General Robert E. Lee. Born at his grandfather's estate Arlington, overlooking Washington, D.C. on the Virginia side of the Potomac River, William H. F. Lee is perhaps better known to history as "Rooney" Lee, a nickname given him by his father because at his birth, the little fellow apparently resembled the black-haired, red-faced Irish gardener, one "Mr. Rooney." The nickname stuck to him the rest of his life, though there exists evidence in his younger sister's diary that he tried as early as age 15 to convince family and friends to call him Fitzhugh. Only his father seems to have achieved any success in that regard, for Rooney Lee served in the cavalry corps of the Army of Northern Virginia with his first cousin, Fitzhugh Lee, who had no other names from which to choose.

Rooney Lee attended Harvard University as a young man. He completed nearly all the four-year course of study, but gave it all up just shy of graduation because he was offered a post in the United States Army as a second lieutenant by his father's commanding officer and patriot, General Winfield Scott.

Sent out West, young Lieutenant Lee served creditably with the 6th U.S. Infantry under Albert Sidney Johnston in the Mormon Campaign. But when the campaign was over Rooney resigned his commission to marry his cousin, Charlotte Wickham, in 1859. The newlyweds settled down at an estate known as White House, which Rooney inherited from his grandfather; it had been the home of Martha Custis, Rooney's great-great grandmother, at the time of her marriage to George Washington.

The outbreak of the war in 1861 found Rooney Lee, now the father of his parents' only grandchild, uncertain of what to do. He felt in his heart that secession was wrong, but Virginia was his home—and like the rest of his family, he placed his sword in defense of Virginia when it sided with the South. He organized a cavalry company at the request of the governor and was appointed its captain; less than a month later he had been promoted to major and was assigned to command the cavalry under General William W. Loring. He was with the last male heir of the Washington family, Colonel John Augustine Washington, when the colonel was killed by Federal pickets in the West Virginia Campaign in the summer of 1861. That winter Lee was reassigned to Fredericksburg, where he was promoted to lieutenant colonel and made second in command of the 9th Virginia Cavalry regiment; very shortly thereafter he won the confidence of his men in the regimental election and became their colonel. The regiment was assigned to the cavalry corps under General Jeb Stuart, who remained Rooney Lee's commander until Stuart's death in 1864.

Through all the major campaigns of 1862 and early 1863, Rooney Lee's name appears in the records with great honor. He participated in all of Stuart's rides around George McClellan's army, during one of which his home was burned to the ground, and was at the Second Battle of Manassas (Second Bull Run); in the fighting before the battle of Antietam, Lee was injured and left unconscious in the street in an

unusually confusing fight at Boonsboro, Maryland, when his horse fell on him during the action. He made his way back to the army under cover of darkness and was hailed by his comrades as if returning from the dead—for so he had been reported to be. Late in 1862, he was appointed brigadier general and received a cavalry brigade that included his old regiment. He led this brigade through the Battles of Fredericksburg and Chancellorsville, to great credit in the reports of his superiors.

At the beginning of the Gettysburg Campaign, Rooney Lee was severely wounded in the upper thigh at the Battle of Brandy Station, the largest cavalry battle ever fought on American soil, on June 9, 1863. He was taken to the home of his wife's relatives at Hickory Hill, near Hanover, Virginia, to recover; but while he was there, barely two weeks after his wounding, he was taken prisoner during a raid that was later found to have been planned specifically to capture him, in addition to its other objectives. The Union Secretary of War, Edwin Stanton, needed a hostage to use against the Confederate government, owing to an extremely unpleasant political situation. General Ambrose Burnside had captured a number of Confederate soldiers in Kentucky and, because they were wearing civilian clothing to supplement their meager uniforms, he had them hanged as spies. Outraged Southern commanders, calling this "military murder," captured some of Burnside's men in full uniform and had hanged them in retaliation. There were more hangings of Confederate soldiers, and casualties of this sort were traded back and forth until the Confederate government chose two officers from Libby Prison in Richmond, and notified Abraham Lincoln's government that the men would be hanged if any more Confederate soldiers died in this fashion. Stanton then made it clear he would do likewise: he chose Robert E. Lee's wounded son and one other officer as hostages for the good behavior of their government, and the matter came to a tense stand-off that lasted several months.

While Rooney Lee was thus awaiting the sentence of death, two remarkable things happened.

A Union officer of some note, imprisoned at Richmond, asked a local clergyman to try and arrange a one-for-one exchange: he felt he could convince his government to trade Rooney Lee for him, if only General Robert E. Lee could be gotten to ask for the deal. The clergyman dutifully relayed the message and received a sad response: the commanding general would not ask for his own son what could not be asked on behalf of the lowliest soldier in his army. The minister later remarked that only one who knew how much Robert Lee loved his children could possibly have known how much such a decision had cost him. And in early December 1863, with Rooney's wife dying in Richmond, his brother, General Custis Lee, tried to arrange to take Rooney's place in prison, even if it meant dying in his stead, so his brother could come home for even a day to say good-bye to her. The Federal response, since the Burnside situation had not resolved, was that the fortunes of war had to remain with those upon whom they had fallen—and they refused the exchange. Charlotte Lee died on the day after Christmas.

Three months later, in March 1864, Rooney Lee was finally included in what proved to be one of the last official prisoner exchanges. Right afterward, U.S. government policy was changed: all Southern prisoners were to be sent North, in an attempt to prevent the Confederate army from having enough men in the field to defend their nation. Rooney returned to Stuart's command, promoted to major general—the youngest in Confederate service by one week's age difference—and went back to the fighting almost immediately. When Stuart was killed at Yellow Tavern in May, Rooney Lee and his fellow division commanders, Wade Hampton and Fitz Lee, each received independent command until arrangements could be made for one of them to succeed the much-lamented Stuart. Rooney led his division against the raid of Union General Wilson in June 1864, and was in command of the cavalry at the Battle of Globe Tavern in August.

At the end, in the desperate fighting of the Appomattox Campaign, Rooney valiantly tried to protect his father's starving army, joining his fellow cavalrymen in the heroic but vain attempt to be everywhere at once against the attacks of Union General Philip Sheridan. At Five Forks on April 1, 1865, Lee commanded the right wing of the Confederate forces—but was unaware of how many men he had to command, because his superiors, Fitz Lee and General George Pickett, had gone off to a shad bake with cavalryman Tom Rosser, and all three of them had failed to inform anyone of where they would be. In the closing days of the war, Rooney Lee was second in command of the Confederate cavalry in Virginia and was the only senior cavalry officer present at the surrender, Rosser having been captured, and Fitz Lee having broken away when the end seemed near, to attempt to join Joseph Johnston's army in North Carolina and make a last stand. One witness to the surrender described having seen numerous officers and men awaiting Robert E. Lee's departure from the McLean House, all of them deeply saddened at the tragic turn of events; sitting among them, tears streaming down his face, was Rooney Lee.

After the war, Lee returned to White House, built a new home, and settled down with a new wife to try and farm the land. He became president of the Virginia Agricultural Society and served in the state legislature as a representative from New Kent County from 1875 to 1879. Inheriting his great-uncle's plantation "Ravensworth" in Fairfax County, Rooney Lee moved back to the part of the state where he had been born, and in 1887 was elected to the U.S. Congress, when the former Confederate states received the right to vote once more. People came to him often with requests for assistance. He helped many families who had been left destitute by the war—both black and white—and once he filibustered on the House floor for several hours, making speeches and impassioned pleas, until Congress agreed to pay damages to the Virginia Theological Seminary in Alexandria, which had suffered a great deal of property and personal loss during the Union occupation. At that time he was told by an annoyed fellow congressman that he had the gentleman's vote in favor of the request, if he could tell them how the professors and clergy at the seminary had prayed during the war: for the president of the United States, or for the president of the Confederacy. Rooney's answer was: "They prayed for all sinners." The bill passed.

Shortly after being elected to his third term in 1891, Rooney Lee suffered a stroke following a lengthy illness. He was seriously ill throughout the spring and summer, and toward the autumn could barely speak; a friend said at the time that so highly did Virginians esteem him, it seemed the whole state was on its knees praying for his recovery. But on October 15—the twenty-first anniversary of his father's funeral—just around sunset, Rooney Lee died. He was buried first at Ravensworth, and then reinterred in the Lee Chapel crypt in Lexington, Virginia, where he rests today with his second wife and five of his seven children. He left behind him what was perhaps most important to the Lees, namely a reputation of honor, charity, duty, and responsibility.

Lincoln, Abraham

1809–1865

The mythic proportions to which the sixteenth United States president have risen are, by and large, well deserved. Lincoln's intelligence, personal integrity, and moral courage saw the country through its most difficult challenge, the Civil War. His Emancipation Proclamation of 1863, although passed with a careful eye to its political consequences, was an act of humanity and vision not yet experienced in American history. A gentle, reflective man, but one prone to self-doubt and depression, Lincoln nevertheless prosecuted the war with remarkable aggressiveness and with a surprisingly tenacious will to win.

Lincoln's humble roots in Kentucky, Indiana, and Illinois are well known. Lincoln spent his childhood chopping wood and farming, but also reading voraciously. Early on, he chose George Washington and other Revolutionary War figures as his heroes, later writing, "I recall think-

ing that, boy even though I was, that there must have been something more than common that these men struggled for." By the time he was 21, he was a well-respected shop owner in New Salem, Illinois and, by the age of 23, a state legislator.

It was during his four terms in the legislature from 1832 to 1838 that his reputation as a man of integrity, wit, and strong opinions first developed. His skill in party management enabled him to become the Whig floor leader at the beginning of his second term. He took a leading role in the establishment of the Bank of Illinois and led a successful campaign for moving the state capital from Vandalia to Springfield.

The issue of slavery in the territories arose in 1837, when the Illinois legislature passed a series of resolutions condemning abolitionist societies. Lincoln took his first stand on slavery at this time by filing a protest. While he admitted that Congress had no power to interfere with slavery in the states where it already existed, Lincoln insisted that the institution of slavery itself was founded on "both injustice and bad policy" and therefore should not be allowed to spread further. Until he issued the Emancipation Proclamation in the fall of 1862, those sentiments formed the basis of his policy toward slavery and the South.

In 1836, Lincoln passed the state bar and, moving to Springfield a year later, opened a law practice that soon became one of the most prominent in the capital. As a "circuit lawyer," Lincoln traveled around 15 counties of the state during six months of every year, affording him a chance to meet many people and discover what they considered the important issues of the day.

In 1840, Lincoln made a speaking tour of the state for William Henry Harrison, the Whig candidate for president, and used his platform to support a central banking system. Lincoln lost his bid for the Whig nomination to Congress in 1843 and 1844, but, two years after campaigning for Henry Clay, won election to the U.S. House of Representatives.

In 1842, Lincoln married Mary Todd, a Kentucky woman living with her sister in Springfield. High-strung and ambitious, Mary would be a source of both comfort and distress to Lincoln throughout his life. Their family life would be difficult; two of his four sons would perish before Lincoln himself lost his life.

During his term in Congress, Lincoln spoke out against what he considered the folly of the Mexican War and supported the Wilmot Pro-

Abraham Lincoln in Washington, April 10, 1865

viso, an act that would have banned slavery in any territory acquired from Mexico had it not been defeated by Congress. When his term ended in 1849, Lincoln returned to build his law practice in Springfield into one of the most important corporate firms in the state.

He remained in private life until 1854, when the Kansas-Nebraska Act spurred his return to politics. Campaigning against the act throughout the state, Lincoln was elected to the state legislature as the leader of the Illinois forces opposing the spread of slavery into the territories. Within months, he resigned to undertake an unsuccessful run for the U.S. Senate. Lincoln joined the antislavery Republican Party in 1856 and made more than 100 speeches in support of John C. Frémont, the Republican presidential nominee.

In 1858, Lincoln was nominated to run against Steven Douglas for the U.S. Senate. In accepting the nomination, he uttered the now famous words that summed up the conflict facing the nation: "A house divided against itself cannot endure, permanently half slave and half free. I do not expect the Union to be dissolved— I do not expect the house to fall—but I do expect it will cease to be divided. It will become all one thing, or all the other." Lincoln then challenged Douglas to a series of seven debates that centered on the extension of slavery into free territory. Lincoln reiterated his long-held position that, although he considered slavery "a moral, social, and political evil," he did not believe the Federal government had the right to interfere with a state's domestic issues. The debates made Lincoln a national figure and impressed the increasingly powerful Republican party in the east. Although Douglas defeated him by a narrow margin, the campaign placed Lincoln front and center on the national Republican stage.

At the 1860 Republican National Convention, Lincoln was considered the most moderate, and most electable, candidate on a roster that included Salmon P. Chase of Ohio and William Seward of New York. Largely due to a split within the Democratic party, Lincoln won the election that November. The election of a Republican administration was the final straw

in the decades-long struggle between North and South. On December 20, 1860, South Carolina began the wave of secession that would eventually sweep across 11 slave states in the South.

By the time Lincoln took the oath of office in Washington, D.C., on March 4, 1861, war with the Confederate States was inevitable and the enemy's capital of Richmond, Virginia, lay just 100 miles southwest of Washington, D.C. Although he hoped a compromise could be reached, he warned that he would use the full power of the nation to "hold, occupy, and possess" the property and places belonging to the federal government, including forts and arsenals now being eyed by the Confederates.

The probability of war became a certainty when shots were fired at Fort Sumter on April 14, 1861. Lincoln met the crisis with action, raising troops, calling for a blockade of Southern ports, and arresting Southern sympathizers in Union territory by suspending the writ of habeas corpus. Although many of his opening moves were criticized, even by members of his own party, Lincoln believed that his actions were within the war powers granted the president by the U.S. Constitution; he stated that opinion when Congress met for the first time in his administration on July 4, 1861.

Despite persistent interference from Radical Republicans and with inconsistent support from the people of the North, Lincoln prosecuted the war aggressively and with excellent strategic instincts. He immediately grasped the importance of a naval blockade and urged Secretary of the Navy Gideon Welles to execute one as quickly as possible. Although current thinking demanded that the only way to win a war was by concentrating one's forces and destroying the enemy's army in one large battle, Lincoln spread his armies out and attacked the enemy in several theaters at once. He also withstood pressure from Radical Republicans to make the end of slavery the goal of the war until the North was sufficiently strong militarily to handle the controversy such a move was sure to stir. He did so in the fall of 1862, after the battle of Antietam; the Emancipation Proclamation was officially enacted January 1, 1863.

On the home front, Lincoln's skill as an orator inspired and sustained the people whose sons were being slaughtered in the battlefield. His Gettysburg Address, issued on November 18, 1863, remains one of the greatest pieces of American oratory in history. Its ten lines summed up the purpose of the war as nothing else had before or since. He ended it by saying, ". . . we here highly resolve that these dead shall not have died in vain—that this nation, under God, shall have a new birth of freedom—and that government of the people, by the people, for the people, shall not perish from the earth."

By the spring and summer of 1864, Lincoln worried that the war's mounting toll of casualties and Union defeats would spell his defeat in the November election. A string of military victories, starting with David G. Farragut's capture of Mobile Bay, William Tecumseh Sherman's victory at Atlanta, and Ulysses S. Grant's success in the Shenandoah Valley restored Northern faith in the president. Lincoln and Vice-President Andrew Johnson handily won the November election.

When Lincoln took his second oath of office on March 4, 1865, the end of the war was clearly in sight. Grant had surrounded Robert E. Lee's troops at Petersburg, and when Petersburg fell, the Confederate capital of Richmond would fall as well. In his second inaugural address, Lincoln urged reconciliation with the soon-to-be-vanquished South, calling for the Northerners to have "malice toward none" and "charity for all." On April 9, 1865, Robert E. Lee surrendered his forces to Ulysses S. Grant at Appomattox Court House, effectively ending the Civil War.

On April 11, in his last public address, Lincoln spoke of his intention to accept the seceded states back into the Union with a minimum of conditions. Four days later, he was shot by an assassin at Ford's Theater in Washington, D.C. Carried unconscious to a neighboring house, Lincoln died at 7:22 A.M. the next morning. After lying in state for two weeks in the East Room of the White House, then in the Capitol Rotunda, Lincoln's body was carried by train west from Washington to Springfield, Illinois. Mourners lined the tracks as the train made its journey across the country so recently divided by war. "Mankind has lost a friend and we a president" read a sign held by one of the millions of grieving Americans.

Lincoln Assassination

APRIL 14, 1865

"Our country owed all our troubles to [Lincoln]," John Wilkes Booth wrote soon after this fateful event. "God . . . made me the instrument of his punishment."

Less than a week after Confederate General Robert E. Lee surrendered at Appomattox Court House, an exhausted President Abraham Lincoln decided to attend the theater for an evening of relaxation. With the war almost over, a sense of calm swept over Washington and security around the president was lax. However, John Wilkes Booth, an actor, and six cohorts (Lewis Paine, Samuel Arnold, Michael O'Laughlin, Mary Surratt, David Herold, and George Atzerodt) were prepared to carry out a plan to murder the president and other high-ranking officials that very night. The first of their schemes to kidnap the president had failed; now, with the surrender of the Army of Northern Virginia, Booth believed that only Lincoln's assassination would avenge the humiliating Confederate defeat.

According to Booth's plan, he would shoot the president at Ford's Theater, Lewis Paine would stab Secretary William H. Seward at his home, and George Atzerodt would kill Vice President Andrew Johnson, also at home. Only Booth succeeded, although Seward was seriously wounded. (Atzerodt apparently was too afraid to even attempt his mission.)

After drinking two snifters of brandy at a nearby bar, Booth arrived at the theater during the first act of the play, *Our American Cousin*, a light comedy starring British actress Laura Keene. Lincoln, his wife, and friends Major Henry Rathbone and his fiancée, Clara Harris, occupied the presidential box and appeared to

President Lincoln's box at Ford's Theater.

be enjoying the show. At about 10:15 P.M., Booth slipped in behind Lincoln, shot him once in the head with a .44 caliber gun, stabbed Rathbone with a hunting knife, and jumped ten feet down to the stage. Although his leg snapped on impact, Booth, ever the performer, stood on stage to shout Virginia's state motto—*"Sic semper tyrannis"*, "Thus be it ever to tyrants"—to the stunned audience. Limping backstage and out into an alley, Booth managed to escape on a horse held for him by stagehand, Edward Spangler, a fellow conspirator.

In the meantime, the president was examined by a surgeon present in the theater. The bullet from Booth's gun had entered the back of Lincoln's head, torn through his brain, and lodged behind his right eye; the doctor proclaimed the wound fatal. Soldiers from among the audience carried the president from the theater to a boardinghouse on Tenth Street. Mary, overcome with grief and terror, was sent home by her physician to await the news of her husband's certain death. Lincoln died the following morning at 7:22 A.M. with his eldest son, Robert, at his side.

Within hours, the country was shrouded in mourning over the loss of its great leader. Federal troops took to the streets, searching for clues to the assailants' whereabouts. On April 26, 1865, Booth and David Herold were cor-

nered in a barn near Port Royal, Virginia. Herold surrendered, but Booth was shot and killed. Eventually all of Booth's co-conspirators were captured and tried before a nine-man military tribunal.

The trial, which began on May 10, 1865, lasted for about six weeks and ended with the conviction of all eight defendants. Atzerodt, Herold, Pain, and Surratt were sentenced to death and hanged on July 7. The remainder received life sentences, with the exception of the stagehand, Edward Spangler, who was sentenced to six years. O'Laughlin died in prison of yellow fever, but the other three were pardoned

Execution of the conspirators, July 7, 1865.

in 1869 by President Andrew Johnson, who was convinced that their orders to kill the president came not merely from the fanatic John Wilkes Booth, but from the defeated Confederate leadership.

Lincoln, Mary Todd

1818–1882

Mary Lincoln, the devoted wife of the nation's sixteenth president, was a deeply disturbed woman throughout most of her marriage to Abraham Lincoln. The daughter of a wealthy Lexington, Kentucky, banker, Mary grew up to

Mary Todd Lincoln

become a socially ambitious young woman. In 1839, at the age of 21, she moved to Springfield, Illinois, to live with a married sister. Mary Todd was one of the most popular young women in the political circles to which her sister's father-in-law, Governor Ninian Edwards, belonged.

In Springfield, she met Abraham Lincoln, a young lawyer with social and political ambitions of his own. Their courtship was a stormy one; Mary was nervous and tense while her beau was moody and absentminded, but the two became engaged and prepared to marry in the summer of 1842. The first wedding was called off, however, when the groom experienced a fit of nervousness. The wedding finally took place on November 4, 1842, when Lincoln was 33 and Mary, 23.

Mary gave birth to the first of four sons, Robert, just nine months after the marriage; tragically, her firstborn was the only one to survive into adulthood. The Lincoln's second son, Edward Baker, was born in 1846, but died four years later. Without doubt, the loss of her children deeply affected the already overwrought Mary Lincoln. Even the ascension of her husband to the highest office in the land disappointed her; her taste for luxury and her haughty manner alienated most of Washington, as did her frequent outbursts of jealousy and temper. The fact that many of her relatives were fighting for the Confederacy further exacerbated her situation, despite the fact that she vowed loyalty to the Union cause. Not only did the war politically and physically separate her from her family, but her Southern roots caused the Washington crowd to view her with suspicion.

When her 11-year-old son, William, died of fever in 1861, Mary was inconsolable. She believed that his death was divine punishment for the way the Lincolns had lived their lives, "so wrapped up in the world, so devoted to our own advancement." For more than three months, she was so depressed that Lincoln feared he would have to institutionalize his wife. Although she rallied, she never fully recovered from William's death and was largely unable to provide emotional support to her husband through the difficult years of his presidency, instead requiring a great deal of his attention. Nevertheless, the two remained devoted to one another.

Not surprisingly, Lincoln's assassination further devastated her. In fact, she was too overwhelmed with grief to accompany the body to Springfield for burial. Although left a wealthy woman, Mary's spendthrift ways soon found her nearly poverty-stricken after she left the White House. An act of Congress granted her a generous pension that enabled her to survive. When her son Tad died, her emotional anguish was so great that her fourth son, Robert, had her committed to a mental institution for several months. Mary spent the last years of her troubled life in her sister's Springfield home, where she had first met her husband nearly 40 years before. She died on July 16, 1882.

Longstreet, James

1821–1904

"Old Pete" to his troops, the man Robert E. Lee called "my old war horse" may have been ineffectual in independent command, but despite the opinion of his detractors, he was a superb corps leader. Longstreet grew up in the deep South and graduated near the bottom of his class at West Point. Serving in the Mexican War and on the frontier, he became an army paymaster, and when he resigned from the U.S. military in June 1861, he hoped for a similar administrative post in the Confederacy. Instead, Longstreet, a master at field fortifications, was given command of a brigade, and after a solid showing at First Bull Run, he was promoted to major general.

Criticized for misconstruing orders at Seven Pines in spring 1862, Longstreet still emerged after the Seven Days Campaign as one of Lee's ablest subordinates and was placed in charge of an infantry corps. He played a key role in the Second Bull Run campaign in August, holding back on the battle's first day, then successfully launching a crushing counterassault on the sec-

ond. Instrumental at Antietam and Fredericksburg later in the year and promoted to lieutenant general, Longstreet was dispatched on an independent mission to the southeastern Virginia coast in April 1863, where he collected much-needed supplies but showed little initiative in confronting Union forces.

He rejoined Lee in time for the South's fateful invasion of Pennsylvania, about which, with his habitual preference for a tactical defensive position, he had great misgivings. Commanding the right wing at Gettysburg, Longstreet urgently counseled the Southern commander to maneuver the army between the Union troops and Washington and force the Federals to attack. But Lee remained on the offensive, and Longstreet's delay in launching the main assault on the battle's second day until the late afternoon is blamed by some for the Confederate defeat. Certain that it would fail horribly, he was even more reluctant to mount "Pickett's Charge" the following day and could barely nod the order to begin the doomed offensive.

With no bad feelings between him and Lee, Longstreet was sent west in September, where he reinforced Braxton Bragg's force in northern Georgia. Routing the Union army at Chickamauga, he was outraged that no follow-up attack on the vulnerable Federals was ordered, and demanded Bragg's removal. To ease tensions, Longstreet was given another independent command, assigned to retake Knoxville, Tennessee. His siege and attacks on the city were unsuccessful, however, and by April 1864, Longstreet was back serving under Lee in Virginia. During the chaotic Battle of the Wilderness, his troops accidentally shot him in the shoulder, and he was out of action until November. Returning to participate in the siege of Petersburg, he surrendered with Lee at Appomattox Court House in April 1865.

After the war, Longstreet became an insurance executive and scandalized the South by joining the Republican party. A longtime friend of Ulysses Grant (to whom he was related by marriage), he accepted several positions in the U.S. government, including minister to Turkey. He also published his controversial memoirs, in which he dared to criticize—albeit judi-

General James Longstreet

ciously—several aspects of Lee's command and defended himself against charges lingering since Gettysburg that his own actions in the decisive battle lost the war for the South.

Lowe, Thaddeus Sobieski

1832–1913

Impressed with the intelligence-gathering possibilities of manned hot-air balloons, Abraham Lincoln appointed Thaddeus Lowe chief of army aeronautics in 1861; by the time he re-signed his post in 1863, Lowe and his crew had made more than 3,000 flights over enemy territory.

A few months before he received his appointment, Lowe, a renowned aeronautic scientist, made a 9-hour, 900-mile flight from Cincinnati, Ohio to Unionville, South Carolina. Unfortunately, his trip followed the fall of Fort Sumter by just a week; when he arrived in South Carolina, the Confederate army summarily arrested him on charges of spying for the Union. Lowe managed to convince them of his innocence but, being a die-hard Union man, immediately rushed back to Washington to do just what he'd been accused of doing: he offered his services for intelligence-gathering to the Union army.

Working under the auspices of the War Department, Lowe received the pay of a colonel, plus materials and labor. His first mission involved gathering information on Confederate troop deployment shortly after First Bull Run in mid-July 1861. During George B. McClellan's Peninsula Campaign in the summer and fall of the same year, Lowe conducted almost daily flights over the Virginia landscape, producing reports and photographs of the Confederate position.

Thanks to additional army appropriations, Lowe was able to expand and improve his fleet. He built seven airships of various sizes and equipped them with newly designed generators that could produce hydrogen gas in the air. The largest of his ships, the *Intrepid*, was 32,000 cubic feet in size and required 1,200 yards of silk. He used it to conduct survellience during and after Fredericksburg.

Although the Confederate Army lacked the resources to launch its own full-scale aeronautics program, Captain E. Porter Alexander oversaw several ascensions by Confederate aeronauts in 1861 and 1862, who reported on Union troop deployment during the Peninsula and Seven Days campaigns. Balloons were often shot down behind enemy lines or, due to the unpredictable nature of balloon flights, were unable to return to camp in time to provide crucial information to the command. The last use of balloons by the Confederate army took place

Professor Lowe in his balloon.

in 1863, after its largest balloon was swept away by a strong, high wind.

The Union soon abandoned the often risky use of surveillance balloons as well. Lowe ended his career with the Union army when the newly appointed commander, Joseph Hooker, sharply reduced the role of aeronautics in the Army of the Potomac in late 1863. Shortly after the war ended, Lowe moved to California, where he continued experimenting with aeronautics and other new technologies. The Lowe Observatory in Pasadena, California, was built as a testament to his scientific accomplishments.

M

Mallory, Stephen Russell

1813–1873

The only Confederate cabinet officer to keep his position throughout the Civil War, Secretary of the Navy Stephen Mallory built and managed a formidable navy with scant resources and little support from his government. Realizing early on that he could not compete with the Northern navy's superior strength, Mallory instead concentrated on developing innovative technologies, such as ironclad ships, torpedos, and submarines.

Mallory's fascination with ships and the sea stemmed from his childhood on Key West, Florida, which was then an isolated, sparsely populated territory almost completely surrounded by water. His military experience before the Civil War consisted of patrolling the coast and the Everglades near Tampa Bay during the Seminole War from 1835 to 1840. Upon his return from the war, he passed the bar and began to practice maritime law in Key West.

In 1851, he was elected to the U.S. Senate, where he became an important member of the Committee on Naval Affairs. As a committee member, and as its chairman from 1855 to early 1861, he pushed for a larger and stronger navy. When on January 10, 1861, Florida became the third state to secede, he resigned his seat and joined the new Confederate government as secretary of its Navy Department.

Mallory faced a formidable task in preparing the South's navy for war. On the day he took his oath of office, the navy consisted of just ten vessels mounting fifteen guns and had virtually no organizational framework. Another obstacle was the opinion of many in the Confederate administration, including President Jefferson Davis, that the navy was a mere auxiliary to the army. Mallory worked hard throughout the spring of 1861 to pry scant resources from the government to strengthen its maritime forces. Funds would, however, remain in short supply throughout the war. Despite this lack of wherewithal, Mallory began to create a creditable navy department, modeling it after the one he had known in Washington.

He then attempted to build up the navy's supply of ships. From April 20 to 21, 1861, the South's navy received its biggest boon when the Norfolk Navy Yard fell into Confederate hands after Virginia seceded and Union attempts to destroy the yard failed. Not only did the South gain the yard, but also its vast stores of supplies, 11 ships, its dry dock and industrial plant, and its ironclad ship, the *Merrimack*. Nevertheless, because the South had few shipyards or materials, Mallory sent envoys to the North, to Canada, and to Europe to purchase vessels.

By the summer, Mallory had made considerable headway, but still faced the biggest chal-

Stephen R. Mallory

lenge to the future of the Confederacy, the Northern blockade. For the South to survive, the Union blockade would have to be broken. To accomplish this, Mallory developed two strategies. First, by using cruise ships constructed and purchased in England to disrupt Northern shipping, he hoped to draw the enemy's ships away from the coast and hurt the Northern economy at the same time. Second, if

he could raise the navy to sufficient strength, the South could directly attack the blockaders. Instead of attempting to compete with the North's vast superiority in numbers of vessels, however, Mallory concentrated his efforts on building ironclad ships, which, as he stated in a letter to the chairman of the House Committee of Naval Affairs, would compensate for "inequality of numbers" with "invulnerability."

Despite Mallory's valiant efforts, the effects of the blockade and the North's superior strength combined to overwhelm the Confederate navy rather quickly. The loss of New Orleans during a naval battle in April 1862—a battle also resulting in the loss of two Confederate ironclads—was a devastating blow to the Confederacy and to Mallory, who, as head of the navy, was blamed for the debacle. In a letter to his wife, he wrote that after receiving the news of New Orleans, he lay "awake night after night with my heart depressed and sore, and my eyes filled with tears."

After the loss of the ironclad *Arkansas* on its way to Baton Rouge from Vicksburg in August, 1862, some members of the Confederate Congress accused Mallory of stupidity and incompetence. Nevertheless, he remained in his position until the end of the war, when he fled Richmond for Georgia with Davis and other members of the cabinet on the evening of April 2, 1865.

After receiving reports of the surrenders by Generals Robert E. Lee, Pierre G. T. Beauregard, and Albert Sidney Johnston, Mallory tendered his resignation on May 2. He was arrested by Federal forces a few days later and spent the next ten months in prison at Fort Lafayette. After a full pardon by President Andrew Johnson, Mallory returned to Pensacola, Florida, and his law practice. He died on November 12, 1873.

Manassas, First

Manassas (First), Campaign and Battle of

JULY 16–21, 1861

The first battle of the Civil War was fought at Manassas Junction, Virginia, near a creek called Bull Run. Confederate forces at Manassas were led by General Pierre T. Beauregard, while General Irvin McDowell led the Federal army. At First Manassas, also known as First Bull Run, the South successfully stopped the Union's advance toward Richmond, the Confederate capital.

Manassas (Second), Campaign and Battle of

AUGUST 26–SEPTEMBER 1, 1862

Second Manassas, also known as Second Bull Run, was fought over the same territory as First Manassas. Confederate troops under the leadership of Major Generals Robert E. Lee and James Longstreet clashed with the Union forces of Major Generals George McClellan and John Pope. Despite being outnumbered, the South won this battle, and the North retreated back to Washington, D.C.

Marine Corps, Confederate

On March 16, 1861, the Confederate Congress established the Confederate States Marine Corps (CSMC). Commanded largely by former United States Marine officers, the CSMC played a relatively small role in the Civil War. Its highest level of enrollment was approximately 540 enlisted men and officers. As in most branches of the armed services, the CSMC suffered from desertions and a lack of new recruits as the war continued; the fact that the pay of enlisted marines was $3 less per month than that of equivalent army grades did not help matters. Confederate marines served mainly as guard detachments for naval stations at Confederate ports and as personnel at naval shore batteries along the

Southern coast. The largest engagement involving Confederate marines was at the battle of the *Monitor* vs. the *Merrimack* (CSS *Virginia*) at Hampton Roads, Virginia, from March 8 to 9, 1862.

Marines, United States

Like their Confederate counterparts, United States Marines played a limited role in the Civil War. A lack of cooperation between the navy and the army accounted for their virtual invisibility. A branch of the Department of the Navy, its commanders, Marine Commandant John C. Harris (1861–1864) and his successor Major Jacob Zeilin, generally steered clear of all army operations. In addition, at the start of the war, the corps suffered from a shortage of personnel, especially after most of its officers resigned to join the Confederacy. By 1864, however, the corps operated at full-strength; with 5,000 enlisted marines serving as ship guards and manning naval batteries. Most of the shore operations in which the U.S. Marines participated were unsuccessful, including First Bull Run and Fort Fisher. Altogether, approximately 150 Union marines were killed in action during the Civil War.

Six Marines with fixed bayonets.

Mason-Dixon Line, the

Named for the men who surveyed it between 1763–1767, English astronomers Charles Mason and Jeremiah Dixon, the Mason-Dixon line runs along the northernmost border of Maryland and Pennsylvania, and includes the northern border of Delaware, as well. The line was surveyed and created to settle a boundary dispute between Maryland and Pennsylvania, though the question was not quite resolved; not too long after the maps were changed to reflect the new border, a Marylander visiting Philadelphia was heard to remark that it certainly was a nice little Maryland city. Before the Civil War, this line was generally regarded as the demarcation between the northern "free states" and the southern "slave states," though this was of course a very broad generalization. Nowadays the line is regarded as the separation point between states considered Northern or Southern.

There is some likelihood that the Dixon portion of the line's name may be responsible for the South's nickname of "Dixie," though an equally strong argument can be made for it coming from a ten-dollar note issued by the state of Louisiana; owing to the strong French influence in that state's history and culture, the "ten" was written as the French "dix," and the notes themselves seem at one point to have been popularly known as "dixies."

Maury, Dabney Herndon

1822–1900

Dabney H. Maury was an illustrious son of a noted line of Virginians and one of the heroes of the Confederate Western theater. Descended from Huguenots who emigrated to America in the early 1700s, Maury was the great-grandson of Reverend James Maury, Patrick Henry's opponent in the famous "Parson's Cause" debates. His paternal uncle was the famed navy officer, oceanographer, meterological and hydrographic scientist Matthew Fontaine Maury, the "Scientist of the Seas," who also gave his time and talents to the Confederate States of America.

Born in Fredericksburg, Virginia, Dabney Maury first studied to be a lawyer at the University of Virginia. He discovered, however, that he loathed the law—and procured an appointment to West Point, graduating in the class of 1846 along with George Pickett—though significantly higher in the class standings. He served gallantly in the Mexican War as a lieutenant in the Mounted Rifles (later known as the 3rd Cavalry) and was given a brevet, or honorary, rank of first lieutenant for bravery in the siege of Cerro Gordo. That brevet was later confirmed as a permanent rank, the first of many promotions Maury would earn for his bravery.

Between 1847 and 1852, Maury was back at West Point as an instructor of infantry tactics and a professor of geography, history, and ethics; after a four-year stint in Texas, he returned to the East, married, and became superintendent of the cavalry school in Carlisle Barracks, Pennsylvania. In 1859, he produced a skirmish drill manual for mounted troops; the next year, he was appointed assistant adjutant-general of the Department of New Mexico, and it is there the Civil War broke upon him. Immediately upon hearing of Virginia's secession, Maury resigned his commission, bade a tearful farewell to his friends, and returned to the East again; this was at Santa Fe in the first weeks of May 1861. On June 25, he was informed he had been dismissed from the service, "it having

been ascertained to the satisfaction of the War Department that he entertained and had expressed treasonable designs." By that time, Maury had already secured a position as captain of cavalry in the Confederate army, more than amply proving to any military court where his loyalties had to rest.

By early 1862, Dabney Maury was a colonel and an aide to General Earl Van Dorn, commander of the Trans-Mississippi Department. On March 7 and 8, Maury was involved in the fighting at the Battle of Pea Ridge, Arkansas; for his bravery, he was made a brigadier general and was praised by Van Dorn as a courageous patriot.

For gallant service in the Battles of Iuka, Corinth, and Hatchie Bridge, Maury was promoted to major general on November 4, 1862; at Corinth, he attacked the Federal enemy with such force that he drove them through and out of the town, then harrassed them all through the later retreat. In July 1863, Maury was appointed commander of the district of the Gulf, taking command at Mobile; he defended the Gulf with all his capacity until the close of the war, when he was compelled to yield to overwhelming odds against him.

If such bravery were rewarded by fate, Dabney Maury would have spent the remaining years of his life in calm, plentiful retirement. But after the defeat of the Confederacy, Maury found his personal fortune gone, and the one thing for which he was best suited—military service—was denied to him as having been branded a traitor along with the rest of his Confederate comrades. He taught in various schools for a few years, then went into business on his own; during a yellow fever epidemic in New Orleans, he closed his business at a loss and volunteered as a nurse in the overcrowded hospitals of the city.

Maury was the founder in 1868 of the Southern Historical Society and a frequent contributor to their publication. He also wrote copiously, out of an apparent desire to keep the record straight. He published a history of Virginia for young people and wrote a witty, charming memoir entitled *Recollections of a Virginian* published in 1894. He was one of the organizers of the famed Westmoreland Club of Richmond, a band of famous Confederate Veterans who met for a while at 707 East Franklin Street—famed as the wartime residence of the Robert E. Lee family. Never one to forget his beloved army, Maury spearheaded a drive to improve the training and preparation of volunteer troops; he was also a member of the National Guard Association's executive committee for nearly 15 years. In the mid to late 1880s, Maury served his country once more, as minister to Colombia; offered a position as superintendent of the drawings of the infamous Louisiana Lottery, with a handsome salary, Maury refused the position as a matter of principle and was proven right when the lottery turned out to be an unmitigated disaster in which many Southerners lost all they had left.

Shortly after the turn of 1899, Dabney Maury passed away peacefully at the home of his son in Peoria, Illinois. He is buried in the Confederate Cemetery in Fredericksburg, Virginia, the town of his birth.

McClellan, George Brinton

1826–1885

"Just don't let them hurry me" may well have been the motto of the general hailed as the "Young Napoleon" at the beginning of the Civil War. Unwilling to take an aggressive approach and lead his men into battle, McClellan missed several opportunities to crush the enemy in the early stages of the war.

At first, McClellan appeared to be the best and the brightest of the Union army. Born into a wealthy Philadelphia family, McClellan earned high honors at the University of Pennsylvania in 1842. At the age of 16, he entered West Point and graduated second in the class of 1846, which voted him "most likely to succeed." Upon graduation, he was appointed brevet second lieutenant in the engineer corps and sent to the Mexican War. He distinguished

himself at the Battles of Malan, Camargo, Tampico, and Vera Cruz; his performance at the battle of Cerro Gordo won him a brevet second lieutenant on April 24, 1847. "Gallant and meritorious conduct" at Churubusco and Chapultepec earned him the rank of captain.

From 1848 until 1852, he taught practical engineering at West Point, then was transferred to the West for another two years. In the spring of 1855, he was sent on a military commission to Europe to report on operations in the Crimean War; his report, *The Armies of Europe*, was published in 1861. Shortly after his return, McClellan resigned his commission and became a civil engineer in the railroad industry.

When the Civil War began, he was made major general of the Ohio Volunteers, commanding the Department of the Ohio. By the end of May 1861, he and his troops had pushed the Confederates out of western Virginia as far as the Alleghenies, in essence carving out the new pro-Union state of West Virginia. For his efforts, McClellan was made major general in the Regular army.

After First Bull Run, Lincoln called him to Washington and gave him command of what would soon be known as the Army of the Potomac. Although he appeared to have all the attributes of a great leader, including an aura of success emanating from his victories in Virginia, McClellan also had an alienating air of self-importance about him. When he received his command, he wrote to his wife, "Who should have thought, when we were married, that I should so soon be called on to save my country?"

In addition to his arrogance, McClellan had his politics: he was a Democrat—a War Democrat to be sure, but certainly opposed to Lincoln's Republican approach to the war. His politics put him up against many of his superiors, especially Secretary of War William Stanton.

McClellan devoted the summer of 1861 to organizing and training the army, spending eight hours or more a day drilling the men. Instilling discipline in his troops appeared to be his main objective: "Let an honest pride be felt in pos-

Major General George McClellan

sessing that high virtue of a soldier, *obedience*," he wrote. His men, who had been humiliated at First Bull Run, came to adore their strong and optimistic commander. Despite having successfully prepared and equipped his 110,000-man army, McClellan refused to move against the Confederates at Manassas Junction and continue "on to Richmond." Claiming that the Confederates outnumbered him by tens of thousands, when in fact he had almost twice

their strength, McClellan insisted he would not advance until he had at least 270,000 men. Whether McClellan truly believed himself outnumbered or whether he was, in fact, timid to the point of cowardice, remains a matter of debate. In any case, Lincoln denied him his request and strongly urged him to take action.

Although disturbed by the 34-year-old general's hesitancy, Lincoln remained confident enough in McClellan's abilities to promote him to general-in-chief of all the federal armies after Winfield Scott retired in October. On January 27, 1862, Lincoln issued McClellan a direct command to advance through a document known as the President's General War Orders No. 1, issued on January 27, 1862. It took McClellan another two months, but he finally embarked on his brilliantly planned but poorly executed Peninsula campaign. His continued reluctance to seize the initiative allowed his superior army to be stopped by a much smaller Confederate force.

Despite winning several victories during Robert E. Lee's Seven Days campaign, McClellan was still convinced that the enemy outnumbered him and chose to retreat back to the Potomac by the end of July 1862. Frustrated with "Young Napoleon," as McClellan became known, Lincoln replaced him with Henry Halleck as general-in-chief, gave John Pope command of all Federal troops north and west of Virginia, and left McClellan in command, under Pope, of only the Army of the Potomac.

Just one month later, however, McClellan was back in charge after Pope was humiliated at Second Bull Run on September 1. As he had after First Bull Run, McClellan spent crucial weeks reorganizing his demoralized troops; then, instead of moving quickly to stop Lee's first invasion of the North, McClellan moved with typical caution, enabling forces under Stonewall Jackson to capture the Union garrison at Harpers Ferry in time to join Lee at Antietam. In fact, had Lee's battle orders not fallen into McClellan's hands in August, Lee's plan to capture Harrisburg, Pennsylvania, may have succeeded. Instead, McClellan forced a bloody showdown at Antietam on September

17, 1862. At the end of the day, when a final push against Lee may have completely crushed the rebel army, McClellan once again hesitated.

On October 1, Lincoln traveled to Sharpsburg to urge his commander to take the initiative. Later, he would make his request a direct order. Still, McClellan hung back. Finally, after nearly a month of inaction, Lincoln relieved McClellan of both commands, and the former golden boy of Lincoln's army retreated into civilian life.

Unable to fight on the battlefield, McClellan took up politics, where his charm and self-confidence appealed to many in his Democratic party, who nominated him for president in the Election of 1864. Confederate Vice-President Alexander Stephens saw McClellan's candidacy as the "first ray of real light since the war began," as did many others in the South, but McClellan lost the election to Lincoln in a near-landslide.

Immediately following his defeat, he left on a three-year trip to Europe. He returned to the United States and reentered politics, serving as governor of New Jersey for one term in 1878. After leaving office, he resumed his work as an engineer. In 1887, he published *McClellan's Own Story*, a defense of his tactics during the war. He died on October 29, 1885.

McLean, Wilmer

(dates unknown)

As one of the Civil War's noteworthy bystanders, McLean, in whose Appomattox Court House, Virginia, home Robert E. Lee surrendered to Ulysses S. Grant, could say without much exaggeration, "The war began in my front yard and ended in my front parlor."

In June 1861, the McLean family estates "Yorkshire," located near Manassas Junction on the banks of Bull Run, was in the path of the war's first major campaign. Confererederate soldiers built defensive works in McLean's fields, while commanding General Pierre G. T. Beau-

regard used the family home as his headquarters, querying McLean about the terrrain. During the First Bull Run, June 21, 1861, a shell tore through the kitchen while Beauregard was having his breakfast. That taste of war was sufficient fot the McLeans, who moved to a two-story brick house in the small village of Appomattox, southwest of Richmond, where they hoped they would remain far from the conflict. For nearly four years, they did indeed enjoy relative peace.

But on the morning of April 9, 1865, McLean was approached in the street by an aide to Lee, who was seeking a location where the generals would meet to discuss surrender terms. An abandoned building that McLean suggested was judged unacceptable, so McLean reluctantly showed the officer his own ohome.

Arrangements were quickly made; Lee arrived first, Grant appeared soon after, and the meeting transpired over the next three hours in McLean's living room. Once the geneals departed, officers and other onlookers descended on the room, bargaining for the furniture and bric-a-brac. They filched souvenirs when McLean angrily refused money and ripped apart the heavier objects to grab a piece of history.

McPherson, James Birdseye

1828–1864

Perhaps the most able Union soldier never to hold independent command, McPherson was instrumental in the Union victories at Forts Henry and Donelson, the Battle of Shiloh, during the Vicksburg campaign, and during William T. Sherman's Atlanta campaign, until he met his death on the battlefield at the age of 35.

Handsome, brilliant, and with easy good humor, McPherson was also one of the most well-liked men in the Union army. First in the West Point class of 1853, McPherson spent the beginning of his military career as a professor of engineering at his alma mater. When war broke out, his first assignment as a member of the

Wilmer McLean's historic house.

Corps of Engineers involved improving Union harbors and seacoast fortifications; his success earned him promotion to captain on August 6, 1861.

For a short time, he served as an aide to Henry W. Halleck, then was transferred to Ulysses S. Grant's command in Tennessee as a lieutenant colonel. McPherson's top-notch engineering skills impressed the general. He gained Grant's trust by informing him of rumors perpetuated by Halleck and others pertaining to Grant's drinking habits. Grant's faith in McPherson was well-rewarded during the next several months, as he assisted in the captures of Forts Henry and Donelson, at the Battle of Shiloh, and the siege of Corinth.

On May 1, 1862, McPherson was promoted to brigadier general; two months later, he rose to the rank of major general. In January 1863, just as Grant began to plan his Vicksburg campaign, McPherson was appointed commander of the 17th Corps in Grant's army. His skills as an engineer were in great demand as Grant realized the technical feat required to maneuver an army through the swamps and bayous of Mississippi. Once engaged in battle, McPherson's bravery and leadership were equally appreciated. His corps played particularly important roles in the capture of Raymond and Champions' Hill in May 1863.

When Sherman succeeded Grant as head of the Union forces in the West in March 1864, Abraham Lincoln put McPherson into Sherman's former position as commander of the

34,000-man Army of the Tennessee. McPherson and his army then played an important role in Sherman's Atlanta campaign. McPherson was particularly adept at accomplishing flanking maneuvers designed to crush the Confederate defensive lines. Although he was beaten back while attempting to stop Joseph E. Johnston's retreat at Snake Creek Gap, he succeeded in several other attempts.

His last battle took place on July 22, 1864. Attempting to maneuver around Confederate General John B. Hood's troops, McPherson and his men were ambushed by a surprise counterattack. In the confusion of the battle, McPherson, trying to cross from one column to another, instead rode into enemy lines, where he was killed by Confederate infantry. Sherman, it is reported, wept openly at the news of the brave young soldier's death.

Meade, George Gordon

1815–1872

Once referred to by his men as "a damned goggle-eyed old snapping turtle," the ill-tempered George Meade replaced Joseph Hooker as commander of the Army of the Potomac on June 28, 1863, just in time to lead it into battle at Gettysburg.

George Meade was born in Cadiz, Spain, where his father was a naval agent for the United States government. The Meade family moved back to the United States when Meade was about three years old; he received his education in Philadelphia and Washington. On September 1, 1831, he entered West Point and graduated in the top third of his class four years later. He resigned from the army a year after graduation in order to become a civil engineer. He reentered the army in 1842 as a second lieutenant in the Corps of Topographical Engineers and spent much of the following four years surveying various military sites, including Delaware Bay.

During the Mexican War, he was connected with the staff of General Zachary Taylor and saw action at Palo Alto and Resaca de la Palma. His first service of note took place at the Battle of Monterey, during which he led the advance on Independence Hill and earned himself a brevet first lieutenant. Serving under General Winfield Scott, Meade also participated at the Battle of Vera Cruz. Upon his return to the United States, Meade resumed his survey work for the Corps of Topographical Engineers. In 1851, he was sent to the Florida reefs,

Major General James Birdseye McPherson

General George G. Meade

where he was engaged for five years in lighthouse construction, and in 1856 he was made captain of the corps conducting the geodetic survey of the Northern Lakes. At the opening of the Civil War, Meade was appointed brigadier general of volunteers in command of the 2nd Brigade of Pennsylvania reserves; as he gained in command and battle experience, he rose steadily in the military ranks.

In 1862, he saw action at Mechanicsville, Gaines' Mills, and White Oak Swamp. In the latter battle, Meade was badly wounded and was forced to leave the army for a number of weeks. After a short period of recovery, Meade returned in time to lead his brigade in the battle of Second Bull Run; by the Battle of Antietam, less than a month later, he was in command of the whole division.

On November 29, 1862, he was made major general of volunteers in command of the 5th Corps. As its leader, he participated in the Battle of Chancellorsville on May 4, 1863, under Joseph Hooker. The badly injured Hooker seriously misused Meade's forces, pulling them back just as they assumed a strong position, but his men acquitted themselves well under the circumstances. At the close of the battle, which had been a surprising and devastating defeat for the Union, Hooker demurred in pursuing the Confederate army under Robert E. Lee, pleading to Lincoln for more troops.

Impatient with the lack of aggression displayed by yet another commander of the Army of the Potomac, Abraham Lincoln replaced Hooker with Meade, who had proved himself a dependable and capable leader. Unfortunately for Meade, Lee was attempting to consolidate his victory at Chancellorsville with a second northern invasion; it was now up to the irascible general to stop him. Just five days after he took command of the army, Meade faced the enemy at Gettysburg from July 1 to 3, 1863, the deadliest battle of the war. The Union managed to drive back the Confederate advance, but at great cost—more than a quarter of Meade's men had been injured or killed. Perhaps devastated by his losses and overestimating the strength of his equally devastated enemy, Meade, like his predecessors at the head of Lincoln's army, failed to pursue the retreating Confederates aggressively. Nevertheless, Meade received a citation from Congress and was promoted to brigadier general in the Regular army on July 3, 1863.

During the summer and fall, Meade stayed close to Lee along the Rapidan Ring, planning to retake the ground between the Rapidan and the Rappahannock. Realizing the odds were against him, Lee withdrew south of the Rapidan on November 10, 1863, without a major battle. On November 26, Meade planned another offensive, this one aimed at Lee's right flank at Mine Run. His advance was slow, due largely to the ineffectiveness of his corps commander, William French. The languid pace gave Lee time to reinforce and extend his line, making an attack against the Confederates futile. Instead, Meade ordered his men to fall back. Although Meade was probably correct to avoid a battle he could not win, he again appeared to lack the battle-readiness necessary to defeat the tenacious Southerners.

Disappointed in Meade's performance, Lin-coln promoted General Ulysses S. Grant to lieutenant general in charge of all the Union forces shortly after the Mine Run operation. Although Meade offered to resign, both Lincoln and Grant insisted he remain as commander of the Army of the Potomac. Grant would, however, move with Meade's army and, as his superior, largely control its actions. Throughout the rest of the war, Meade remained in Grant's shadow, carrying out his orders effectively and apparently without complaint.

On August 18, 1864, he was promoted to major general in the Regular army. Present at the Confederate surrender at Appomattox Court House, Meade was overjoyed at the war's end. Elisha Rhodes, a soldier from Rhode Island, described Meade as riding "like mad down the road with his hat off shouting 'the war is over and we are going home.'"

After the war, Meade commanded successively the Department of the East, the Military District of Georgia, and the Military Division of the Atlantic. He died of pneumonia, which was aggravated by the old war wounds received at White Oak Swamp, on November 6, 1872.

Medal of Honor, the Congressional

The first military decoration formally authorized by the American government to be worn as a badge of honor, the Medal of Honor was created by an act of Congress in December 1861. Senator James W. Grimes of Iowa, the chairman of the Senate Naval Committee, proposed that a medal of honor, similar to the Victoria Cross of England and the Iron Cross of Germany, be given to naval personnel for acts of bravery in action. His bill was passed by both Houses of Congress and approved by President Abraham Lincoln on December 21, 1861. It established a Medal of Honor for enlisted men of the United States Navy and Marine Corps.

Two months later, Senator Henry Wilson of Massachusetts introduced a Senate resolution extending eligibility for the medal to enlisted men of the U.S. Army and making eligibility retroactive to the beginning of the war. On March 3, 1863, army officers were made eligible through another act of Congress; naval and marine officers were not included until 1915.

According to the act establishing the army medal, the award was to be given to those members of the armed forces who "shall distinguish themselves by their gallantry in action, and other soldierlike qualities." Because of the act's vague wording and because the United States gave no other medal to its armed services, the Medal of Honor was awarded liberally during the Civil War to about 1,200 men.

The first to receive medals were the six survivors of Andrew's Raid. In 1916, Congress considerably tightened the rules for eligibility, requiring that a serviceman come into actual contact with an enemy and perform bravely at the risk of his own life above and beyond the call of duty. Congress also created a board of five retired generals to review all previous award recipients for eligibility and found that about 911—most of them Civil War veterans—did not meet the new standards and thus struck them from the list.

Medical Care, Battle Wounds and Disease

The Civil War was fought, claimed the Union army surgeon general, "at the end of the medical Middle Ages." Little was known about what caused disease, how to stop it from spreading, or how to cure it. Surgical techniques ranged from the barbaric to the barely competent.

A Civil War soldier's chances of not surviving the war was about one in four. These fallen men were cared for by a woefully underqualified, understaffed, and undersupplied medical corps. Working against incredible odds, however, the medical corps increased in size, improved its techniques, and gained a greater understanding of medicine and disease every year the war was fought.

During the period just before the Civil War, a physician received minimal training. Nearly all the older doctors served as apprentices in lieu of formal education. Even those who had attended one of the few medical schools were poorly trained. In Europe, four-year medical schools were common, laboratory training was widespread, and a greater understanding of disease and infection existed. The average medical student in the United States, on the other hand, trained for two years or less, received practically no clinical experience, and was given virtually no laboratory instruction. Harvard University, for instance, did not own a single stethoscope or microscope until after the war.

When the war began, the Federal army had a total of about 98 medical officers, the Confederacy just 24. By 1865, some 13,000 Union doctors had served in the field and in the hospitals; in the Confederacy, about 4,000 medical officers and an unknown number of volunteers treated war casualties. In both the North and South, these men were assisted by thousands of women who donated their time and energy to help the wounded. It is estimated that more than 4,000 women served as nurses in Union hospitals; Confederate women contributed much to the effort as well.

Although Civil War doctors were commonly referred to as "butchers" by their patients and the press, they managed to treat more than 10 million cases of injury and illness in just 48 months and most did it with as much compassion and competency as possible. Poet Walt Whitman, who served as a volunteer in Union army hospitals, had great respect for the hardworking physicians, claiming that "All but a few are excellent men...."

Approximately 620,000 men—360,000 Northerners and 260,000 Southerners—died in the four-year conflict, a figure that tops the total fatalities of all other wars in which America has fought. Of these numbers, approximately 110,000 Union and 94,000 Confederate men died of wounds received in battle. Every effort was made to treat wounded men within 48 hours; most primary care was administered at

Ambulance wagons and drivers.

field hospitals located far behind the front lines. Those who survived were then transported by unreliable and overcrowded ambulances—two-wheeled carts or four-wheeled wagons—to army hospitals located in nearby cities and towns.

The most common Civil War small arms ammunition was the dreadful minié ball, which tore an enormous wound on impact: it was so heavy that an abdominal or head wound was almost always fatal, and a hit to an extremity usually shattered any bone encountered. In addition, bullets carried dirt and germs into the wound that often caused infection.

Of the approximately 175,000 wounds to the extremities received among Federal troops, about 30,000 led to amputation; roughly the same proportion occurred in the Confederacy. One witness described a common surgeon's

tent this way: "Tables about breast high had been erected upon which the screaming victims were having legs and arms cut off. The surgeons and their assistants, stripped to the waist and bespattered with blood, stood around, some holding the poor fellows while others, armed with long, bloody knives and saws, cut and sawed away with frightful rapidity, throwing the mangled limbs on a pile nearby as soon as removed."

Contrary to popular myth, most amputees did not experience the surgery without anesthetic. Ample doses of chloroform were administered beforehand; the screams heard were usually from soldiers just informed that they would lose a limb or who were witness to the plight of other soldiers under the knife.

Those who survived their wounds and surgeries still had another hurdle, however: the

Wards like this one at Harewood Hospital in Washington, D.C. were filled with wounded and diseased soldiers.

high risk of infection. While most surgeons were aware of a relationship between cleanliness and low infection rates, they did not know how to sterilize their equipment. Due to a frequent shortage of water, surgeons often went days without washing their hands or instruments, thereby passing germs from one patient to another as he treated them. The resulting vicious infections, commonly known as "surgical fevers," are believed to have been caused largely by *Staphylococcus aureus* and *Streptococcus pyogenes*, bacterial cells which generate pus, destroy tissue, and release deadly toxins into the bloodstream. Gangrene, the rotting away of flesh caused by the obstruction of blood

flow, was also common after surgery. Despite these fearful odds, nearly 75 percent of the amputees survived.

While the average soldier believed the bullet was his most nefarious foe, disease was the biggest killer of the war. Of the Federal dead, roughly three out of five died of disease, and of the Confederate, perhaps two out of three. One of the reasons for the high rates of disease was the slipshod recruiting process that allowed under- or over-age men and those in noticeably poor health to join the armies on both sides, especially in the first year of the war. In fact, by late 1862, some 200,000 recruits originally accepted for service were judged physically unfit and discharged, either because they had fallen ill or because a routine examination revealed their frail condition.

About half of the deaths from disease during the Civil War were caused by intestinal disorders, mainly typhoid fever, diarrhea, and dysentery. The remainder died from pneumonia and tuberculosis. Camps populated by young soldiers who had never before been exposed to a large variety of common contagious diseases were plagued by outbreaks of measles, chicken-pox, mumps, and whooping cough.

The culprit in most cases of wartime illness, however, was the shocking filth of the army camp itself. An inspector in late 1861 found most Federal camps "littered with refuse, food, and other rubbish, sometimes in an offensive state of decomposition; slops deposited in pits within the camp limits or thrown out of broadcast; heaps of manure and offal close to the camp." As a result, bacteria and viruses spread through the camp like wildfire. Bowel disorders constituted the soldiers' most common complaint. The Union army reported that more than 995 out of every 1,000 men eventually contracted chronic diarrhea or dysentery during the war; the Confederates fared no better.

Typhoid fever was even more devastating. Perhaps one-quarter of noncombat deaths in the Confederacy resulted from this disease, caused by the consumption of food or water contaminated by *salmonella* bacteria. Epidemics of malaria spread through camps located next to stagnant swamps teeming with *anopheles* mosquito. Although treatment with quinine reduced fatalities, malaria nevertheless struck approximately one quarter of all servicemen; the Union army alone reported one million cases of it during the course of the war. Poor diet and exposure to the elements only added to the burden. A simple cold often developed into pneumonia, which was the third leading killer disease of the war, after typhoid and dysentery.

Throughout the war, both the South and the North struggled to improve the level of medical care given to their men. In many ways, their efforts assisted in the birth of modern medicine in the United States. More complete records on medical and surgical activities were kept during the war than ever before, doctors became more adept at surgery and at the use of anesthesia, and perhaps most importantly, a greater understanding of the relationship between cleanliness, diet, and disease was gained not only by the medical establishment but by the public at large. Another important advance took place in the field of nursing, where respect for the role of women in medicine rose considerably among both doctors and patients.

Mexican War

1846–1848

This two-year war over 525,000 square miles of territory laid the groundwork for the Civil War in several respects. First, Texas, the largest acquisition of land since the Louisiana Purchase, revived the nation's political and moral debate over slavery. Second, the battlefields of Mexico proved excellent training ground for many soldiers and generals who would later fight in the Civil War.

The roots of the Mexican War date back to the early 1820s, when the Mexican government granted permission to Stephen Austin, an American citizen, to settle its sparsely populated northern territories. Within a decade, more than 30,000 Americans—many of them slave owners—called the territory home, outnumbering Mexican residents four to one.

The Mexican government attempted to regain control of the land by enacting laws that abolished slavery and controlled the number of weapons brought in by the Americans. These and other invasive measures were met with an armed insurrection led by Sam Houston, an American frontiersman and politician. After the settlers won a decisive victory at San Jacinto on April 26, 1836, the Mexican government agreed to grant independence to the new Republic of Texas. The size of the territory was in dispute, however, with Texas claiming the

General Scott entering Mexico.

Rio Grande as its southwestern border and the Mexicans limiting it to the Nueces River.

For about three years, the future of the new republic remained unsettled. In the United States, Southerners saw its acquisition as a way to gain the upper hand in the ongoing fight with Northern states for political power: below the 36° 30' parallel designated as the boundary for slavery in the Missouri Compromise and with slaveholders already residing in the territory, Texas would certainly come into the Union as a slave state.

Equally important was a growing sense of "manifest destiny," the feeling among many Americans that the country had a kind of divine right to expand its territory on the continent. President James Polk, a Southerner from Virginia, attained congressional approval for the annexation of Texas on March 1, 1845; it was formally admitted into the Union on December 29, 1845. In the meantime, Polk attempted to secure the disputed territory for the United States as well as acquire additional land (California and New Mexico) from the Mexican government. In November 1845, he sent an emissary to Mexico City with an offer to purchase the new land for about $30 million, an offer that was immediately rejected.

Relations between the two countries continued to deteriorate. Matters were brought to a head when Polk ordered Major General Zachary Taylor, who was stationed with about 4,000 men on the Nueces River, to advance to the Rio Grande. Taylor reached the river in April 1846.

On April 25, a party of Mexican soldiers surprised and defeated American cavalry just north of the Rio Grande. The news of the battle provoked Congress to declare war on Mexico on May 13, 1846.

The ensuing conflict pitched a well-equipped, well-trained but relatively small American army against large numbers of underfed, poorly armed Mexicans. Although in unfamiliar territory and greatly outnumbered in nearly every battle, American forces under Taylor and, in 1847, General Winfield Scott, eventually outfought their spirited opponents led by the indomitable president of Mexico, Antonio López de Santa Anna. Thousands of American soldiers who later fought on both sides of the Civil War participated in the conquest, including Ulysses S. Grant, William T. Sherman, George B. McClellan, George Meade, Robert E. Lee, Thomas "Stonewall" Jackson, and Confederate President Jefferson Davis.

The Mexican War ended after American forces, victorious at the fierce battle of Chapultepec, occupied Mexico City on September 14, 1847. For months, however, the Mexican government refused to negotiate a peace treaty until a new president ready to compromise replaced the intransigent Santa Anna. On February 2, 1848, the Treaty of Guadalupe Hidalgo ceded to the United States more than 525,000 square miles of territory, which would eventually comprise the states of California, Nevada, and Utah, most of Arizona, and New Mexico, and parts of Colorado and Wyoming.

The question of whether these territories would become slave or free states caused great controversy in the U.S. Congress. The South believed its survival was, in part, contingent upon the spread of slavery throughout the West; without this proliferation, the South would find itself at the mercy of Northern senators. The issue was resolved, however temporarily, with the Compromise of 1850.

Minié Ball

The development of this half-inch lead rifle bullet revolutionized warfare, while the slowness of Civil War military leaders to adapt their tactics to adjust to the new technology was greatly responsible for the overwhelming number of battlefield deaths.

Before the introduction of what soldiers commonly called the "minnie ball"—even though it was indeed bullet-shaped—the use of rifles in battle was impractical and largely limited to corps of elite marksmen. Expensive, tight-fitting projectiles had to be jammed into the grooves of the rifle's muzzle, a time-consuming process.

In 1848, however, French army Captain Claude F. Minié created a smaller, hollow-based bullet that could far more quickly and easily be rammed into the bore, expanding when the weapon was fired to catch in the rifling and be shot spinning out of the barrel. That spin made the minié ball, like other, more expensive and unwieldy rifle bullets, a highly precise and far-traveling projectile. They could reach half-a-mile or more, and an average soldier could easily hit a target 250 yards away.

By 1855, Harpers Ferry Armory worker James H. Burton had honed an even cheaper version of the minié ball, which, along with the rifle itself, soon became widely used in the U.S. Army. It was the standard bullet for both sides in the Civil War, although neither anticipated the enormous difference this would make on the battlefield. Against a defensive line using musket fire—requiring a 25-second reloading period and accurate to only 50 feet or less—a frontal infantry charge was likely to be successful if the assaulting force moved quickly enough.

The widespread use of the minié bullet, however, shifted the balance greatly to the defense's favor. Nevertheless, Civil War generals continued ordering such attacks, learning only after hard and bloody battlefield experience—from the assault on Marye's Heights at Fredericksburg to Pickett's Charge at Gettysburg—that their strategy would have to be altered.

The ordinance abolishing slavery in Missouri, formally nullifying the Missouri Compromise of 1820.

Missouri Compromise

1820

For more than three decades following the ratification of the U.S. Constitution in 1783, the issue of slavery remained largely uncontroversial. The Northwest Ordinance, enacted in 1787, provided that all territories north of the Ohio River were to be free and those south were to be slave; so far, the process of settlement and organization had proceeded smoothly.

Following the Louisiana Purchase of 1803, the United States expanded quickly into western territory. By 1819, nine new states had been added, bringing the total to 22, of which half were slave and half were free. However, of the land that remained unsettled west of the Mississippi, only Louisiana (which had been admitted as a slave state in 1812) and the Arkansas Territory would allow slavery if the rules outlined in the 1787 ordinance were obeyed.

The first crisis arose in 1819, when Missouri requested admittance to the Union as a slave state. As most of the territory lay above the Ohio River, such an action would require nullification of the Northwest Ordinance. Moreover, it would create an imbalance in the U.S.

Senate, with slave states gaining a majority for the first time. Luckily, the newly formed territory of Maine requested admittance—as a free state—at about the same time.

In an attempt to solve not only the immediate crisis but to provide a framework for coping with the conflicts that could arise as more states were created, members of Congress, led by the brilliant Henry Clay, negotiated the Missouri Compromise. Broken down into three parts, each of which was voted on and passed separately, the Missouri Compromise succeeded in admitting Missouri as a slave state, admitting Maine as a free state, and nullifying the Northwest Ordinance by redefining the boundaries of slavery from north of the Ohio River to north of the 36° 30' parallel.

In addition to offering a practical answer to the question of slavery in the territories—which satisfied both sides of the issue for three decades—the Missouri Compromise implicitly gave to the federal government the power to decide such issues, a power many people did not agree it had. "To compromise," wrote North Carolina Senator Nathaniel Macon, "is to acknowledge the right of Congress to interfere and to legislate on the subject [of slavery], this would be acknowledging too much." Indeed, in many ways, the balance of power between individual states and the federal government would become as important in the development of the Civil War as the question of slavery itself.

Mobile Bay, Battle of

AUGUST 5, 1864

This naval engagement determined the fate of the Confederacy's last major open Gulf port east of Texas. While the Union blockade was in place elsewhere, Alabama's Mobile Bay became a center for the receipt of critically needed provisions smuggled into the South from Europe. U.S. Rear Admiral David G. Farragut wanted to try taking the port after he captured New Or-

leans in April 1862, but he was not able to begin his preparations until January 1864.

After more than half a year of planning, Farragut's fleet of 14 wooden ships and four ironclads began its attack shortly after dawn on August 5, entering the bay's heavily mined main channel at 6 A.M., with the monitors in front. The Confederates started firing as the Union boats approached the bay's main defense, Fort Morgan. Leading a flotilla of three small, wooden gunboats and the CSS *Tennessee*—the South's largest ironclad—Confederate Admiral Franklin Buchanan commanded the defensive naval forces against an attack for which he had prepared for two years.

Farragut had himself lashed to the mast of his flagship, the *Hartford*, so he could better direct his forces, and watched as his lead ironclad, the *Tecumseh*, struck a mine. Blown out of the water, the ship sank in minutes with most of its crew. The Federal fleet halted in alarm as the firing continued from Fort Morgan, until Farragut's famous command, "Damn the torpedoes! Full speed ahead." Moving the *Hartford* in front, the Union admiral led his fleet through the minefield with no additional sinkings and past the fort into the bay.

The *Tennessee*, with Buchanan aboard, attempted to ram the Union ships, then traded fire with the vessels before taking refuge at Fort Morgan. While the Union crews began taking the opportunity to have some breakfast, Buchanan pulled the *Tennessee* out from the fort for another attack. The Confederate ironclad, imposing but unwieldy, was quickly surrounded by Federal boats and fired on and rammed repeatedly. Soon adrift and helpless, with commander Buchanan himself seriously wounded, the *Tennessee* surrendered at approximately 10 A.M., and the battle was over.

Union forces, which totaled nearly 3,000, suffered 319 casualties; of the 470 Confederates engaged, there were 312 casualties, most taken as prisoner. The Union navy now effectively controlled Mobile Bay for the remainder of the war, although Fort Morgan was not captured until August 23, and the city of Mobile itself, 30 miles to the north, remained in Confederate

The USS Monitor *and the CSS* Merrimack *(renamed the CSS* Virginia*) at war.*

control until the following April—three days, in fact, after Lee surrendered.

The *Monitor* vs. the *Merrimack* (CSS *Virginia*)

MARCH 8, 1862

Ushering in a revolution in sea combat, the single, inconclusive March 1862 encounter between the Union and the Confederacy's first ironclads was perhaps the most sensational naval battle of the Civil War.

The *Merrimack* (sometimes spelled without the "k") had been one of the U.S. Navy's finest wood steam frigates before Northern forces scuttled it when they were forced to abandon the Norfolk shipyards one week after the fall of Fort Sumter. Salvaging the wreck in the summer of 1861, Confederate engineers bolted 2- to 4-inch-thick armor plates on the hull and deck,

constructed casemate ports for ten guns, and fitted a cast-iron ram to the prow. Most of the peculiar-looking vessel was submerged, with the exposed portion sloped on a 35 degree angle to increase the chances that enemy shells would simply ricochet off its sides. Slow and unwieldy, too unseaworthy for ocean service yet with too deep a draft for shallow rivers, it was still a fearsome craft that could outmatch any wooden ship that came against it.

Reports of the refashioned *Merrimack*, renamed the CSS *Virginia*, drifted north and compelled the Union navy to hasten its own efforts at building an ironclad. The renowned Swedish-American inventor, John Ericsson, who had been tinkering with armored vessel designs for 20 years, developed a unique new ship for the North, protected by four and one half inches of iron plating, with two guns mounted on an innovative revolving turret. Smaller, swifter, and more maneuverable than the *Merrimack*, the *Monitor*, also mostly submerged, was an even odder-looking vessel, described as resembling a "cheesebox on a raft."

Construction was completed in a remarkable

101 days, beating the South's ironclad to the launching slip, and on March 4, 1862, the *Monitor* was towed out of Brooklyn, New York, to join the Federal blockading squadrons off the Carolina coast.

The CSS *Virginia* (though it often remains better known by its former name), was launched at Norfolk Shipyard on March 5. Its crew thinking they were on a trial run, the Confederate ship headed right for battle at Hampton Roads, Virginia, a channel off Newport News at the entrance of the Chesapeake Bay that was a major Union blockading base.

At about 1 P.M. on March 8, the *Virginia* confronted a fleet of five wooden Federal ships. Enemy broadsides bounced off the ironclad as it rammed and sank the *Cumberland*, the Union's mightiest frigate, ran aground and burned the 50-gun *Congress*, and incapacitated the huge flagship *Minnesota* before withdrawing for the night. The Union navy would not suffer such great losses again until the World War II attack on Pearl Harbor. Though its ram had broken off in the fighting and its captain, Franklin Buchanan, had been wounded, the *Virginia* was little damaged, poised to destroy the rest of the Hampton Roads fleet and then to go on and threaten the entire Union blockade.

The *Monitor*'s hasty arrival in the channel at 1 A.M. on March 9 did not initially calm the mounting panic in Washington, D.C. Nearly sinking on its voyage south, the Union vessel seemed barely able to float, let alone fight. But in battle, the *Monitor* proved an equal match to the *Virginia*. Only 100 yards apart, the two ironclads began a furious four-hour duel at 9 A.M. that morning, pounding out artillery fire that scarcely made a dent and colliding several times, both accidentally and in unsuccessful attempts to ram each other. Neither ship could gain the advantage, and when the *Monitor* pulled back after its captain, John L. Worden, was temporarily blinded by a shell blast, the *Virginia*, beginning to leak and have engine problems, withdrew.

The first battle in history between ironclads ended in a draw, though the Union blockade at Hampton Roads held and the North's fears of losing its naval superiority were allayed. Still, the Confederacy proved it could mount a formidable challenge to the Union fleet, as both sides acknowledged the obvious superiority of armored ships and hurried to build more.

The *Monitor* and the *Virginia*, however, never confronted each other again—neither, in fact, remained afloat for long. On May 11, little more than two months after the *Virginia* was launched, the Confederates blew up their pioneer ironclad in Norfolk harbor to prevent its seizure by Union forces that had captured the port. And on December 31, the *Monitor* sank in a storm off the coast of Cape Hatteras, North Carolina.

Morgan's Raids

OCTOBER 1862–JULY 1863

Confederate Brigadier General John Hunt Morgan's three spectacular cavalry raids in Kentucky and Tennessee so disrupted the Union army in the west that President Abraham Lincoln himself sent an urgent missive to commander Henry W. Halleck: "They are having a stampede in Kentucky. Please look to it."

John Hunt Morgan—the epitome of a cavalry commander sitting straight, tall, and fearless in the saddle—had served in the Mexican War but otherwise had no professional military training. He began his Civil War service as captain, incorporating the Lexington Rifles, a local militia he had organized in 1857, into the Confederate effort when the war began. By the end of 1862, he had been made a brigadier general in command of the 2nd Kentucky Cavalry and was serving under Major General Joseph Wheeler in the western theater.

Morgan's first raid undermined Union Major General Don Carlos Buell's attempts to capture Chattanooga, Tennessee. From July 4 to August 1, 1862, he and his men covered more than 1,000 miles, captured more than 1,200 prisoners, and destroyed several Union supply depots along the way. Morgan himself lost just 100 men.

Three months later, after serving under General Braxton Bragg during his Kentucky campaign, the clever horseman and his unit joined Lieutenant General Kirby Smith as he attempted to retreat from Kentucky while under fire from pursuing Union troops. With 1,800 men, he circled eastward, captured Lexington, Kentucky, and destroyed Union transportation and communication lines before returning to Tennessee at the beginning of November.

Morgan's third raid, also known as his "Christmas Raid," was designed to help Bragg counter Union Major General William S. Rosecrans' advance through Tennessee. After organizing a division of two brigades totalling about 4,000 men, Morgan headed north from Alexandria, Tennessee, on December 21, 1862, to raid Rosecrans' lines of communication and supply.

Brigadier General John H. Morgan

Riding through Glasgow and Bardstown, he reached the Louisville & Nashville Railroad and followed it to Rolling Fork, near Elizabethtown, capturing the town and severing Rosecrans' lines.

By this time, the Union army had tracked the cavalrymen and were preparing to attack them as they headed back to Confederate lines. Morgan, realizing the danger, made his escape during the night with minimal loss of life, returning to camp on January 2, 1863. In just over a week, he and his men managed to destroy more than two million dollars worth of Union property and capture about 1,900 troops.

Morgan's final raid took place during July 1863. While his commander, Braxton Bragg, had directed him merely to slow Rosecrans' advance on Chattanooga, Morgan instead invaded Ohio. He hoped that a show of Confederate strength would raise support for the Southern cause among Yankees who were both tired of the war and sympathetic in some manner to the South. Although he did inflict damage on the Union supply lines, this raid appeared to more like a reckless adventure than a well-planned offensive.

On July 2, Morgan managed to elude more than 10,000 Union troops and took about 2,500 men across the Cumberland River. Wreaking his usual havoc on his way north, he joined in several skirmishes with Federals while completing the longest continuous march of the war, covering 90 miles in just 35 hours.

On the afternoon of July 13, he arrived in Harrison, Ohio, with a reduced force of 2,000 and with the Union already planning his capture. Indeed, his men had already captured 6,000 men, mobilized thousands of Union troops, destroyed 25 bridges, and demolished scores of railroads. By July 18, however, Morgan began to encounter serious enemy action; the next day, he was badly beaten by forces under Union Brigadier General Edward H. Hobson at Buffington Island. Supported by militia and gunboats, the Union troops managed to devastate Morgan's crew, killing about 120 and capturing another 700.

Morgan himself managed to escape with about 300 men and made a desperate effort to reach Pennsylvania. Hobson pursued relentlessly, finally capturing the wily horseman on July 26, at New Lisbon. Morgan and his raiders were then imprisoned in the Ohio State Penitentiary. Remarkably, Morgan was able to escape, although he was killed just about a month later during a cavalry encounter at Greeneville, Tennessee, on September 3, 1864.

Mormons in the Civil War

The Mormons, a religious group living primarily in the American West around Utah at the time of the Civil War, were not actively involved in the secession crisis back East. Having come out of what they considered to be the "sinful, fleshly world" to follow their charismatic young leaders Joseph Smith and Brigham Young, the Mormons established what they hoped would be a New Jerusalem in a land set aside for them by God. They believed that the Native Americans were the lost tribe of Israel and moved west to be with them. At this time in their development the Mormons practiced polygamy, the taking of more than one wife in marriage. They believed such marriages were legally binding, though the territorial law of the United States did not agree.

By coincidence, the Mormons provided an opportunity for the up and coming young men of the U.S. Army to practice for what would become the all encompassing Civil War. Between 1857 and 1860, the Mormons were the focus of a great deal of military activity as a sizeable force under the command of Colonel Albert Sidney Johnston was sent to prevent Smith's followers from taking control of sections of Nevada and Utah—with every intent of seceding from the Union and forming their own nation. Soldiers whose names would be emblazoned on the annals of the Civil War had to confront many of the same issues they would be dealing with on a national scale very soon: the right of a state or territory to disalign itself from the government if its needs and preferences were not being met or respected; the level to which the government ought to be allowed to gain involvement in the religious, civil and legal customs of a state or territory, and at what point armed intervention can go before the local citizenry exercises the right of self-defense.

Just a small sampling of names from the expedition's rosters is sufficient to indicate the men to whom these formerly abstract concepts became daily reality under fire: Philip St. George Cooke, father-in-law of Jeb Stuart; G. W. Custis and William H. F. "Rooney" Lee, sons of Robert E. Lee; Fitz-John Porter; Stephen Dill Lee; and John Bell Hood.

Once these men and their comrades were involved in their own secession war in the East, the Mormons found themselves being left largely alone, save for being under the watchful eye of the few U.S. troops left in the territories during the period of 1861 to 1865. Dedicated to the preservation of their way of life and beliefs, the Mormons passed the ongoing years in peaceful, even friendly relations with the Native American population of their area. They eventually put aside some of the more extreme practices of their faith and distilled Joseph Smith's teachings down to an essential kernel of belief that has sustained them in the twentieth century.

Mosby's Rangers

Numbering about 800 at its greatest strength, this corps of partisan rangers sabotaged Union efforts in northern and western Virginia so successfully that historians believe they prolonged the life of the Confederacy for more than a year.

Formed in December 1862 by Confederate cavalry commander Jeb Stuart, the Rangers were made up of men on leave from army units, convalescents, and civilians unwilling to enlist in the Confederate army. Leading the men was the clever and fearless John Mosby (1833–1916). A diminutive man of just 125 pounds, Mosby had fought in the cavalry corps at First Bull

Run, then joined Stuart's cavalry as a scout; Mosby originated the idea for Stuart's ride around Major General George B. McClellan's Union army during the Peninsula campaign. An impetuous, independent man—he became an attorney by studying for the law while in prison for shooting a fellow student at the University of Virginia—Mosby chafed under strict army rules.

After the Confederate Congress authorized the organization of partisan bands through the 1862 Partisan Ranger Act, Mosby convinced Stuart to give him an independent command. Mosby's Rangers operated from private homes and individual camps in western Virginia and only met as a group when Mosby called them together. Their military techniques were equally unconventional. They usually attacked in small groups in the dead of night, carried Colt .44 revolvers rather than swords or rifles, and more than once kidnapped Union officers and enlisted men after waking them from a sound sleep.

On March 8, 1863, Mosby and 29 of his men managed to capture Brigadier General Edwin Stoughton, two captains, and 30 enlisted men in the middle of the night in Fairfax Court House, Virginia. In addition, they also managed to garner 58 horses from the raid, the loss of which apparently upset Union President Abraham Lincoln more than the lost personnel. "I can make new brigadier generals," Lincoln remarked, "but I can't make new horses."

For the most part, Mosby's Rangers focused

Clash between Union soldiers and Mosby's Rangers.

on attacking Union trains and supply depots, destroying them after appropriating their contents. In the summer of 1863, as Robert E. Lee made his second invasion of the North after his victory at Chancellorsville, Mosby and his men followed, undermining Union efforts to mount an effective counterattack. On June 10, shortly after hearing they had been officially designated the 43rd Battalion of Partisan Rangers, Mosby and his men rode into Maryland and burned a Union camp at Seneca Mills to the ground. "Mosby is an old rat and has a great many holes," wrote one of the many Union soldiers trying to put an end to the costly war of attrition Mosby was waging.

By August 1863, at least two prominent cavalry companies—the 2nd Massachusetts and the 13th New York—were ordered to pursue the clever horsemen on a full-time basis, but Mosby's Rangers remained elusive. In fact, just before and during Philip Henry Sheridan's Shenandoah Valley campaign of 1864–1865, the Rangers reached their peak in terms of manpower, activity, and effectiveness. On July 6, 1864, Mosby's guerrillas swooped down upon a camp at Mount Zion Church, killing 40 Union cavalrymen and taking about 60 others prisoner. Their attack several days later at Fairfax Station achieved nearly the same results, as did another outside of Falls Church a few weeks after that. In late summer, Robert E. Lee noted that during the previous six months alone, Mosby and his men had killed, wounded, or captured 1,200 Federals and had taken more than 1,600 horses and mules, 230 head of cattle, and 85 wagons.

During the fall of 1864, Mosby's Rangers continued to wreak havoc by upsetting Union plans to repair the vital Orange & Alexandria rail line at Manassas. The Rangers derailed trains, tore up tracks, and shot construction workers, so terrorizing Union forces that Secretary of War Edwin Stanton ordered that every house within five miles of the tracks be burned unless its owner was "known to be friendly." The threat was carried out, but the guerrillas continued their activities.

During the fall of 1864, Sheridan ordered Captain Richard Blazer to recruit 100 men and,

equipping them with repeating rifles, led them on a search-and-destroy mission against Mosby's band. The "Gray Ghost," as Mosby was known, outmaneuvered Blazer on November 18; during a surprise attack, the Rangers killed or wounded all but two of Blazer's men and captured their weapons.

By the spring of 1865, the clever horsemen controlled a vast stretch of land between the Potomac and the Rappahannock known by friend and enemy alike as "Mosby's Confederacy." Hardly a day went by without a Ranger attack; even after word reached them of Lee's April 9, 1865, surrender at Appomattox Court House, they continued to fight in the mountains.

After General Joseph E. Johnston's surrender about two weeks later, however, Mosby called his partisans together and urged them to surrender. Mosby, who had been wounded seven times during the course of the war, returned to Warrenton, Virginia, and practiced law until his death on May 30, 1916.

Murfreesboro, Battle of

DECEMBER 31, 1862–JANUARY 2, 1863

The close of the war's first full year brought action at last on the Tennessee front between Confederate defender Braxton Bragg and his Union opponent William S. Rosecrans. After several days of impending attack, both generals curiously enough came to nearly exact conclusions: it was the last day of the year, they must make some sort of demonstration, and it would be to fling the left extreme of their line against the right flank of the enemy. Bragg, however, put his plan into motion while Rosecrans was still trying to feel his way; just after dawn William Hardee sent his corps smashing into the Union right. This set what would be the Federal standard for the day, as Rosecrans' forces remained essentially on the defensive throughout the fighting.

As each Confederate move was made, a mir-

Sheridan's Union forces at Murfreesboro.

ror maneuver was enacted on the Union side to attempt to counter it; the Federals fell back to the difficult position of trying to hold the turnpike which ran between Murfreesboro and Nashville, with Stone's River at their back— never a good tactical position in which to find oneself, but worse in the dead of winter with the water high and cold. Constantly under attack from the cavalry under General Joseph Wheeler, and knowing he was in a daunting position, Rosecrans ordered the assault abandoned and concentrated his line on the turnpike. The fighting continued without conclusion until well into the afternoon; the Federals held on stubbornly, inflicting heavy casualties on the Confederates.

By the end of the day, the two armies settled in for a long, cold night, each expecting to continue in the morning. In one of the more poignant incidents of the war, a military band on one side began to play "Home, Sweet Home." As the notes sounded across the cold ground that had been a killing field in the daylight, a band on the opposing side joined in to play along in the darkness. In the silence that followed the tune, the two armies caught what little sleep they could almost within sight of one another on the field of battle.

The Confederates used the darkness to entrench; the Federal commanders met in an attempt to design a new strategy. After much discussion, it was decided they would remain

Rebel soldiers of the 9th Mississippi Infantry at Murfreesboro.

and fight it out. Curiously enough, however, as the new day and new year dawned, almost nothing of a military nature occurred; there were occasional sporadic outbreaks of firing, and once or twice a brief artillery duel, but neither army came forward on the muddy ground to offer battle.

It was not until the early morning hours of January 2, 1863, that anything substantive happened—and that turned out to be very gallant, very bloody, and tactically pointless. Confederate John C. Breckinridge led his men to take a hill to the northeast of Stone's River, which they did with accompanying high casualties, only to be attacked in force and pushed back by superior strength bolstered by a shattering ar-

tillery barrage. The two armies did nothing more for the rest of the day, but sat back to contemplate their heavy losses: between wounded, killed or missing, the Federal forces had been depleted by almost 13,000 out of over 40,000; the Confederates suffered nearly 12,000 out of 35,000 men lost or no longer able to fight.

There was a brief attack the following day, January 3, as the Federals demonstrated against Bragg's lines near the river, but very little came of it, and there was no return to the general conflict. The Federals were astounded but gratified when, for no reason they could see, Bragg withdrew his forces from Murfreesboro along the Manchester Turnpike for the next day or so. Rosecrans moved his men into the town on

January 5, 1863, and was wired by Abraham Lincoln that he had the admiration and congratulations of his country for the victory. Two weeks later, on January 21, Braxton Bragg discovered what his country thought of him for his curious retreat: President Jefferson Davis sent General Joseph E. Johnston to investigate the Army of Tennessee's commander, looking into reasons he had for abandoning Murfreesboro, and to see if there was any substance to criticisms of Bragg that had reached Richmond. Bragg would not be relieved of command, but Davis' confidence in him was seriously impaired for a long time to come.

N

Nashville, Battle of

DECEMBER 15–16, 1864

The Confederate Army of Tennessee under John Bell Hood was crushed after a two-day on-slaught by George Henry Thomas' Union troops outside Nashville in December 1864, a decisive clash that ended the major fighting in the Civil War's western theater.

Fresh from the catastrophic November 30 de-feat at Franklin, 75 miles south of the state cap-ital, Hood refused to abandon his quixotic invasion of Tennessee, still irrationally hoping his army could retake the state, collect rein-forcements, and mount new assaults on Union forces in Virginia and the Ohio Valley. Also thinking that a retreat would invite large-scale desertion, the undaunted Confederate com-mander ordered his demoralized troops—one quarter of whom were marching barefoot—for-ward toward Nashville. There, they faced a Union force twice as large as their own—Thomas' 30,000 troops, sent earlier by William T. Sherman to ward off the Confederate ad-vance, joined by John Schofield's equally large army that had just come up from Franklin.

Occupying the Tennessee capital since early 1862, the Union military had already turned the city into a near-impenetrable fortress. By the time Hood's army arrived in the hills a few miles south on December 2, there was little the Confederates could do either to dislodge or pass the enemy. With far too few troops for an effec-tive siege or a direct assault, and unable to ad-vance around the city without exposing their rear and flank, the Southerners dug in and formed a wide defensive line, hoping for rein-forcements and waiting for Thomas' attack.

Recognizing his adversary's dire position, the methodical Union commander took his time preparing his army's offensive. Back in Virginia, Ulysses S. Grant was livid at the delay. Overestimating Hood and underestimating Thomas, the Union general-in-chief feared that the Army of Tennessee was poised to prolong the nearly concluded war by invading Northern territory and wired several urgent messages to Nashville ordering an immediate attack. Thomas ignored the directives as he waited for a heavy sleet storm to pass, while Grant headed to Tennessee to relieve the general and take charge of the operation himself.

Before he arrived, Thomas struck at last. On the morning of December 15, three Union corps began hammering the Confederate left while an ancillary infantry and cavalry attack kept Southern troops busy at the other end of the line. Barely holding on until sundown, Hood's army finally fell back two miles that night to a new defensive position extending between two hills.

Thomas did not know whether the Confeder-

1st Tennessee Colored Battery on its way to Nashville, November 23, 1864.

ates had retreated altogether in the dark and waited until the following afternoon to mount a renewed assault. Hood's troops were able to repel a charge on Overton Hill to their right, but by 4 P.M. his entire left flank was virtually surrounded by Union infantry, cavalry, and artillery. Smashing suddenly through the line with astonishing force as a hard rain fell, the Northerners utterly routed the Confederate army. Nearly an entire division—cannon and

all—was captured as hundreds of Southern troops surrendered, while others abandoned their weapons and supplies to flee more quickly.

Followed closely by Union horsemen, the splintered remnants of the Army of Tennessee continued retreating for the next two weeks all the way to Mississippi, covered in the rear by Nathan Bedford Forrest's fighting cavalry. For such a conclusive battle, the casualties were surprisingly light—fewer than 400 Federals killed and about 1,500 Confederates killed or wounded. But with its twin defeats at Franklin and Nashville and its subsequent headlong retreat, John Bell Hood's army was demolished.

In January 1865, the general resigned a command that had all but ceased to exist, while most of his surviving troops were sent back into combat in the East to stem Sherman's unstoppable advance through the Carolinas.

Native Americans in the Civil War

Despite decades of scholarship, many misperceptions persist concerning the Civil War. The war is often viewed, for example, as solely a white man's war; it is also often thought to have taken place solely in the East and South. Modern historians are attempting to dispel these notions, both of which serve to obscure the participation of Native Americans in the Civil War.

During the period of 1861 to 1865, Native Americans all over the continent were struggling for autonomy, as peoples with their own organization, culture, and life-style. Some tribes, like the Cherokees, were directly involved in the war. Other Native Americans living in the war-torn areas of the East made individual decisions as to whether they wished to have anything to do with the situation. Still others, living in the mountains, prairies, and deserts of the rest of the country, suddenly realized they had a chance to take back some of their own land, as they saw fewer and fewer U.S. Army soldiers assigned to forts in their tribal areas.

Statistics show that just under 3,600 Native Americans served in the Union Army during the war. Perhaps the best known of their number was Colonel Ely Parker, who served as an aide to General U. S. Grant, and was present at Robert E. Lee's surrender at Appomattox Court House. Statistics for the Confederacy are not re-

liably available, but most scholars of Native American involvement in the actual fighting of the war are very well acquainted with the major Southern figure among them: Brigadier General Chief Stand Watie, a three-quarter blood Cherokee who was born in December 1806 near what

Chippewa agent, Hole-in-the-Day.

would become Rome, Georgia. Stand Watie was one of the signers of a treaty that agreed to the removal of the Cherokee from their home in Georgia to what was then the Oklahoma territory; this split the tribes into two factions, and Stand Watie became the leader of the minority party.

At the outbreak of the Civil War, the minority party gave its allegiance to the Confederacy, while the majority party went for the North. Watie organized a company, then a regiment known as the First Cherokee Mounted Rifles; the regiment fought at Wilson's Creek, Elk-horn, and in numerous smaller fights and skirmishes along the border with what was known as Indian Territory. The warriors found curious the white man's strategy of standing still and allowing people to shoot at them, or lob artillery shells at them; the Cherokee tended to be spectacular at wildly brave mounted charges, but once the artillery began to fire, the warriors wanted nothing to do with it. Stand Watie was unreconstructed to the end; it is believed he never surrendered until June 23, 1865, well after other Confederate commanders had given up. He died in 1871 and is buried in the Old

Wounded Native American sharpshooters on Mayre's Heights near Fredericksburg.

Ridge Cemetery in Delaware County, Oklahoma.

While the war was raging back East, out in the West things were seldom quiet or peaceful. Statistics show that nearly 90 engagements were fought by U.S. troops in the West during the war, most of them involving Native American tribespeople. From January to May 1863, there were almost continuous fights in the New Mexico territory, as part of a concerted effort by the Federal government to contain and control the Apache; in the midst of all this, Abraham Lincoln met with representatives from several major tribes, and informed them he felt they would never attain the prosperity of the white race unless they turned to farming as a way of life.

In July 1864, there was fighting against Native Americans in Minnesota; fighting continued throughout the year in New Mexico, as well. Then in November, on the twenty-ninth, there occurred what some historians have called the first major blot of the so-called Indian Wars: the Sand Creek Massacre. Frightened by raids made by warriors in the area around Denver as a result of a reduced military presence in the West, Colorado settlers asked Colonel J. M. Chivington to punish the raiders. Chivington, with 900 volunteer militiamen, attacked a peaceful village of some five hundred or more Arapaho and Cheyenne natives, killing women and children as well as warriors. In his report, Chivington chillingly stated: "It may perhaps be unnecessary for me to state that I captured no prisoners."

Some of the people escaped, however, and at least one of them was pursued by irony in the years to come: Chief Black Kettle of the Cheyenne survived the massacre at Sand Creek, only to die at the hands of George Armstrong Custer's 7th Cavalry in a second attack on a peaceful village some three years later, at a place called the Washita River.

After the Civil War, the white presence in the West rose to new levels. Numerous financial crises and depressions hit the East after the boom of the war years, and many families chose to move onward in hopes of finding gold, or purchasing cheap land to start a farm. Men unable to find work in the cities joined the army. As the tribal peoples fought to defend their sacred places, hunting grounds, and even their very way of life, they attacked crews building railroads and sought to drive off hunters and gold prospectors. Conflicting views of what ownership of the land meant, as well as numerous other cultural misunderstandings, led to bloodbath after bloodbath; at Little Big Horn and Beecher's Island, the tribes defeated the white man, only to be battered into defeat themselves at places like Wounded Knee. The official army policy was to provide necessities for the tribes during the winter, then to face the reality of fighting the same people when the weather cleared and they wished to change hunting grounds; this policy was known ironically to the common soldier as "feed 'em in winter, fight 'em in summer."

The unofficial government policy, however, was summed up curtly by General Philip Sheridan, the man who in 1864 stated he would so devastate the Shenandoah Valley, breadbasket of the Confederacy, that a crow flying through it would have to "carry his own rations." Sheridan, appointed to command of one of the major administrative departments of the territories in the years after the war, made the now-infamous statement: "The only good Indian I ever saw was dead." With an attitude such as this, it was only a matter of time and attrition before the Native Americans saw their way of life taken from them—not forever, though, as the descendants of those who fought to save the Way are even today striving to bring back the old knowledge and customs.

Navy

Both the Federal and Confederate navies played crucial roles in the Civil War; the Union blockade and naval operations in the western theater were at least as important to the Northern victory as its successful land war. Moreover, the technical and strategic advances made

Gunboat USS Mendota.

by both sides during the period effectively ush- ered in the era of modern warfare at sea.

When the Civil War began, neither the Union nor the Confederacy had strong naval capabili- ties. The Union had just 90 ships, half of which were out of commission. Its 1,500 officers and 75,000 enlisted men were scattered around the globe; more than 10 percent of its officers would resign to join the Confederacy. Another Union loss to the Confederacy near the begin- ning of the war was the Norfolk Navy Yard on April 20–21, 1861. However, with its vast in- dustrial and financial resources, the Union quickly established a naval force powerful enough to devastate the South.

At the beginning of the war, the Confederate navy consisted of just 10 ships and 15 guns, and it would struggle throughout the war to main- tain its ranks at full strength. At the time of the Civil War, the world's navies were just making the transition from sail to steam and from wooden ships to ironclads. To compensate for its dearth of resources, the Confederate navy at- tempted to appropriate some of these new tech- nologies. The South was the first to build an ironclad, to experiment with submarine tech- nology, and to use torpedoes during battle (at Yorktown, Virginia, May 1862).

Without question, the major naval operation of the war, for both sides, was the Northern blockade of Southern ports. Under orders from U.S. Navy Secretary Gideon Welles, the Union concentrated its force along the Southern coast in order to strangle the Confederate government economically. David Farragut's capture of New Orleans on April 25, 1862, solidified Union control of the seas. In turn, most of the South's scant naval resources were devoted to efforts at circumventing the blockade; in fact, Confederate Secretary of the Navy Stephen Mallory was criticized for spending too much time and money on building blockade runners and in conducting raids on Northern shipping, neither of which did much damage to the blockade in the end. In fact, the North's foreign trade actually increased between 1861 and 1865, while the South's barely survived.

Second in importance only to the blockade were U.S. naval operations on the western rivers. With their potent firepower, Union gunboats helped to capture Fort Henry, Fort Donelson, and Vicksburg, thereby providing secure arteries for moving Union men and matériel across an otherwise impenetrable landscape of lowland mire.

The number of successful combined navy-army operations was limited, however, largely due to lack of a proper chain of command and cooperation between the two branches of the service. In addition, naval commanders, convinced of the ironclads' invincibility, often underestimated the need for the army's help to subdue the enemy. By the end of the war, due to its vast technical and industrial advances, the U.S. Navy had become one of the most powerful forces in the world, with more than 600 ships and 50,000 men.

New Orleans, Battle of

APRIL 25, 1862

David Farragut's impressive April 1862 naval victory placed the Confederacy's largest city and most vital port in the hands of the Union. A hundred miles above the mouth of the Mississippi, New Orleans was the gateway to the great river and to the entire deep South, and its capture could almost divide the Confederacy in two. Military actions elsewhere left the city itself lightly defended, dependent on the protection of Forts Jackson and St. Philip, which guarded the river approach 75 miles downstream. But the garrisons were heavily fortified, and a barricade of hulks in the water stalled vessels right in front of their heavy guns.

With Union naval commander David Porter arguing that sustained mortar fire from boats on the river would disable the forts and allow a fleet of ships to pass all the way to New Orleans, preparations were begun for the attempt in early 1862. Army General Benjamin Butler captured Ship Island near the mouth of the Mississippi, where David Farragut, squadron captain and Porter's adopted brother, gathered 24 wooden sloops and gunboats, along with Porter's 19 mortar schooners. After delays to make the vessels light enough to pass over the many sand bars, Farragut's fleet started ascending the river in April, supported by 15,000 troops under Butler for possible land battle.

On April 18, Porter commenced a six-day barrage of cannon fire on the two forts, an incessant bombardment of over 3,000 shells a day that did more to rattle Union crews with the constant pounding than to weaken the Confederate defenses. Perhaps distracted by the shelling, however, the Southerners did not seem to notice when two Federal gunboats approached the river barricade on the night of April 20 and cleared a small passageway through. With Porter's bombardment making little impact, Farragut ordered his fleet to proceed anyway. Hidden by the dark, the boats started their audacious run at 2 A.M. on April 24.

Cannon fire from the forts, answered by Union shelling from the river, quickly lit up the sky in a dazzling nighttime fireworks display. Their two nearby ironclads not yet fully operational, the Confederates launched a small squadron of wooden ships to ram the Federal boats and sent rafts set ablaze to impede the advance. Farragut's flagship, the *Hartford*, caught fire and ran aground, but was afloat again shortly as the Union fleet proceeded to sink or disable the enemy vessels. After an hour and a half of pounding battle, all but four of Farragut's

Battle of New Orleans.

boats managed to pass the Confederate forts, despite some heavy damage and nearly 170 men killed or injured.

On April 25, Farragut steamed into New Orleans, defended now only by angry pistol-bearing citizens, and captured the city without further combat, though the mayor refused to formally surrender. Butler's troops arrived on April 29, beginning their harsh occupation, while the day before, Forts Jackson and St. Philip, whose disheartened soldiers had begun to mutiny, surrendered, too.

It was a disastrous defeat for the South. Although the Union did not yet control the entire Mississippi, the entrance to the waterway that bisected the Confederacy and served as its life-line would remain cut off for the rest of the war.

New York Draft Riots

JULY 11–13, 1863

"The nation is at this time in a state of Revolution, North, South, East and West," wrote the editor of the Washington *Times* during the of-

Confederate outer works. The structures in the left background, chevaux-de-frise, are made of sharpened stakes and used as infantry obstacles.

few years of the war, won spectacular battles at Second Bull Run, Fredericksburg, and Chancellorsville.

Lee's second failed northern invasion, which culminated in the Battle of Gettysburg at the beginning of July 1863, marked the turning point for the army and the Confederacy. The Wilderness campaign of the following spring decimated the Confederate troops; in one month, the army lost more than 30,000 on the battlefield, while disease and desertion took thousands more. By the time Lee surrendered at Appomattox Court House on April 9, 1865, the once-mighty Army of Northern Virginia numbered just 28,000 hungry, poorly clad soldiers, exhausted after three years of brutal war.

O

Orphan Brigade

Declared one of the best brigades in the army by top Confederate command, this Confederate unit of 4,000 hard-fighting Kentucky men earned its odd nickname because it originated in Kentucky, which remained a Union state throughout the war. The 1st Kentucky Brigade trained and organized in Tennessee, then defended their home state against Union general Ulysses S. Grant's offensive during the winter of 1862. In fact, the 1st Kentucky Brigade fought on its native soil for the last time in February, when Grant succeeded in pushing the Confederate army out of Kentucky. After being absorbed into the Army of Tennessee, the brigade fought at several major Civil War battles, including Shiloh, Corinth, Vicksburg, Chickamauga, and throughout the Atlanta campaign. By the time the brigade surrendered at Washington, Georgia, in May 1865, its original members numbered just 500.

P

Pacifists

Thousands of citizens in both the North and South, mostly members of pacifist churches, objected to the Civil War on moral and/or religious grounds. In the nineteenth century, a number of so-called "peace churches," most prominently the Society of Friends (Quakers), with over 200,000 members, but also sects like the Mennonites, Shakers, and Dunkers, were thriving in America. With resolute tenets advocating nonviolence, they denied the obligation of military service. These beliefs were shared as well by individual members of churches without a pacifist canon, along with secular organizations like the New England Non-Resistance Society and utopian communities scattered across the country.

Because Quakers and other pacifists were among the most committed abolitionists, the Civil War created a moral dilemma for them, especially after Lincoln's 1862 Emancipation Proclamation made the eradication of Confederate slavery a war policy. Abolitionist leader William Lloyd Garrison, for one, who before the war had opposed the use of military force to achieve emancipation, guardedly supported Lincoln and the Union case. There were even a few dozen peace church members of military age who, facing reproach from their sects, volunteered for the army on both sides.

Other Confederate and Union pacifists alike engaged in nonmilitary work, including service in hospitals and industry; Northerners were often especially eager to teach and work with free blacks. Still, there were large numbers of conscientious objectors who opposed any kind of participation—including payment of taxes—in the war effort, and encountered vocal, even violent, hostility toward their beliefs. The New England writer Henry David Thoreau was jailed for nonpayment of his taxes during the war, and was harassed by his community.

When conscription of soldiers was introduced in both the North and South, pacifists faced further pressures. The Union's draft laws did exempt conscientious objectors from combat, but required alternative service or an exemption fee. Pacifist groups denounced those conditions, even when Secretary of War Edwin Stanton promised that their payments would be earmarked for an education fund for emancipated slaves.

Conscientious objectors remained subject to arrest and seizure of their property in some Northern communities, but the federal government routinely worked to release those who could prove membership in a peace church. Harder pressed for soldiers, the Confederate government tended to be less sympathetic to pacifists. Quaker lobbyists did get the Conscription laws amended to allow nonservice options for peace church members, although those provisions were largely ignored as the war situation grew more desperate.

On both sides, pacifists unable or unwilling to buy their exemption found themselves in uniform. Sometimes deserting, sometimes simply refusing to take up arms, they created problems in the ranks. Although none was executed, rebellious pacifist soldiers were given punishments ranging from bread-and-water diets and sleep deprivation to beatings and assaults by bayonets. Regimental officers tended to come down hardest on conscientious objectors, while their superiors had took a more balanced approach. Recognizing that pacifists did not make good soldiers, most commanding generals simply wanted to send them home.

Parker, Ely

1828–1895

The highest ranking Native American officer in the Union army, Parker was present at the surrender of Robert E. Lee as a member of Ulysses S. Grant's staff.

Parker was a full-blooded Seneca, born on a tribal reservation in New York. Although he had studied law, Parker was refused admittance to his home state's bar because he was not officially an American citizen. He then earned an engineering degree from Rennselaer Polytechnic Institute in Troy, New York.

When the Civil War began, Parker was denied a commission in both the Union army and the New York state militia. In 1863, the army, now desperate enough for capable personnel to overcome its prejudice, reconsidered, and Parker was appointed division engineer under Brigadier General John Smith.

While serving at Vicksburg, he became reacquainted with Ulysses S. Grant, whom he knew before the war, and joined Grant's staff during the 1864 Petersburg campaign as his military secretary with the rank of lieutenant colonel. Parker, despite his position, was not spared in-

Lieutenant Colonel Ely Parker

sult in the army, often referred to contemptuously by his fellow officers as "the Indian."

At the April 9, 1865, meeting between Grant and Lee at Appomattox Court House, he was responsible for transcribing the terms of surrender. The Confederate commander, according to witnesses, seemed startled by Parker's presence, evidently mistaking the dark-skinned Native American as a black man. Once he learned that Parker was a Seneca, Lee commented, "I am glad to see one real American here." Parker's reply, famous in Civil War lore, was, "We are all Americans."

Continuing to serve on Grant's staff after the

war, Parker became his aide-de-camp in 1867. As president, in a bold but controversial move, Grant appointed him Commissioner of Indian Affairs in 1869, a position that no Native American had ever previously held. Parker's tenure was a troubled one, however, as his department was plagued by corruption. A congressional investigation cleared Parker himself of any wrongdoing, but he was nevertheless compelled to resign. Suffering a series of setbacks in his subsequent business career, Parker died destitute in 1895.

Partisans

Confederate guerrilla activity, designed to terrorize and undermine Union troops and operations, occurred almost from the beginning of the war and increased as the months and years of bloodshed dragged on. Fighting on their home turf, these army irregulars knew every mountain pass and path in the area and could strike suddenly at unsuspecting Union troops. Sometimes they attacked in small bands of just five or ten, sometimes in groups of several hundred. Their targets ranged from wagon trains and supply depots to Union outposts and camps.

Smoldering railroad iron, the work of Confederate partisans.

In April 1862, the Confederate Congress, perhaps realizing that the Confederates could not win the war with the Regular army alone, enacted the Partisan Ranger Law. Calling for the formal organization of companies, battalions, and regiments of partisans, the Ranger Law entitled partisans to receive the same rations and allowances as regular soldiers. In addition, guerrillas would be paid the full value of any arms or ammunition they managed to capture from the enemy.

Partisan forces fought in both the Eastern and Western theaters. In the East, such clever and generally honorable men such as John Mosby, J. H. MacNeil, and Harry Gilmore fought a war of attrition against Ulysses S. Grant and Philip Sheridan. In the West the partisan fight, as led by William Clarke Quantrill, Bill Anderson, and George Todd, was distinctly more vicious. Quantrill, a former gambler and horsethief, and his men rampaged along the border of Kentucky and Missouri, robbing Union mails, ambushing Federal patrols, attacking boats on the Missouri River, and frequently murdering civilians they deemed disloyal to the Confederate cause. On August 25, 1863, Quantrill and about 300 others swept down upon the town of Lawrence, Kansas, and slaughtered 17 Federal recruits and at least 150 Union civilians.

Apart from such blatant brutality, guerrilla warfare against the Union army was quite effective. In February 1863, Abraham Lincoln wrote, "In no other way does the enemy give us so much trouble, at so little expense to himself, as by the raids of rapidly moving small bodies of troops (largely, if not wholly, mounted), harassing and discouraging local residents, supplying themselves with provisions . . . and breaking our communications." The Confederate Congress repealed the Partisan Ranger Law in 1864, partly because of Quantrill's scourge at Lawrence and partly because partisans engendered jealousy among troops in the Regular army.

Partisans enjoyed relative freedom from military restrictions; living away from camp, they avoided most of the tedium experienced by Regular soldiers. In addition, their exploits—tricky maneuvers only possible if performed by a small group of men—soon became legendary. Despite the law's repeal, the Confederate secretary of war was authorized to allow certain bands to continue at his discretion, including Mosby and others in the Eastern theater.

Peace Democrats

The Peace Democrats were a vocal group within the Democratic party who were opposed to saving the Union through military force. One of their supporters was Clement Vallandigham, one of the so-called Copperheads. The Peace Democrats wanted the swiftest possible end to the Civil War by means of peace conferences between the two opposing governments.

In the months leading up to the 1864 election, the Peace Democrats were successful in getting their party to agree to a "peace plank," or peace proposal, into the platform on which the party candidates would run for election; this plank stated that "immediate efforts be made for a cessation of hostilities," and detailed some of the means by which they would seek this result if elected.

The Democratic candidate for the presidency was General George B. McClellan; when he accepted the nomination of his party on September 8, 1864, he insisted that "the Union is the one condition of peace." He refused to agree to the peace plank unless it stipulated that any peace proposal should include the country being reunited. The Peace Democrats were split over this issue, some strongly believing that the war should end regardless of the cost, while others were just as insistent that the Confederacy not be recognized as an independent nation by any means but be made to rejoin the Union.

Ultimately, their platform would fail, very likely because of the split in policy; Abraham Lincoln would be reelected in November 1864, and the war would continue toward a military resolution that was still another six months away.

Pemberton, John Clifford

1814–1881

The man who was forced to surrender the Confederate stronghold of Vicksburg on July 4, 1863, was a Northerner by birth. Despite his heritage, however, Pemberton fought hard and well for the Confederate cause; his failure at Vicksburg was due more to the conflicting orders he received from his commanders, President Jefferson Davis and Joseph E. Johnston, than poor generalship on his part.

Pemberton was born into a family populated largely by antislavery, antiwar activists, including his father, who was a Quaker minister. Somehow drawn to the military in spite of his family's pacifism, his application to West Point was successful in large part because of a long-standing friendship between his father and President Andrew Jackson.

Pemberton graduated in 1833, twenty-seventh in his class of 50. Appointed second lieutenant and assigned to the 4th Artillery, he first served in the Seminole War in Florida from 1837 to 1839, then performed garrison duty until the opening of the Mexican War. Twice brevetted for gallantry at Monterey and Molino del Rey, Pemberton had advanced to the rank of major by the end of the war. His longheld pro-Southern and pro-states' rights opinions were further solidified upon his 1848 marriage to Martha Thompson, the daughter of a wealthy Virginia family.

On April 24, 1861, he resigned from the army to accept Jefferson Davis' offer of a brigadier general's commission. His first assignment was as commander of the relatively minor Department of South Carolina, Georgia, and Florida. Earning two promotions, one to major general and the second to lieutenant general, he remained in the post until October 14, when he

was given command of the Department of Mississippi and Louisiana.

Considering his reportedly less than inspiring personality and lack of command experience, some military historians see this appointment as one of "Jefferson Davis' major mistakes." With approximately 40,000 men, Pemberton faced the armies of Ulysses S. Grant and William Tecumseh Sherman, who were determined to capture the city of Vicksburg, thereby opening the Mississippi River to the North and cutting the Confederacy in half. In the winter of 1862, Pemberton's first advance stopped Grant at the Battle of Chickasaw Bluffs, during which the Federal army lost some 1,700 men.

Grant embarked upon a new approach in the spring, and Pemberton received contradicting sets of orders from his commanding officers in response to the renewed offensive. Joseph E. Johnston wanted Pemberton to abandon the city and save his army, while Jefferson Davis ordered Pemberton to hold the city at all costs. On May 14, Johnston sent word to Pemberton to come northeast and join him at Jackson, where he hoped they could defeat Grant together. Instead, Pemberton tried to stay close to Vicksburg and fight Grant from there. Just east of the city, Grant brought him to battle at Champion's Hill on May 16, beat him badly, and forced him back into Vicksburg with about 30,000 Confederates.

On May 22, the two-and-half month long siege of Vicksburg began. Pemberton watched his men grow ever more hungry and exhausted as Grant tightened his line around the city, cutting off communication and supplies. Finally, on July 3, Pemberton reluctantly gave the city over to the Federals, claiming that it would be "an act of cruel inhumanity to subject [the troops] any longer to the terrible ordeal."

Hoping to win easier terms of surrender, Pemberton shocked many Southerners by agreeing to allow the Union to declare victory on the national holiday of July 4. Some accused Pemberton of treason, pointing to his Northern roots as further proof of his disloyalty, but no formal charges were ever brought. Pemberton's men were indeed allowed to resign from the

General John C. Pemberton discussing the terms of surrender with Grant at Vicksburg.

army and return home rather than face Federal imprisonment.

Following the surrender of Vicksburg, no command could be given Pemberton commensurate with his rank; he therefore resigned and accepted appointment as a colonel of artillery. At the end of the war, he settled for a time at Warrenton, Virginia, but finally returned to his home state of Pennsylvania, where he died on July 13, 1881.

Peninsula Campaign

MARCH–AUGUST 1862

The direct approach to the Confederate capital having failed at First Bull Run, commander-in-chief of the Federal armies, George B. McClellan, planned to attack Richmond, Virginia, by-passing what he believed was an enormous Confederate force led by Major General Joseph E. Johnston at Manassas Junction. Transporting his men by ship down the Chesapeake Bay to the mouth of the Rappahannock, he would then lead them on foot across the peninsula to Richmond before Johnston could stop him. Although taking this course would leave Washington, D.C., exposed to the Rebel army, Lincoln—desperate for any action—agreed to the plan.

On March 17, McClellan began his advance. About 400 vessels carried more than 100,000 men from the Washington area to Fortress Monroe at the tip of the Virginia peninsula. Once ashore, however, poor weather, impassable roads, and flooding considerably slowed his march. On April 5, the Union advance reached Yorktown, where about 11,000 Confederates, led by the wily John Bankhead Magruder, waited in a solid defensive position.

Although vastly outnumbered by McClellan, Magruder used tricks—including marching one battalion in and out of a clearing several times—to convince McClellan that his force was enormous. Instead of attacking and annihilating his enemy, McClellan cabled Washington to send reinforcements. "It seems clear that I shall have the whole force of the enemy on my hands," he wrote, and informed Lincoln that he was settling in for a siege on Yorktown.

Lincoln begged the commander to push ahead, but McClellan refused. For more than a month, he did little more than wait, allowing Johnston to bring most of his army onto the peninsula to oppose his advance. Nevertheless, McClellan's troops could still easily overwhelm Johnston's 60,000 men.

On May 3, with 100 Federal guns in place, McClellan was at last prepared to attack. That night, the Confederates surprised the Union army by launching a massive artillery attack.

Federal encampment at Cumberland Landing, Virginia, during the Peninsula Campaign.

The surprise turned to shock in the morning when they realized that the Confederates had abandoned Yorktown during the barrage, retreating to a better defensive position to the south at Williamsburg. McClellan ordered his men to pursue and attack the Confederate line.

A brutal day of fighting ensued, with the Confederates losing about 1,700 men and the Union about 2,200, until the Rebels were forced to resume their withdrawal up the peninsula. By doing so, the Confederates essentially surrended most of eastern Virginia, including Norfolk Naval Yard. The Confederate navy was forced to destroy its ironclad, the CSS *Virginia (Merrimack),* housed at the yard, to keep the Union from obtaining it.

By the end of May, the two armies opposed each other just outside of Richmond. McClellan again requested reinforcements; specifically he wanted Irvin McDowell and his 40,000-man army to join him. McDowell, however, was occupied with the maneuvering of Stonewall Jackson in the Shenandoah Valley. On May 31, nature struck a blow against McClellan by flooding the Chickahominy River, thus isolating two Union corps near the villages of Fair Oaks and Seven Pines. Johnston immediately took advantage of the situation, ordering corps commanders James Longstreet and William Whitings to make a strong attack. In what one historian called "A Battle of Strange Errors," a series of miscommunications and mistakes on the part of the Confederates turned what might have been a victory into a draw. The day-long battle was a bitter one, however, killing or wounding more than 11,000 men—about 5,000 Federals and 6,000 Confederates.

The battle had two significant results. First, the fierce fighting frightened an already overcautious McClellan, who wrote home that he was "tired of the sickening sight of the battlefield with its mangled corpses and poor wounded." Second, the Confederate failure to fully exploit the situation caused President Jefferson Davis to replace Johnston with a more aggressive leader, Robert E. Lee.

Although McClellan continued to advance slowly during the next few weeks, his Peninsula campaign effectively ended when Lee assumed command. Lee did not plan to simply defend the Confederate capital, but instead devised his own offensive strategy known as the Seven Days Campaign, which pushed McClellan all the way back to Harrison's Landing at the edge of the Potomac.

Perryville, Battle of

OCTOBER 8, 1862

This battle, Kentucky's only major conflict in the war, ranks as one of the stranger fights engaged in by Civil War soldiers. Fought essentially by accident, the battle was precipitated by a Confederate chance encounter with Union reconnaissance troops in search of water on a hot, terribly dry day. The commander of the Union forces at Perryville, the dapper General Don Carlos Buell, had been thrown from his horse the morning of the battle, and so had remained at headquarters taking a leisurely luncheon with General Gilbert, one of his subordinates. Owing to an atmospheric phenomenon concerning the terrain and the direction of the wind, the noise of the battle did not carry back in the direction of headquarters—with the result that Buell was unaware anything was going on and consequently did not field the majority of his troops until after four o'clock in the afternoon. His opponent, Confederate General Braxton Bragg, did not fare significantly better; portions of his army were not present on the field either, still being in the vicinity of nearby Frankfort.

Bragg's second-in-command, Episcopal Bishop and Confederate General Leonidas K. Polk, very nearly got himself captured by the troops of the 87th Indiana Infantry (the Hoosiers), in yet another confused accident in the action of the day. Polk mistook the Hoosiers for Confederates and rode up to them with the command that they cease firing into the ranks of their own army. The 87th's commander, Colonel Shryock, responded with a demand to know who Polk was, since Shryock was certain his fire was directed appropriately. Polk realized he was speaking with the enemy, and made a hasty retreat before his confusion could lead to further embarrassment.

Buell's Federals managed to win the engagement despite the confusion. It was a costly defeat for the Confederates in terms of fighting force, as well as loss of territory; estimates of Bragg's casualties are near a fourth of his available 16,000 men. Buell's losses, on the other hand, taking into account that not all of his men even saw action, run just under one-tenth, with a little over 4,000 soldiers killed, missing, or wounded out of 37,000.

In the aftermath of Perryville, both Buell and Bragg would receive censure from their respective presidents, Buell for having failed to destroy the retreating Southerners, and Bragg for failing to hold Kentucky. Buell was relieved of command; Bragg would keep his job a little while longer, owing almost entirely to the patronage of President Jefferson Davis.

Petersburg, Siege of

JUNE 1864–MAY 1865

The climax of the fighting in Virginia was an agonizing 10-month deadlock between deeply entrenched Union and Confederate forces, broken only when the worn-down Southern army was finally unable to withstand a frontal assault.

Nine days after his devastating defeat at Cold Harbor in early June 1864, Ulysses S. Grant furtively began advancing the Army of the Potomac, leaving Robert E. Lee baffled about where the Federals were heading. Grant's target was Petersburg, the vital rail and communications center 20 miles south of Richmond through which most of the Confederate capital's supply lines ran. By capturing Petersburg, the Union commander recognized, he would ensure the capitulation of Richmond.

The 1st Pennsylvania Light Artillery on the front lines at Petersburg.

Army engineers, in an extraordinary feat of construction, briskly built a 2,100-foot pontoon bridge for the huge Federal force to cross the James River, and by June 15, William F. Smith's advance guard of over 10,000 was poised to begin the attack on Petersburg. Unaware that Confederate Pierre G. T. Beauregard had fewer than 2,500 men defending the heavily fortified city, the Union general struck far too cautiously, to the disgust of his troops. Smith still managed to make headway, coming close, in fact, to taking the town, but the Confederates held off the Federals until Lee and the Army of Northern Virginia arrived to fill Petersburg's expansive trenches.

His chances for a quick victory spoiled, Grant commenced a daily artillery bombardment of Petersburg and reluctantly settled in for what he knew would be a long siege. Lee was no happier about the situation. With his vastly outnumbered force pinned down in an urgent defense of the South's capital, the Confederate commander lost the mobility that had been his greatest advantage and suspected that it would be "a mere question of time."

Grant himself wasted little time in putting his superior numbers to use. Constructing a formidable labyrinth of trenches, the Federals extended their line in both directions, swinging down from due east of Richmond more than 40

A captured Confederate encampment at Petersburg.

miles around to the southwest of Petersburg. Lee was forced to do the same, dangerously attenuating Confederate defenses. The South was so desperate for able bodies to line its defenses that it resorted to using old men, boys—and two unwilling members of the Confederate cabinet.

Life in the trenches was brutal for both sides. Numbing boredom was accompanied by the constant threat from sharpshooters and artillery fire. Burrowed in dirt and filth, exposed to the summer heat and the winter cold, the troops suffered even greater losses through disease. But while the Federals were regularly reinforced and kept decently fed and supplied, the Confederates nearly starved, and with thousands deserting or surrendering simply to get food, their numbers diminished further.

Yet, Lee's position was still sufficiently fortified to hold off a Union assault. One audacious attempt to break the Confederate defense in late July, the "Battle of the Crater," was a fiasco. After a regiment of Pennsylvania coal miners set off a huge explosion in a 500-foot tunnel dug right under the enemy, advancing Union troops were pulverized when they were trapped in the deep hole created by the blast.

The Federals were more successful in tightening the stranglehold on the Southerners. In August, they captured one of Virginia's key lifelines, the Weldon Railroad, after a failed attempt two months earlier. In October, Union forces repulsed a Confederate attempt to retake two vital roads, though later in the month they were unable to seize the Southside Railroad. By late winter 1865, Grant's army had grown to nearly 125,000 with reinforcements, while Lee's had dwindled to under 50,000.

With the besieging Union forces threatening to encircle him, the Confederate commander's one remote chance to survive involved leaving the Petersburg trenches and combining forces with Joseph E. Johnston's army in North Carolina. On March 25, John B. Gordon launched an abrupt attack on the Union line east of the town in an attempt to force the Federals to pull back and to create a breach through which Lee's army could escape south. Capturing Fort Stedman and a half mile of Union trenches, the

Confederates seemed close to a breakthrough, only to be forced back after rallying Union troops counterattacked.

To forestall any further such attempts, Grant sent a force miles to the west of the Confederate defenses, trying to stretch Lee's weakened line to the breaking point. On April 1, infantry and cavalry from both sides battled at the Five Forks junction, and George Pickett's Confederate division was routed. When Grant received word of the victory, he ordered the conclusive blow. At 4:30 A.M. the next morning, the Federals launched an overwhelming onslaught along the entire Petersburg front. The Confederates simply could not hold; Union troops smashed through their line at several points.

After sending word to Jefferson Davis that the Confederate capital had to be evacuated, Lee ordered his men to retreat. Petersburg was occupied the evening of April 2, Richmond the following day.

Meanwhile, Lee's army headed west along the Appomattox River—desperately searching for food and for a way to cut south to join Johnston—with Ulysses Grant and the Federals in close pursuit.

Pickets

Pickets in the Civil War were at the same time a very necessary segment of the armies and a nearly invisible object of annoyance and derision to their comrades.

They were the soldiers detailed to stand guard outside the perimeter of an encamped army, as a first line of defense against attack. Seldom if ever stationed at a watchpost alone, there were often as many as four or five soldiers per position; they were charged with keeping one another awake, alert, and ready to raise the alarm if the enemy came too close.

Night and day, these men would be posted as much as a quarter mile from camp or along the army's line of march; if the enemy were sighted, one or two of the pickets would remain quietly to watch them and take note of regimental or corps badges or information written on flags, while the other pickets would hurry into camp to report the enemy's presence to the commanding officer.

This was very often a thankless job, for those who were good at it tended to get stuck with the duty on a regular basis; comrades believed they had the easy life out on the picket line, smoking, talking, perhaps playing cards and taking the occasional forbidden drink of whiskey. But in actual fact, pickets were in constant danger of being killed or captured, for guard duty was a critical but deadly job.

If a soldier fell asleep at his post, he endangered his entire camp as well as himself. Pick-

Pickets warming themselves over a fire.

ets were a favorite target of snipers from both sides, because they knew it was possible to excite a general alarm by gunning one down and making the enemy think there was an attack coming. While they were responding to an imagined threat, a real one could erupt from an entirely different part of the line.

Perhaps the most common phrases associated with the duties of a picket are these: "setting pickets," which simply means placing groups of them on the edges of one's camp; "being picketed" to a certain place, which meant being assigned to a post; and "having one's pickets driven in," which refers to an encounter of a large body of the enemy and one's own picket post, requiring the pickets to run into camp to raise the alarm. A truly careful attacker could see to it the driving in of pickets was the first hint the enemy had of an impending assault, for by then it would almost be too late to prepare for a strong attack.

When an army was in camp, pickets were usually drawn from the ranks of the infantry, though the cavalry picketed their own camps in the main; on the march, with a whole army in motion, it was the cavalry's duty to "ride picket" along the roads and forests near the route to protect the army from attack. Once the cavalry raised an alert, they either fought it off on their own, to their great credit, or gave warning to the infantry commanders—who would then wheel their soldiers from lines of march into lines of battle, a truly daunting sight to an enemy who thought he had taken them by surprise. Many a great battle began in just that way, by virtue of armies and pickets stumbling into one another without warning.

Pickett, George

1825–1875

He neither ordered nor planned the assault, his troops comprised less than half of the attacking force, and the rest of his Civil War service was rather undistinguished, but because he

Major General George E. Pickett

spearheaded the gallant, doomed Confederate charge that climaxed the Battle of Gettysburg, George Pickett's enduring fame is assured.

Graduating at the very bottom of his West Point class, the elegant, almost foppish Virginian performed ably in the Mexican War and on the western frontier. After joining the Confederate army, he led the "Gamecock Brigade" in the Peninsula campaign, where he was seriously wounded during the Seven Days battles in June 1862. Though he was promoted to major general that October and was present at Fredericksburg, Pickett saw little further action until Gettysburg.

Guarding the South's rear during much of the battle, he and his all-Virginian division did not arrive on the field until early the third day, July 3, 1863. James Longstreet, ordered by Confederate commander Robert E. Lee to mount an all-out assault on the center of the Union line,

asked Pickett, one of his favorite officers, to coordinate the attack.

Eager to lead the South to glory, he confidently launched the charge with Longstreet's dubious nodded assent at about 3 P.M. Pickett stayed to the rear, as was customary for a division commander, while his three brigades and another six under A.P. Hill—a force totaling over 14,000—marched deliberately over three-quarters of a mile of open field toward the waiting Federals.

In less than an hour, Pickett's Charge was over, a magnificent effort but the disastrous failure that Longstreet predicted, with barely half of the attacking troops making it back to the Confederate line. When Lee told him to ready his division for a Union offensive, Pickett had to inform the general, "I have no division."

He continued to serve under Lee in the Petersburg campaign. On April 1, 1865, Pickett's troops were nearly wiped out at the Battle of Five Forks, presaging the fall of Richmond. After he was defeated again four days later at Sayler's Creek, Lee relieved him of his command just prior to the Appomattox surrender.

Once wanted by the Union as a war criminal for executing deserters, Pickett eschewed further military service—turning down a marshalcy from President Grant and a generalship from the Khedive of Egypt—to work in insurance back in Virginia. He never forgot the sad outcome of Pickett's Charge and, overlooking his own enthusiasm for the gamble, blamed Robert E. Lee. "That old man," Pickett insisted stubbornly and simply, "had my division massacred."

Pickett's Charge

JULY 3, 1863

"Whatever my fate, I shall do my duty like a brave man," declared George Pickett just before he led 14,000 Virginians across an open field in one last-gasp effort to win a Confederate victory at Gettysburg.

After troops led by Richard Ewell had been driven back from Culp's Hill and Jeb Stuart's attack on the Federal rear was foiled, the Confederates' last hope for victory centered on breaking through the Union center at Cemetery Ridge. All afternoon, the Confederates had bombarded the ridge with artillery fire. When an eerie silence descended on the field at about 3:00 P.M., Generals Robert E. Lee and James Longstreet mistakenly assumed they had destroyed the Union batteries and ordered 14,000 Confederate infantry to move forward.

They emerged from the woods on Seminary Ridge and organized themselves into one mile-long line, complete with mounted infantry and colorful battle flags. The only avenue of approach open to the Confederates was across a mile-wide, empty field. With parade-ground precision, the Confederates marched down a small hill. The Union battery had not been destroyed, however; they had merely been saving ammunition to thwart just such an assault.

Within moments after the Confederates started across the field, Union artillery fire began to mow down row after row of the Confederate column. When the thinned-out ranks were within a short distance of the Federal line, their rebel yells could be heard above the thundering of guns as they made their last dash to the front. Although the first line of Federals was driven back upon the earthworks near the artillery, Union fire and a sudden, furious hand-to-hand battle finally stopped the charge. In less than an hour, more than half of the brave men of Pickett's Charge had been killed and nothing had been gained. The Union claimed victory at Gettysburg and Lee was forced to retreat.

Pinkerton, Allan

1819–1884

The noted detective proved to be no military intelligence expert when he served as the Union's head of Secret Service. The son of a

Pickett's charge on the Union center, July 3, 1863.

Scottish policeman, Pinkerton emigrated to the United States in 1842, settling in Illinois and becoming a staunch abolitionist whose home was a station on the Underground Railroad. He originally worked as a cooper, but entered law enforcement after stumbling upon a counterfeiting ring. Named Chicago's first police detective in 1850, Pinkerton resigned the same year to form a private agency under his own name, with a watchful-eye logo that became synonymous with the profession. The business flourished, and while conducting investigations for the Illinois Central Railroad, Pinkerton became acquainted with the company's lawyer, Abraham Lincoln.

En route to the inauguration in 1861, he informed the president-elect about an assassination plot being hatched in Baltimore, rumors some suspected that he invented himself. Pinkerton arranged Lincoln's secret passage to Washington, getting him to his destination safely but earning the incoming president much derision for supposedly sneaking ignominiously into the capital under disguise. Lincoln was grateful to Pinkerton nevertheless, and in April the master detective was asked to organize secret service operations for the Union.

Excelling at counterespionage, he and his agents uncovered a Confederate spy ring in the nation's capital operated by prominent Washington socialite Rose O'Neal Greenhow. While assigned to George McClellan's Department of the Ohio, Pinkerton personally embarked on clandestine missions into the deep South. He came back east when McClellan was named commander of the Army of the Potomac and, often going under the code name "Major E. J. Allen," joined him on his spring 1862 Peninsula campaign in Virginia.

Including fugitive slaves among his operatives, Pinkerton attempted to collect information on Confederate troop strength and movement, but this kind of intelligence-gathering was not his strength. His reports wildly overestimated the force mounted against the Northern army by two to three times its actual size, confirming McClellan's mistaken fears that he was outnumbered. The Union commander used these erroneous counts to demand reinforcements and to justify stalling his advance, squandering his advantage and dooming the campaign in the process.

Returning to Chicago after McClellan was relieved of command in the fall of 1862, Pinkerton limited his further Civil War service to investigations of fraud among Union military suppliers. He continued to build his agency and won further fame writing 18 self-serving books about his detective work.

Polk, Leonidas

1806–1864

Having abandoned an early army career for the clergy, the Episcopal bishop returned to military service during the Civil War and rose to high Confederate command, more through the support of his close friend, Jefferson Davis, than through his battlefield achievements.

Polk, a tall, gallant figure, came from a prominent North Carolina family and was a relative of President James K. Polk. Graduating from West Point near the top of his class, he left the army after six months to study for the Episcopal ministry. Polk was ordained as a deacon in 1830 and in 11 years was named bishop of Louisiana, where he owned a plantation and 400 slaves.

At the start of the war, Davis, a former West Point classmate, convinced the staunch secessionist that he would lend great prestige and legitimacy to the Southern cause by serving with the Confederate army. Bishop Polk was made a major general and assigned to supervise the fortification of the Mississippi Valley.

Determined to be more than a figurehead, Polk raced against Union officer Ulysses S. Grant to occupy the river stronghold of Columbus, Kentucky, in September 1861. In the process, however, he violated the border state's neutral-

Leonidas Polk

The bishop did not forsake his clerical work altogether during his Civil War service, taking time to baptize both John Bell Hood and Joseph E. Johnston and to perform celebrated raider John Hunt Morgan's wedding ceremony during lulls in the fighting. Leading a corps under Johnston during the 1864 Atlanta campaign, Polk was killed at Pine Mountain on June 14, by a stray round of enemy artillery fire while conferring with his commander. Jefferson Davis considered his death one of the South's worst setbacks. But while Polk was well-liked and respected, not many other Confederates agreed with Davis' assessment.

Pope, John

1822–1892

A skilled and courageous commander, John Pope held command of the Union's Army of the Virginia (later the Army of the Potomac) just long enough to suffer defeat at Second Bull Run before being replaced by his predecessor, George B. McClellan.

Described by contemporaries as dashing and a fine horseman, Pope was also known to be arrogant, abrasive, and incapable of inspiring loyalty among his officers or troops. After graduating seventeenth in his West Point class of 1842, the former Illinois farmboy entered the Mexican War as part of the Corps of Topographical Engineers; for his actions there he was brevetted captain for gallantry. From 1846 until the opening of the Civil War, he worked as an army engineer in the West.

On May 17, 1861, Pope was appointed brigadier general of volunteers in Missouri, then given command of the Army of the Mississippi the following February. He and his army played a major role in the campaign to open up the Mississippi River to Federal navigation, helping to capture New Madrid and Corinth at the beginning of March 1862. Just a few weeks later, President Abraham Lincoln

ity, causing its legislature to throw its support to the North. Placed under his West Point roommate Albert Sidney Johnston, Polk repelled Grant's attack on the citadel two months later and led four assaults against the Union general's troops the following April in the Battle of Shiloh.

As second-in-command to Braxton Bragg at Perryville, he was promoted to lieutenant general. Although Polk continued serving with Bragg, the two did not get along. After the New Year's 1863 Battle of Murfreesboro, Polk suggested that his superior be replaced, and nine months later Bragg was ready to court-martial him for his supposedly sluggish performance at Chickamauga. Standing behind his friend, Davis reassigned Polk to Mississippi, where, indeed showing a tendency for slowness, he was unable to stop the advance of William T. Sherman's forces from Vicksburg.

called the victorious and apparently aggressive young general east to take over the new Army of the Virginia, a well-equipped, well-trained army that George McClellan, a hesitant and ineffectual general, resisted sending into battle.

Pope's first action was to issue a high-handed, condescending statement that alienated officers and soldiers alike. Addressed to his troops, the statement suggested that McClellan, whom the troops adored and whose dismissal outraged the ranks, had taken a faulty approach to the war and that the soldiers themselves had not performed well. Pope also encouraged his men to seize food and supplies from Virginia farms and suggested that anyone suspected of aiding the Confederacy be hanged for treason without trial. Such opinions earned him the enmity of some of the more circumspect Northerners and certainly that of every Southerner, including General Robert E. Lee, who described Pope as a "miscreant."

That Pope entered the eastern theater at a time when the Confederates had the upper hand did not help matters, either. After pushing the Federals back from Richmond during the Seven Days Campaign in the spring, Lee made a daring move to invade the North. Lee's brilliant strategy simply overwhelmed the relatively inexperienced commander. When the armies met from August 28 to September 2, Lee's 55,000 troops outmaneuvered and outfought Pope's Army of the Virginia at Second Bull Run. The next day, Lincoln removed Pope from command, replacing him with the problematic but beloved "Little Mac" McClellan.

Pope's Civil War career effectively ended; he was sent to command the Department of the Northwest, where he became somewhat of an expert in Indian affairs. Promoted major general in the U.S. Army in 1882, Pope retired four years later. He died at the Old Soldiers' and Sailors' Home in Sandusky, Ohio, September 23, 1892.

Porter, David Dixon

1813–1891

By the time the Civil War began, 48-year-old David Porter, soon to become one of the greatest naval heros of the war, had been engaged in naval affairs for more than 35 years.

A member of the most distinguished family in United States naval history, David Dixon Porter literally grew up on the sea. At the age of 10, he accompanied his father, a naval officer and diplomat, on an expedition to suppress piracy in the West Indies. At the age of 14, he was made midshipman in the Mexican Navy. In 1829, Porter returned to the United States and joined the navy, serving in the Mediterranean and the South Atlantic. First as lieutenant and then as commander of the *Spitfire*, Porter took part in every coastal engagement during the Mexican War from 1846 to 1848.

On April 1, 1861, he was given command of the powerful steamer the *Powhatan* and sent to the Gulf of Mexico, a promising start to his Civil War service. As commander of the *Powhatan*, Porter sailed to the Gulf of Mexico to relieve Fort Pickens at Pensacola, Florida, which had been under siege for several months. He stayed in the gulf for the remainder of the war's first year.

To assist David Farragut's assault on New Orleans in April 1862, Porter led a flotilla of small sailing vessels, equipped with mortar and shells, into the harbor in hopes of diminishing Forts Jackson and St. Philip. His plan failed, however, and Farragut's larger, more powerful fleet was necessary to take the forts; the forts finally surrendered on April 28, 1862.

Two months later, Porter was appointed acting rear admiral of the Mississippi Squadron and assumed naval responsibility for the Mississippi and its northern tributaries. His first action, taken in cooperation with William Tecumseh Sherman, was to capture the Arkansas Post in January 1863, thereby opening the Mississippi to Federal navigation. In the spring, Porter assisted Ulysses S. Grant in his move against Vicksburg. In one attempt to reach the city, Porter sailed his fleet from the Mississippi through Steele Bayou, then into and across the Yazoo River below the heavily fortified Fort Pemberton. Porter's gunboats, however, were caught in the narrow, swampy streams that crisscrossed the region. When Confederates began felling trees behind the fleet in an attempt to trap the Union ships, Porter was forced to call to Sherman for army support. Once extricated, Porter headed back to the Mississippi, his first mission at Vicksburg a failure.

On April 30, however, he came through for Grant by taking a dozen vessels loaded with supplies and soldiers across the Mississippi through heavy Confederate gunfire. The passage took more than two hours, but Porter managed to lose just one transport. For his actions at Vicksburg, he was promoted to rear admiral and given increased responsibility for a larger territory: the Mississippi River system north of New Orleans.

The spring of 1864 found Porter ready to undertake what was to be a dreadful failure for the Federal forces during the Red River Campaign.

Admiral David Dixon Porter

Nature and poor planning scuttled the mission to secure the important river for the Federals. Porter nearly lost his fleet during the expedition, but managed to save most of his ships. In October 1864, Porter was sent east to take command of the North Atlantic Blockading Squadron, which was responsible for blockading the coast north of South Carolina. Under orders from Grant to capture Fort Fisher at Wilmington, Porter and army Brigadier General Alfred H. Terry planned a combined naval-land offensive.

On the morning of January 14, 1865, Porter's fleet of 40 warships—the largest ever assembled—began to bombard the fort. At 4:00 P.M., 1,600 of Porter's sailors and 400 marines stormed the northeastern end of the fort while brigades of infantry scaled the parapet. Fierce hand-to-hand combat continued for several hours, until the garrison finally fell at 9:00 P.M., closing the Confederacy's last open port on the East Coast.

After his victory at Fort Fisher, Porter's Civil War career ended, but he continued to serve in the military for the rest of his life. He was promoted to vice-admiral in 1866 and to admiral in 1870. He served as superintendent of the Naval Academy for several years before being appointed head of the Navy Department. David Dixon Porter's remarkable life-long record as a naval officer appeared to run in the Porter family. David Farragut, under whom he served at the capture of New Orleans, was his foster brother. Another brother, Commodore William D. Porter, assisted Andrew H. Foote as commander of the *Essex* in the campaign up the Tennessee River early in 1862. Porter's cousin, Fitz-John Porter, another promising Civil War officer, won accolades for his performance as a soldier during George McClellan's Peninsula Campaign, but gained many detractors after Second Bull Run. Author of several books about his remarkable life, Porter remained active until his death at the age of 78.

Porter, Fitz-John

1822–1901

The story of Union General Fitz-John Porter must surely rank as one of the most frustrating and difficult in the annals of the war. Born to a Portsmouth, New Hampshire, navy family that included Commodore David Porter and Admiral David Dixon Porter, young Fitz-John nevertheless chose the army, graduating from West Point high in his class in 1845. He served for a time in the 4th Artillery, until the outbreak of the Mexican War took him to that training ground for future Civil War generals. Serving under Zachary Taylor, Porter was later transferred to Winfield Scott's army, with whom he saw action from Vera Cruz to Mexico City. He was brevetted for gallantry at Molino del Rey and Chapultepec, and finished the war with a rank of major.

From 1849 to 1855 he was an instructor at West Point, teaching artillery and cavalry tactics. Eventually returning to more active service, Porter was involved in the 1857 Mormon Expedition to Utah, where he served with many men who would later fight alongside or opposite him in the Civil War. On the eve of the nation's breakup, Porter was assigned to numerous difficult tasks associated with the secession of the Confederate states: inspecting Charleston's defenses, lest it should become necessary to level them; finding the means to withdraw loyal troops from Texas after that state's secession; and keeping the trains running between Washington City and the Northern states.

When the fighting began, Porter received a number of assignments, including an appointment on May 17 as brigadier general of Volunteers, and was sent to fight with Nathaniel Banks and Robert Patterson in the Shenandoah Valley. During George McClellan's Peninsula campaign, Porter, who was initially an intimate of McClellan, rose from division command under General Heintzelman to command of the 5th Corps. Attacked in force at Mechanicsville and Gaines Mill, Virginia, during the drive to take Richmond, Porter offered a valiant defense of his position; after a hard fight, he withdrew in good order across the Chickahominy River. Porter's corps was responsible for the safety of the wagon train as McClellan finally began moving across the peninsula, and had orders to occupy and hold Malvern Hill as a protective point for the entire Union army in the campaign.

McClellan's troops were later reassigned to Major General John Pope, in the Union entity known as the Army of Virginia. Porter's men reached the rendezvous by way of the Rappahannock River at Falmouth, Virginia—just in time to receive the brunt of a startling attack by Robert E. Lee and Stonewall Jackson, as they moved Jackson's corps in an attempt to skirt Pope's right flank and break for Thorofare Gap. It took Pope some time to realize what was afoot, whereupon he sent Porter to try and contain the elusive Jackson before he could reunite with the rest of Lee's army. The plan was to attack Jackson's right flank on August 29, 1862, and defeat him before turning to deal with James Longstreet, but Porter failed to follow through on this task. At Second Bull Run (Second Battle of Manassas), Jackson was able to decisively defeat Pope on the old familiar battlefield, sending the scattered and demoralized Northerners back to Washington, D.C., where

General Fitz-John Porter and staff, June 1862.

the army was reshuffled and Porter's corps was returned to McClellan's command.

The following November, General Porter was relieved of command and summoned to a court martial; the charges, leveled by John Pope, included failure to obey orders, disloyalty, and misconduct in the face of the enemy, any one of which was a serious charge all on its own. Pope was clearly looking for a scapegoat, and though Porter offered a rigid defense along the lines that Pope had not given clear orders at any time, and that the Confederates had been in such position as to render impossible the orders he did receive, he was found guilty and dishonorably dismissed from the army on January 21, 1863—coincidentally the thirty-ninth birthday of Stonewall Jackson, the author of Porter's troubles.

Porter began immediately trying to clear his name, but was unable to secure a review of the proceedings until 1879. The wait was worth it, for a board of generals appointed to look into the matter found in Porter's favor. However, it was not until 1882 that the president took some action on Porter's behalf; part of the sentence was remitted to allow him to hold office in the United States. During this time, Ulysses S. Grant wrote an unsolicited testimony in Porter's favor, publishing an article in the *North American Review,* "An Undeserved Stigma." Four years later, on August 5, 1886, ironically owing to the intervention of Congressman Joseph Wheeler, formerly a Confederate cavalry commander in the Army of Tennessee, Porter was reappointed to the rank of colonel of infantry from May of 1861—unfortunately without remuneration of back pay—and then was promptly placed on the retired list two days later.

Porter was finally able to get on with his life and moved to Colorado, where he was involved in mining. He had not been entirely idle during the years that he spent waiting for exoneration, however; he ran a mercantile business in New York, and reluctantly turned down an offer from the Khedive of Egypt of command of the entire Egyptian Army. Porter held such disparate positions as construction superintendent for the State Asylum in New Jersey; receiver of

accounts for the Central Railroad of New Jersey; and public works, fire and police commissioner for the city of New York. At the age of seventy-nine, General Porter died of natural causes in Morristown, New Jersey, leaving behind a widow and four children.

Potomac, U.S. Army and Department of the

The North's most famous army in the Civil War lost more men, proportionately, than any army before or since. Nevertheless, it emerged victorious after Appomattox and its service to the United States reached legendary status almost immediately.

Charged with protecting Washington and capturing Richmond, the Army and Department of the Potomac was created on August 15, 1861. Until that time, it had been known as the Military District, then the Military Department, of the Potomac. The number of corps attached to it, and the geographical area it covered, would fluctuate during four years of war, as would its commanders.

The first to take the helm of "Mr. Lincoln's Army" was George B. McClellan, who instilled a sense of discipline, pride, and respect for training the army retained throughout the war. After McClellan failed to make headway during his Peninsula campaign or stop Lee's advance during the Seven Days campaign, President Abraham Lincoln reorganized his command, splitting off the Army of the Potomac and creating a new Army of the Virginia headed by John Pope.

After Pope lost at Second Bull Run, Lincoln returned McClellan to command and the Army of the Potomac remained the largest army in the North ever after. When McClellan again failed to take aggressive action following his victory at Antietam, Ambrose Everett Burnside took command and led the now battle-ready troops to their third major loss at Fredericksburg. Immediately following the debacle, he was replaced with Joseph E. Hooker, who led

Army of the Potomac before Chancellorsville.

the army to another devastating defeat at the hands of Robert E. Lee at Chancellorsville.

On June 28, 1863, Lincoln chose George Gordon Meade, who had proven himself an able and consistent corps commander during the first two years of the war, to head the army. It won its first major victory at Gettysburg, in July 1863. Although Meade perhaps missed an opportunity to crush Lee's forces by not vigorously pursuing them after the defeat, the battle was nonetheless a turning point both in the war and in the fortunes of the Army of the Potomac itself.

After Ulysses S. Grant was appointed lieutenant general-in-chief of all the Union forces, the Army of the Potomac went on to victory at Petersburg, Richmond, and at Appomattox, where Lee finally surrendered. On May 23,

1865, the Army of the Potomac was formally disbanded.

Prisoner Exchange

Captured soldiers of both the North and South languished in deplorable prison camps once the delicate prisoner exchange program fell apart over the Confederacy's refusal to include black troops in the deal and the Union's realization that the policy aided the enemy's war effort.

Field officers had informally traded captives after battles since the early days of the conflict. With a far smaller reserve of able-bodied men

Generals McClellan and Burnside with the Army of the Potomac at Rectortown, Virginia, November 10, 1862.

and with fewer resources to keep prisoners, the South was eager to formalize the arrangement. Although Abraham Lincoln hesitated entering into an agreement that would tacitly recognize the Confederacy, he was swayed by public pressure, and an official exchange cartel was concluded in July 1862. The policy called for captured soldiers of equal rank to be traded on a one-for-one basis, with four privates equaling one lieutenant, 60 a commanding general, and so forth.

Despite occasional disputes, most concerning when and whether released prisoners could return to armed service, the arrangement lasted for ten months, freeing about 200,000. The breakdown came when African-American troops began serving in the Union army. Outraged at what it saw as the arming of fugitive slaves, the Confederate Congress in May 1863 declared that captured black soldiers, fugitive

or not, would be reenslaved and that they—and their white commanders—could also be subject to execution. The North, demanding that the captured blacks be acknowledged as legitimate prisoners of war and included in exchanges, promptly suspended the agreement and the Union and Confederate prison camp populations swelled.

Late that year, the South altered its stance by promising that only actual runaways would be returned to bondage, but the impasse remained. Ulysses S. Grant reiterated the North's position in an April 1864 order, stating that "no distinction whatever will be made in the exchange between white and colored prisoners." Some claimed that the Union's new general-in-chief had another purpose in mind—that he was willing to sacrifice thousands of soldiers to the enemy's prisons because the South would be hurt even more by the depletion of manpower.

Rations served to exchanged Union prisoners on board the New York.

Desperate inmates at Andersonville prison sent petitions to Lincoln urging him to resume prisoner exchanges, physicians and clergymen lobbied the president as well, and the Democrats tried making the government's "cruel" inflexibility into an election issue. But Lincoln, believing the principle outweighed the suffering, would not yield. Finally in January 1865, as the faltering Confederacy was contemplating the use of armed slaves in its own military, it agreed to include blacks in prisoner exchanges. By the time the practice resumed, with three months left in the war, nearly 50,000 captured soldiers had died in prison.

Prison Life

One of the difficult realities of military service in the Civil War was the ever-present possibility that a soldier might be taken prisoner as a result of action undertaken by his regiment.

Because this war took place during the Victorian Era, a time of great civility, there was very little mistreatment of prisoners on the actual field of battle; the men of the two armies seemed to instinctively understand they could just as easily have been in the other fellow's shoes, and so behaved toward captured enemy soldiers with a polite gentlemanliness. If captured, one could expect to be required to give one's parole: that is, to make some sort of promise not to attempt to escape. If offered and accepted, parole made it possible for the cap-

Three Confederate soldiers after their capture at Gettysburg.

tives to be sent back under flag of truce to their own lines—whereupon the paroled soldiers would be sent home until an exchange was effected between the Confederate and United States governments, allowing the parolees to return to active duty. If a paroled soldier went back to the field unexchanged, he was liable to be shot, or in times of low ammunition, hanged, for having broken one of the more curious and seldom transgressed gentlemen's agreements of the army tradition.

As the war went on, however, the simple parole of captured soldiers became a less often seen phenomenon. It became the policy of the Union in 1864 to cease offering exchanges altogether, in hopes of wearing down Confederate resistance by draining their manpower. Confederate soldiers captured in battle were most often sent to prisons in the North. Some of the best-known Union prisons were Point Lookout, Maryland; Johnson's Island, the Ohio State Penitentiary, and Camp Chase, Ohio; and Rock Island, Illinois; in the South, there was a Union prison mostly for captured Confederate officers at Fortress Monroe, Virginia. Confederate prisons included Danville, Virginia; Camp Oglethorpe, Georgia; Mobile, Alabama, and Salisbury, North Carolina. Prisons in the South were constructed wherever there was room; Libby prison in Richmond was a converted tobacco warehouse, while the infamous Andersonville was in a field in Georgia.

Until fairly recently, it was widely believed that Confederate prisoners in Northern hands were treated decently, fed abundantly, and sent home in good physical condition, while Union prisoners in Southern facilities were starved, brutalized, beaten, and murdered. In each case, there is exaggeration.

Men of rank could generally expect a certain

level of good treatment, as the officer in charge of the prison could be expected to sympathize with a fellow officer. Many an officer both North and South was indeed fed well, treated well, and—oddly enough—was frequently given a new uniform upon his exchange, minus the military buttons. And there are ample stories of acts of kindness and gentlemanly conduct between prisoners and their keepers; the otherwise loathed Union General Benjamin Butler went to great difficulty to find a warhorse belonging to Robert E. Lee's son, cavalry brigadier William H. F. Lee, which had been stolen from him during his capture in 1863. As there is almost always a reverse side to the coin, however, one must look at the brutal treatment accorded to the brother of Confederate raider John Hunt Morgan, when he was captured during an expedition into the Ohio Valley. Incarcerated in the Ohio State Penitentiary, Morgan and his companions were stripped, had their heads shaved, and were imprisoned in cells that were 38 inches wide by six and a half feet long; when it was believed they might try to escape, they were put into unheated cells at one end of the prison with no blankets or beds, and no room to move in order to warm themselves, in sub-zero weather. They languished in this state for 16 days, because they would not confess the details of an escape plan no one was entirely certain even existed.

The 35,000 men incarcerated in Andersonville could certainly speak of the horror of being a prisoner of war, and there was general acclaim at the war's conclusion when the commandant, Henry Wirz, became the only Confederate official actually prosecuted for war crimes. Undeniably terrible as the overcrowded conditions in Andersonville were, Wirz was not entirely lacking an explanation for his actions: the Confederate Congress passed a law stating that prisoners were to have as their daily ration the same allowances made for Southern soldiers in the field, and they were starving as well. As for medical supplies for the prisoners, there were none to be had—as a result of the Northern blockade of Southern ports. The unhappy fact of life for prisoners on both sides was that measures taken to shorten the war often trickled down to those who were least able to take action for their own comfort and safety.

Q

Quantrill, William Clarke

1837–1865

The most notorious of the Confederate "bushwhackers" terrorized Union troops and pro-North civilians alike in Kansas and Missouri. An aspiring schoolteacher from Ohio, Quantrill headed west in 1857, where he turned to gambling and theft and joined local antislavery partisans in factional disputes. With the start of the Civil War, however, he switched sides and fought with the South during the August 1861 Battle of Wilson's Creek.

Abandoning regular military service thereafter, he commanded a loosely knit guerrilla band, its members motivated more by personal animosities, expectations of booty, and a taste for mayhem than by political convictions or sectional loyalties. His followers included such future Wild West desperados as the Younger brothers, Frank James, and later, Jesse James. In an area where atrocities were committed by both sides, these partisans stood out for the particular delight they took in the butchery.

Attached to a formal cavalry unit, Quantrill captured Independence, Missouri, in August 1862 and won a captain's commission in the Confederate army. But Southern commanders

August 1863: Quantrill and his band go on a rampage through the antislavery town of Lawrence, Kansas, killing 150 civilians.

had little control over the bushwhackers' actions or methods, which they tended to consider counterproductive at the very least. In his most infamous foray, Quantrill led an August 1863 attack on Lawrence, Kansas. His 400 raiders pillaged and burned the antislavery town and killed over 150 unarmed civilian men and boys before fleeing into the Missouri woods.

Expressing the North's outrage, a Union general responded by banishing over 10,000 civilians from four counties believed to harbor Quantrill supporters. The guerrillas themselves were hard to pin down, however; a nebulous, anarchic bunch that frequently went off on separate raiding parties. One offshoot, led by the psychotic William "Bloody Bill" Anderson, committed acts even more shocking than Quantrill chanced, such as a train ambush in which 24 unarmed Union soldiers on leave were murdered, along with over 120 members of the posse that went in pursuit of the band.

By the fall of 1864, Union forces managed to curtail much of the guerrilla activity in Kansas and Missouri, and Quantrill went east intending to assassinate Abraham Lincoln. Waylaid by Federal troops in Kentucky, he was mortally wounded in May 1865 and died a prisoner 20 days later.

R

Radical Republicans

The most extreme and ultimately most powerful wing of the Republican Party during the Civil War, the Radicals saw the goals of the Civil War to be the immediate emancipation of the slaves and the complete reorganization and subjugation of the South's political and economic power.

Comprising about one-third of their party, the Radicals were led by outspoken and influential members of Congress, including Senator Charles Sumner, chairman of the Senate Foreign Relations Committee; Senator Benjamin Wade, who established the Joint Committee on the Conduct of the War; Representative Thaddeus Stevens, chairman of the House Ways and Means Committee; and Henry Davis, chairman of the House Foreign Relations Committee.

Lincoln's secretary of the treasury, Salmon P. Chase, and Secretary of War Edwin M. Stanton were both Radicals and, as such, did much to undermine the president's efforts to present a united front to the Northern public. Although Lincoln personally opposed slavery, he was much more moderate in his approach to the conduct of the war, and to the relationship between North and South once the war was over, than were the Radicals. During the 1862 state and local elections, the Radicals refused to campaign for more moderate members of their

party, causing Lincoln to remark, "If there is a hell, I am in it."

They were particularly disappointed over the limited scope of Lincoln's Emancipation Proclamation, which did not, in fact, free the slaves outright. Instead, it freed only those living in rebellious states; for those living in loyal slave states, such as Maryland and Delaware, Lincoln favored paying slave owners compensation for the release of their slaves.

In addition, in attempting to control war strategy, the Radicals created and administrated the Joint Committee on the Conduct of the War, which harassed generals perceived as being "soft" on the South. Lincoln's first general-in-chief and commander of the Army of the Potomac, George B. McClellan was a prime target of the committee. It was largely through Radical Republican efforts that the Confiscation Acts were passed and that black soldiers were allowed to fight.

The division between moderate and Radical Republicans was widest over the issue of Reconstruction. The moderates urged a more benign and gradual reunion, while the Radicals saw the war as an opportunity to completely restructure the South by establishing Northern-run schools, hospitals, and local and state governments. Many Radicals favored refusing suffrage to ex-Confederates for at least 10 years, during which time they hoped to alter social mores and customs peculiar to the South, par-

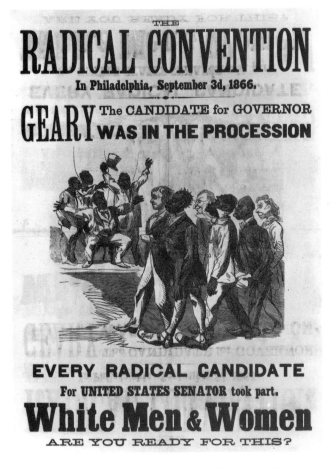

RADICAL CONVENTION

In Philadelphia, September 3d, 1866.

GEARY The CANDIDATE for GOVERNOR WAS IN THE PROCESSION

EVERY RADICAL CANDIDATE

For UNITED STATES SENATOR took part.

White Men & Women

ARE YOU READY FOR THIS?

A racist campaign poster, attacking Radical Republican support of voting rights for African-Americans.

ticularly its racist attitudes toward blacks and its inbred suspicion of the North.

After the Lincoln assassination, the Radicals gained and kept control over Reconstruction policies and national politics until the end of Ulysses S. Grant's second term in 1876. An economic recession, coupled with charges of vice and corruption against the Grant administration, brought the era of Radical Republicanism to a close.

"Rebel Yell"

The Confederate troops' shrill, exultant battle cry became an enormously effective weapon of war. A strange scream, possibly a variation on the houndlike yelp that Southern sportsmen would call out during a fox hunt, it routinely unsettled Federal troops. The Rebel yell made a distinctive counterpoint to the typical Union soldier's cry, which was described by one Northerner as a "deep, manly, generous shout." The Confederates' version was much higher pitched, but no less manly—and quite a bit more effective.

Probably used at First Bull Run on the afternoon of July 19, 1861, the war's earliest battle, it proved instantly successful, exhilarating the Rebels and terrifying the Yankees. After 14 hours of fighting, a massed corps of Confederate forces under the command of Pierre G. T. Beauregard began a counterattack and rather spontaneously commenced with the piercing wail. Whether it was the yell itself, the sheer size of the attacking force, or more likely a combination of both, the Union troops beat a retreat.

Thereafter, the Rebel yell could be heard in practically every Civil War engagement. From the time of Robert E. Lee's surrender at Appomattox Court House, Civil War historians, veterans, and novelists have tried vainly to capture in words the precise sound of the yell—and the queasy feeling it evoked in Union soldiers on the receiving end. The best descriptions are the ones admitting that words must fail. "There is nothing like it on this side of the infernal region," one Northern veteran explained. "The peculiar corkscrew sensation that it sends down your backbone under these circumstances can never be told."

Asked to reproduce the Rebel yell years later, an aging ex-Confederate from Tennessee explained it could never be done "unless made at a dead run in full charge against the enemy." Moreover, he concluded, it was impossible "to try to imitate it with a stomach full of food and a mouth full of false teeth."

Confederate troops led into battle by the shrill, exultant "Rebel Yell."

Reconstruction

1865–1877

Following the Confederate surrender, a series of measures designed to "reconstruct" the South were enacted by President Andrew Johnson and by the United States Congress. Although some measures were clearly retributive in nature, Reconstruction was designed to bring the Southern states back into the Union, rebuild the devastated Southern economy, and empower newly freed blacks.

Long before the end of the war, a debate over how to deal with seceded states if and when the North claimed victory raged within the Lincoln administration and across the nation. On what terms should the defeated Confederacy be reunited with the Union and who should establish the terms, Congress or the president? What kind of economy would the South have after slavery had been abolished? What role should blacks play in the politics and economy of the new South?

The first official act concerning Reconstruction was issued on October 8, 1863, by Abraham Lincoln. Called the Proclamation of Amnesty and Reconstruction, the act offered full pardon and the restoration of all rights "except as to slaves" to anyone who reaffirmed their allegiance to the Union by taking an oath of loyalty and by pledging to accept the abolition of slavery. Former high-ranking Confederate military personnel, however, would remain subject to prosecution by the Union government. When 10 percent of a state's population (based on 1860 voting rolls) accepted these conditions, this minority could establish a new state government and the state could be represented in the U.S. Congress. Its new constitution would have to abolish slavery, but the government could adopt temporary measures to ease the transition between a slave and free labor economy.

Both Radical Republicans and abolitionists were disappointed with Lincoln's moderate approach. First, his plan did not include any punitive measures against most former Confederates and made it relatively easy for the previously rebellious to rejoin the Union. Second, it did not provide for black suffrage or define any role for African-Americans in the Reconstruction process.

The first Radical Republican response to Lincoln's plan came in the form of the Wade-Davis Bill, which insisted on much more stringent criteria for rejoining the Union. Lincoln pocket-vetoed the bill (he simply did not sign or return

Illustration of African-American men voting for the first time.

the bill to Congress before it adjourned for the year). By the time the war ended, Congress had passed the 13th Amendment, abolishing slavery throughout the Union and empowering Congress to enforce abolition with "appropriate legislation." Shortly after this historic legisla-

tion was passed, Congress established the Freedmen's Bureau, a federally funded organization to distribute clothing, food, and fuel to destitute freedmen and to oversee "all subjects" relating to their condition in the South.

After the Lincoln assassination, President

"One Vote Less."

Andrew Johnson attempted to remain true to Lincoln's moderate course. In May 1865, Johnson conferred amnesty and pardon, including the restoration of all property rights—except for slaves—upon participants in the rebellion who took an oath of loyalty to the Union and accepted emancipation. He also appointed provisional governors to lead those Southern states in rewriting their constitutions using language that would allow them to rejoin the Union.

Again, no provisions other than emancipation were made for blacks. Johnson believed that the states should decide for themselves the future of freedmen within their borders. Such a policy led to the enactment of Black Codes in several Southern states; these state laws essentially kept blacks out of the political and social mainstream.

Although Johnson had attempted to create a new political order by appointing men loyal to the Union to head the readmitted states, Radical Republicans insisted that a more aggressive approach be taken. They asserted that rebel states had lost all their former rights and having been defeated were now to be treated as conquered provinces or federal territories. To the Republicans, black suffrage and equality before the law were the most important aims of the reconstruction process. As violence against African-Americans mounted in the years following the war—between 1865–1866 alone, more than 5,000 blacks were killed by Southern whites—the need for military control became evident.

In addition, many in Congress believed that Johnson had overstepped his authority and that Reconstruction should be the responsibility of the legislative and not the executive branch of the government. To that end, congressional Reconstruction began with the Reconstruction Act of 1867, which fundamentally altered Johnson's plans for the new South. The eleven Confederate states were divided into five military districts under commanders empowered to employ the army to protect life and property. New constitutions were to include a promise to ratify the 14th Amendment (which granted citizenship to the newly freed slaves and directed

the federal government to protect the citizens of a state against arbitrary state actions, including the black codes), a loyalty oath swearing the state's allegiance to the Union, and a ban prohibiting former Confederate leaders from holding office.

During the next ten years, Radical Reconstruction achieved a wide range of accomplishments, some more successful than others. The Reconstruction governments established the first public, tax-supported school systems in most states of the South. Attempts were made to broaden the South's economy by offering aid to railroads and other industries. Black suffrage was achieved, and blacks were included for the first time in the political process.

Many of the changes made were illusory or short-lived. Despite attempts to lure industry to the region, the South remained dependent on agriculture throughout the rest of the nineteenth century and into the twentieth. Southern states continued to violate the rights of blacks by enacting laws such as the poll tax, which severely curtailed many blacks' ability to vote. Few African-Americans acquired land during this period, making it impossible for them to gain economic independence.

Nevertheless, the passage of the 14th and 15th Amendments to the Constitution, which established a national system of equal protection under the law, laid the basis for the civil rights movement of the twentieth century and remains Reconstruction's most enduring legacy.

Red River Campaign

MARCH–MAY 1864

Eager to capture the city of Shreveport, Louisiana, and secure East Texas, President Abraham Lincoln authorized an ill-fated expedition up the unpredictable Red River from New Orleans.

Lincoln and his general-in-chief Henry Halleck hoped that a successful thrust into the heartland of Louisiana might convince large numbers of the state's silent Unionists to join the Federal cause. In addition, the Red River area was rich with cotton ready to go to market; at high wartime prices, the incentive for garnering the cotton and selling it to the highest bidder was great.

Although the commander in charge of the expedition, David Dixon Porter, expressed concern about the falling level of the Red River, the plan got underway at the beginning of March. Setting out from New Orleans, Porter took 12 ironclad gunboats, two large wooden steamers, and four smaller steamers. On board were 10,000 men sent by William Tecumseh Sherman and commanded by Brigadier General Andrew J. Smith. Another 15,000 troops, dispatched from the corps of Union General Nathaniel Banks, planned to join them before the contingent reached Shreveport.

After achieving initial success at Fort De Russy below Alexandria, Louisiana, the campaign was delayed by weather and bureaucratic maneuvering by Ulysses S. Grant, who wanted to detach Sherman's contingent to proceed with the Atlanta campaign later in April. As Porter headed toward Alexandria, the Red River began to fall and Confederates lining its banks showered the slow-moving flotilla with an endless barrage of small arms and artillery fire.

On land, the army fared no better. Eight thousand Confederate troops led by Major General Richard Taylor forced Banks' men to retreat at Mansfield. In the meantime, Porter, under constant fire, lost a gunboat and a steamer to artillery shells. When he reached Alexandria, the situation grew critical. The water level had plummeted to just three feet; his gunboats needed at least seven feet of water to pass.

Porter faced two equally bleak alternatives:

Building a dam on the unpredictable Red River.

he could destroy his flotilla before the Confederates captured it, or he could watch it, and his men, be devastated by Confederate fire. It was, Porter wrote his mother, "a hard and anxious time" for the admiral and his men. A Wisconsin engineer named Lieutenant Colonel Joseph Bailey, however, saved the day with an ingenious plan. By building a dam across the river, the Union could raise the water level high enough to at least forge a hasty retreat down to the Mississippi. Approximately 3,000 troops, using nothing but trees, rocks, and bags of dirt, constructed an enormous dam that spanned nearly the whole width of the river.

To finish the job, Porter ordered the sinking of four barges lined up in a row to completely fill the 758-foot expanse. Four of the gunboats managed to pass over the rapids created by the improvised structure before it fell apart; Bailey and his men spent another few days rebuilding before the rest of the squadron could move. Porter's escape to the relative safety of the Mississippi ended the disastrous campaign, gaining nothing for the Union except humiliation.

Republican Party

Out of the political chaos that greeted the passage of the Kansas-Nebraska Act of 1854 sprang a new political organization, the Republican party. It boosted a broad alliance of former Whigs, Free-Soilers, business and industry leaders who supported a central economic policy, and abolitionists.

The South immediately perceived the Republican Party as a great threat to its economy and way of life. High tariffs, free land for homesteaders in the territories, and other economic issues were included in the party's platform, but without question, slavery and its future formed its core. The party formed out of the antislavery rallies that greeted the passage of the Kansas-Nebraska Act throughout the Midwest and North.

In 1856, John Frémont, already famous for his exploration and conquest of California, became the party's first nominee for president. Although defeated by James Buchanan, Frémont and his nascent party made a good showing in the North. By the time the election of 1860 was held, sectional tension was at an all-time high. The Democratic party, which had held the White House for most of the past 40 years, had splintered over the issue of slavery, giving the Republicans a clear shot at capturing the presidency. Abraham Lincoln, former senator from Illinois, became the nominee at the Republican Convention in the summer of 1860. He won the election in November with a majority in the electoral college, but only 40 percent of the popular vote.

Although Lincoln espoused relatively moderate views on slavery—insisting that the federal government had no right to put an end to slavery where it already existed—the South saw his election and the ascension of the Republicans as paramount to the destruction of the South. The process of secession began at once.

During the war, the Republican party itself splintered into three sections: conservatives, moderates, and Radical Republicans. Conservatives favored gradual emancipation of the slaves and benevolent treatment of the South after the war; moderates saw the need for more rapid emancipation and for some economic and political sanctions; Radicals favored immediate emancipation, equated the Civil War with a war for abolition, and pushed for harsh recriminations against the South during Reconstruction.

By 1864, with the war into its third bloody year, the Republicans faced a formidable challenge from Democrat George B. McClellan. In order to appeal to a broader range of constituents, the Republicans dropped Lincoln's Republican vice-president, Hannibal Hamlin, from the ticket and replaced him with War Democrat Andrew Johnson; for a brief time, the Republicans called themselves the National Union Party as evidence of this change. Thanks to a series of military victories during the summer, Lincoln won the election handily.

After the war and the Lincoln assassination,

the division widened between moderates and Radicals over Reconstruction. The Radicals gained the upper hand during the impeachment hearings of Andrew Johnson and the subsequent election of Ulysses S. Grant in 1868. The 1876 election of Rutherford B. Hayes, a decided moderate, proved that the balance had shifted, due in part to corruption in Grant's administration. Hayes embarked on a course of reconciliation with the South, withdrawing Federal troops from the South and appointing ex-Confederates to his cabinet and to other positions in the federal government. By instituting strong central economic policies, he restored the economy while, at the same time, his personal integrity helped repair Republican credibility damaged during Grant's terms.

Richmond, Virginia

"On to Richmond" was the rallying cry in the North from the early days of the Civil War. Although the lines of battle would widen considerably, capturing the seat of Confederate power would remain an important goal of the

1856 Republican presidential candidates Fremont and Dayton.

Union army. In many ways, the manpower and attention the Confederacy mustered for Richmond's defense left the Confederacy vulnerable in other military theaters, thereby hastening its defeat.

Located at the head of the James River just 100 miles away from Washington, D.C., Richmond acted as the capital of the Confederacy from May 1861 until the end of the Civil War. In 1861, Richmond was the third most populated city in the South (38,000 residents) and ranked first in manufacturing. The center for the tobacco, flour, and corn meal industries, Richmond was also home to the South's only iron factory, the Tredegar Iron Works, by far the most valuable Confederate foundry for the manufacture of large guns and other munitions.

Within a few months of being named the Confederate capital, the tenor of the city changed dramatically. Defenses in the form of ordnance and earthworks rimmed the city. Hundreds of bureaucrats and thousands of Confederate soldiers arrived to take up short- and long-term residence. As the war dragged on, the city would become home to the South's largest hospital,

Chimborazo, and two of the largest Confederate military prisons, Libby and Belle Island. Since the stretch of territory that lay between the Union and Confederate capitals would be the site of heavy fighting throughout the war, these institutions were usually filled to capacity, especially during and after the Peninsula campaign and throughout the siege of Petersburg and Richmond's final defense.

As the fortunes of the Confederacy fell, so too did the quality of life in its capital. While food and other necessities grew scarce, crime, gambling, and prostitution flourished. In April 1863, this dissatisfaction erupted into the Rich-

The ruins of Richmond, April 1865.

mond Bread Riot. Nearly 1,000 Richmond women, angry over skyrocketing prices and an alarming scarcity of staples, marched through the streets, looting stores and bakeries. It took action from Jefferson Davis to quell the disturbance.

On April 2, 1865, just hours after Confederate troops relinquished Petersburg, Richmond fell to the Union. Southerners burned what they did not want the Union to have, and Federal artillery finished destroying what had once been an elegant Southern capital. On the morning of April 3, Federal troops entered Richmond and placed a Union flag on top of the Confederate capitol building. Although Robert E. Lee did not surrender for another week, and Albert Sidney Johnston did not lay down his arms for several days after that, the flying of the Union flag in Richmond represented to many Confederates the rebellion's humiliating end.

Ruffin, Edmund

1794–1865

The Virginia agricultural innovator and impassioned secessionist has been popularly, though erroneously, credited with firing the first shot of the Civil War.

Born into plantation society, Ruffin turned to the study of scientific farming methods to combat the soil depletion ravaging the upper South. A pioneer in the use of fertilizer and legumes, he advocated diversified planting and crop rotation that went against the region's prevailing one-crop system.

The president of the Virginia Agricultural Society and editor of the *Farmer's Register*, Ruffin put those aside in the 1850s to become a leader in the growing Southern movement toward secession. He wrote fiery tracts, traveled throughout the region giving speeches for the cause, and attended the December 1859 execution of terrorist abolitionist John Brown with great satisfaction. Maddened by Virginia's reluctance to leave the Union, Ruffin headed to South Car-

olina, the state that led the South's secessionist parade.

Despite his age of 65, he became an honorary member of the state's Palmetto Guard. Ruffin was with that unit at Charleston Harbor on April 12, 1861, during the Fort Sumter standoff. Stationed at Cummings Point on Morris Island, he gladly accepted the honor—after others refused it—of firing a symbolic first shot on the fort. It was merely symbolic, however; artillery fire had already commenced from other locations, the first blast probably discharged by Confederate soldier Henry S. Farley.

But Ruffin, a striking figure with a flowing

Edmund Ruffin

mane of white hair, made the most of his formal status as the man who led off the Civil War. Remaining with the Palmetto Guard at First Bull Run, he also claimed more credit than he possibly deserved in the rout of Federal forces there, maintaining that he fired the cannon shot that launched the Union's panicked retreat. Ruffin was too old to continue military service and sat out the rest of the war in Richmond. Crushed by the South's defeat, Ruffin committed suicide, on June 17, 1865, a few months after the Confederate surrender.

S

Salem Church, Battle of

MAY 3–4, 1863

Part of the Battle of Chancellorsville, the fighting around the little edifice known as Salem Church was among the hottest in the larger picture of the campaign.

On the day after Stonewall Jackson's critical wounding, with the main body of the Army of Northern Virginia at the Chancellor house crossroads some ten miles from Fredericksburg, Virginia, preparations were made for an assault that never materialized. The majority of Union General Joseph Hooker's men were in Fredericksburg proper under command of General John Sedgwick, advancing over the old familiar ground of Marye's Heights, scene of the terrible fighting in December 1862, with as little success in the springtime as had been procured the previous winter.

Twice, in action sometimes referred to as the Second Battle of Fredericksburg, Sedgwick's men tried to take the heights; on the third try, after high losses, they finally succeeded in breaking the Confederate line. The Southern defenders, commanded by General Jubal Early, were driven back to the south, leaving the road back to Chancellorsville invitingly open. As Sedgwick accepted the invitation, Robert E. Lee turned his army to meet their advance, using Salem Church as the pivot. All around the small brick church, fighting raged for the remainder of the day until nearly full dark.

That night, the church became a hospital for the wounded and dying of both sides. Badly knocked about and exhausted, the Federals did very little effective movement in the early part of May 4, with the result that Lee was able to bring up the rest of his troops to reinforce Confederate lines around Salem Church. Early moved up from Fredericksburg, and the Federals found themselves assailed from three directions. Unfortunately, the Southern forces had left the back door open, and Sedgwick escaped with his men across the Rappahannock at Banks Ford, crossing the pontoons there under cover of darkness.

Sanitary Commission, United States

Fueled by the volunteer work of legions of women and frequently at odds with the Union war department, this instrumental private organization, the largest venture of its kind yet attempted in America, lobbied Congress, raised money, and dispatched field agents to raise the standard of health care in the military.

In the Civil War's opening days, women's groups throughout the North started local soldier-relief agencies, recognizing that squalid camp conditions, inadequate medical care, and the rampant spread of disease would be as devastating to the nation's war effort as battlefield defeats. Consolidating these efforts and gaining influence over military leaders hostile to such civilian interference, a group of prominent physicians and other influential Easterners such as clergyman Henry W. Bellows met with Abraham Lincoln, who, though skeptical, authorized the creation of the United States Sanitary Commission in June 1861.

The agency was supposed to limit itself to an advisory capacity, but quickly took a far more active role in addressing military health concerns and opposing the inadequate measures being taken by the Army Medical Bureau. Within a year, the Sanitary Commission had gained enough political power to get congressional legislation passed implementing crucial staffing reforms in the bureau. Soon the army's ineffectual surgeon general and other recalcitrant administrators were replaced by officials far more responsive to the Sanitary Commission, and thenceforth the military worked in concert with the agency.

A Sanitary Commission nurse surrounded by her patients, Fredericksburg, Virginia.

By 1863, there were 7,000 local branches across the nation, with 500 paid employees—mostly men—and thousands of volunteers—mostly women. Two of the more prominent were Mary Livermore and Jane Hoge, who organized hundreds of chapters in the Midwest. The Sanitary Commission workers took on a multitude of responsibilities: obtaining and distributing medical supplies, food, and clothing; providing nurses, ambulance drivers, and other health care workers; and sending agents to army camps and hospitals to conduct inspections, supervise cleanups, and furnish advice on disease prevention, sewage disposal, hygiene, and nutrition.

The Sanitary Commission also ran a Washington, D.C., veterans' home, fed and lodged soldiers heading home on leave, and equipped trains and boats to transport the wounded from battlefield to hospital. To finance all these enterprises, commission officials solicited corporate donations and sponsored rallies and benefit performances.

But the most elaborate and successful fundraising events were the legendary "sanitary fairs," gala festivals held in cities and towns throughout the North featuring bazaars, exhibitions, games and contests, and abundant entertainment and refreshments. The first sanitary fair, held in Chicago for two weeks in fall 1863 and highlighted by the auction of Lincoln's original draft of the Emancipation Proclamation, raised $300,000, topped by fairs in New York and Philadelphia the following year that brought in over $1 million each.

Spending well over $20 million on its efforts by the end of the Civil War, the Sanitary Commission had not only vastly improved conditions in the military, but it had encouraged the involvement of women in American public affairs on an unprecedented level.

Scalawags

"We can appreciate a man who lived north, and even for fighting against us," wrote a for-mer North Carolina governor, "but a traitor to his own home cannot be trusted or respected." Contemporary slang for "no good scoundrels," the term scalawags was used to describe Southern whites who joined the Republican party after the Civil War. In so doing, they became traitors to many who remained loyal to the Confederate cause.

More than 20 million white Southerners from all walks of life joined the Republican party in the years following the war. Several prominent war veterans, such as Charles Hays—a wealthy Alabama planter, ardent secessionist, and Confederate soldier—and James Longstreet, one of the Rebels finest corps commanders, joined. So did entrepreneurs seeking new capital, and yeoman farmers hoping to preserve their age-old way of life. In fact, the majority of white Southern Republicans were semi-subsistence farmers who occupied the hill country between West Virginia and the foothills of the Appalachians in Alabama. Poor and isolated, the Civil War for these farmers had been "a rich man's war" fought largely in their backyards; many of them were Unionists at heart to begin with.

Because the large numbers of these disaffected people became Republicans, the term scalawag also came to denote "poor white trash." Others who embraced the Republican party at the end of the war were native Southern reformers of all types, who saw a change in administration as a chance to bring economic and political change to the South. Whatever the motivation, all scalawags had one thing in common: they felt they stood a better chance of achieving their goals by cooperating with a Republican administration than by joining the anti-Reconstructionist camp.

Mistrusted and disliked by those even moderately loyal to the Southern cause, scalawags were frequent targets of violent reprisals by unrepentant ex-Confederates, some of whom formed the secret white supremacist organization, the Ku Klux Klan.

Scandinavian-Americans in the Civil War

Americans of Scandinavian descent during the Civil War period were largely to be found in the Northern sections of the continent, and consequently the majority of them served in the Union army. Fiercely antislavery, the freedom-loving Swedes, Norwegians, and Danes could not bring themselves to support the Confederate cause in any great number, no matter how admirable some of the infant nation's aims and goals might be.

Extensive genealogical research can uncover only about 1,000 Scandinavian-Americans living in states that joined the Confederacy; among the Southern forces only 19 soldiers can be found who claimed Scandinavian descent. Therefore, the majority of Scandinavians were Federal sympathizers. It has been rightly said that the Scandinavians who enlisted in Union regiments went forth "in the firm belief that they were helping to make the United States what it was supposed to be—a free land where all men, white or black, were equal."

Among the few Confederate Scandinavians, we do find one young hero: Augustus Forsberg, who served first as a lieutenant in the 51st Virginia Infantry Regiment, then was promoted successively to colonel. He commanded a brigade that included four Virginia regiments, though he apparently never officially received the rank of general. Reports of him cite his gallantry, efficient service, bravery, and "soldierly bearing."

There were a great many more Scandinavians to be counted among the soldiers of the Union, from a far larger population. Census figures for the decade between 1850 and 1860 show a jump of nearly 55,000 Americans claiming to have been born in Scandinavia. Among them are some of the most resounding names of the history of the Federal forces—and one obligatory rogue.

It would be unusual for Scandinavians not to be attracted to the sea, given their Viking ancestry, and one of Scandinavia's most famous immigrant sons surely must be John Ericsson, a Swede, inventor of the propeller, so critical to naval maneuvering—and designer of the Union ironclad ship the *Monitor*. Two members of the ironclad's crew were also Swedish: M. P. Sunstrum, assistant engineer, and seaman Hans Anderson. Ericsson fought ridicule and design prejudice to convince the Lincoln administration of the fact that an iron ship could not only stay afloat but maneuver tactically and withstand solid shot in battle.

Admiral John Adolph Dahlgren of the U.S. Navy was also the son of Swedish immigrants, and went on to great fame as the inventor of the so-called "Dahlgren Gun," an Artillery piece. Commanding the Washington Navy Yard at the beginning of the war, Dahlgren was given charge of the blockade that kept Southern ports from receiving or shipping forth any goods, supplies, foodstuffs, or luxuries for the Confederacy. He assisted in the taking of Savannah, Georgia, in 1864, and was instrumental in the siege of Charleston, South Carolina, in 1865, where his flagship was torpedoed and sank. Dahlgren escaped, however, to live another five years in relative peace.

Many other Scandinavians served creditably in the Union forces: Oscar Malmborg, a hero of the Mexican War, who was so bad-tempered in spite of his heroics in the Civil War that he was relieved of duty—only to have the general in command, John Logan, criticize Malmborg's replacement as not being nearly as gallant and effective as the man he replaced; General Charles Stolbrand, personally commissioned a general of artillery by Lincoln, and who fought bravely at Vicksburg and Savannah; and Ernst von Vegesack, who served for two years in the Union army, rose to the rank of brigadier general, and was cited frequently by his superiors in their reports for his "admirable example . . . calm courage . . . and meritorious conduct."

Scott, Winfield

1786–1866

Having already served as the country's general-in-chief for two decades, America's preeminent military figure—perhaps the most celebrated since George Washington—was nearly 75 when he commanded the Union armies at the start of the Civil War. By that time, Scott, a Virginia native who refused to join the Confederacy, was clearly nearing the end of his brilliant career.

Hero of the War of 1812 and Black Hawk War, commander of U.S. forces in the Mexican War, unsuccessful Whig presidential candidate in 1852, Scott, called "Old Fuss and Feathers" because of his devotion to military pomp and protocol, now suffered from gout and vertigo, weighed more than 300 pounds, and could no longer ride his horse. Because of his infirmities, he required a field commander and urged Lincoln to appoint his fellow Virginian Robert E. Lee to the position. George B. McClellan, who got the post after Lee turned down the Union commander's personal appeal, soon began to resent Scott and took to contradicting him in staff meetings and snubbing him in public.

By then, however, the general-in-chief was being amply ridiculed elsewhere as well. Blamed for the Union's dismal showing in the first months of the war, Scott received sharp criticism for his "Anaconda Plan," in which he recommended a naval blockade to press the

General Winfield Scott

Confederacy while the Union gradually developed its armed forces for what he anticipated to be a long struggle. Although Scott was more clearheaded on the subject than the majority of military and political figures—Union and Confederate alike—who believed the war would conclude quickly, many suspected Old Fuss and Feathers was growing senile.

On November 1, 1861, after another Union battlefield defeat at Ball's Bluff, Lincoln accepted Scott's standing offer to resign. Succeeded the same day by McClellan, he retired to write his two-volume memoirs, travel through Europe, and see the essential elements of his Anaconda Plan ultimately prove effective in the waging of the war.

Secession

Decades of increasing tension between Northern and Southern states over slavery and other economic and political issues reached a breaking point when Republican Abraham Lincoln was elected president of the United States in November 1860.

Since the beginning of the nineteenth century, the North had been steadily gaining in population and expanding economically. In 1800, half the nation's five million people lived in the South; by 1850, only a third lived there. Of the nine largest cities in the United States, only New Orleans was located in the lower South.

At the same time, the South continued to base their economy on agriculture, while the North entered the Industrial Revolution with enthusiasm. By 1852, only a tenth of the goods manufactured in America came from Southern mills and factories. A French visitor wrote, "Every day the North grows more wealthy and densely populated, while the South is stationary or growing power . . . The first result of this disproportionate growth is a violent change in the equilibrium of power and political influence . . . These changes cannot take place with-

out injuring interests, without exciting passions."

At the center of the crisis in 1860 was the question of slavery. Apart from the moral issues involved, slavery also touched upon almost every aspect of relations between individuals and their government and between the states, including interstate commerce, protection of private property, and the tallying of population to determine congressional apportionment. Moreover, slavery—and its spread to other states and territories—was deemed imperative to the Southern economy.

By the 1850s, many parts of the South had been over-farmed; after two centuries of planting soil-depleting crops like cotton and tobacco, much of the land was no longer arable. Only with the spread of slavery into other parts of the country could the wealthy Southern planters continue to make profits and to sustain what they considered a gracious way of life.

With Lincoln's election, the delicate balance of power between North and South tilted sharply in the North's favor; the South felt that with Lincoln in the Oval Office, slavery's days were numbered. Secessionists argued that since sovereign states had created the Union for their mutual benefit, any state that felt injured by the government it had helped create had a right to withdraw rather than submit to laws with which it disagreed.

South Carolina was the first to secede, issuing the Ordinance of Secession on December 20, 1860. Passed by a unanimous vote of its 169 members, the state convention repealed the ratification of the 1788 Constitution of the United States, stating that "the Union now subsisting between South Carolina and the other states, under the name of the United States of America, is hereby dissolved." Six other states adopted similar statutes: Mississippi seceded on January 9, 1861; Florida, January 10; Alabama, January 11; Georgia, January 19; Louisiana, January 26; and Texas, February 1.

From February 4 to 9, the first convention of Confederate states was held in Montgomery, Alabama, with representatives from each seceded state in attendance. A provisional constitution creating the Confederate States of

MERCURY

EXTRA:

Passed unanimously at 1.15 o'clock, P. M. December 20th, 1860.

AN ORDINANCE

To dissolve the Union between the State of South Carolina and other States united with her under the compact entitled " The Constitution of the United States of America."

We, the People of the State of South Carolina, in Convention assembled, do declare and ordain, and it is hereby declared and ordained,

That the Ordinance adopted by us in Convention, on the twenty-third day of May, in the year of our Lord one thousand seven hundred and eighty-eight, whereby the Constitution of the United States of America was ratified, and also, all Acts and parts of Acts of the General Assembly of this State, ratifying amendments of the said Constitution, are hereby repealed; and that the union now subsisting between South Carolina and other States, under the name of "The United States of America," is hereby dissolved.

THE

UNION

IS

DISSOLVED!

Special edition of the Charleston Mercury announces South Carolina's secession.

America was adopted on February 8, and Jefferson Davis and Alexander Stevens were chosen as president and vice-president on February 9.

After Fort Sumter fell on April 14, 1861, four other states joined the Confederacy, beginning with Virginia on April 17, followed by Arkansas on May 6, North Carolina on May 20, and Tennessee on June 8. In addition to these 11 states, Confederate governments vied with Union regimes in Kentucky and Missouri throughout the war. The Confederate States of America was dissolved after the military surrender at Appomattox Court House and reunited with the Union during the process of Reconstruction.

Secret Service

In the strictest sense of the title, the Secret Service in the United States was originally an outgrowth of the Treasury Department, only becoming a protective unit for the chief executive, the president, later on. In terms of the Civil War, the term conjures up exactly what it was at that time: an organization of spies and paid informers, to be found in both the Confederate nation and the Union. Not a great deal of scholarship has been presented on the background of these groups, though a great deal has been written on the lives and actions of various individual spies.

Uniformed soldiers scouting, observing, talking to civilians, and questioning captured enemies was not considered to be spying. However, if the exact same activities were done in civilian clothing, or while wearing the uniform of the opposite army, with every effort made to hide the truth, that was most decidedly spying—and both sides considered it an offense to be punished with at least imprisonment, more usually with death by hanging.

With all the dangers to life, limb, and loved ones that spying potentially included, there was seldom a lack of willing volunteers. Some backed into working for the Secret Service on both sides because they were bored or wanted to participate in the thrill of doing something they would not ordinarily have done. Many of these were women, bound by the strictures of Victorian society. Wartime, with its ready excuse of patriotism, allowed women freedoms they would never have had in peacetime, and so society ladies such as Rose O'Neal Greenhow and Belle Boyd donned disguises, flirted with enemy officers, eavesdropped on conversations, and then carried what they had learned to their contacts. The danger was very real, and very seldom did a spy make it through the entire war without being captured at least once.

There were those who fell into spying without quite realizing what was happening, like tragic young Sam Davis of Tennessee, who insisted to the end of his life, try though his captors might to make him say otherwise, that he was no spy—and that he would not reveal the identity of his sought-after commanding officer, the spy Henry Shaw. And then there were those who, once realizing they were in a situation where they might overhear sensitive information, happily collected it and passed it on. Such a one was Miss Antonia Ford of Fairfax, Virginia, whose parents entertained Jeb Stuart and John Mosby when the town was in Confederate hands, and were questioned by the Federals when Fairfax became occupied once more. Antonia blushingly accepted a joke commission as a Confederate cavalry captain from the gallant Stuart; the commission was used as evidence against her when she was arrested, and she was locked up in Old Capitol Prison in Washington, D.C. Her story has a happier ending than most, for her chief guard, Captain Willard of a famous hotel family, fell in love with her—and married her as soon as she was released from jail.

Both sides actually had formally organized Secret Service groups, though it was widely believed for many years that the South's network was highly informal. In Washington, the organization was headed by Lafayette "Lafe" Baker, a shadowy figure of a man about whom little was

Execution of a Confederate spy.

known during his career. A believer in temperance, who never touched a drop of alcohol and never swore, Baker was nevertheless a cold-blooded man beneath his mild exterior; a dead shot with pistol and rifle, he was known among his few friends as a man who would not hesitate in the least to kill someone if it seemed the right thing for him to do. Baker went to great lengths to prove his loyalty to General Winfield Scott, traveling extensively in the Confederacy for several months gathering information at great personal risk. When he returned to Washington, Scott became his patron. Baker was interested mostly in personal advancement and very much wanted to be in charge of the Secret Service, but one man stood in his way: Allan Pinkerton, the current head of national security. However, Baker had only to wait patiently; Pinkerton supported General George McClellan, and when McClellan annoyed President Lincoln for the last time, Pinkerton's organization fell apart. Baker only had to step into his rival's shoes to accomplish his goal.

It is now believed by scholars that there was no one head of the Secret Service in the Confederate States, but rather that high-level members of the government acted in concert with the military commanders to get information, or to stop secrets from being sent North by counter-spies. Surely among those involved at the highest level were President Jefferson Davis, Judah Benjamin, Secretary of War James Seddons, and Richmond's provost marshal, General John H. Winder. Winder was charged with seeing to it that spies were prevented from getting information out of the Confederate capital, but in one spectacular case he consistently failed. Living in Richmond, the Unionist daughter of an old Virginia family sent information of all sorts to the Federals on a constant basis. Her name was Elizabeth Van Lew, and when the war was over she lived on, safe in her home, as her neighbors believed she was insane and referred to her as "Crazy Bet."

On the military end of things, perhaps the most effective scout on both sides was the Con-

Spies in Buell's army abandoning their stolen train in Georgia. They would eventually be caught and executed.

federate raider John Singleton Mosby. For most of the war he commanded the fabled 43rd Battalion of Cavalry, or Mosby's Rangers known to the Union as "Mosby's Guerillas" in addition to a host of less pleasant things. The bane of most Federals' existence, Mosby gained more information on troop movements, changes in command, and battlefield effective strength of the Union forces than perhaps any other operative.

In the long run, the duty of the Secret Service on both sides was to keep an eye on the enemy, find ways to strike at their effectiveness, and halt their access to information about their opponent while gathering as much information as possible about themselves. The activities of these spies, many of whom simply preferred to be called patriots, enliven the pages of the war's history with equal gallantry, bravery, and honor to the exploits of the uniformed soldiers of the armies.

Seven Days Campaign

JUNE 25–JULY 1, 1862

Putting an end to the Union's first attempt to capture the Confederate capital of Richmond, Robert E. Lee's campaign of deception was a devastating defeat for the Union army. Although the Union technically won almost all seven of the battles fought during the last week of June 1862, the army found itself pushed back all the way to Harrison's Landing, largely because of Union Major General George B. McClellan's fear and indecision.

After the battle of Seven Pines, McClellan divided his army, moving about 80,000 men south of the Chickahominy River. About 20,000 Union troops under Fitz-John Porter remained on the north side of the river to await the arrival of Irwin McDowell's troops on their way from Fredericksburg. As McClellan prepared to move against Richmond, however, Robert E. Lee devised a brilliant plan to move the action away from the capital and take the offensive. His first move was to divide his own army of about 55,000, leaving about 20,000 men with corps commander John Magruder, who would try to detain McClellan, while he himself took about 25,000 men to attack Porter's weak right flank.

The first engagement of the Seven Days Campaign took place on June 25, when a Union reconnaissance division under Joseph Hooker met Confederate troops at Oak Grove. After a full day of fighting, the Union managed to dislodge the Confederates, but at a loss of more than 625 Federal soldiers. From then on, Lee took the offensive, assisted by his three able corps commanders, Ambrose P. Hill, Daniel H. Hill, and James Longstreet. Also expected to participate was Thomas "Stonewall" Jackson. Exhausted after his successful and brilliant campaign in the Shenandoah Valley, however, Jackson was more a hindrance than a help to Lee.

On June 26, Lee dispatched Hill with five infantry brigades and artillery across the Chickahominy to launch a frontal attack on Porter, who had assumed a defensive position behind Beaver Creek Dam about a mile from a small town called Mechanicsville. In the meantime, Jackson would arrive in time to hit Porter from the rear. Jackson, however, never arrived at the battle site, leaving Hill to attack Porter on his own.

The Confederates fought for more than six hours against a well-prepared Union force; by the end of the day, they had lost nearly 1,500 men while only 360 Union men fell. Under orders from McClellan, Porter then withdrew to another prepared position at Gaines' Mill, which he was ordered to hold at all costs. Hill renewed his attacked there the next morning, only to be stopped by the main Federal line located on a high plateau near Boatswain's Swamp.

Longstreet joined Hill on the Union left in the middle of the afternoon, but was ordered by Lee to delay his attack until Jackson and his men could get in position to hit the opposite flank. Once again, however, Jackson failed to appear when expected, upsetting the battle plan. After a long day of intermittent but heavy skirmishing, the Confederates suddenly launched a full frontal assault, piercing the Federal line.

The day's losses were devastating to both the Union and Confederacy. Out of approximately 34,000 Federals engaged, there were more than 6,800 casualties; about 8,700 out of 57,000 Confederates were lost. Unnerved by Lee's aggression, and believing false reports estimating his enemy's strength at double his own, McClellan ordered a strategic withdrawal.

For the next three days, Lee pursued the retreating Federal army, forcing battles at Savage's Station and White Oak Swamp that did little damage to the Union army but lost him valuable manpower. Nevertheless, his offensive kept the Union army on the run until June 30, when McClellan halted at a strong position on Malvern Hill.

Organizing his defenses throughout the day,

McClellan amassed some 250 guns to cover enemy approaches. Although Lee had been warned of the position's impregnability, he decided to attack on the morning of June 1. He first attempted to establish an artillery line of his own, but problems with organization gave the Union the upper hand. Later, as Confederate troops stormed the hill, they were mown down by Union artillery fire. This last day of the campaign was later described by Daniel H. Hill: "It was not war, it was murder." Lee lost more than 5,300 men; McClellan about 3,200.

Despite the fact that McClellan won the battle at Malvern Hill, and even though his corps commanders urged him to hold the position and launch a counterattack, the reticent Union general chose instead to withdraw further. By July 2, he and his troops were entrenched at Harrison's Landing on the James River. Lee would continue his offensive by launching the

Over 15,000 men died in a single day of fighting during the Seven Days Campaign. Here, Federal troops operate Parrott guns.

first eastern invasion of the North by Confederate forces.

Seward, William Henry

1801–1872

Called the "evil genius" of the Abraham Lincoln administration by Radical Republicans, the Union secretary of state steered a relatively even and successful course through the thicket of international and internal affairs during the Civil War.

After graduating from Union College in Schenectady, New York, Seward passed the New York State bar at age 21. His interest in local politics encouraged him to make a successful run for state senator as a staunch Whig in 1830. His 1834 bid for the governorship was unsuccessful, but he was elected to the office in 1838.

For four years, he served New York well, lobbying for equal rights for blacks and for changes in the educational system. Although he failed to win reelection in 1842, he remained a prominent member of the Whig party in New York and was elected to the U.S. Senate in 1849. As a senator, he vigorously opposed the spread of slavery into the territories on both moral and political grounds. His speeches were often inflammatory: in March 1850, he urged the Free-Soilers to "remain true to a higher law" than the U.S. Constitution.

Seward, however, was as ambitious as he was principled, and when he felt he had gone too far, he retreated to a more moderate ground. During the debate over the Kansas-Nebraska Act in 1854, he sided with Stephen Douglas, embracing his theory of popular sovereignty. Astute and insightful, Seward predicted that the compromises that had so far held the country together were no longer strong enough to sustain it. In 1858, he warned that the fight over slavery formed the basis for an "irrepressible conflict" between the North and South.

Having joined the nascent Republican Party in 1856, he was a front-runner for the presidential nomination in 1860, but lost out to a more consistently moderate Abraham Lincoln. Considering himself cheated out of the presidency by political maneuvering within the party, Seward almost rejected Lincoln's appointment to secretary of state, but he eventually accepted. Once in the cabinet post, Seward tried to exert his influence throughout the administration.

One of his first actions was to initiate a covert operation that would send the powerful warship the *Powhatan* to defend Fort Pickens in Pensacola, Florida. He did this without consulting Secretary of War Edwin Stanton or Secretary of the Navy Gideon Welles, who was especially perturbed because the *Powhatan* had been promised to him for his actions at Fort Sumter.

Once he realized he had overstepped his bounds, Seward attempted to call back the ship and its commander, David Dixon Porter, by sending a message through army Captain Montgomery Meigs. The message arrived too late; the *Powhatan* had already set sail. Seward apologized to the president and to Welles, and promised to refrain from meddling in military affairs outside his realm in the future.

He broke his word soon after by sending Lincoln a missive entitled, "Some Thoughts for the President's Consideration." In it, he pressed for a peaceful surrender of Fort Sumter and suggested that the United States instigate a war with a foreign power (Great Britain or France) in order to reunite the country against a common enemy.

Once Lincoln reined in his overly ambitious cabinet member, Seward proved to be an adept and even-handed secretary of state. In 1861, Seward managed to avoid the war he had once encouraged between England and the United States by negotiating a compromise solution to the *Trent* Affair. His greatest challenge in the international arena during the course of the war involved England's relationship with the Confederacy. In particular, he monitored England's manufacture and sale to the South of blockade runners; by doing so, he laid the basis for the successful prosecution of the *Alabama* claims at the end of the war.

One of Seward's most important roles involved supporting the president in his struggle to resist pressure from the Radical Republicans to emancipate the slaves. Although he supported emancipation, Seward urged Lincoln to wait until the Union had won a few major military victories before making such a controversial move; Lincoln heeded his advice and announced his Emancipation Proclamation only after the victory at Antietam in the fall of 1862.

On the night of April 14, 1865, Seward was attacked and seriously wounded by an accomplice in the Lincoln assassination. He recovered and was able to retain his post under Lincoln's successor, Andrew Johnson. He further earned the enmity of Radical Republicans by supporting Johnson's more conciliatory approach to Reconstruction. In 1867, amidst a power struggle between Congress and the executive branch, Seward managed to negotiate the purchase of Alaska from Russia at the cost of $8.7 million, an act described as "Seward's Folly."

After leaving the State Department, Seward embarked on a world tour, returning to Auburn, New York, where he died on October 10, 1872.

Shaw, Robert Gould

1837–1863

Dubbed "the blue-eyed Child of Fortune" by philosopher William James, Robert Gould Shaw—the son of wealthy Boston abolitionists—reluctantly became the commanding officer of the 54th Massachusetts Regiment, the first Northern regiment comprised of free black soldiers and noncommissioned officers, led by white ranking officers.

Shaw was a Harvard man from a period when Henry Adams, grandson and great-grandson of presidents, and William H. F. Lee, son of Confederate commander Robert E. Lee, also attended the school. He had seen some combat before accepting a new assignment at the urging of his mother: to train and lead a regiment of free blacks. Though not particularly in sym-

pathy with abolitionist goals, the young white commander—he was barely twenty-six when he took command—began to respect the courage and resolve of his untrained soldiers.

Many people believed at the time that black men were not brave enough to withstand combat, and though Shaw's correspondence shows he had some anxiety along that line, nevertheless he continued to build the 54th into a trained fighting unit.

Their first major fight was almost their last, and certainly was the end of Shaw; the 54th was assigned on July 18, 1863, to make an impossible assault on Fort Wagner, one of the harbor defenses of Charleston, South Carolina. Shaw led the attack on foot, and made it as far as the parapets before he was shot dead. At least twenty of Shaw's men were killed by his side, but they had reached the fort itself, and forever laid to rest the belief that former slaves would not fight for their freedom.

Shaw and his comrades were buried in a trench grave, almost where they had fallen. When it was suggested that he bring his son's remains home to Boston, Shaw's father refused, saying Robert was where he belonged: in the same grave with the gallant men he had commanded.

With doubts quelled as to the courage of the freedman, the North incorporated more than 50 new black regiments before the end of the year.

Shenandoah Valley Campaign, Jackson's

MAY–JUNE 1862

Swerving, feinting, and racing up and down Virginia's Shenandoah Valley, Thomas J. "Stonewall" Jackson utterly flummoxed three separate Union commands for more than a month in the spring of 1862 in a brilliant series of maneuvers that diverted thousands of much-needed Federal troops from the North's advance on Richmond. It was Robert E. Lee's idea to have Jackson take the offensive in the valley and prevent George B. McClellan from receiving reinforcements for his Peninsula campaign. The eccentric Confederate general faced superior numbers—both Nathaniel Banks' corps, based in Winchester to protect Washington, and John Frémont's force, preparing to invade east Tennessee.

But strengthened by Richard B. Ewell's division, Jackson was ready to move in early May with 17,000 troops, putting his strategy, "Always mystify, mislead, and surprise the enemy," into action. He ordered his equally mystified men east, pretending to head for Richmond, then suddenly put them on trains to return west. Disembarking at Staunton, the Confederates marched through the Alleghenies and smashed Frémont's unsuspecting front guard at the small town of McDowell on May 8. Jackson then scurried back into the valley to confront Banks' force, rumored to be preparing to join McClellan. Aided by intricate maps detailing the tortuous terrain and local scouts and civilian spies reporting the enemy's troop movements, he pressed his infantry north at a grueling pace. After fooling Banks into expecting an attack on his entrenched troops at Strasburg, Jackson swung east and hit one of his small, detached forces at Front Royal on May 23.

Jackson continued north, and with the Union capital now threatened, Banks, who earned his command more through political connections than military prowess, was forced to rush back

200 of Jackson's soldiers captured in the Shenandoah Valley, May 1862.

to his base at Winchester. Outnumbering the Federals more than two to one, the Confederates attacked at dawn on May 25 in a rout that sent the Union troops fleeing 35 miles, all the way back to the Potomac River and into Northern territory. In the process, Jackson's troops netted a treasure trove of food, weapons, and medical supplies.

The Union's panicked leaders assumed the Confederates were preparing to invade. Abraham Lincoln called for a massive convergence on Jackson: Frémont was ordered into the valley from the west, Banks was directed to regroup and hit the Confederate rear from the north, and at Fredericksburg, Irvin McDowell was told to shelve plans to reinforce McClellan on the Peninsula and send several additional divisions from the east. Ready with another surprise, Jackson led his army further north toward Harpers Ferry, as if preparing to cross into Maryland, then turned around and began an incredible dash south all the way to the other end of the Shenandoah Valley to evade the approaching forces. He relentlessly drove his troops—already exhausted by the three battles—marching them a punishing 25 miles a day. Their efforts poorly coordinated, Frémont, Banks, and McDowell could not catch the swiftly moving Confederates. Frémont and James Shields, leading one of McDowell's divisions, did manage to follow behind, fighting several rear actions, and when Jackson crossed the Shenandoah River at Port Republic, they had him caught between their two forces.

On June 8, however, the Confederates fought off a poorly mounted assault by Frémont near the small village of Cross Keys, and the next morning, Jackson took the offensive against Shields back at Port Republic, defeating the Federals after a tough three-hour battle. That night, the Confederates withdrew from the valley and boarded trains the following week to join Robert E. Lee's army outside Richmond.

The Shenandoah campaign made Stonewall Jackson a hero throughout the South. It was a legendary strategic triumph: outmaneuvering three armies and winning five straight combat victories, managing in all but one to mount a larger force despite being badly outnumbered overall. And it was a triumph of sheer courage, with Jackson's stalwart infantrymen covering over 350 miles and showing just why they were known as "the Foot Cavalry." Robert E. Lee's purpose was achieved; kept on the run and in the dark, surprised by lightning attacks and defeated in battle, nearly 60,000 Union were held in the Shenandoah Valley during a crucial period when the South was struggling to defend its capital.

Shenandoah Valley, Campaign of Philip Sheridan

AUGUST 7, 1864–MARCH 2, 1865

Ordered to put a decisive stop to Jubal Early's activities near Washington, D.C., Philip Sheridan organized the Army of the Shenandoah and began a seven-month rampage through the fertile Virginia valley, destroying the land as well as Early's forces before he was through. Commanding approximately 40,000 battle-tested cavalry and infantry troops, Sheridan began his advance up the valley in early August.

With reservations both military and political in nature—Lee had recently reinforced Early with infantry, cavalry, and artillery and Lincoln wanted to avoid a major defeat before his election in November—Sheridan's initial advance was quite cautious; he only skirmished with his Confederate enemies during August and early September. In fact, it was not until William Tecumseh Sherman had captured Atlanta on September 2 that Sheridan was encouraged enough in the Union position to take a more aggressive approach. After that, Sheridan attacked mercilessly.

On September 19, his troops met the Confederates on a field near the town of Winchester for a vicious, all-day battle that ended with a Confederate retreat to safe ground at Fisher's Hill. The total losses at the battle of Winchester amounted to more than 8,500 men. Three days later, on September 22, Sheridan sent three divisions under George Crook to attack the Confederate left while he led the remaining Federals on a frontal assault of the Confederate position at Fisher's Hill.

With another Union victory under his belt, Sheridan decided to return to Winchester to reinforce Grant. Early, meanwhile, retreated to Mount Jackson, near the Blue Ridge Mountains. Sheridan grouped his forces at Harrisonburg for a few weeks, then headed back down the valley toward Winchester.

As he withdrew, Sheridan stripped the country of provisions and stock, burned crops, and destroyed property, adhering to the "scorched earth" policy also promulgated by his commander, Sherman. By doing so, he stripped not only the Southerner's land, but their dignity as well. He was so successful in his efforts to devastate the countryside, he bragged that "a crow would

have had to carry its rations if it had flown across the Valley."

He was furiously pursued by Confederate cavalry, who so harassed his troops that he finally ordered commander Alfred Torbert to "either whip the enemy or get whipped yourself." On October 9, Torbert indeed whipped the Confederate cavalry at Tom's Brook. By the middle of October, the Union army was camped at Cedar Creek, while its commander was traveling to meet with Secretary of War Edwin Stanton in Washington, D.C. It was during Sheridan's absence that Early decided to make another attempt to beat the Army of the Shenandoah.

Launching a surprise attack at dawn on October 19, Early managed to drive the Federals back from several successive positions during the morning and early afternoon. Sheridan made it back to the front in time to rally his re-

Sheridan and his men moving up the Shenandoah Valley, December 1864.

treating forces and deliver a devastating counterattack that essentially crushed Early's army. On March 2, Sheridan and Early met in one futile skirmish that ended in another Confederate defeat at Waynesborough. This engagement marked the end of major military action in the Shenandoah Valley; Early's career was over and Sheridan joined with Grant for the final assault against the Confederates at Appomattox Station.

Sheridan, Philip Henry

1831–1888

One of the youngest commanders to serve in the Civil War, Philip Sheridan was known for both his extraordinary skills as a cavalry commander and his uncompromising attitude toward the enemy. "Smash 'em up, smash 'em up!" he would urge his calvary before they embarked upon one of their many devastating raids through Southern territory during the course of the Civil War.

Sheridan fought in several important battles in both the Western and Eastern theaters of the war, but was best known for the "scorched earth" policy he followed during his infamous Shenandoah Valley campaign (Sheridan's) from 1864 to 1865.

The son of Irish immigrants, Sheridan was born in Albany, New York, and brought up in Ohio. Too young to serve in the Mexican War, Sheridan was nonetheless so eager to pursue a military career that he falsified his birth date by one year to gain early admittance to West Point in 1848. Just five feet five inches tall and barely 115 pounds, this whip of a man was known as much for his bad temper as his fine horsemanship and fighting spirit. In fact, he was nearly expelled during his first year at the academy for attacking a cadet officer with a fixed bayonet during an argument. After serving a one-year suspension, Sheridan was allowed to return.

He graduated from West Point in 1853, thirty-fourth in his class of 49 members. His first assignment, as brevet second lieutenant in the 3rd Infantry, took him to the Rio Grande in Texas in 1854; he was transferred a short time later to the 4th Infantry in the Northwest. In 1861, Sheridan was promoted to first lieutenant, then captain of the 13th Infantry. Following the fall of Fort Sumter, he worked as chief quartermaster and commissary of the army in Southwestern Missouri until May 1862, when he was promoted to colonel of the 2nd Michigan Cavalry under Henry Halleck during the campaign for Corinth, Mississippi. Although he also acted as quartermaster—keeping track of supplies for the camp—during this period, his performance at Corinth marked the turning point of his career. Just a month later, at Boonesville, Mississippi, he and his troops experienced their first victory. The triumph at Boonesville earned him the rank of brigadier of volunteers in October, as well as a

Major General Philip H. Sheridan

transfer to the 11th Division of the Army of the Ohio, enabling him to participate in the Battle of Perryville. At Murfreesboro on December 31, 1862, his division of 5,000 held back more than twice that number of troops under Confederate General Braxton Bragg, allowing Sheridan's commander, General William Rosecrans, to form new lines and finally defeat the enemy.

As major general of volunteers, to which he was promoted on March 16, 1863, Sheridan participated in the capture of Winchester and assisted in the battle of Chickamauga in September, where his division sustained terrible losses at the hands of James Longstreet. At Chattanooga, Sheridan not only broke the Confederate line by storming Missionary Ridge, he also almost succeeded in capturing Braxton Bragg and several of his generals. By the end of the battle, his division was the only Union force able to pursue the retreating Confederates.

Impressed with Sheridan's stamina, bravery, and ruthlessness, General Ulysses S. Grant selected "Little Phil," as he was now known by his men, to head the cavalry corps of the Army of the Potomac. In that capacity, he participated with Grant in the Battle of the Wilderness and at Spotsylvania. From May 9 to 24, 1864, he undertook what became known as "Sheridan's Richmond Raid." His goal during this campaign was to destroy his counterpart at the head of the Confederate cavalry, the equally clever and daring Jeb Stuart. In addition, he hoped to raid the city of Richmond, damaging its communications and supply lines. Sheridan's first independent cavalry action was successful on both counts: on May 11, Sheridan defeated Stuart, mortally wounding him at the Battle of Yellow Tavern. By the time he returned to Grant on May 24, he had ridden completely around Lee's army, severed many vital communication lines around Richmond—including 10 miles of railroad track on three different lines and its telegraph system—and captured vast quantities of supplies.

In August 1864, Grant made the now famous Sheridan commander of the new Army of the Shenandoah. In this capacity, his primary objectives were to stop Jubal Early, who had made several raids on Washington, D.C., and to decimate the Confederate bread basket of the Shenandoah Valley. By August 7, Sheridan's Shenandoah Valley campaign was underway. Seven months later, Early had retreated and the once fertile valley lay in ruin. Sheridan's actions during this campaign earned him the undying enmity of the Southerners and two promotions from the Northern army, the first to brigadier general in the Regular army in September and the second to major general on November 8. By the spring of 1865, the Siege of Petersburg was nearing its final days.

On April 1, when Union commander Gouvernor Warren miscalculated the Confederate position at the Battle of Five Forks, Sheridan's quick thinking managed to transform what might have been a devastating loss into a resounding victory. Sheridan was able to readjust his cavalry divisions in time to turn the Confederates back and force a surrender. Sheridan captured four cannon, eleven flags, and about 5,200 Confederates. He and his troops were present at Appomattox Court House when Grant accepted Robert E. Lee's surrender.

Following the war, Sheridan served as commander in various departments throughout the country, including in the Department of the Gulf and the Department of the Missouri. In early 1869, he was placed in command of the Military Division of the Mississippi during Reconstruction. His unforgiving treatment of Southerners, so effective in war, was counterproductive in peace, and he was removed after just six months.

When Grant became president in 1869, William Tecumseh Sherman was elevated to general-in-chief and Sheridan was promoted to lieutenant general. During the 1870s, he spent much time in Europe and was present in Germany during a portion of the Franco-Prussian War. When Sherman retired in 1883, he left Sheridan his successor as general-in-chief of the United States Army. He was promoted to full general June 1, 1888, just two months before he died in Nosquitt, Massachusetts, on August 5, 1888.

and then to capture the Confederacy's last major rail center at Atlanta. However, when Johnston's army proved both more elusive and more tenacious than Sherman expected, Sherman decided to take a different approach: he would destroy not the army, but the South itself. With about 100,000 men, Sherman descended through Georgia on his way to Atlanta, decimating Confederate supply lines and property along the way. He arrived near Atlanta on July 17 and, after several battles in and around the city during the following six weeks, finally took the last bastion of Confederate strength by forcing General John Bell Hood to evacuate Southern troops on September 1.

After being promoted to major general for his victory, Sherman evacuated the civilian population from Atlanta and commenced to destroy the city's military resources. During his efforts there, a fire was started—most likely by civilians—that eventually gutted a large section of Georgia's capital. After abandoning the city, Sherman sent about 30,000 troops to defend Tennessee and took the rest southward on his famous March to the Sea. Along the way, he and his men set fire to crops and plantation homes, cut every conceivable supply line, and in doing so, crushed whatever spirit the exhausted Confederates had left. Turning north to attempt another offensive against the elusive Johnston in North Carolina, Sherman had arrived near Richmond in time to reinforce Grant in his final encounter with Robert E. Lee.

Five days after Lee surrendered at Appomattox Court House on April 9, 1865, Johnston sent a message asking Sherman to define his terms of surrender. Sherman's unauthorized reply on April 17 caused some controversy. For a man who pursued war with such violence, Sherman's terms were quite benevolent, at least in part because he believed Abraham Lincoln, who had been assassinated just two days before, had not wanted the South to be punished. Called a traitor by War Department chief William Stanton, Sherman was ordered by President Andrew Johnson to renegotiate for stiffer terms.

His extraordinary service during the war more than made up for this gaffe, however, and

Sherman continued to serve the military with distinction following the war. He first served as commander of the Division of the Mississippi; in July 1866, he was promoted to lieutenant general. On the election of General Grant to the presidency in 1869, Sherman succeeded him as general-in-chief in Washington, D.C. He served at that post for 14 years, until November 1, 1883. He formally retired from the military on February 8, 1884; he died on February 14, 1891.

Sherman's March to the Sea

AUGUST–DECEMBER 1864

Fulfilling his vow to "make Georgia howl," Union General William Tecumseh Sherman brought the brutalities of modern total war to the citizens of the deep South in the final months of 1864. "War is cruelty and you cannot refine it," he told Atlanta's mayor after capturing the city in September and forcing most of its inhabitants to evacuate. And it was precisely Sherman's intention to use that cruelty as a weapon against the Confederacy—to strike against civilians as well as armies and crush the spirit of the people who were supporting and sustaining the South's war effort.

Rather than confront John Bell Hood's forces to the west, Sherman wanted to head southeast, rolling through the heartland of Georgia all the way to Savannah on the Atlantic coast. In the process, his troops would wreck the state's transportation system and keep its bountiful supply of crops from reaching hungry Confederate armies. Though Ulysses S. Grant and Abraham Lincoln were both somewhat skeptical, they approved Sherman's plan.

On November 15, the Army of Georgia and Army of the Tennessee began heading out of Atlanta, burning much of the city before they departed. Marching in two columns, Sherman's 62,000-man force created a front 25 to 60 miles wide and proceeded to destroy bridges, factories, warehouses, and supply depots that lay in their broad path. Telegraph lines were cut, and miles of railroad track were torn up and twisted around tree trunks to make what the troops called "Sherman's hairpins." Cut off from its own communications and supply lines, the Union army had to live off the land, a task the soldiers undertook with special vigor. Sherman gave them permission to "forage liberally," and while they were told to avoid undue plunder of private property, discipline was lax and the order was mostly overlooked. In the words of one private, the troops "raised Hell." Livestock was confiscated, driven off, or simply slaughtered. Details of foragers known as "bummers" roamed through the fertile countryside daily, carting back wagonloads of meat, vegetables, and grain. The fall harvest was in and the corn that the onetime cotton planters of Georgia had

begun growing for the soldiers of the Confederacy now fed the Northern invaders.

While Sherman was depriving Robert E. Lee's army of the goods it so desperately needed to continue waging war, his own troops had far more than they could eat or carry, and simply discarded the rest or distributed it among fugitive slaves. The Union commander, no great believer in emancipation, could not stop nearly 25,000 liberated blacks from following the Northern force on foot or by wagon. There were other followers as well: deserters from both armies, Georgia unionists, and sundry renegades, eager to participate in the pillaging but obeying no one's command.

With Sherman doing little to discourage the marauders, they looted mansions, slave quarters, and churches alike, razing plantations, setting fires to houses and barns, and committing

Refugees in Georgia trying to outrun Sherman's March to the Sea.

other pointless acts of vandalism and destruction. To the citizens of Georgia, however—particularly the women and children who felt the brunt of the mayhem—there was little to distinguish the stragglers from the soldiers, and an understandable hatred of Sherman and the North was spawned that endured for generations. But the Federal troops were in high spirits throughout the march, better fed than they had ever been in their army careers and facing little armed resistance. The opposition was limited to a few thousand state troopers, militiamen, and an outnumbered cavalry corps that Sherman's horsemen easily contained. After annihilating a small force that attacked its rearguard at Griswoldville on November 22, the Union army captured and ravaged Milledgeville, Georgia's capital, the following day.

Aside from a few brief skirmishes, there were no other confrontations, and the land mines, felled trees, and burnt bridges that the Confederates desperately hoped would slow Sherman's progress were barely an annoyance. Finishing its nearly 300-mile march to the sea on December 10, the Union troops reached the Atlantic coast just below Savannah, having inflicted, by Sherman's own estimation, over $100 million worth of damage.

He prepared to assault the city, but Confederate general William S. Hardee soon withdrew his 10,000-man defense force. Occupying Savannah on December 22, Sherman sent a telegram to Abraham Lincoln two days later, presenting the city to the president "as a Christmas gift." Then, with central Georgia left devastated and the entire South demoralized, the Union general and his troops turned their relentless attention to the Carolinas.

Shiloh, Battle of

APRIL 6–7, 1862

Essentially a tactical draw, this bloodiest engagement of the war to date came to be recognized as an important Union victory, although commanding general Ulysses S. Grant received much criticism for his efforts. In the North, it was initially referred to as the Battle of Pittsburg Landing, after the Tennessee River embankment the Union forces were defending, but both sides came to call the battle by the name of a small Methodist log meetinghouse near where some of the fiercest fighting occurred—a church known as Shiloh, from the Hebrew word for "place of peace."

Grant and his 42,000 troops had been bivouacked on the west side of the Tennessee River near the Mississippi border for almost a month in early spring 1862, waiting for the arrival of Don Carlos Buell's army. Together, the forces were to head south to attack Corinth, a major Southern railroad center. At Corinth, Confederate General Albert Sidney Johnston decided to go on the offensive and catch the Union troops at their encampment before Buell's forces joined them. His second-in-command, Pierre G. T. Beauregard, originally favored the idea, then became convinced that the 22-mile march of over 20,000 soldiers would be detected and wanted to abandon the whole enterprise, certain that Grant would be receiving his reinforcements.

But by the morning of Sunday, April 6, when the Confederates arrived at Pittsburg Landing, there was no sign of Buell, and Johnston's forces surprised Grant, who was away from the front nursing an injured leg. At 8 A.M. the Southern army attacked, overrunning the divisions of Generals William T. Sherman and Benjamin Prentiss near Shiloh Church after three hours of ferocious fighting, with both sides suffering awful casualties. The Confederates' momentum was slowed, however, as ravenous Southern troops started foraging through the abandoned Federal camps to grab a quick breakfast.

As disorganization mounted, both Northern and Southern soldiers—four-fifths of whom had never been in battle before—scrambled to assemble in their correct units. The fighting soon deteriorated into dozens of furious, confused skirmishes; Confederate troops dressed in both blue and gray started firing on each other, and hundreds of infantrymen from both sides fled the battlefield in fear. Medical personnel and ambulance corps were unequipped to handle such overwhelming numbers of dead and wounded. Attention quickly focussed on one sunken road in a dense thicket where a small line of Union soldiers had been ordered by the newly arrived Grant, to hold the position at all costs.

Swarming with shells and bullets, the area became known as "the Hornet's Nest," and there the Federals beat back a dozen massive Rebel charges. As he directed the assaults, Confederate commander Johnston was shot in the foot and, with his staff keeping the news from his army, bled to death at 2:30 P.M. Three hours

later, under fire from 62 Confederate cannon, the 2,200 defenders of the Hornet's Nest were finally forced to surrender. While the delay gave Grant the chance to amass a line along Pittsburg Landing, supported by two gunboats and heavy artillery, the day had gone badly for the Union, notwithstanding the Confederates' loss of Johnston. As darkness fell—and with it rain—Beauregard, now commanding the Southern forces, suspended a new assault until the following morning.

That night, however, Don Carlos Buell's Federal reinforcements arrived, and Southern forces awoke to face a Union army nearly twice as

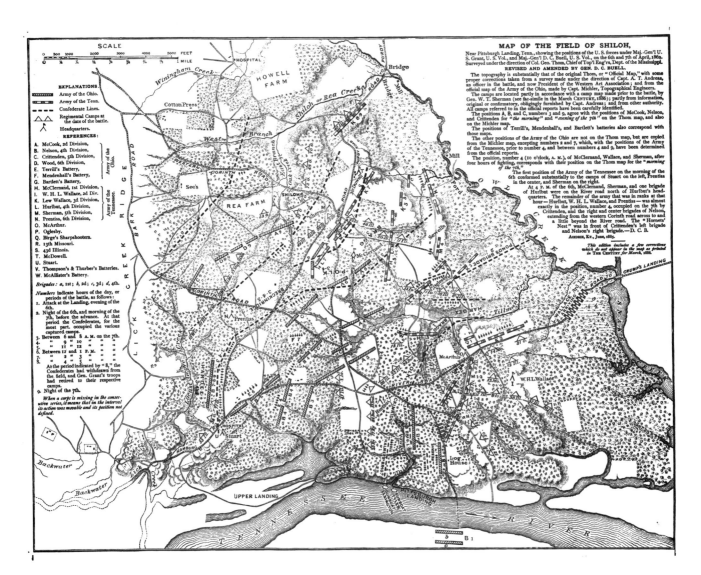

Map

Grant's last line at Shiloh.

large as their own, including 30,000 fresh troops. The fighting resumed at 7:30 A.M. and the Union forces retook almost all the ground they had lost the previous day. Making one counterattack, the Southerners kept falling back until, in the late afternoon, Beauregard ordered a withdrawal back to Corinth. With Nathan Bedford Forrest's aggressive cavalry covering the retreat, the Union army did not pursue.

The Federals could still claim a victory for holding their position, and the battle was indeed a serious setback for the Confederacy's position in the West. But Grant, despite redeeming himself on the battle's second day, was castigated for being caught by surprise in the first place. Falsely accused—by his superior Henry Halleck, among others—of being drunk

in battle, he was also blamed for the huge number of Union deaths. The losses on both sides were appalling. With 13,047 Union and 10,694 Confederate casualties, including a total of nearly 3,500 killed, more than twice the number of soldiers fell at Shiloh than in all the previous engagements of the war *combined*.

The battle may have affirmed the bravery of Union and Confederate soldiers, but it ended any lingering romance in the North and South about the conflict. And it taught its participants a ghastly lesson. After Shiloh, Grant recollected, "I gave up all hope of saving the Union except by complete conquest."

Sickles, Daniel

1819(25?)–1914

Had he not lost a leg during his controversial Gettysburg advance, the New York-born Union general might have been court-martialed rather than given the Medal of Honor. A shameless womanizer and shady attorney indited three times for legal improprieties, Sickles was already a notorious figure before the Civil War. His Tammany Hall political connections got him a seat in the U.S. Congress in 1857, and two years later, he caused the most sensational scandal of the day when he shot and killed his wife's lover—the son of Francis Scott Key—in the streets of Washington, D.C. Defended by Edwin Stanton in a shocking trial, he became the first American acquitted on a murder charge for reason of temporary insanity. Public support for Sickles subsided, however, when he took back his adulterous wife.

Facing a serious setback to his political career, he turned to the military when the war began and raised a rowdy brigade of New Yorkers. Sickles proved a surprisingly adept and stalwart officer in the field. A favorite of his commander, Joseph Hooker, he received several promotions, leading his brigade in the Peninsula campaign, a division at Antietam and Fredericksburg, and a corps at Chancellorsville. Sickles remained a corps commander after Hooker was replaced by George Gordon Meade, who was far less enamored of him.

Still, at Gettysburg, Meade gave Sickles the important assignment of covering the Union's left. On the second day of the July 1863 battle, Sickles decided that his position was vulnerable and, against orders, had his men advance to

General Daniel E. Sickles

higher ground a half mile in front of the Federal line. Separated from the rest of the army, Sickles' troops were even more exposed, and the movement left a big gap in the Union's defenses. A furious Meade ordered the maverick general to return to his former position, but by then James Longstreet's Confederate corps had started to charge. As the advantage seesawed back and forth, Sickles' and Longstreet's troops fought savagely over patches of terrain that have become famous in Civil War lore—the Peach Orchard, the Wheatfield, the Devil's Den. His leg shattered by an enemy bullet, Sickles was carried away from the field calmly smoking a cigar, and the limb was amputated within a half hour.

Meanwhile, his troops were driven back and other Federal generals had difficulty plugging the breach he had created in the line, but the Union's left flank did hold. Some have since suggested that Sickles' advance might actually have helped shield the Union defenses from the full fury of Longstreet's assault. But the Gettysburg debacle damaged Sickles military reputation—the Medal of Honor would not be awarded for three more decades—and his persistent criticism of Meade did not help. Although he remained in the army, Sickles was removed from field command.

After the war, he served as military governor of the Carolinas until Andrew Johnson fired him over his harsh Reconstruction policies. Sickles then reentered politics when he was appointed minister to Spain. He returned to Congress in the 1890s and was said to make several visits to the severed leg he lost at Gettysburg, which was exhibited at the Washington, D.C., Army Medical Museum.

Slavery

By the time the Civil War began in 1861, more than four million slaves lived in the South, comprising about a third of the region's population and forming the backbone of its agriculturally based economy. By far, the South's most important commodity was cotton: by 1860, cotton exports from the South were worth $191 million—57 percent of the value of all American exports. The astounding profits to be made from this crop, as well as from tobacco and rice, depended to a large degree on cheap labor, for all three of the South's main crops required long hours in the fields over many months to plant, cultivate, and harvest. The cheapest form of labor available were slaves: all that owners needed to provide their workers were food, clothing, and shelter, the quality of which varied from poor to barely adequate.

Although it was the dream of most young, white Southerners to own a vast plantation worked by slaves, only about 10,000 families owned more than 50 slaves while most owned 10 or 20. Indeed, just five percent of the white population controlled more than 40 percent of the slaves, cotton output, and total agricultural wealth in the South. These powerful families counted on slave labor to increase profits and sustain their wealthy life-styles; the smaller farmers simply could not afford to pay for the labor they received from slaves for free. In addition to economics, the Southerners fought against the end of slavery because many of them—poor as well as rich—believed that they were racially superior to blacks, that the law of nature permitted the strong to rule the weak. Others claimed that slavery was beneficial to blacks as well as whites. Perhaps most important, proslavery Southerners linked the continuation of slavery to their honor, way of life, and destiny.

Slavery had been practiced in nearly every society across the globe since the beginning of recorded history. Conquered Greeks were sold as slaves by Romans as early as 170 B.C. In about 1300, the first black slaves imported by Europeans were purchased by Italians from North African Arabs with whom they traded; the Arabs had enslaved West Africans for centuries. During the 1400s, the European slave trade began in earnest when Portuguese sailors started to explore the coast of West Africa and to ship black Africans to Europe. Both the practice of slavery and the slave trade quickly spread to other European nations and their colonies in the New World. From 1510 to 1870, nearly 9.6 million Africans were captured, about half of whom were brought to what would become the Southern United States. In 1619, the first slaves brought to the American colonies arrived in Jamestown, Virginia. By 1775, slavery was legal in all 13 colonies, although the practice was dying out in the North.

During the 1787 Constitutional Convention, slavery had been banished in five Northern states, but since about 30 percent of the 55 delegates to the convention were slaveowners, and many others had an economic state in slavery (i.e. shipmasters) no mention of abolishing slavery was made. Almost from the beginning, slavery flourished mostly in the South, where large plantations flourished; in the North, farms tended to be smaller and manufacturing and commerce developed more rapidly.

In 1793, the invention of the cotton gin made the production of cotton faster and more inexpensive than ever before. At the same time, demand was even greater than the supply: cotton was the single most important raw material to both American and British industry. The high demand for cotton led to the establishment of cotton plantations throughout the South. "Cotton is king," said Senator James Henry Hammond of South Carolina in 1860, "and the African must be a slave, or there's an end of all

Slaves on a South Carolina plantation preparing cotton.

things, and soon." Most of the plantation slaves were field hands who planted and picked cotton, although thousands also worked as house slaves in the owners' homes. Some slaves were hired out to factories or small businesses in Southern cities and towns in exchange for cash or barter. As the number of slaves required to work the fields increased, trading in slaves became just as profitable—sometimes more profitable—than the export of crops.

The colonial slave trade was conducted through an elaborate network between North America, the West Indies, and West Africa. The industries connected with it, including ship-building, manning of ships, and providing provisions, also grew in Northern and Southern cities alike. Even after the importation of slaves to the United States was banned in 1808, trading within the United States was common. Slaves were brought to this country under barbaric conditions: the ships were notoriously overcrowded and hundreds of thousands of blacks died along the way.

Once they arrived, they were often physically mistreated by their masters, who insisted on total domination. Slaves had no legal or human rights: they were not allowed to marry, own property, or testify in court, and they were considered to be the property of other human beings. Slave marriages had no legal status, and families were frequently split apart when one slave was sold to another plantation. Although

Dreams of freedom.

conditions under which slaves lived varied from owner to owner, health care and sanitation were universally lax: fewer than four out of 100 slaves lived to be 60.

Many slaves tried to escape the chains of slavery and thousands succeeded, including those who followed the runaway slave Harriet Tubman along an escape system called the Underground Railroad. Some slaves joined organized rebellions led by leaders such as Gabriel Prosser, Nat Turner, and Denmark Vesey. The widespread movement against slavery among whites began during the 1700s, when religious and philosophical leaders condemned the practice as a violation of human rights and God-given law. The westward expansion of slavery during the early and mid-1800s brought the is-

sue to the force in the United States, with pro- and antislavery factions waging a bitter fight over the new land.

Northerners feared that the South would gain control of Congress if Western territories entered the Union as slave states. If the slave trade could not expand, the South had more to lose than their power in Congress: much of its arable land had been overfarmed and could no longer produce the agricultural crops upon which its economy was based. In order to retain its economic and political power, then, the South required no only that slavery be allowed to continue in the states where it already existed, but to expand as well.

For decades, the South and North had attempted to compromise on the issue, but the

African-American family crossing over to Union lines.

simmering hostility between North and South came to a boil when Abraham Lincoln won election to the presidency. The Southern states withdrew from the Union and the Civil War began. In 1863, Abraham Lincoln's Emancipation Proclamation freed all slaves who lived in the rebellious states of the South; the Proclamation is considered the first step in abolishing slavery throughout the United States.

In 1865, adoption of the 13th Amendment to the Constitution legally ended the practice. The effects of more than 200 years of enslave-

ment on black descendants and the racism such enslavement engendered in whites remains a subject of intense debate.

Small Arms

Any weapon smaller than cannon and carried by a soldier was known as a small arm. During the Civil War, small arms included muskets,

Stacked rifles at Petersburg.

which were smoothbore, long-barrelled shoulder arms; rifles, shoulder guns with spiral grooves cut into the inner surface of the barrel; carbines, short-barrelled rifles; and handguns, including pistols and revolvers. Like artillery, small arms also were designated by their caliber, mode of loading (breech or muzzle), and maker. The principal small arms on both sides were the .58 caliber Springfield musket and the .69 caliber Harpers Ferry Rifle, both muzzle-loading arms that fired the deadly minié ball.

The introduction of these rifled pieces compelled a radical change in infantry tactics, which had been based on the use of the shorter range, less accurate smoothbore musket until the Civil War. Using smoothbore muskets, firing lines even 100 yards apart could not inflict much damage upon each other. For an attack to be successful, then, soldiers were forced to mass together and run directly into their enemies. The Civil War rifled musket, with its greater accuracy and longer range, was able to kill at a distance of over a half-mile, making a direct, frontal assault a particularly deadly affair.

One of the greatest small arms controversies during the war involved the debate over breech-loaders and muzzle-loaders. Because breech-loaders were able to fire more rapidly, they created a need for more ammunition, which neither army had in great supply. Breech-loaders were used primarily by the cavalry: one of the most effective was the recently-invented Spencer carbine. The Spencer carbine, which held seven .52 caliber cartridges, was easy to use and lightweight. Other important shoulder arms included the Henry repeating rifle, which carried 15 rounds of .44 caliber cartridges in its magazine, and the Sharps carbine. Hundreds of thousands of revolvers of different makes and models were used by Confederate and Union soldiers. By far, the most common was the Colt revolver, primarily the .44 caliber Model 1860 and the .36 caliber Model 1851 Navy, both of which were lightweight (less than three pounds). The Remington New Model and the Starr Army Percussion revolvers were also purchased in large numbers by both sides.

As in artillery, the North enjoyed an overwhelming advantage over the South in small arms. For much of the war, the Confederacy depended on imports smuggled through the increasingly effective naval blockade. Several different foreign models, particularly from France and England, were imported by the Confederate army, and some were made famous by the generals who used them. The French LeMat revolver, for instance, was favored by Confederate generals Jeb Stuart and P. G. T. Beauregard. Developed by a French-born New Orleans physician, the .44 caliber was produced in France when the Confederates could no longer supply the machinery or metal at home. The English Enfield rifle, which fired a .557 caliber shot, was another important import; about 700,000 were used by Confederates during the war.

Smalls, Robert

1839–1915

His spectacular 1862 escape from slavery, seizing a Confederate steamship in the process, led to Smalls' appointment as the first black captain of a U.S. merchant fleet vessel.

Hired out by his South Carolina owner, Smalls was serving as a pilot aboard the *Planter*, a paddle-wheel boat being used to transport arms and other supplies for the Southern army. On the night of May 13, 1862, the ship was docked in Charleston harbor with six guns aboard. When the *Planter*'s captain went ashore, Smalls and seven other black crew members commandeered the boat and, with Smalls wearing the captain's hat and coat, began sailing it out of the harbor. They passed the heavily armed Confederate forts with a salute and daringly paused beside a merchant vessel to dispatch a rowboat that picked up forewarned family members waiting at the dock.

Delivering the vessel and its supplies to the surprised Union blockade squadron anchored outside of the harbor, Smalls also furnished naval commanders with key information about Charleston's defenses, which was invaluable in

Captain Robert Smalls

subsequent operations against the port city. In recognition of his performance, Smalls was made captain of the *Planter* and served as a naval pilot for the remainder of the war, later becoming a South Carolina state legislator and U.S. congressman during Reconstruction.

Snake Creek Gap

MAY 1864, ATLANTA CAMPAIGN

This broad valley in the mountains near Dalton, Georgia, figured several times in the action surrounding the Atlanta campaign, William T.

Sherman's extended attempt to take and hold the critical railroad city.

At the beginning of the Federal march, Snake Creek Gap was the initial objective of Union General James McPherson's cavalry; between May 7 and 8 the blue horsemen attempted to swing through the gap as part of a three-pronged attack aimed at turning the left flank of Confederate General Joseph E. Johnston's army. Sixty thousand Southern soldiers held a strongly entrenched position on the ridges above Dalton, extending outward across Sherman's front. On the afternoon of the eighth, McPherson's men made a sally against Snake Creek Gap in hopes that Johnston's men would be too preoccupied repulsing the attacks of Sherman and General George Thomas elsewhere along the line. The Federal cavalry, however, met with only limited success.

The next morning, however, saw heavy fighting everywhere along the contested battle line. After another attempt to cut through Snake Creek Gap and attack the rear of Johnston's line, McPherson decided on the basis of reconnaissance that the Confederates were too well dug in and retired to a safer position, from which he sent to Sherman for further instructions. There is still discussion to this day as to why McPherson, normally a combative opponent, would have made such a decision; certainly at the time it annoyed Sherman.

Throughout the next day, May 10, there were more isolated fights and skirmishes. Johnston adopted a holding stance, knowing that reinforcements under Leonidas K. Polk were on their way from Mississippi. Sherman, on the other hand, was goaded by McPherson's inaction into committing his entire army to a passage through Snake Creek Gap. This action was begun the next day, with Resaca the nearest objective beyond the gap. By the end of the day on May 12, almost all of Sherman's men had made it through Snake Creek Gap and were poised to strike Resaca; Johnston evacuated Dalton that evening and arrayed his forces along Sherman's front, preparing to offer battle. Polk's reinforcements arrived, and the stage was set for the bloody two-day attempt to take or hold Resaca, Georgia.

Spanish- and Hispanic-Americans in the Civil War

The majority of scholarship at this time concerning the participation of Hispanic-Americans in the Civil War seems to focus on those Texas natives, known as *Tejanos*, who served with both the Union and Confederate forces. They represent only a portion of the nearly 10,000 Hispanic-Americans who actually participated, but historians have only begun to explore this fascinating aspect of the Civil War.

Long thought to have had high desertion

Union General Edward Ferrero and his staff.

rates, incompetent leaders, a tendency to switch sides at inopportune moments, and a lack of reliability in battle, the *Tejano* regiments—of which the best known are perhaps the 33rd Texas Cavalry and the 2nd Texas Cavalry (Union)—were in actual fact perfectly loyal after their own fashion, for they had very different goals from most Union or Confederate soldiers. Loyal to themselves first, the *Tejanos* had to deal with a great deal of prejudice against them in both armies, and perceptions of their leaders and their behavior in battle is very likely due to the language barrier with which they had to live. Orders given under hurried circumstances in a language one does not understand usually turn out to be orders that are not obeyed. The *Tejanos* were also frequently the last to get supplies, ammunition, feed for their horses, or food for themselves.

The 33rd Texas was commanded by Colonel Santos Benavides, who did his best to overcome poor supply lines and prejudice to take his men into battle. Time and time again they were called upon to fight against Mexican bandits and Union soldiers in Texas and the Southwest. Benavides never lost a single battle and was often praised by the Confederate government. At one point, he was embarrassed to discover that one of his troop commanders, Captain Adrian Vidal, defected with his whole company and joined the Union army. (Vidal would serve creditably for almost a year under the Federal flag, then he would desert again, heading home to Mexico with his men to participate in the revolution against the Imperialist faction. Later, he was to be captured and executed by firing squad.)

Of the 90-odd officially recorded Civil War-related fights in Texas, the *Tejanos* and their brethren were very likely involved in a significant majority. But the reality behind the involvement of Spanish-, Mexican-, and Hispanic-Americans in the Civil War is this: their story remains to be told.

Special Order No. 191

SEPTEMBER 9, 1862

On the ninth of September, Confederate Generals Robert E. Lee and James Longstreet collaborated on the production of a plan of action for the Army of Northern Virginia in its assault upon the Union Army of the Potomac, under command of the notoriously slow General George B. McClellan, in the vicinity of Sharpsburg, Maryland, along Antietam Creek. This plan called for a three-pronged attack upon the Union position at Harpers Ferry, leaving the Federals no means of escape. An order was issued from Lee's headquarters, to take effect on September 10, 1862; it was designated Special Order No. 191, and in great detail outlined the Confederate strategy. Order No. 191 listed which Southern generals were to strike from where, with what troops; it told precisely what each officer's objectives would be, and stated that the attacks would commence on the morning of September 12.

Lee's adjutant, Colonel Chilton, made copies of the order to be delivered by courier to each of the generals named in the document. Upon receipt of his copy of the order, General Stonewall Jackson made another copy for General D. H. Hill, who was on detached service to Longstreet's corps.

On the morning of September 13, with the Confederate plan well underway, two soldiers from the Federal 27th Indiana Infantry, encamped in a meadow outside Frederick, made a startling discovery. Sergeant John Bloss and Corporal Barton Mitchell found a fat envelope in the grass nearby, while they sat in the meadow and passed the time of day. Inside were three cigars, wrapped in a sheet of paper. Tobacco being much beloved of soldiers, and these being good cigars, the men were elated. However, when they looked at the writing on the paper, they went running for their commanding officer, Captain Peter Kop—the paper was a copy of Special Order No. 191, addressed to Major General D. H. Hill. Kop hurried to *his* commander, Colonel Silas Colgrove, and Colgrove went pelting to brigade headquarters, to speak to General Alpheus Williams. Here, in their hands, was the means to destroy the Army of Northern Virginia, to know its every move even as the maneuvers were being made, and to therefore be able to strike in force where resistance was least expected.

The paper was in McClellan's hands before noon, authenticated by Williams—who recognized the handwriting of Lee's adjutant, having known him in the old army before the war. "Little Mac" was delighted, clutching the paper in hand and crying, "Now I know what to do!" He promptly wrote a wire to President Abraham Lincoln, informing him he had the plans of the enemy in hand, and that he would send the president "trophies" when the destruction of Lee's forces was complete. However, he crowed too soon; in customary fashion, McClellan failed to take full advantage of the information that had so luckily fallen into his hands. Delays and failures to move where and when expected plagued him; confused and confusing instructions to subordinates, and inexplicable, inexcusable lack of action on several fronts led to Sharpsburg being a bloody stand-off, with both sides claiming victory in some fashion or another, as Lee slipped out of McClellan's grasp yet again.

In after years, D. H. Hill roundly denied that he had lost his copy of Special Order No. 191, which had come to be known as the "Lost Order." There was no record in his headquarters papers of the dispatch having been received, the careful recording of which would have been a normal and expected duty of the headquarters staff. A fascinating discussion of the order, cross-referencing such details as the dates and times of day that substantiating evidence concerning the document's authenticity, and whether or not Robert E. Lee was aware that the order had been mislaid and fallen into the wrong hands, can be found in *Landscape Turned Red*, an excellent account of the Battle of Antietam by historian Stephen W. Sears.

Spotsylvania, Battle of

MAY 7–19, 1864

Directly on the heels of the bloody Battle of the Wilderness, the armies of Ulysses S. Grant and Robert E. Lee lost thousands more in over a week of equally fierce fighting outside the tiny Virginia crossroads town of Spotsylvania Court House in May 1864. The Federal troops anticipated a retreat following the earlier battle, but instead, Grant ordered them to advance further south. Some contend that he was purposely waging a brutal and costly war of attrition, quite willing to sustain unprecedented Union casualties to wear down the enemy's outnumbered forces. But his actual goal was far more strategic, hoping to force Lee's army into the open, where it could be smashed decisively by the Union's superior numbers and weaponry.

Anticipating Grant's move and not wanting the Federals to block his way to Richmond, Lee and his forces raced south as well and, on May 8, arrived at Spotsylvania first, where they began constructing formidable protective fieldworks. Grant now had to take the offensive and intended to make a showdown of it, proclaiming he would "fight it out on this line if it takes all summer." After an abortive attempt to hit Lee's left flank, he ordered an attack on an arched salient called the "Mule Shoe" near the center of the Confederate line. Supported by heavy artillery fire, a Union division under an intense young colonel, Emory Upton, made a wild, running charge in the late afternoon on May 10, breaking through the enemy's strong defenses and taking 1,000 prisoners before being driven back.

Encouraged by the initial success, Grant decided to mount a larger assault against the Confederate center. At 4:30 A.M. on May 12, Winfield Scott Hancock's 15,000-strong corps led off the attack, breaching the inverted v-shaped Southern line, capturing nearly an entire infantry division, and dividing Lee's army. The Confederates were pushed back almost half a mile while the Federals regrouped in the trenches they had just overrun.

Answering the onslaught, Lee himself prepared to lead a countercharge, but, as they had the week before at the Wilderness, his troops insisted he move to safety in the rear. The two armies then battled for 20 hours straight in some of the most ferocious hand-to-hand combat in the annals of warfare. Soaked in blood and rain, the small piece of land over which they fought—known as "the Bloody Angle" ever after—was soon carpeted with layers of dead and wounded soldiers, while the hail of bullets flying around them sliced down trees nearly two feet thick. Both sides held their ground until well after midnight when Lee finally ordered his exhausted troops to fall back to a new, swiftly dug line of earthworks.

Over the next several days, Grant made unsuccessful attempts in the rain to flank the Confederates, and then, on May 18, tried another frontal assault that merely produced hundreds of new Union casualties. More than 17,500 Union soldiers had been killed, wounded, or captured at Spotsylvania. While the Confederacy's total was significantly smaller—10,000—the losses were far more devastating to the dwindling Southern forces.

Lee's army was hardly finished, however, and on May 19 took the offensive and mounted an assault on Grant's right. Withstanding the attack, Grant finally acknowledged that he could not dislodge and defeat Lee here. The next day, the Army of the Potomac was on the move south once more, with the Army of Northern Virginia scrambling anew to beat them to the next point of confrontation. Again, too locked in conflict to allow the customary period of recuperation following a major battle, both sides would plunge directly into more fighting.

Stanton, Edwin McMasters

1814–1869

Deeply committed to the Union cause, Abraham Lincoln's outspoken—some would say irascible—secretary of war led the Union army with equal parts dedication and ambition.

A pudgy, bustling figure with a scraggly beard, Stanton worked nearly as hard to promote the policies of the Radical Republicans as he did to arm and direct the armies of the North. A lawyer by trade, Stanton acted as counsel for the state of Pennsylvania from 1849 to 1856. His succeeding work as special counsel for the United States government brought him to the attention of President James Buchanan, who appointed him attorney general in 1860.

Edwin M. Stanton

With the election of Abraham Lincoln, Stanton returned to private practice for about a year. In early 1862, Lincoln called Stanton back to service after firing his first secretary of war, Simon Cameron, whose outspoken views against both emancipation and the use of black soldiers disturbed the more circumspect president.

Ironically, Stanton's own bluntness and strident manner made him many enemies among the administration; when Stanton began to press his own Radical Republican agenda, his president would find himself the target of some of Stanton's most cutting remarks. Stanton often accused the commander-in-chief of weakness, or even ignorance, in conducting the war, once referring to him as "the original gorilla."

Nevertheless, Stanton's intelligence and extraordinary administrative abilities did much to organize and sustain the Union army through four long, bloody years of battle. Stanton was one of the first to realize the importance of the ironclads and urged the navy to increase its fleet after witnessing the Confederate *Merrimack* (CSS *Virginia*) in action. Responsible for coordinating requests for troops, matériel, and provisions for the Union's armies across the country—which he did with remarkable success—Stanton was also intimately involved with Lincoln in mapping overall strategy for the war.

Stanton was not afraid of making unpopular decisions; to sustain and protect his army, he enforced the draft laws and instituted restrictions on press coverage of battles. He was tough on his generals, particularly those who did not share his political viewpoint. George B. McClellan, Lincoln's first commander of the Army of the Potomac, was particularly disliked by Stanton. Not only was McClellan an avowed Democrat with proslavery views, the general was also chronically slow in moving his army. "The champagne and oysters on the Potomac must be stopped," Stanton wrote during the spring before McClellan initiated his long-awaited Peninsula Campaign in 1862. "I will *force* this man McClellan to fight."

Stanton continued to express his opinions of Lincoln's commanders, frequently supporting the actions of the Joint Committee on the Conduct of the War. Following the end of the war and the Lincoln assassination, President Andrew Johnson asked Stanton to remain in his cabinet post.

Within a year, however, Stanton found himself at the center of great controversy. Bitterly opposed to Johnson's lenient Reconstruction policies, Stanton was asked by the president to resign his post. When he refused, Johnson suspended him and put Ulysses S. Grant in his place. Infuriated by what they considered an abuse of executive power, the Radical Republicans in Congress reinstated Stanton and began impeachment proceedings against Johnson. Soon after Johnson narrowly escaped removal from office, Stanton resigned his post and returned to private life. Edwin Stanton died on December 24, 1869, just four days after Congress confirmed his nomination to the Supreme Court put forth by President Ulysses S. Grant.

"Stars and Bars"

The famous nickname for the Southern nation's first official banner is often erroneously used to refer to the more familiar Confederate battle flag. Believing their new government the true successor to the original republic, most secessionists wanted to adopt a flag that evoked the "Stars and Stripes"—some even argued they should lay claim to the American banner themselves.

The "Stars and Bars," approved by the provisional Confederate Congress in March 1861, indeed bore a resemblance. Designed by Prussian-American Nicola Marshall, it featured three wide red and white horizontal stripes, with a blue canton (the top inner quarter) containing a circle of seven stars, one for each of the states that had then seceded. Ultimately the flag would have 13 stars—for the 11 Confederate states plus the secessionist governments of Missouri and Kentucky. The resemblance to the

"Stars and Stripes," however, proved to be precisely the drawback to the "Stars and Bars," as Confederate commanders learned from the earliest Civil War engagements.

In the smoke and confusion of battle, the two flags were easily mistaken for one another, particularly when they hung limp. Following First Bull Run, suggestions were sought for a more distinctive battle flag, and General Pierre G. T. Beauregard's design was put into use. This was a square banner featuring a blue St. Andrew's cross containing 13 stars, trimmed in white and set on a red field. The battle flag, often called the "Southern Cross," quickly gained great popularity throughout the South among troops and civilians alike, and it remains the banner most commonly associated with the Confederacy (though today's incarnations are typically rectangular). It was never officially adopted by the government, however.

In May 1863, the Confederate Congress approved a new national flag, which did use the battle flag design as its canton, set on a elongated rectangular all-white field. Known as the "Stainless Banner," this version was flawed as well, looking far too much like a flag of truce.

Trying again, the Southern legislature adopted a third design in March 1865, a truncated variation of the Stainless Banner with a wide vertical red bar on its outer edge, but its wide usage was precluded by the end of the Civil War. ("The Bonnie Blue Flag," nicknamed after a beloved patriotic song of the era, referred not to a Confederate flag but to the national banner of the short-lived Republic of West Florida.)

Though the seceded states all rejoined the Union after the South's defeat, eight of them felt enough continued loyalty or nostalgia for the Confederacy to revise their flags to feature elements of its various banners. The nostalgia lingers more than a century later as the "Southern Cross" continues to be embraced by many, with the emotional debate still raging over whether it is a symbol of slavery and oppression or of a heroic heritage worthy of respect.

States' Rights

When Confederate General Joseph E. Johnston called the Civil War the "War Against States," he was echoing the feelings of most Southerners that what was at issue was not the practice of slavery, per se, but the relationship between the states and the federal government. In the opinion of many in the South, Northerners, who now outnumbered Southerners and therefore controlled Congress, were attempting to enforce their will upon Southern states in the name of the national government.

The doctrine of states' rights is based on the 10th Amendment to the Constitution, which stipulates that the "powers not delegated to the United States by the Constitution, nor prohibited by it to the States, are reserved to the states respectively, or to the people." To strict readers of that clause, the federal government has the right only to declare war and conduct diplomacy in the name of the states. All other matters, including the right to allow slavery to exist within a state's borders, are to be decided by the population of each individual state. Those who believe in broad national powers find their proof in the "elastic clause" in Article 1, Section 8 of the Constitution, which says that the federal government can make any laws that are "necessary and proper" for enforcing its power.

The controversy over the relation between states' and federal rights arose shortly after the Constitution was adopted in 1787 and has never diminished. In 1798, the proposed Kentucky and Virginia Resolutions, passed in opposition to the Alien and Sedition Acts enacted by the federal government, pitched Thomas Jefferson and James Madison, who believed that individual states could decide whether or not to enforce federal legislation, against the Federalists' advocacy of strong central government. Another prominent states' rights controversy took place in 1814 at the Hartford Convention, when New England Federalists used the states' rights argument to claim that the national government had no right to enforce federal shipping policies that were the cause of the War of 1812.

Starting in the 1820s, as the country began to expand westward, the states' rights argument centered more and more upon the practice of slavery. The most extreme states' rights position was taken by South Carolina Senator John Calhoun, who developed the doctrine of *nullification*, which asserts that a state can nullify within its own borders any act of the federal government which it considers an invasion of its own rights. The doctrine was officially adopted by South Carolina in 1832. Such a theory led logically to the doctrine of secession, which viewed the Constitution as a contractual agreement between states and the federal government that could be invalidated as public sentiment within each individual state dictated.

In many ways, the South's insistence on states' rights weakened its position in the Civil War, since it limited its ability to organize a coordinated military and economic front. The Civil War marked a turning point toward government centralization; Constitutional amendments enacted since then have tended to limit the authority of the states and/or expand federal authority.

Perhaps the most sweeping change in the relationship between states and the federal government resulted from the passage of the 14th Amendment, ratified in 1868, which granted due process and equal protection under the law to all United States citizens. This led to the landmark Supreme Court decision, *Brown* v. *Board of Education, Topeka, Kansas* (1954), which held segregation in public school across the country unconstitutional.

As the civil rights movement grew during the 1950s, advocates of states' rights in the South insisted that each state had the right to "interpose the sovereignty of a state against the encroachment upon the reserved power of the state." Under this doctrine, which was struck down by the Supreme Court in 1960, a state would have the power to overrule a decision of a federal agency if it conflicts with a state law— a doctrine remarkably similar to nullification.

Heard most often in relation to black civil rights legislation, the rallying cry for states' rights has been invoked as a defense against a broad range of social and political change, including federal environmental protection regulations, abortion rights, and the extension of federal protection of civil rights to homosexuals and women.

Stephens, Alexander Hamilton

1812–1883

"Our new government is founded on the opposite idea of the equality of the races . . ." the new Confederate vice-president announced as he took his oath of office on February 18, 1861. "Its corner stone rests upon the great truth that the Negro is not equal to the white man. This . . . government is the first in the history of the world, based upon this great physical and moral truth."

A long-standing and vociferous proponent of the institution of slavery, Alexander Stephens was equally committed to the idea of Union, thereby making him odd choice for the Confederacy's second highest office. Born in Georgia, an orphan at 12, Stephens was raised and educated by an uncle. After graduating first in his 1832 class at the University of Georgia, Stephens studied law and passed the bar in 1834. He entered politics when he won election to the Georgia legislature in 1836, serving every year but one until 1843, and earned the respect of both his colleagues and his constituents. The small, frail man also earned the nickname "Little Aleck."

In 1843, he was elected to the U.S. House of Representatives, where he became a strong advocate of states' rights and slavery. Along with Howell Cobb and Robert Toombs, however, Stephens remained adamantly opposed to secession until Georgia officially seceded on January 19, 1861. His strong proslavery and states' rights views won him the support of the firebrands, and his pro-Union leanings struck a chord among the moderates. When the Provisional Congress met on February 9, 1861, Stephens' broadbased appeal won him election to the vice-presidency.

Because of his personal dislike and political animosity toward President Jefferson Davis, however, Stephens spent little time in Richmond or performing official duties. The relationship between Davis and Stephens was sour from the start both personally—Stephens referred to his president as being "weak and vacillating, timid, petulant, peevish, obstinate"—and politically. Stephens became the central spokesman for congressional and cabinet opposition to Davis' increasingly nationalistic approach to the war. He opposed Davis' efforts to institute a draft, to impose taxes, and to suspend the writ of habeas corpus. In fact, Stephens—who also abhorred Richmond's cooler climate—left the capital directly after inauguration.

In his efforts to mitigate Davis' nationalistic tendencies, Stephens elicited the help of his

brother, Linton Stephens, a powerful member of the Georgia legislature. Eleven years younger and much heartier than his brother, Linton had also opposed Georgia's secession, but once the war began had resigned the judgeship he held to join the Confederate army for a short time. Linton was elected to the Georgia state legislature in 1862 and from there coordinated efforts to oppose Davis with "Little Aleck."

From his self-imposed exile in Georgia, Alexander Stephens advocated a few wise policies, including the immediate sale of cotton to Europe before the blockade became effective. He was also at the forefront of efforts to achieve peace. He led the Southern delegation to the unsuccessful Hampton Roads Conference in early February 1865, at which he urged the two nations to put aside their differences and join together to fight the French in Mexico.

After the war, he was arrested and imprisoned at Fort Warren in Boston, Massachusetts, until October 1865. He then returned to Georgia, and to politics, winning election to the United States Senate. Because Reconstruction policies instituted after the election banned former Confederates from holding office, however, Stephens was forced to resign. He returned to private law practice until he reentered politics in 1872—when ex-Confederates were once again allowed to hold office—as a member of the U.S. House of Representatives. In 1882, he won election to the governorship of Georgia, but died just a few months after his inauguration.

Alexander H. Stephens

Stevens, Thaddeus

1792–1868

The most vocal and unrelenting abolitionist and Radical Republican during and after the Civil War, Thaddeus Stevens was known for his biting sarcasm and bitter invectives on the floor of the House of Representatives. After graduating from Dartmouth, Vermont-born Stevens moved to Pennsylvania to open a law practice. It was there that he first came into contact with the South's "peculiar institution," which was being practiced just over the border in Maryland. Finding slavery morally abhorrent, he frequently defended runaway slaves *pro bono* and became an outspoken abolitionist.

In 1848, he was elected as a member of the Whig party to the U.S. House of Representatives, then used his increasing power to organize the Republican party in Pennsylvania. One of Abraham Lincoln's most vocal supporters, Stevens was disappointed by the president's failure to offer him a cabinet position. Stevens' uncompromising stand on the South, combined with his acrimonious personality, alienated the more moderate Lincoln, and he remained in the House throughout the war.

As the chairman of the House Ways and Means Committee, however, Stevens exerted tremendous influence on the conduct of the war by pushing through legislation that supported Lincoln's more controversial actions, including the establishment of taxation and conscription. Lincoln resisted the powerful legislator and his Radical Republican brethren in their attempts to make emancipation the main goal of the war. Stevens urged the president to accept enlistment of black soldiers and expedited bills to abolish slavery in the territories. By doing so, he helped prepare the North for the acceptance of the 13th Amendment in 1865.

After the war, as chairman of the Committee on Reconstruction, Stevens established the Freedmen's Bureau and helped propel the passage of the Civil Rights Act of 1867. An outspoken opponent of Andrew Johnson, Stevens led the impeachment proceedings against Lincoln's successor and helped put an end to the era of presidential Reconstruction. He died on August 11, 1868.

Stonewall Brigade

Originally composed of about 4,500 green volunteers from Virginia, this brigade became one of the most effective fighting forces in the Confederate army. It was organized in April 1861, and, after several weeks of hard training, played a decisive role at First Bull Run.

Thomas "Stonewall" Jackson successfully lobbied to transfer the brigade to his army, where it remained until his death at the Battle of Chancellorsville on May 2, 1863. Like its counterpart in the Northern army, the Iron Brigade of the West, Jackson's force remained effective throughout most of the war despite terrible attrition.

The Stonewall Brigade played significant roles in Jackson's Shenandoah Valley Campaign and at the Battles of Gaines' Mill, Antietam, Fredericksburg, Chancellorsville, the Wilderness, and Spotsylvania. Finally reduced to 200 men after Spotsylvania, the brigade was merged with another regiment. On his deathbed at Chancellorsville, Jackson was heard to say, "The men of the Brigade will be, some day, proud to say to their children, 'I was part of the Stonewall Brigade.'"

Stowe, Harriet Beecher

1811–1896

Remembered chiefly for her antislavery novel, *Uncle Tom's Cabin*, Harriet Beecher Stowe was a dedicated and talented author who published numerous novels in addition to the one that brought her acclaim in the North and enmity in the South.

Born to a prominent Presbyterian minister in Litchfield, Connecticut, Stowe moved to Cincinnati, Ohio, with her family at the age of 21. In 1836, she married Calvin Stowe, a member of the Lane Theological Seminary, where her father was president. The Stowes moved to

Confrontation between members of the Stonewall Brigade.

Maine in 1850 in order for Calvin to accept a professorship at Bowdoin College.

Just two years later, Stowe finished writing *Uncle Tom's Cabin*, a literary account of life in slave-era United States. Despite the fact that Stowe had virtually no firsthand knowledge of the conditions of slavery or of the Southern way of life, she was able to draw convincing—if stereotypical—characters from her imagination and from the abolitionist tracts that flourished in New England. The book became an instant best-seller and a lightning rod for the ongoing slavery debate.

Immediately following its publication, George Aiken wrote and staged a theatrical play loosely based on the book. Aiken's version lowered Stowe's characters to the level of pure car-

icature and probably did far more to fuel the fires of dissension between North and South than did the book. Although *Uncle Tom's Cabin* made her famous, Stowe was only just beginning her literary career.

Over the next several years, she published several novels and collections of short stories, most of which depicted life in nineteenth-century New England. One novel, *Dred, A Tale of the Great Dismal Swamp* published in 1856, also dealt with the issue of slavery in the South. Stowe was the author of one of the most shocking books of the late nineteenth century, *Lady Byron Vindicated* (1870), which described the separation of Lady Byron from her poet-husband, Lord Byron. Stowe died on July 1, 1896, in Hartford, Connecticut.

Harriet Beecher Stowe

Stuart, James Ewell Brown (Jeb)

1833–1864

"We must substitute *esprit* for numbers," Jeb Stuart told his commander, Robert E. Lee. "Therefore I strive to inculcate in my men the spirit of the chase." More than a bit of a show-off in his colorful uniform and long, flowing beard, the Confederate army's best cavalry commander was both a fearless horseman who took incredible risks and a fine soldier who understood strategy and instilled confidence and loyalty in his men.

Deeply religious and, much like his friend Thomas "Stonewall" Jackson, pious and sober in his personal habits, Stuart also had a bit of a wild streak and was prone to both vanity and exhibitionism. However contradictory his personality, however, his skills as a cavalry commander were rarely questioned. Robert E. Lee depended on Stuart's excellent abilities as a scout and a raider throughout the first three years of the war, often referring to him as "the eyes and ears of my army."

Stuart was born and raised in Virginia. He entered West Point in 1850 and graduated thirteenth in his class. Brevetted second lieutenant in the Mounted Rifles, he served on the Texas frontier until he was promoted to first lieutenant on December 20, 1855. The following year, he and his regiment were sent to control the border wars in Kansas; in 1857, Stuart was seriously wounded while fighting the Cheyenne. A part-time inventor, Stuart took time during his recuperation to devise a sabre attachment for the War Department. While in Washington, he volunteered to serve on Robert E. Lee's staff during his mission to capture John Brown after the Harpers Ferry Raid in 1859. Stuart then returned to his regiment in Kansas until his home state of Virginia seceded in April 1861.

Committed to the Confederate cause and to the defense of his home state, Stuart resigned from the U.S. Army and returned to Virginia about a month later. He was commissioned lieutenant colonel of the Virginia Infantry on May 10, 1861, and 13 days later was named captain of the cavalry. At First Bull Run, Stuart's division defended the Confederate left, then performed a sweeping charge upon the rear of the defeated and retreating army. For his actions at Bull Run, he was appointed brigadier general on September 24, 1861, and spent the next several months skirmishing with Federal troops in the Shenandoah Valley.

His talents as a diligent scout and a daring raider were on display during the Peninsula campaign in June 1862. Ordered by Lee to reconnoiter the right flank and rear of George B. McClellan's position along the Chickahominy before the Battle of Mechanicsville, Stuart took 1,000 troops and, going far above and beyond his duty, rode completely around the Union army. Along the more than 150-mile route, he and his men, including the soon-to-be-infamous John Mosby, destroyed considerable Union property and captured dozens of Union soldiers.

Despite the fact that his actions alerted Mc-

Clellan to a possible Confederate attack and allowed the Union general time to prepare, the information and pillage he brought back to Richmond earned him a hero's welcome from Lee. Stuart continued to reconnoiter McClellan's army as it made its retreat during the seven days battles. On July 25, 1862, Stuart was promoted to major general and put in command of all cavalry forces in the Army of Northern Virginia.

Just before the Battle of Second Bull Run, Stuart performed an outrageous, but successful, raid on John Pope's headquarters at Catlett's Station. Covering 60 miles in just 26 hours, Stuart returned with two guns, 1,500 men, and a coat that contained a notebook outlining the disposition of Federal troops. These orders gave Lee vital information that helped him win at Second Bull Run on September 1, 1862. Thanks to this victory, Lee dared to risk an invasion of Maryland soon after and ordered Stuart to lead the advance of Jackson's corps while Jackson rode to Harpers Ferry.

It was good-humored and dedicated Jeb Stuart who was forced to tell Lee that a copy of Lee's battle orders had been appropriated by Union troops, thereby placing the whole campaign in jeopardy. The result was the bloody battle of Antietam on September 17, 1862, during which Stuart and his cavalry fought valiantly to hold the vital gap of the South Mountain. As Lee retreated into Virginia following the battle, Stuart rode north to attempt to cut a Union supply line in Chambersburg, Pennsylvania. Although he failed in that effort, he and his 1,800 men managed to ride 126 miles in just three days, circling McClellan's army again. Along the way, they destroyed a machine shop, raided several private stores, and captured about 500 horses before recrossing the Potomac on October 12.

At the Battle of Fredericksburg two months later, Stuart's cavalry guarded the extreme right of the Confederate line throughout this surprise Confederate victory. During the following winter and spring, Stuart was able to give Lee information on Joseph Hooker's crossing of the Rappahannock River in time for Lee to prepare a brilliant strategy for the Battle of Chancel-

lorsville on May 3, 1863. Stuart's cavalry also controlled all of the roads around Chancellorsville, keeping Hooker from discerning the Confederate position. When Stonewall Jackson was killed and his second-in-command, Ambrose P. Hill, was wounded during the battle itself, Stuart ably took command of Jackson's corps.

Following the spectacular Confederate win at Chancellorsville, Lee planned another Northern invasion, and once again counted on Stuart to provide reconnaissance. On June 9, 1863, he and his men encountered a Union cavalry patrol and there ensued the Battle of Brandy Station, Virginia, the largest cavalry engagement in American history and one that brought Stu-

Brigadier General J.E.B. Stuart

art another victory. His next endeavor, however, was less than successful.

To prepare for the Battle of Gettysburg, Lee sent Stuart out on another scouting mission to locate and report on Union troop movements. As was his habit, Stuart decided to push forward and take another "ride around McClellan." The Federal army, however, occupied much more ground and was much more active than Stuart had assumed. Driven far to the east, the "eyes and ears" of Lee's army was out of touch with his commander for more than 10 days. At least part of the blame for the devastating Confederate defeat belongs to Stuart, who did not arrive on the field until the second day of battle. Apparently learning his lesson, Stuart stayed in close contact with Lee during the next few months as he tracked Grant's movements during the devastating Wilderness campaign.

After the vicious Battle of Spotsylvania, Philip H. Sheridan, the Union cavalry leader, and 12,000 cavalry began moving toward Richmond with Stuart following in close pursuit with 4,500 exhausted men. They met in the Wilderness at a place called Yellow Tavern. During a desperate charge, Stuart was mortally wounded. He was immediately taken to Richmond, but died the following day on May 12, 1864. The personal and military loss to Lee and to the Army of Northern Virginia was incalculable.

Substitutes

During the Civil War, well-heeled men of the North actually considered it a patriotic act to hire someone else to serve for them in the Union military. There were several other options, after all, for affluent draftees who did not fancy themselves as soldiers, from an above-board payment of a $300 "commutation" fee each time their name was drawn to such under-the-table maneuverings such as being declared physically unfit for service by a bribed doctor.

Arranging for a substitute provided the army with the able bodies it needed, while allowing professionals and skilled laborers, at least in theory, to pursue work just as vital to the war effort. As a symbolic gesture to encourage the practice, even Abraham Lincoln hired a substitute—paying $500 to 20-year-old Pennsylvanian John Summerfield Staples, who had been discharged from the Union army once before when he contracted typhoid. So did draft-age future presidents Chester Arthur and Grover Cleveland, neither of whom would suffer politically for avoiding Civil War military service. Though little more than legalized draft evasion, substitution was a commonly accepted wartime practice, with a long tradition in Europe and a Revolution-era precedent in American history as well.

The Union's March 1863 Conscription Act exempted for the duration any draftee who could arrange for someone to join the army in his place. The price was agreed upon by the two men involved, usually with the assistance of one of the increasing number of "substitute brokers" who created a new, lucrative enterprise handling the arrangements. The pool of potential substitutes included teens under draft age and immigrants, often recruited by brokers back in their home country and occasionally tricked into a long-term commitment they never intended. Lacking a real motivation to fight, substitutes did not usually make the best soldiers, and army officials could be bribed to overlook physical and mental impairments. On the front, the veteran troops deeply resented these mostly undistinguished recruits, who would frequently desert or get themselves captured at the first opportunity. The government hoped to keep down the rates for hiring replacements, and communities attempted to raise the money for less affluent draftees, but it was not enough to ease the growing sense that substitution was a policy meant to benefit the rich.

A similar conclusion was reached sooner in the Confederacy, whose 1862 conscription law also sanctioned the practice. With no commutation fee option and a dearth of healthy men, the cost of hiring a substitute quickly skyrocketed in the South, reaching as high as $6,000—three years wages for an average worker. A luxury only very wealthy Southerners could enjoy, substitution fell into disfavor, and in November 1863, the Confederate Congress banned it altogether.

The Union, however, continued to allow the hiring of substitutes throughout the conflict. There, the cost remained within the reach at least of the middle class, and the practice continued to be endorsed by the president himself. By the end of the war, 118,000 men, six percent of the total fighting force, would join the Union military as substitutes for other men who were able-bodied—but also able to afford to dodge the draft.

Sumner, Charles

1811–1874

"We must not stop till we have laid the Slave Power on its back," urged Senator Charles Sumner at the Republican party's first state convention held in his home state of Massachusetts. The leading Radical Republican in the U.S. Senate before, during, and after the Civil War, Sumner fought for emancipation and against Southern interests throughout his career.

A member of a prominent New England family, he graduated from Harvard Law School in 1833 and was admitted to the bar the following year. For several years, Sumner worked as a reporter for the U.S circuit, then traveled extensively in Europe. In 1840, he opened his own law practice in Boston, where his interest in the antislavery movement blossomed.

As a leading abolitionist, Sumner developed a compelling oratorical style, lecturing on emancipation and the threat posed by the extension of slavery into the territories. Elected to the U.S. Senate as a Whig in 1850, Sumner quickly became a powerful advocate of abolition and Northern economic interests. He vehemently opposed the Kansas-Nebraska Act of 1854; when a vicious border war occurred in Kansas following the act's passage, Sumner delivered

his "Crime Against Kansas" speech from May 19 to 20, 1856.

Tall and handsome, but equally arrogant and self-righteous, the Massachusetts senator stood on the floor of the Senate and raged for several hours over two consecutive days about the evils of slavery and the shortcomings of those who supported it. Rather shockingly, Sumner constructed the speech around the metaphor of the "rape of a virgin territory" and filled it with sexual innuendo. He claimed that the "harlot . . . slavery" was the only mistress to whom Southern senators could pledge their loyalty and denounced the proslavery Missourians who were fighting in Kansas as "hirelings picked from the drunken spew and vomit of an uneasy

Charles Sumner

civilization." The inflammatory speech enraged citizens throughout the South. Preston Brooks, a representative from South Carolina, expressed his resentment quite violently.

On May 22, after the Senate had adjourned for the day, Sumner sat at his desk writing letters. Brooks, wielding a gold-headed walking stick, approached him from behind and accused him of libel. As Sumner began to rise, Brooks repeatedly bludgeoned him with the cane until the senator was bleeding and unconscious. "I did not intend to kill him, but I did intend to whip him," admitted Sumner's attacker, who was arrested on assault charges, then freed on $500 bail.

Brooks quickly became a hero of the country's proslavery faction; although the House of Representatives attempted to expel him, the 121–95 vote against him fell short of the two-thirds majority required to do so. Brooks pled guilty to the criminal charges and paid $30 in fines.

Sumner, who never fully recovered from his injuries, became the North's first Civil War martyr and the "caning of Sumner" became a symbol of the barbaric extent to which proponents of slavery would go to preserve their way of life. In 1857, Sumner, who was one of the first politicians in Massachusetts to join the antislavery, pro-Union Republican party, was elected to the Senate as a Republican and campaigned for the election of Abraham Lincoln in 1860.

During the war, however, Sumner emerged as a leader of the radical wing of the Republican Party, pressuring Lincoln to make emancipation and equal rights for blacks the war's true goals. Despite their differences, Lincoln appointed Sumner chairman of the Senate Foreign Relations Committee. In that capacity, Sumner worked with Secretary of War Edwin Stanton to avert war with Great Britain during the Trent Affair. The greatest area of disagreement between Sumner and more moderate Republicans, including Lincoln, concerned Reconstruction. By the end of 1862, Sumner had developed his "Southern Suicide" theory which argued that, by the very act of secession, the Southern states had forfeited any and all rights under the U.S. Constitution; when they reentered the Union after the war, therefore, they would be completely at the mercy of the federal government. In addition, according to Sumner, readmission to the Union should be made contingent upon equal-suffrage clauses written into new state constitutions.

After the war, Sumner joined other Radicals in demanding that the federal government seize the land of former Confederates and redistribute it to former slaves and/or Union veterans. Sumner softened his approach after taking a tour of the devastated South in 1867; although he still insisted upon black suffrage, he urged Congress to place far less harsh economic sanctions on the former Confederacy.

Despite his more balanced approach, Sumner believed that it was the responsibility of Congress—not of the executive branch—to devise and enforce Reconstruction. To that end, he took a leading role in the 1868 impeachment of President Andrew Johnson, whose attempt to control Reconstruction efforts was opposed by Congress. With the election of Ulysses S. Grant in 1868, Sumner was removed from his post as chairman of the Senate Foreign Relations Committee, largely because of his unwillingness to negotiate a moderate settlement with Great Britain on the *Alabama* claims.

Despite failing health, Sumner worked tirelessly to produce a Civil Rights Act in the early 1870s. As envisioned by Sumner, the bill would extend the 14th Amendment's principle of political equality into social relations by desegregating schools, juries, churches, cemeteries, and all public accommodations. Far too sweeping for most Republicans, the bill languished in the Senate for three years until its sponsor, the Radical war-horse Sumner, was stricken by a heart attack on March 10, 1874. He died the following day.

Surrenders, Confederate

Although the surrender of Robert E. Lee at Appomattox Court House on April 9, 1865, is generally considered to mark the official end of the Civil War, at least three other Confederate commanders extended their battle against the North for another two and a half months. General Joseph E. Johnston continued to follow William Tecumseh Sherman's devastating march northward through North Carolina, even after hearing of the loss of Petersburg and Richmond, and of Lee's surrender. Finally, on April 17, Johnston agreed to discuss surrender with the enemy he had been stalking for more than two years. Although the first peace terms offered by Sherman were rejected by the Federal govern-

ment, the two generals were able to negotiate an agreement acceptable to Ulysses S. Grant on April 26, 1865. Johnston's troops formally surrendered on May 3.

Still holding out with some 15,000 troops in Mobile, Alabama, was Confederate Lieutenant Richard Taylor, the son of former U.S. president Zachary Taylor. Taylor finally surrendered to E. R. S. Canby on May 4, 1865. Lieutenant General E. Kirby Smith waged the last land fight of the Civil War in West Texas from May 12 to 13, 1865. Unaware that Lee had surrendered more than a month before, 350 of Smith's stalwart Confederates won a surprising victory over more than 800 of Theodore H. Barrett's Federals at Palmito Ranch.

After hearing of the Confederate surrender at Appomattox and the loss of Richmond, how-

Confederate General Joseph Johnson surrenders near Greensboro, North Carolina, April 26, 1865.

ever, Smith's troops disbanded. Smith, however, was ready to fight another day and went to Houston to rally more troops. His plans were dashed when Lieutenant Simon B. Buckner, acting in Smith's name, surrendered the Trans-Mississippi Department on May 25 in New Orleans, Louisiana.

For nearly a month after that, Stand Watie, leader of the Cherokee Nation and commander of the largest Native American force in the Confederate army, kept his troops in the field. He was finally convinced to surrender on June 23, 1865, to Lieutenant Colonel Asa C. Matthews.

T

Taney, Roger

1777–1864

Supreme Court chief justice under ten presidents, Taney was already 80 years old when he issued the bombshell Dred Scott decision and went on to oppose several of Abraham Lincoln's controversial emergency policies during the first three years of the Civil War.

The Maryland politician, an ardent supporter of the South, served as Andrew Jackson's attorney general and secretary of treasury before reaching the high court in 1836. Over his 28-year tenure, Taney routinely supported states' rights over federal authority. Although he had freed his own slaves, he saw the "peculiar institution" as integral to the South's economy and denied that Congress had the constitutional right to pass legislation limiting its existence.

The 1857 case of Dred Scott, a black man who sued for his freedom because he had been brought to live in the North for two years, offered Taney the chance to try to settle the slavery issue conclusively in the South's favor. Intending to confront what he considered "Northern aggression" against the Southern way of life, challenge the concept of popular sovereignty, and cripple the nascent Republican Party in one judicial blow, the aged chief justice wrote a 55-page opinion.

Taney, fixated with the issue of black citizenship, based his decision against Scott on the idea that blacks not only could not sue in U.S.

Chief Justice Roger Taney

courts, but—slave or free—"had no rights which a white man was bound to respect." Also ruling that the Missouri Compromise, which had defined slave and free territories for over 35 years, was unconstitutional, the decision vastly intensified the festering sectional conflict. Many believed, with some justification, that the Taney court would soon sanction the return of slavery throughout the North, a possibility that subsided with the South's secession. Perhaps quietly supporting the Confederacy while remaining the Union's chief justice, Taney sought to curb the war powers invoked by the government and military.

In a May 1861 decision concerning the questionable arrest of a Maryland secessionist, he ruled that Lincoln did not have the authority to suspend the writ of habeus corpus. With no power to enforce the ruling, however, the chief justice was simply ignored by the president. Two years later, Taney was unable to get the court to find that the president could not order a blockade of the South without a formal declaration of war.

Undaunted, he longed to have the opportunity to overrule both the conscription act and the Emancipation Proclamation. Eagerly awaiting the ancient justice's retirement, Lincoln continued disregarding him. Taney's departure from the court, however, did not come until his death at age 87.

Taxation

The huge cost of waging the Civil War required both the Union and Confederate governments to implement an array of new levies, including the first income tax in American history.

The Northern Congress began in 1861 by boosting tariffs—which would be raised again several times over the next four years—and then turned its attention to internal duties. Opting against property taxes, the legislature authorized a semi-progressive income tax that

August. Families with an annual income above $600 would pay a three percent rate; those earning less were exempt.

With Congress' passage of the Internal Revenue Act of 1862 the following July, the Union inaugurated a comprehensive federal tax program. The catalogue of taxable effects was encyclopedic—from sin items such as liquor and tobacco to luxury goods like carriages and jewelry. Professionals paid a tax on their licenses, banks and corporations on their gross receipts, and patients on their medication. There were stamp taxes, inheritance taxes, and value-added taxes. Income taxes were increased to five percent for those earning over $10,000 a year, and rates across the board would be raised again to a maximum ten percent in 1864.

Predictably, Democrats opposed the Lincoln administration's tax policy, but it was undeniably effective in generating revenue for the government, raising nearly $700 million and covering over one-fifth of the North's entire war expenditures. The South obtained a far smaller proportion of its revenues through taxation, as little as six percent. Because there was little tradition of taxation in the region, the Confederate government preferred to finance its war effort through loans and the printing of paper money (the Union government also printed paper money).

That policy resulted in runaway inflation, however, and in April 1863, at the urging of Treasury Secretary Christopher Memminger, the Southern Congress finally passed a comprehensive tax program of its own. It featured a national income tax, though with rates held from one to two percent, the program was far more circumscribed than that which Memminger had envisioned, and neither produced much capital nor slowed inflation. The legislation also included profit taxes and excise and license duties, but its most controversial element was a ten percent "tax in kind" on farm produce and livestock. Over the sharp objection of small farmers, who felt unfairly burdened by the policy, government agents collected perhaps as much as $150 million in foodstuffs, most delivered to the needy Confederate military. Passing

Southern armies were also given leeway to expropriate goods from farms, leaving behind nearly worthless vouchers.

To ease the mounting criticism and devise a more equitable system, the Confederate Congress revised its tax laws in February 1864. Southerners whose property was worth less than $500 were exempted from the tax in kind, while the affluent were assessed a five percent duty on the value of their land and slaves, the funds earmarked to assist indigent military families. After the war, the federal government repealed its income tax, and most of the other levies imposed during the conflict were allowed to expire. The Bureau of Internal Revenue, however, created by the 1862 tax law, has remained in existence ever since.

Thirteenth Amendment

Ratified at the end of 1865, the 13th Amendment to the U.S. Constitution officially abolished slavery "within the United States or any place subject to their jurisdiction," emancipating four million blacks who had not been freed over the course of the Civil War.

More than 60 years had passed since the Constitution had been amended, and the purpose of the twelve previous changes had been far different—limiting governmental authority rather than expanding it by mandating national reform. Ironically, a thirteenth amendment authorizing the *continuation* of slavery had been proposed in 1861 as a desperate attempt to prevent the country's imminent disunion. Supported by almost half of the congressional Republicans as well as the vast majority of Democrats, it had passed in both the House and Senate by the two-thirds majority required, but the war erupted before it could be ratified by the necessary three-quarters of the states.

During the conflict, the abolition of slavery emerged as a Union war goal, confirmed in September 1862 by Abraham Lincoln's Emancipation Proclamation. But since the presidential edict was a war measure, freeing only those slaves from states in armed rebellion, it might not apply once that rebellion concluded. There was a good chance that the Supreme Court would even rule the proclamation itself unconstitutional.

To circumvent any future attempts to preserve slavery, Lincoln and other Republican leaders began efforts in 1864 for a constitutional amendment that would unequivocally ban the practice altogether. The Democratic party opposed its ratification, even though Lincoln continued to advocate financial compensation for former slaveholders by the federal government.

Nevertheless, the Republican-dominated Senate quickly passed the proposed 13th Amendment by a 38 to 6 vote in April. Two months later, however, the House, with its larger contingent of Democrats, failed to give its two-thirds support. Lincoln called for another vote after his reelection indicated popular backing for emancipation. This time, following the president's tireless lobbying efforts and offers of tempting governmental appointments and other administration favors to undecided congressmen, the legislature passed the amendment on January 31, 1865, by only a few votes—119 to 56. The historic moment was greeted with prolonged cheers in the House chambers and with artillery batteries on Capitol Hill firing a hundred-gun salute.

The next day, the president signed the amendment in a purely symbolic gesture, proclaiming it a "great moral victory." Within a week, eight states ratified the amendment, as ultimately did all the others that had remained in the Union, except for the slave states of Delaware and Kentucky. But because the North had never recognized the legality of secession, the approval of several Southern states was needed as well to obtain the necessary three-quarters majority.

Although it took eight months after the war's conclusion for the abolition of slavery to be constitutionally guaranteed, by the time the 13th Amendment was officially ratified on December 18, 1865, the Reconstruction governments of eight former Confederate states had added their support.

Thomas, George Henry

1816–1870

Earning his famous nickname "The Rock of Chickamauga" for steadfastly holding his position during the Georgia battle after most of the Federal troops had been wiped from the field, the Virginia-born Union general proved to be one of the North's greatest military assets.

Thomas' gutsy boyhood ride to warn isolated neighbors of Nat Turner's slave uprising helped him win an appointment to West Point. Becoming an artillery and cavalry instructor at his alma mater, he also fought in the Mexican War and served with the famous 2nd Cavalry alongside future battlefield opponents John Bell Hood and Albert Sidney Johnston. Although Thomas was physically as rock-solid as his future nickname would suggest, an 1860 frontier wound almost ended his army career.

But at the outbreak of the Civil War, he returned to active duty—remaining with the Union, however, to the disgust of Confederate family members and colleagues and the suspicion of some among the North's high command. Initially stationed in Virginia, Thomas was transferred west, where he brought the Confederacy one of its first defeats near Mill Springs, Kentucky, in January 1862, routing a small force under A. S. Johnston.

After a solid performance at Perryville in October, he refused an order to take over the command of his superior Don Carlos Buell. Thomas remained Buell's ranking officer in the New Years' 1863 Battle of Murfreesboro, where he stolidly protected the Union center. In a still more dazzling display of his matchless defensive skills, he made his legendary stand at Chickamauga in September, rallying his troops to hold their ground at Snodgrass Hill for hours after Union commander William Rosecrans had

retreated. Thomas finally ordered a withdrawal at dusk, saving the Union force from destruction.

Rewarding him with the command of the Army of the Cumberland, Ulysses S. Grant did not want to assign a primary role to Thomas' troops in the following month's actions at Chattanooga, thinking they were still too demoralized from the earlier engagement. Thomas and his men were eager to prove otherwise and, ordered merely to make a limited assault on the Confederate line at the base of Missionary Ridge, sent an attack force of 23,000 that had little trouble overrunning the enemy trenches. Lacking further instructions, the exhilarated troops continued up the slope and swept the Confederates off the ridge altogether, winning a stunning victory and avenging their loss at Chickamauga. Thomas' army provided less dramatic but still invaluable support for William T. Sherman's advance on Atlanta in 1864.

Later in the year, he was sent back to Tennessee to challenge John Bell Hood's desperate attempt to retake the eastern portion of the state. Assembling a force of over 60,000 outside Nashville in his characteristically calm and methodical fashion, Thomas ignored Grant's insistent orders to attack immediately. He was about to be relieved of command when he finally launched his offense on December 16, an overwhelming assault that all but annihilated Hood's army.

With Thomas' conclusive victory, the Confederate military was essentially finished in the West. Thomas remained in the Regular army at the war's conclusion, serving as commander of the Military Division of the Pacific when he died.

Toombs, Robert Augustus

1810–1885

After resigning his Georgia Senate seat following the election of Abraham Lincoln, Robert Toombs stormed out of the Senate chamber, demanded from the bursar his salary due plus mileage back to Georgia, and went home to organize secession in his state. Brilliant but unpredictable, Toombs would serve not only as Jefferson Davis' secretary of state, but as brigadier general in the Confederate army.

One of the wealthiest planters and most powerful politicians in Georgia, Toombs received his education at the University of Georgia and Union College, New York, then went on to be-

Robert A. Toombs

come a lawyer. He became a state legislator in 1837, serving there for six years, after which he went to the United States House of Representatives from 1844 to 1852, then won election to the U.S. Senate. Throughout his early career, Toombs, like many of his fellow Southerners, was anxious to effect a compromise between North and South that would maintain the Union. In this respect, he was aligned most closely with colleagues Howell Cobb and Alexander Stephens.

Like many Southerners, however, Toombs saw the election of Republican Abraham Lincoln as a sign that compromise was no longer possible and strongly urged Georgia to secede. In February 1861, he was sent as a delegate to the Montgomery convention and lobbied hard to be elected to a high office, preferably to the presidency. With several powerful Georgian candidates, including Cobb and Stephens, splitting the vote, Toombs lost out to Jefferson Davis.

Bitterly disappointed, he nearly refused appointment to secretary of state. After initially urging restraint at Fort Sumter, Toombs became an ardent supporter of all-out war once the first shots had been fired. It quickly became clear to both Toombs and the president that the State Department was not the place for him. His restless energy found little outlet in the department, especially since the Confederacy was not yet recognized by any foreign power, nor would it ever be.

On July 24, 1861, Toombs resigned his cabinet post to take a more active, and certainly more exciting, role on the battlefield. Despite the fact that he had no military training, he asked Davis to appoint him as brigadier general; Davis, with misgivings, obliged. Toombs first saw battle during the Seven Days campaign, where he fought aggressively but unwisely. At White Oak Swamp, he took it upon himself to convert a minor military demonstration into a full-scale assault on the heavily-manned Federal entrenchments and was repulsed with a great loss of men.

Later in the campaign, he was arrested for allowing his troops to leave their posts without first gaining permission from his own commander to do so. This breach of duty caused him to lose his command for several weeks, until Second Bull Run. His careless disregard of military tack caused Toombs to be loathed by most of his men and passed over for promotion by his superiors. Although he fought well at Antietam, where 550 men under his command successfully challenged more than 20 times their number, he was disappointed at his lack of advancement and chafed under military rules and regulations. Mary Chesnut wrote in her diary: "Toombs is ready for a revolution. He curses freely everything Confederate from a president to a horse boy and thinks there is a conspiracy against him in the army." He finally resigned his commission on March 3, 1863, and returned to Georgia, where he remained an unrelenting critic of the Davis administration.

He returned to uniform just once, joining the militia to oppose William Tecumseh Sherman during his devastating March through Georgia. Barely escaping arrest at the war's end, Toombs fled to Cuba and Europe, returning to Georgia in 1867. Because he refused to apply for a pardon, however, he was unable to hold public office. He died in Washington, Georgia, on December 15, 1885.

Traveller

A "Confederate gray" five-year-old horse caught Robert E. Lee's eye during his West Virginia campaign in 1861. A year later, he purchased him for $200. Originally named Jeff Davis, Lee called the 16-hand high, black-pointed horse Traveller, and travel he did, for Lee rode the horse in nearly every battle of the war and across thousands of miles of terrain.

In addition, the solitary, often lonely general found that an evening ride astride Traveller relieved him of the cares of the day. "Traveller is my only companion; I may say my only pleasure," the Confederate general once wrote to his wife. Traveller outlived his master by several years, reportedly dying of lockjaw. His

skeleton now stands in the Washington and Lee Museum.

Tredegar Iron Works

By far the most valuable Confederate foundry for the manufacture of large guns and other munitions, the iron works at Richmond produced approximately 50 percent of the South's domestically produced cannon during the course of the Civil War.

The only major steel mill in the South when the war started, Tredegar was the larger of the Confederacy's two first-class foundries and machines shops; the other was Leed's Co. in New Orleans. Until the beginning of the hostilities, Tredegar Iron Works employed about 800 people and primarily produced revolvers and gun carriages. As soon as Virginia seceded and war was imminent, the works were flooded with military contracts.

However, the early loss of Tennessee—the state that had produced most of the South's iron for all military and industrial purposes, and much of its gunpowder, rifles, artillery, and other essential material, including locomotives—robbed Tredegar of a major portion of its resources, subsequently devastating the Confederacy, which was already overwhelmed by the North's superior industrial strength. During one month in the late summer of 1861, Tredegar did not have the material to produce a single cannon. It was left to John R. Anderson, the foundry's owner since 1843, to try to stimulate iron production in the Shenandoah Valley and around Birmingham, Alabama, but with little success.

A West Point graduate, Anderson left the foundry to join the Confederate army in September 1861 and fought in several early battles until wounded during the Seven Days Campaign in July 1862. Returning to direct Tredegar, Anderson attempted to cope with a profound lack of materials that only worsened as the Federals captured more and more South-

Robert E. Lee sitting on "Traveller."

ern territory. Despite its lack of supplies, Tredegar expanded its workforce to include about 2,500 men, including many slaves, and manufactured thousands of three-inch ordnance guns, 12-pounder Napoleons, siege artillery, as well as armor for ironclads.

During the four-year conflict, however, Southern foundries produced just 25 percent of the cannon turned out by Northern companies. By the end of the war, the production of artillery at Tredegar and elsewhere in the South had ceased altogether.

Trent Affair

NOVEMBER 1861

The United States and Great Britain nearly came to war over the seizure of two Confederate diplomats traveling aboard a British vessel. The officials, James M. Mason of Virginia and John Slidell of Louisiana, had recently been appointed the South's envoys to England and France, respectively. Their departure from Charleston, South Carolina, in October 1861, on a blockade runner was an open secret. At Havana, Mason and Slidell transferred to the *Trent*, a British mail steamer, to continue their

Tredegar Iron Works

passage to Europe. Patrolling the waters off Cuba was the Union naval sloop *San Jacinto*, whose captain, Charles Wilkes, acting without orders from his government, decided to intervene. On November 7, the *San Jacinto* fired on the *Trent*, halting the British vessel.

Wilkes sent his crew aboard, allegedly in search of diplomatic dispatches, which, according to international law, could be legally seized in wartime. Arresting Mason and Slidell instead, Wilkes had them removed to the *San Jacinto*, and then sailed to Boston. There, the navy captain was greeted with a hero's welcome by a public eager for any Union military success, while the two Confederates, well-known and despised in the North, were jailed in Fort Warren.

The dubious Union triumph was short-lived, however. Outraged by the episode, the British government issued an ultimatum, demanding the immediate release of Mason and Slidell and an apology. The two countries already had a long, contentious history of such high-seas disputes—a major cause of the War of 1812—and this was promising to be the most calamitous one yet. England sent 11,000 troops to Canada, put its naval fleet on war alert, and placed an embargo on saltpeter from India, desperately needed by the Union military for the production of gunpowder. In the United States, many welcomed a confrontation with Britain, while the crisis was beginning to cause a panic in the stock and bond market and a run on the banks. The Union's minister to England, Charles Fran-

Union agents capturing Mason and Slidell aboard the Trent.

cis Adams, and British foreign minister Lord John Russell both labored, lacking clear instructions from their governments, to ease the tensions. Even Prince Albert, Queen Victoria's consort, entered the mediation.

Finally, Abraham Lincoln, convinced by Secretary of State William H. Seward, decided that the Union could not afford entering into another armed conflict. "One war at a time," the president was said to have remarked. In a Christmas Day 1861 cabinet meeting, a face-saving proposal was concocted where Mason and Slidell would be released while the United States would maintain its right to have arrested them. The British government accepted the offer, and the Confederate envoys were freed to resume their interrupted voyage to Europe on New Year's Day, 1862.

With war averted by the amicable settlement of the *Trent* Affair, relations between the United States and England were perhaps actually friendlier than before the dispute.

Trevilian Station, Battle of

JUNE 11–12, 1864

In the aftermath of the bloody fighting at Cold Harbor at the beginning of June 1864, General U. S. Grant began maneuvering his army to take the best advantage of successes gained in the fighting around Richmond.

Robert E. Lee sent his cavalry corps to try and prevent the Federal cavalry, under the command of General Philip Sheridan, from joining up with the Union forces under General David Hunter, moving through the Shenandoah Valley. The Confederate cavalry was in a state of some confusion, owing to the death in May of their fabled leader, Jeb Stuart; neither Wade Hampton nor Fitzhugh Lee had yet been named to replace the fallen commander, and the two men, who disliked one another, were not entirely in accord as to how they should move. But they did manage to get their troops into position around Trevilian Station, blocking Sheridan's path.

The fighting was incredibly confused. Sheridan's protégé, General George Custer, attacked the rear of Hampton's line—but Fitz Lee came to Hampton's rescue. Custer found himself facing his old friend and West Point classmate, General Thomas Rosser, who foiled the attack. Hampton was able to retire in good order, but Lee took the brunt of the attack and was driven back in disarray. During the night, Hampton's men dug in across Sheridan's path, causing the Federal commander to abandon his plan of linking up with Hunter.

The next day, Sheridan repeatedly attacked the entrenchment put up by the Confederates, but it was to no avail. Unable to root out or ride around the men of Hampton and Lee, Sheridan was forced to return the way he had come. The cost was high—slightly over 1,000 of his 8,000 effective troopers were killed, captured or wounded—and the end result was an embarrassing defeat. But the Confederate losses had been costly, too, for of 5,000 men engaged, Hampton and Lee lost more than 600 soldiers—

men they could not spare, as Confederate resources continued to dwindle.

Truth, Sojourner

1797(?)–1883

Born Isabella Baumfree, Sojourner Truth was one of the earliest and most passionate of female abolitionists—for she herself had once been a slave.

In the 1820s, when still quite a young woman, she escaped from her New York owner after being brutally treated and sold away from her family. By the 1840s, Truth had become a

Sojourner Truth with Abraham Lincoln.

powerful speaker against slavery, often moving her audiences to tears and exclamations of horror with her firsthand accounts of what many of her black brethren and sisters were enduring at the hands of cruel masters. She would tell listeners of how some slaves were kept cowed and afraid to act by beatings, sometimes with spiked sticks and chains; she herself, as a teenager, had been taken into the barn by her master one afternoon for absolutely no reason and tied up by the wrists. Then he tore the shirt from her back and whipped her with a bundle of sticks until her back bled. In a voice contemporaries described as rich and deep, she described how she refused to give him the satisfaction of screaming, by clenching her fists so hard her fingernails drew blood from her palms.

She also spoke of the living conditions many slaves were forced to endure, crowded together into cabins with no privacy, overworked, fed scraps in many cases, and clothed in threadbare hand-me-downs. Her audiences must have felt the shame as Truth recalled the auction block, upon which men and women alike were frequently forced to strip and stand before potential buyers, who would search their bodies for marks of the whip or of wrist or leg irons, the presence of which would indicate the slave had been frequently punished. The slaves would be forced to endure impersonal and degrading inspections of their teeth, muscles, and other body parts, depending on what the buyer was looking for in the purchase.

Truth was self-educated, and much of her speaking bore the stamp of a deep love of and acquaintance with Scripture. When explaining to Harriet Beecher Stowe how she came to change her name, Truth said she felt God had called her "to travel up and down the land, showing the people their sins and being a sign unto them." She also possessed a quick wit, coupled with an ability to think fast and turn the unkind words of others against them. Facing a heckler once who told her he did not care for her antislavery talk anymore than he would for the bite of a flea, Truth retorted, "Perhaps not, but Lord willing I'll keep you scratching."

She was very involved in political causes, and strongly supported suffrage. During the Civil War, she gathered supplies for black volunteer regiments, and, in tribute to her efforts, was received at the White House by President Lincoln in 1864. Truth was appointed to the National Freedman's Relief Association in 1864, where she worked diligently to better conditions for African-Americans.

She lived long enough to see her people brought to freedom, but never stopped in her efforts to win more equality for them. Right up until her death, in Battle Creek, Michigan, she continued to speak out for her race; when she died in 1883, she went to her grave a much-lamented and beloved figure in abolitionist lore.

Tubman, Harriet

1820(?)–1913

Reverently called "Moses" by the hundreds of slaves she helped to freedom and the thousands of others she inspired, Harriet Tubman became the most famous leader of the Underground Railroad to aid slaves escaping to free states or Canada.

Born into slavery in Bucktown, Maryland, Tubman escaped her own chains in 1849 to find safe haven in Philadelphia, Pennsylvania. She did so through the underground railroad, an elaborate and secret series of houses, tunnels, and roads set up by abolitionists and former slaves. "When I found I had crossed the [Mason-Dixon] line, I looked at my hands to see if I were the same person," Tubman later wrote. ". . . the sun came like gold through the tree and over the field and I felt like I was in heaven." She would spend the rest of her life helping other slaves escape to freedom.

Her early life as a slave had been filled with abuse; at the age of 13, when she attempted to save another slave from punishment, she was struck in the head with a two-pound iron weight. She would suffer periodic blackouts from the injury for the rest of her life.

After her escape, Tubman worked as a maid

in Philadelphia and joined the large and active abolitionist group in the city. In 1850, after Congress passed the Fugitive Slave Act, making it illegal to help a runaway slave, Tubman decided to join the Underground Railroad. Her first expedition took place in 1851, when she managed to thread her way through the backwoods to Baltimore and return to the North with her sister and her sister's children. From that time until the onset of the Civil War, Tubman traveled to the South about 18 times and helped close to 300 slaves escape. In 1857, Tubman led her parents to freedom in Auburn, New York, which became her home as well.

Tubman was never caught and never lost a slave to the Southern militia, and as her reputation grew, so too did the desire among Southerners to put a stop to her activities; rewards for her capture once totaled about $40,000. During the Civil War, Tubman served as a nurse, scout, and sometime-spy for the Union army, mainly in South Carolina. She also took part in a military campaign that resulted in the rescue of 756 slaves and destroyed millions of dollars' worth of enemy property.

After the war, Tubman returned to Auburn and continued her involvement in social issues, including the women's rights movement. In 1908, she established a home in Auburn for elderly and indigent blacks that later became known as the Harriet Tubman Home. She died on March 10, 1913, at the approximate age of 93.

several revisions made to the conscription laws by the Confederate Congress throughout 1862. Recognizing the need to draft, or conscript, men into the Confederate army, President Jefferson Davis had difficulty from the first with people who disapproved of the necessity to force men to serve. Almost as soon as he approved the Conscription Bill in April 1862, Davis began receiving amendments to it. There was a limitation on ages, so that at this early stage of the war only men between the ages of 35 and 45 were required to serve; another amendment exempted men in a number of occupations deemed necessary to the war effort. But the most controversial, the least beloved by the poorer and non-slaveholding Confederate soldiers, was the amendment which exempted from service any overseer or owner of 20 or more slaves.

The rationale behind this act was that such a large black population would require the controling hand of a man with authority. Soldiers already in the army who were fighting for love of state, defense of home and family, or similar reasons, saw this as a way of letting the rich men off the hook. It would not be until December 1863 that any form of draft-dodging, generally lumped under the heading of substitution, was discouraged by stringent tightening of the remaining exemptions; desperate for manpower, the Confederates made it very difficult for anyone to get out of serving in the military. No matter what one did for a living, or how rich they might be, or how many slaves they might own, they were required to enter the army.

20 Negro Law

Though popularly referred to as a "law," the 20 Negro Act was actually a clause in one of

U

Uncle Tom's Cabin

1851–1852

Bitter feelings between Northerners and Southerners increased dramatically after the publication of this novel about slavery and the Southern way of life.

Written by an Ohio-born woman living in Vermont, Harriet Beecher Stowe, *Uncle Tom's Cabin* describes the experiences of a dignified old slave named Uncle Tom and his three slaveholders. Two of his masters treat Tom kindly, but the third, Simon Legree, severely abuses him and finally beats him to death for refusing to reveal the whereabouts of two runaway slaves. A subplot of the story concerns the plight of George and Eliza, a married slave couple, and their efforts to escape to freedom with their baby.

Although the novel was written with a sense of balance—the vicious slave owner Simon Legree is a Northerner and Augustine St. Clair, one of Tom's kind owners, is a Southerner who questions the morality of slavery—the book was hailed as an antislavery masterpiece in the North and condemned as an insulting lie in the South.

In addition to its historical importance as a contributing factor to the Civil War, *Uncle Tom's Cabin* is also considered to be a literary achievement. Critic Edmund Wilson wrote that "it is a much more remarkable book than one had ever been allowed to suspect," chiefly because of its vivid descriptions of American life and its finely drawn, enduring characters.

Underground Railroad

An informal system that helped slaves escape to the North and Canada during the mid-1800s, the Underground Railroad exacerbated tensions between North and South and helped produce the divisive Fugitive Slave Act of 1850. The system was neither underground nor a railroad; the slaves traveled by any means possible—by foot, wagon, train, and boat—and stayed in shelters, nicknamed "stations," provided by those sympathetic with their efforts to gain freedom.

The term "Underground Railroad" was first used about 1830; during the next 30 years the system brought thousands of blacks to freedom. Free-soil party members, free blacks, women's antislavery societies, and others worked together and individually to provide food, clothing, money, and shelter to the escaping slaves. Fugitives were hidden in livery stables, attics, and secret passageways. They often traveled in disguise and moved from station to station at

Harriet Tubman led thousands of slaves to freedom via the Underground Railroad.

night. The most heavily traveled routes of the railroad ran through Ohio, Indiana, and western Pennsylvania.

Once in the North, many slaves decided to continue on to Canada, usually via Detroit or Niagara Falls to southern Ontario and Quebec. White abolitionists contributed a great deal to the effort, particularly William Lloyd Garrison and women's rights activists like Lucretia Mott and Susan B. Anthony. Levi Coffin, a Quaker, was called the "president of the underground railroad" in honor of his success in helping 3,000 slaves find freedom. Recent evidence sug-

gests, however, that free blacks and former slaves had as much to do with the success of the railroad as did whites.

Uniforms, Union and Confederate Army

Although commonly described as the War Between the Blue (Union) and Gray (Confederate), an immense variety of uniforms appeared on both armies, especially at the beginning of the war. Of particular interest were the colorful uniforms of the Zouaves, based on the French uniforms worn in colonial Africa. By the end of 1862, however, most units adopted the dress officially prescribed in the *U.S. Army Regulations* or the *Regulations for the Army of the Confederate States.*

The Federal infantryman generally wore a dark blue, loose flannel sack coat that hung to the mid-thigh, blue woolen or jersey trousers, and blocky leather brogans nicknamed "gunboats." Extra clothing and protective gear included a blue-caped overcoat, a gray wool blanket weighing about five pounds; a gum blanket that could double as tent floor and poncho; a heavy white flannel pull-over shirt, and a pair of wool socks. Affiliation with a particular branch of the service was denoted by stripes down the outer seam of the uniform: yellow for cavalry, red for artillery, sky-blue for infantry, emerald-green for mounted rifleman, and crimson for ordnance and hospital personnel.

Distinctions of rank were indicated by the type of frock coat worn: majors, lieutenant colonels, colonels, and all general officers' coats were double-breasted. Those ranking lower wore single-breasted coats. Other rank distinctions included the number and placement of buttons and shoulder boards or sleeve chevrons: major generals' coats had nine buttons in each of three rows and wore two stars; brigadier generals wore four rows of two buttons each and one star. Colonels, lieutenant colonels, and majors each wore two rows of seven buttons. In addition, colonels had an eagle emblazoned on their shoulder boards; lieutenant colonels had two silver embroidered leaves; majors, two gold embroidered leaves; captains, two groups of gold bars; a first lieutenant, a gold bar; and a second lieutenant wore boards with no insignia.

All noncommissioned officers wore a single row of nine buttons. Sergeants wore three chevrons on their sleeves, and corporals wore two chevrons. Regular troops were distinguished by one stripe sewn on the lower sleeve for each five years of service.

Confederate troop uniforms were similar, but gray or butternut (yellow-brown) in color. A gray or butternut wool shell jacket; gray, butternut or blue trousers; and low-heeled brogans comprised the Confederate infantryman's wardrobe. Mid-thigh length frock coats, similar to the Federal design, were also prescribed to

the Rebel troops, although these were always in short supply. Other garments included a home-made coverlet, a homespun cotton shirt, a wool vest, and wool socks. All officers and enlisted men in both armies were also supplied with ankle-high Jefferson boots.

Affiliation with a particular branch of service was denoted by colored facing on the coats of army personnel: yellow for cavalry, red for artillery, sky-blue for infantry, and black for medical. Distinctions of rank within each branch was designated by colored stripes on outer trouser seams: Regimental officers had one ¼-inch stripe; generals wore 2⅝-inch stripes; adjutant, quartermaster, commissary, and engineer officers wore one gold ¼-inch stripe. Sergeants and other noncommissioned officers were expected to wear a ¼-inch cotton stripe of colors appropriate to their branch of service. Buttons and insignias were also used to designate rank:

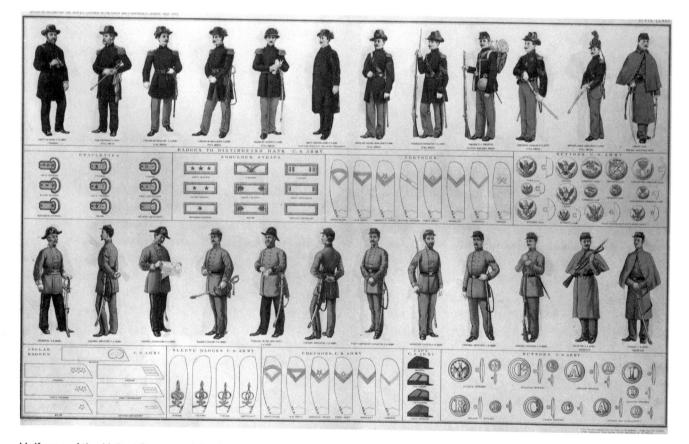

Uniforms of the United States and Confederate Armies.

generals, lieutenant generals, major generals, and brigadier generals wore three gold stars—the middle one larger than the other two—within a wreath on their collars. Colonels wore three equal-size stars; lieutenant colonels, two stars; majors, one star; captains, two gold bars; first lieutenants, two bars; second lieutenants, one bar. All sergeants wore three chevrons on their sleeves; corporals wore two. A brigadier general's coat had two rows of eight buttons, junior officers had two rows of seven buttons each.

Both armies were also supplied with kepis, loose-fitting forage caps, also called slouch caps, with visors that are most closely associated with the Civil War. The Civil War soldier was expected to carry on his back everything he would need, both in battle and in camp. A fully equipped infantryman might carry more than 50 pounds. Basic gear included the items listed above as well as a rifle, cartridge box, sheathed bayonet, cap box, cotton haversack, and a tin or wooden canteen and cup.

A pipe, writing kit, soap and towel, jackknife, sewing kit, cartes de visite, razor, and eating utensils might also find their way into the haversacks carried by the soldiers, who were often away from home for more than a year at a stretch.

V

Vallandigham, Clement Laird

1820–1871

Known as "Valiant Val" by his supporters, the Ohio politician and head of the Peace Democrats was one of Abraham Lincoln's most outspoken critics during the Civil War. When his relentless campaigning against the war threatened to undermine Lincoln's 1864 reelection bid, Vallandigham was arrested, and eventually he was exiled to the Confederacy.

A lawyer by trade, Vallandigham began his political career in 1844 as a member of the Ohio state legislature. At the same time, he gained prominence in the state as editor of the Dayton *Empire* newspaper from 1847 to 1849. Turning his interest to the national arena, the ardent states' rights activist attempted to win election to Congress, but failed in the elections of 1852 and 1854. He contested his third defeat in 1856 and, after nearly two years of legal and political maneuvering, finally was seated in the United States House of Representatives in May 1858.

A staunch, conservative Democrat who urged a moderate course in the mounting secession crisis, Vallandigham supported Stephen A. Douglas for president in 1860. Within days of the action at Fort Sumter, Vallandigham pronounced the war unconstitutional and further described it as an attempt by the Republican party to enhance their own power. From his seat in the House, he publically criticized almost every aspect of Lincoln's prosecution of the war, including the conscription acts and the suspension of the writ of habeas corpus.

By 1862, his extreme views had alienated him from the mainstream of the Democratic party; by gerrymandering his district, the Ohio Democrats kept him from being reelected to the U.S. House that year.

Undeterred and supported by a growing constituency of Copperheads, or Peace Democrats, Vallandigham continued his campaign against the war by running for governor of Ohio under the slogan, "The Constitution as it is, the Union as it was." In the meantime, Ambrose B. Burnside, commander of the Department of the Ohio, issued General Order No. 38 in April, 1863, which expressly forbade any expression of sympathy for the enemy. Hoping to garner more support, Vallandigham did his best to provoke his own arrest by making a series of speeches calling for soldiers on both sides of the conflict to desert, declaring the South invincible and warning of the potential for the Western states to leave the Union and join the Confederacy. Burnside declared Vallandigham a traitor and, without Lincoln's prior approval, had him arrested on May 5, tried by a military court from May 6 to 7, denied a writ of habeas corpus, and sentenced to two years in a military prison.

Lincoln, perceiving that this action would

make a martyr out of the Copperhead and further alienate Democrats before the upcoming 1864 election, cancelled the order of imprisonment. In order to support Burnside, however, he then sent the troublesome politician into exile, banishing him to the Confederacy. Vallandigham was escorted to the South through Murfreesboro, Tennessee, at the end of May 1863, and from there, he fled to Canada by sea via Nassau. Nominated for governor by outraged Ohio Democrats, Vallandigham ran his campaign from his home in southern Ontario. He lost by more than 100,000 votes to Republican John Brough.

Vallandigham's return to Ohio in June 1864, was ignored by a Lincoln administration confident of its own reelection. That month, at the Democratic convention, Vallandigham helped devise George B. McClellan's peace platform, which so split the party that Lincoln won the November election easily.

After the war, Vallandigham was unable to find a place for himself in the reconstructed Democratic party and, after losing a bid for the state legislature, returned to private law practice. He died on June 16, 1871, under rather bizarre circumstances—while demonstrating to fellow attorneys how one of his clients may

Arrest of C.L. Vallandigham in Dayton, Ohio, May 5, 1863.

have accidentally shot himself, Vallandigham did the very same thing to himself. His gun fired and the shot killed him.

Van Lew, Elizabeth

1818–1900(?)

The first Union flag to wave over Richmond in four years was raised in 1865 by this famous and effective Union spy. Born into a prominent Richmond family, Elizabeth Van Lew returned from her schooling in Philadelphia as an adamant abolitionist determined to fight slavery in the bastion of the South. "Slave power," she wrote in her diary, "is arrogant, is jealous and intrusive, is cruel, is despotic." Outspoken and rebellious, she appeared to her neighbors to be more than a little eccentric and soon became known as "Crazy Bet."

After Virginia seceded and Fort Sumter fell, she used her reputation for innocuous idiosyncracy as a shield behind which her shrewd and resourceful mind devised schemes to abet the Union cause from within Richmond. Her first target was the Confederate Libby Prison, which imprisoned Union captives. Pretending to make a merely humanitarian gesture, Van Lew brought baskets of food, medicine, and books to the prisoners. What she brought out would have shocked the guards she learned to charm and deceive.

Not only did Van Lew help some prisoners escape, she also gleaned valuable information from various sources inside the prison. Newly

Union spy Elizabeth Van Lew infiltrated the Confederate Libby Prison in Richmond, Virginia.

arrived Union prisoners secretly recounted the strength and dispositions of Confederate troops they had seen on their way from the front to Richmond. Of even more use was information carelessly conveyed to the "harmless Crazy Bet" by Confederate guards and by the prison's Confederate commandant, Lieutenant David H. Todd (Mary Todd Lincoln's half-brother).

She even managed to penetrate the home of President Jefferson Davis by convincing one of her former servants to secure a position in the Davis household staff. At first, Van Lew simply mailed the information she retrieved in letters posted to Federal authorities. As her work continued, her methods grew more sophisticated. She devised a code involving words and letters that prisoners would underline in the books she lent them.

Van Lew also sent her household servants—though she had freed the family's slaves, many of them chose to stay with her—northward carrying baskets of farm produce. Each basket held some eggs, one of which contained encoded messages in place of its natural contents. She sent her information directly to BenjAMIN Butler as well as to Grant through an elaborate courier system. It was so fast and effective that General Grant often received flowers still fresh from his spy's large garden. Grant would later say of her efforts, "You have sent me the most valuable information received from Richmond during the war."

After the war, President Grant rewarded Van Lew with a job as postmistress of Richmond, which she held from 1869 to 1877. Although revered in the North, she was, needless to say, ostracized by her Richmond neighbors. "No one will walk with us on the street," she wrote, "no one will go with us anywhere; and it grows worse and worse as the years roll on." Failing to be reappointed postmistress under Rutherford B. Hayes, she lived on a annuity from the family of a Union soldier she had helped in Libby Prison. She died in Richmond, probably in 1900.

Veteran Reserve Corps

Allowing sick and disabled Union soldiers to continue their military service, this large U.S. Army outfit performed necessary wartime duties that freed other troops for the front lines.

A policy of discharging most wounded or otherwise incapacitated combat veterans badly depleted the North's forces early in the Civil War. Recognizing that not every casualty had to be written off, the military began to allow soldiers who had sufficiently recovered from their injuries or illnesses to return to active duty, and to find other noncombat work for those needing an extended recuperation or whose permanent disabilities still permitted them to perform useful labor.

Medical officers had been employing convalescing soldiers since 1862, and in April 1863, the army formally established a volunteer Invalid Corps. Its less infirm members were given guard assignments at prison camps, armories, and garrisons, or served as military police, while the more incapacitated received lighter duties as nurses, orderlies, and clerks at army hospitals. Headquartered near Alexandria, Virginia, the corps was organized similarly to other Union outfits, with companies, regiments, and battalions and a full measure of military discipline.

Still, many wounded soldiers would not join, not wanting to be stigmatized as "invalids," while the ones who did volunteer were sensitive—for good reason—about not being taken seriously. They resented the light-blue uniforms that distinguished them from the other Northern troops, and loathed the demeaning name of their outfit—whose initials, I.C., also happened to be the "Inspected/Condemned" code stamped on rejected army goods.

Redesignated the Veteran Reserve Corps in March 1864 and finally authorized to issue regular army uniforms to its troops, it became a more attractive option for servicemen who did not want their injuries to end their military careers.

By the end of the war, more than 50,000 soldiers had joined the corps, forming nearly 200 companies. The work was mostly unglamorous and usually took place far behind the lines, but some members did see action. Helping to quell the New York City draft riots, aiding in the defense of Washington, D.C., against Jubal Early's Confederate raiders, and fighting off Wade Hampton's attack on Port Royal, the ostensibly infirm troops of the Veteran Reserve Corps proved as valuable as the "able-bodied" soldiers they served alongside.

Vicksburg, Campaign and Siege of

APRIL–JULY 4, 1863

Abraham Lincoln called the capture of Confederate Vicksburg "the key" to Union victory.

By seizing the Mississippi city, the Union would gain control of the Mississippi River, thereby cutting the Confederacy in half and taking its most important supply line. Although the war would drag on for two more years, the death knell for the Confederacy was sounded when the Union plan to win Vicksburg succeeded.

The strategic penetration of the South down the Mississippi started with Ulysses S. Grant's capture of Fort Donelson and Fort Henry early in 1862. In April of the same year, David Farragut had seized New Orleans and, with Nathaniel Banks, took control of the river north almost to the border of Mississippi. The Confederates remained in control of the part of the river that lay adjacent to the southern half of Mississippi, a segment heavily guarded by the strongholds of Vicksburg and Port Hudson.

In the fall of 1862, Ulysses S. Grant was or-

Battery Sherman, just before the Battle of Vicksburg.

dered to take Vicksburg and secure the river for the North. The challenge was formidable. Vicksburg was well defended; its strategic importance was not underestimated by the South. Confederate forces under Lieutenant John C. Pemberton, who would be assisted by his commander Joseph E. Johnston, were charged with defending the city. In addition to a strong Confederate military presence, the city was protected by its geographic position. Nearly surrounded by low-lying delta, Vicksburg's location at the mouth of the Yazoo River and the Mississippi made a successful Union approach almost impossible.

During the fall and spring of 1862 to 1863, Grant and his corps commanders, William Tecumseh Sherman, John A. McClernand, and James B. McPherson had made four equally frustrating attempts to penetrate the swamps, bayous, and woods around Vicksburg. Finally, by April 1863, Grant devised a brilliant, albeit risky, plan to take the city. On April 30, with naval support from David Dixon Porter, he and his troops traveled by ship across from the west bank of the Mississippi to Grand Gulf on the east bank south of Vicksburg. From here, he would launch an infantry attack on the city.

The key to the success of Grant's plan lay in keeping the two Confederate forces—Pemberton's at Vicksburg and reinforcements soon to be commanded by Johnston about 45 miles to the east at Jackson—from combining. Grant decided to turn first against Jackson. By attacking and defeating that force, he could concentrate on Vicksburg without fear of a threat to his northern flank or rear. By the time Confederate General Johnston arrived at Jackson on May 13, he saw the impossibility of holding the city. He had just 6,000 men to oppose the approximately 25,000-man Union army. Johnston evacuated the city, freeing Grant to concentrate on Vicksburg. Leaving Sherman with two divisions to finish destroying the supply and communication lines at Jackson, Grant ordered McClernand to march westward, roughly following the route of the Southern Mississippi Railroad.

In the meantime, confusion and miscalculation reigned within the Confederate army. Although ordered by Johnston to move northwest

to reunite the two forces, Pemberton instead chose to attempt an attack on Grant's line of communications to the south. On May 13, his advance stalled due to drenching rain and flood waters. While waiting for a bridge across the swollen Baker's Creek to be completed, he received another directive from Johnston to move north. This time he complied and countermarched.

Meanwhile, Johnston, north of Jackson, moved further away to avoid a perceived threat from Sherman. By May 16, Pemberton was essentially trapped. McPherson and McClernand's corps were rapidly closing in from the west, and Grant moved toward Vicksburg from the east. Pemberton deployed his three divisions of about 22,000 men at Champion's Hill, a prominent knoll covered with woods east of Vicksburg. McClernand arrived at about 6:00 A.M. and McPherson a few hours later; between them they had about 29,000 men. The ensuing battle was a bitter, day-long event in which more than 6,000 men were killed. Forced to withdraw, Pemberton attempted to delay the pursuing Federals by destroying the bridges across the Big Black River. The Union simply rebuilt the bridges and continued their pursuit, engaging the Confederates in another battle at the river which lost the Rebels another 1,700 men.

By May 18, Pemberton and about 32,000 men were trapped behind the defenses of Vicksburg. The next day, all of Grant's forces, about 45,000 men, had closed in. Grant hoped to capitalize on the demoralized state of the Confederate defenders by launching a frontal assault on the city. The attack began at 2:00 P.M. and raged for hours; the Confederates were far more tenacious and stubborn than Grant had anticipated. When a similar approach failed on May 22, Grant settled his troops in for what he knew would be a long and arduous siege.

Standard siege works were quickly constructed and mines were planted. The opposing trenches grew so close that hand grenades could be thrown and then returned before the devices exploded. Constant shelling and the growing shortage of rations made Pemberton's plight more hopeless each day. Sickness and wounds

A woman running a sutler's cart, boosting morale at Bailey's Cross Roads, Virginia.

had rendered about 50 percent of his men unfit for active service. Civilians also suffered from the unceasing bombardment and shortage of food. "We are utterly cut off from the world," wrote one resident, "surrounded by a circle of fire. . . . The fiery shower of shells goes on, day and night . . . People do nothing but eat what they can get, sleep *when* they can, and dodge the shells."

Finally, six weeks after Pemberton had withdrawn into Vicksburg, he was ready to relinquish the city. The opposing commanders met on July 2 to discuss terms of surrender; hoping to gain paroles for his men, Pemberton agreed to surrender on Independence Day. Thirty-one thousand Confederates surrendered on July 4, 1863, and the Stars and Stripes was raised above the Vicksburg Court House. Coming the day after the Federal victory at Gettysburg, the fall of Vicksburg marked the beginning of the end of the Confederacy.

W

Wade-Davis Bill

JULY 1806

Anticipating the Confederacy's collapse, Radical Republicans in Congress attempted in July 1864 to name their own terms for the Union's Reconstruction in a stunning challenge to Abraham Lincoln's leadership. The occupied states of Louisiana, Arkansas, and Tennessee were close to seeking readmittance into the Union, and Lincoln hoped that a lenient policy would encourage other Southern states to follow and hasten the end of the war.

In his 1863 Proclamation of Amnesty and Reconstruction, the president declared a state could be eligible for readmission once 10 percent of its white male citizens took an oath of loyalty to the United States. Implicit in this was an acceptance of the country's emancipation policy. The Radical Republicans, however, feared that the total abolition of slavery might be negotiated away in a peace settlement with the South. Moreover, they claimed that because the seceding governments had forfeited their rights as states, the conditions for their return to the Union were to be dictated by Congress, not the president.

Those conditions were spelled out in the Wade-Davis Bill, and they were far harsher than Lincoln's. One half, not ten percent, of the state's white male population had to swear allegiance to the Union before a civil government would be restored. Only then could a convention be called to adopt a new state constitution, which had to guarantee emancipation. Confederate office holders and those who voluntarily fought in the Southern military would be forbidden ever to serve in the restored government. Initially, black suffrage was also mandated, but the sponsors of the legislation, Republican Ohio Senator Benjamin F. Wade and Maryland Representative Henry Winter Davis, dropped that requirement to improve its chances of approval.

By a narrow margin, both houses of Congress passed the Wade-Davis Bill on July 2. Lincoln refused to sign the legislation in a "pocket veto," and released a statement outlining his reasons. Primary among them was his insistence that Congress could not summarily demand the abolition of slavery. Furious at the president's veto, Wade and Davis issued a "manifesto" of their own, a stunning attack on Lincoln by members of his own party. "The authority of Congress is paramount and must be respected," they asserted, warning the president to "confine himself to Executive duties—to obey and execute, not make the laws," or risk losing Republican support in his reelection campaign.

Reconstruction was essentially tabled until after the war, precisely what the Radicals intended by their restrictive legislation. Likewise, the Republican-dominated Congress intended to continue trying to set the nation's Reconstruction policy itself, a resolve that would lead to a grim and ugly conflict with Lincoln's successor, Andrew Johnson.

Walker, Mary Edwards

1832–1919

The first woman commissioned as an army surgeon, she also became the first of her gender to receive the Medal of Honor.

Walker graduated from Syracuse Medical College in 1855, the only woman in her class, and set up a struggling practice in Cincinnati. At the start of the Civil War, she left that practice to volunteer her services to the Union army. Despite an acute shortage of trained medical professionals, she was denied a surgeon commission, though allowed to serve for nearly three years as an army nurse. In September 1863, she finally received an appointment—at first temporary—as an assistant surgeon for an Ohio regiment under General George Thomas. Tending to wounded soldiers and ill civilians on both sides, Walker moved between the lines freely and, according to some accounts, also served as a spy.

She was once captured while treating a Confederate and was held for four months until an August 1864 prisoner exchange. Thereafter, Walker no longer served in the field, although she continued her army duties until June 1865. A "Bloomer Girl" since the 1850s, who advocated women's dress reform, Walker wore army uniforms during her service and civilian male clothing thereafter. In her postwar years, she resumed her work as a suffragist and equal rights activist, founding a shortlived women's separatist colony, Adamless Eden, in 1897. Walker's radical views estranged her from not only her family but from others in the women's movement as well.

Losing her living from speaking and writing

fees, Walker still received a monthly military pension, which she had to supplement with humiliating appearances on the sideshow circuit, and she further damaged her reputation with mean-spirited vendettas against her enemies. In addition, Walker's Medal of Honor, bestowed shortly after the war, was revoked during a World War I-era review of every prior recipient of the decoration, when awards for noncombat service were ruled invalid.

Walker angrily refused to return the medal and fought against the decision until her poverty-stricken death. Nearly 60 years later,

Dr. Mary Edwards Walker

Walker posthumously won her battle with the official reinstatement of her medal in 1977.

War Correspondents

Newspaper coverage of the Civil War brought about a major transformation of the American art and practice of journalism. Before the war, newspapers across the country paid scant attention to national news or issues; in fact, fewer than a dozen papers employed full-time reporters in Washington, D.C. Moreover, most were little more than eight-page editorials that attempted to mold public opinion rather than report objective fact. Only a few reporters, such as Henry Raymond of the *New York Times*, had had any war-reporting experience at the start of the conflict.

Nevertheless, newspapers from both the North and South sent several reporters to cover First Bull Run and to most of the battles that followed. During the course of the war, however, the number of Southern reporters and Southern newspapers diminished as paper supplies became scarce and all able-bodied men—including journalists—were required to fight. In fact, most Confederate war correspondents were also soldiers who reported from the front. Reporters on both sides frequently used pseudonyms to evade the censorship imposed by the army: before releasing any information about a battle or troop movement, the journalist was required to obtain permission from the commanding major general.

Since permission was rarely forthcoming from generals wishing to retain as much secrecy as possible, journalists did so secretly. Altogether, about 100 Southerners reported on the war. Perhaps the most famous Confederate journalist was Felix G. DeFontaine, formerly of the *New York Herald*, who wrote for several Southern newspapers and was a member of the Confederate Press Association.

In the North, where manpower and material were more plentiful, the press corps grew as the war continued; about 350 Northerners wrote about the war for newspapers, including many soldier correspondents. In the spirit of the times, the Northern war correspondents joined together and called themselves the "Bohemian Brigade." Sharing information and often traveling in groups, they formed the first true American press corps.

Like their counterparts in contemporary America, these journalists developed a reputation (some of it earned) for both hard living and executing daring exploits in search of a story from the front. Charles Anderson Page, George Alfred Townsend, Samuel Wilkeson, and John Russell Young were some of the best known journalists covering the Eastern theater. Their counterparts in the West included Jerome Bonaparte Stillson, Franc Bangs Wilkie, and John B. McCullagh.

War Democrats

Crucial to Abraham Lincoln's war efforts was the support of the Northern Democrats. Overwhelmed in Congress by the Republican party after the defection of the Southern Democrats to the Confederacy, the Democrats who remained in the Union—and who did not defect to the Republican party—struggled to carve out a role as a minority party in the Union Congress.

The party was split into two factions: the Peace Democrats (Copperheads), who generally supported the South and considered the war unconstitutional, and the War Democrats, who believed in the Union and, for the most part, supported the Lincoln administration. War Democrats generally had little or no objection to the continued existence of slavery in the South and insisted that they wanted to restore the Union without interfering with states' rights to conduct their own domestic affairs.

Nevertheless, they were willing to fight against the South in order to restore the Union. In that matter, they were heirs to the philosophy of Stephen A. Douglas who, despite his adamant support of states' rights, remained in

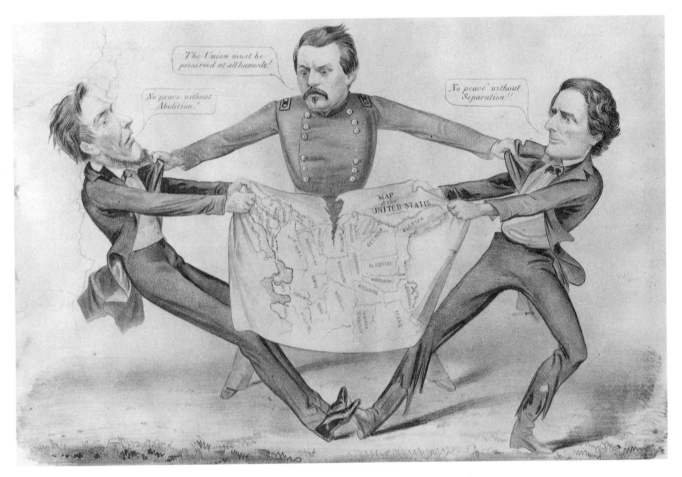

Cartoon depicting War Democrat George McClellan mediating between Lincoln and Davis.

favor of the Union until his death in 1861. It was largely to appease the War Democrats, and thus present a united front in the execution of the war, that Lincoln delayed passage of the Emancipation Proclamation.

Like their counterparts, the Copperheads, the ranks of the War Democrats rose and fell according to the way the North fared during the war. As the war dragged on and casualties increased, the already small number of Democrats willing to align themselves with Lincoln diminished. This loss of support influenced both Lincoln's prosecution of the war and his reelection campaign in 1864 when War Democrat George B. McClellan ran against him. Revealing the rift in the Democratic party, McClellan, who had fought against the South as Lincoln's general-in-chief during the first

year of the war, offered a peace platform to the voters.

Perhaps the most ardent War Democrats were the Union soldiers fighting in the field. Although 40 to 45 percent of the soldiers had been Democrats when they joined the army, more than 75 percent of them voted for Abraham Lincoln in the 1864 election.

Washington, D.C.

At the beginning of the war, all that stood between the Rebel army and the nation's capital were a few Regular troops and a scattering of neighborhood militia units. Within months, however, Washington, D.C. would become one of the most heavily fortified cities on earth, ringed by 93 batteries and 60 forts creating a 37-mile circle of protection.

When Union troops first started to amass in the capital in early 1861, many were dismayed to find that it was still a rather shabby city more than 70 years after its establishment. Many buildings, including the Capitol, were unfinished, as was its sewer system and many of its roads. Nevertheless, the city was and would remain the enduring symbol and center of the Union; its protection was an essential goal of the Union army.

Like Richmond, Virginia, its Confederate counterpart, Washington, D.C. would undergo tumultuous change during the course of the war. From 1860 to 1865, its population grew

from about 40,000 people to more than 150,000. Along with soldiers and politicians came speculators and entrepreneurs, as well as so many gamblers and prostitutes that Washington, like Richmond, developed an often overwhelming problem with crime. New hospitals and prisons were built to handle the tens of thousands of wounded and captured from the battles that raged in nearby Maryland and Virginia. Although Washingtonians rarely experienced severe shortages of food or supplies, they shared with their Confederate counterparts the enduring fear that the war would somehow make its way into the city.

Washington experienced only two major threats to its safety. The first occurred in the weeks just before and after First Bull Run as the defenseless city awaited the arrival of Federal

Defending Washington.

troops to protect it against any well-coordinated Confederate approach. In fact, the Confederates managed to effectively blockade one avenue of approach to the city by constructing three fortifications on the Potomac in the spring of 1861. The Army of the Potomac's first commander, George B. McClellan, was quick to remedy the situation, creating formidable Washington defenses within a few months' time that would improve as the war continued.

The only other major threat occurred in 1864 when Jubal Early invaded Maryland and, from his base there, conducted a series of raids upon the outskirts of the capital city. In May 1865, the two armies, one vanquished and one victorious, marched down Pennsylvania Avenue in the capital of a nation once again whole.

Watie, Stand

1806–1871

The highest ranking Native American in either force, the Cherokee leader was the last Confederate general to surrender—more than two months after Appomattox.

Watie was born in Georgia, educated in Connecticut, and became a prominent planter and journalist. He was also instrumental in negotiating the controversial 1835 treaty with the United States that relocated the Cherokee Nation from the Southeast to the Indian Territory (present-day Oklahoma). An early supporter of the Confederacy, Watie raised a pro-secession home guard as the Civil War commenced. It was an unofficial command, for the Cherokees initially intended to remain neutral in the conflict, despite the fact that many of the more affluent owned black slaves. The Confederacy, however, eager to protect its vulnerable Western border and hoping to gain as many as 20,000 new army recruits, sought the support of the Indian Territory tribes. Promised better treatment than it had received from the federal government and guaranteed rights long denied,

the Cherokee Nation entered into an alliance with the South in 1861.

Watie, a principal backer of the bargain, entered the Confederate military later in the year and was appointed colonel of the "Cherokee Mounted Rifles." The Southern armies attracted far fewer Indian troops than had first been envisioned, and many of the several thousand who did enlist, frustrated at being kept poorly supplied, soon abandoned the cause. Watie and his cavalry, however, served throughout the war.

After participating in the fighting at Wilson's Creek, Missouri, in August 1861, they distinguished themselves the following March during the Battle of Pea Ridge, Arkansas, in a bold charge on a federal artillery battery. With the Union occupation of the Indian Territories in 1863, most of Watie's subsequent Civil War service involved local raids and skirmishes, fre-

General Stand Watie

quently vying against pro-North Native American units.

That same year, the Cherokee Nation repudiated its treaty with the Confederacy and allied with the Union, while Watie continued to lead a large pro-South faction, his battalion also including Creek, Seminole, and Osage troops. Promoted to brigadier general in May 1864, he gained a reputation as an expert guerrilla fighter for such successful actions as the capture of a Union steamship on the Arkansas River carrying a cargo worth over $100,000. The Northern press paid great attention to these forays, printing highly exaggerated accounts of atrocities the Indians allegedly committed against the Union boys. As the North's victory was assured in 1865, Watie proved to be the Confederate general most reluctant to accept defeat. Lee and Johnston had surrendered in the East in April; even headstrong Department of the Trans-Mississippi commander E. Kirby Smith capitulated the following month.

But Watie did not give up until four weeks later, finally surrendering at Doaksville on June 23, 1865. His own fight lasting months longer than the Civil War, he went back to planting and the tobacco business.

Welles, Gideon

1802–1878

Although a former Democrat who had almost no prior naval experience, Abraham Lincoln's secretary of the navy was one of the most effective and loyal members of his cabinet.

Born in Connecticut, Welles was a taciturn New Englander from a prominent family. During the 1820s, he worked as a newspaper editor while holding minor political offices such as state legislator and comptroller. A staunch supporter of states' rights, Welles went against New England tradition by embracing the Democratic party in 1824 and working to elect Andrew Jackson in 1828. His support of Jackson won him an appointment as postmaster of Hartford in 1836.

He remained in this post until 1844 when, after campaigning for James Polk during his successful 1844 run for president, he was rewarded with an appointment to a minor position within the Navy Department. Four years later, after Polk lost reelection to Zachary Taylor, Welles returned to Connecticut as a political reporter for the *Hartford Times*, and by the middle of the 1850s had become so opposed to slavery that he reluctantly joined the nascent Republican party.

In 1856, he ran for governor of Connecticut as a Republican; although he lost, he garnered national attention and a seat on the Republican National Committee in 1860. Despite the fact that he opposed Abraham Lincoln in favor of the more adamant antislavery candidate, Salmon P. Chase, Lincoln appointed Welles secretary of the navy in the spring of 1861.

Unlike many of his fellow cabinet members, he did not take part in any factional efforts to influence the president on the conduct of the war; instead, he concentrated on the task at hand, namely, preparing the navy to meet the enemy. Stern-faced and with a bushy white beard, Welles prepared the strategy for and oversaw the execution of the successful Union blockade of Southern ports and strongly recommended the construction of ironclads. Dissatisfied with the quality of his naval officers—he felt they were "without audacity, desire for fierce encounter, and in that respect almost utterly deficient as commanders"—Welles engendered resentment among his staff by constantly shuffling and reshuffling commands.

Nicknamed "Father Neptune" by Lincoln, Welles nevertheless conducted the Union's naval war with efficiency and success. He remained in his post after the Lincoln assassination until 1869. During his retirement, he remained outspoken on public issues and published several articles and books on the Civil War. Although self-serving, his three-volume autobiography, *Diary of Gideon Welles*, is a fascinating account of the Civil War from inside the Lincoln administration. Welles died on February 11, 1878, in Hartford, Connecticut.

West Virginia

The Civil War brought longstanding internecine disputes in Virginia to a climax, with 50 western counties seceding from the Confederacy to rejoin the Union as a new state. Far removed socially, economically, and even geographically from the rest of Virginia, citizens of the mountainous region west of the Alleghenies felt habitually slighted by the slaveholder aristocracy that dominated the state government. Fiscal policies and public improvements tended to favor the tidewater plantations of the east over the small farms and mining and manufacturing concerns of the western hills. Slavery was never widespread in that region, which had more in common with its neighbors to the North than with the rest of Virginia—let alone with the deep South—and there was little support there for joining the Confederacy as the Civil War began.

In a spring 1861 statewide referendum, voters in the western counties unsuccessfully opposed secession from the Union by a three-to-one margin. Now determined to break off from Virginia and ally with the North, regional leaders hastily gathered for a convention in Wheeling. By June 20, they formed a rump pro-Union state government that was eagerly recognized by the Lincoln administration. Senators and representatives were elected to take Virginia's vacated seats in the U.S. Congress, as formal steps commenced to create from the western counties an entirely new state that was originally going to be named "Kanawha."

This breach in Confederate unity certainly had political significance, and with the Baltimore & Ohio Railroad and Chesapeake & Ohio Canal—vital links between Washington and the West—running through the region and the Ohio River on its border, the military significance was just as great. To gain control of western Virginia and encourage the statehood movement, the Union army dispatched 20,000 troops under its rising star George B. McClellan. In July, he drove out a small Confederate force and proclaimed that "secession is killed in this country."

The South then called on its own military luminary, Robert E. Lee. Making a disappointing showing in his Civil War field debut, Lee, "outwitted, outmaneuvered, outgeneraled," according to a Richmond newspaper, was unable to reverse the situation. With the region largely free of Southern troops, an October 1861 referendum boycotted by pro-Confederates showed overwhelming support for forming a new Union-loyal state.

A constitutional convention was held the following January, and in May, West Virginia formally requested statehood. After agreeing to the U.S. Congress' demand for gradual emancipation of its relatively few slaves (freeing them on their 25th birthday), it officially entered the Union on June 20, 1863. For a time, other pro-North regions of the upper South, particularly eastern Tennessee, seemed inspired to take similar action, but those statehood movements wound up faltering. Not that conflict in West Virginia was resolved by the decision to return to the Union. Support for the South persisted in some portions of the new state, which would continue to be ravaged by partisan fighting until the Civil War ended.

Though tensions remained after the war's conclusion, West Virginia rejected overtures to merge back with its parent state and opted to retain its separate status in the reunified nation.

Wheeler, Joseph

1836–1906

"Fighting Joe" Wheeler was a man to whom the ordinary rarely applied. Born of New England parents who migrated to Augusta, Georgia, before Wheeler's birth, he is nevertheless remembered as one of the Confederacy's finest cavalry commanders. More, he is one of the few generals to whom Robert E. Lee gave the term outstanding. Graduating from West Point in 1859 with high standings in military subjects and poor standings in academics, Wheeler spent two years fighting Indians in New Mexico before his native state seceded from the Union; on April 22, 1861, he resigned his U.S. commission and offered his sword to his new country.

At first commissioned anew as a first lieutenant in the Confederate Regular army, Wheeler very soon received a post and promotion to colonel of the 19th Alabama Infantry; he led this regiment in the bloody fighting at Shiloh, received an infantry brigade very soon after—and on the heels of that assignment, Wheeler suddenly found himself in command

Lieutenant General Joseph Wheeler

of the cavalry in the Army of Mississippi. By the end of the war, Wheeler had risen successively through the ranks to finish as a lieutenant general, but he always retained command of the cavalry in the Western theater of the war.

There is almost no action in the West that Wheeler was not somehow a part of. At Murfreesboro and Chickamauga, he was instrumental in keeping the commanders of the army aware of Federal maneuvers. He was heavily engaged in the Knoxville campaign and was a constant thorn in the side of William T. Sherman throughout the Atlanta campaign. Wheeler's men were effectively the only troops to have any success in the attempt to contain Sherman's March to the Sea. His cavalrymen, known to the Federal enemy as "Wheeler's Raiders," were feared by opponents far more thoroughly armed and better supplied than he, and right up to the end, his very name caused the upset of many a Federal commander's equilibrium.

Before the surrender of Joseph Johnston, Wheeler's men broke away and, to their discredit, were involved in less than admirable excesses against isolated groups of Federal soldiers in the closing days of the war. But even that could not diminish the fame of their young commander, who had, it was said, participated in over 800 skirmishes, 200 engagements, and had been wounded three times in the course of the war's four years.

After the war, Wheeler settled into what must have seemed a rather commonplace life. He married and relocated to a town in Alabama that was instituted and named in his honor. He planted cotton and practiced law, until Reconstruction ended and politics became a major interest in his life. In 1881, he initially won election to the Forty-seventh Congress, but the election was contested; in the end, his seat was taken by a Mr. Lowe. Before the end of the term, however, Lowe died—and Wheeler was elected to take his place. He was also a member of the Forty-ninth Congress, involved in military and fiscal policy-making, to no one's surprise. He became the senior Democrat on the House Ways and Means Committee, and in a show of "no hard feelings" was involved in the revocation of the harsher sentences of Union General Fitz-John Porter's court-martial decision. For the most part, however, Wheeler was known as a man whose interests primarily lay with his own people. Everything he did, even his work toward the continuing reconciliation between North and South, he did for Alabama.

Such a career would have been enough for an ordinary man, but Wheeler was hardly ordinary. When the Spanish-American War flared in the 1890s, Wheeler was appointed a major general in command of Volunteers, one of three Con-

federate cavalry generals to serve in this war; he commanded a cavalry division in the Santiago Expedition, was present at the landing at Daiquiri, Cuba, and started the fighting at Las Guasimas in 1898. He was present at the Battle of San Juan Hill on July 1, 1898, though illness prevented him from participating. Recovering in time to join the siege of Santiago, Wheeler figures prominently in reports of the action. Ever busy, Wheeler was in charge of the convalescent camp in Montauk Point, Long Island, when the wounded of the war were returned to the United States; he was then given a brigade

Union blockhouse garrisoned against Wheeler's Raiders.

of cavalry in the Philippines. On July 16, 1900, he was appointed a brigadier general in the U.S. Army, and finally retired three months later at the age of 64. Wheeler was an ardent writer and champion of the South; he wrote an innovative cavalry tactics manual during the Civil War, as well as articles concerning the operations of his Confederate troopers, and his interests in genealogy are evidenced by a book he coauthored with his wife on the ancestry of their children.

Wheeler lived out the remainder of his life in peace and quiet, passing away in Brooklyn, New York, in 1906. He is buried in Arlington National Cemetery, Arlington, Virginia.

Wilderness, Battle of the

MAY 5–6, 1864

The first battlefield confrontation between Ulysses S. Grant and Robert E. Lee, this engagement in Virginia's Rapidan basin marked the beginning of a 40-day campaign that included some of the bloodiest fighting of the Civil War. Grant, who had been appointed the Union's general-in-chief two months earlier, intended nothing less than a showdown between Meade's Army of the Potomac and Lee's Army of Northern Virginia that, together with coordinated efforts by other Federal forces elsewhere, would bring about the Confederacy's defeat by the end of the year.

On May 4, Union troops began crossing the Rapidan River and marching south to face the Confederates, returning to the location of the Battle of Chancellorsville. Grant had hoped his troops could avoid a clash with the enemy until they passed the notorious dense forest of trees and shrubs known as "the Wilderness." Choked with heavy underbrush and still littered with human bones and other battle debris, this was the spot where Lee's army achieved such devastating success exactly one year earlier.

The Confederate general relied on the Wilder-

ness once again, reckoning that the Union army's great numerical advantage—115,000 to his force of 60,000—would be offset by the difficult terrain. The battle began early on the morning of May 5, when Union and Confederate troops stumbled upon each other as the Federals attempted to cross the forest. Both sides received reinforcements, and by 1 P.M., the Union mounted a major assault. With the troops soon swallowed up in the impenetrable thickets, however, the fighting plunged into total chaos. Visibility was less than 50 yards, hampered even further by the smoke of battle and brushfires ignited by bursting shells. Having few discernible targets, many soldiers just shot blindly into the woods, sometimes hitting their own men, while entire units got lost in the tangled undergrowth, forcing their commanders to resort to compasses to find their way.

As Lee anticipated, the terrain did even the odds. With far fewer experienced woodsmen among the Northern troops, the superior size of the Union force created more of a logistical problem than a tactical advantage. But the greater numbers did allow the Federals to absorb greater casualties. Commanded by the resolute Grant, they continued making relentless assaults, repulsed each time by Confederate counterattacks. By the end of the first day's fighting, Grant managed to weaken Lee's right flank, and was positioned for attack.

At dawn on May 6, Union forces began slamming through the Confederate center, advancing almost a mile, nearly all the way to Lee's field headquarters. By this time, however, much-needed Confederate reinforcements from James Longstreet's corps were beginning to arrive on the field. Hood's Texas Brigades, the celebrated infantry unit now actually under John Gregg, was soon poised for a counterattack. Lee himself intended to lead the charge, but the Texas troops refused to begin their assault until the Confederate commander was safely behind the lines.

Throughout the morning, Longstreet's fresh troops pushed the flustered Union men back. Following an unfinished railroad line all but hidden under bushes and vines, the Confederates had a makeshift pathway for a massive attack on the Union's left flank. Their momentum was crushed, though, when Longstreet was accidentally shot and wounded by his own troops. By the time Lee mounted a new assault in the late afternoon, Union forces had regrouped and were able to hold their position.

Meanwhile, in a late attack on the Union's right, Confederate John B. Gordon drove Federal troops back one mile, although they managed to regain most of the ground by nightfall. Still, the setback caused great alarm at Grant's headquarters. While the Union commander kept his composure, even chastising his gloomy aides for bemoaning Lee's supposed superior prowess, some eyewitnesses reported that Grant himself broke down in tears when he retired to his tent.

Both commanders had good reason to be upset. The two-day battle cost the Union army 17,500 casualties to the Confederates' 7,750, with neither side gaining much ground. At several points, the fighting had to be halted while both sides attempted to rescue wounded comrades being burned alive by the uncontrolled brushfires raging through the Wilderness. The following day, however, as the two armies began skirmishing, Grant did not call for the expected retreat. To the contrary, notwithstanding his far heavier losses and a tactical draw on the battlefield, he ordered an advance.

Intent on keeping his promise to Abraham Lincoln that "whatever happens, there will be no turning back," Grant's plan now was for George Meade's army to move further south—past Lee's right—and position itself provocatively between the Confederate forces and their capital, Richmond. The fighting would resume within days, 12 miles away at the strategic crossroads town of Spotsylvania Court House.

The Battle of the Wilderness, May 5 and 6, 1864.

Wilson's Creek, Battle of

AUGUST 10, 1861

The second military engagement of the war after First Bull Run was a small but vicious battle over the future of the border state Missouri. The commander of Federal forces was Nathaniel Lyon, who had amassed some 5,500 troops at Springfield, Missouri. The Confederate army of about 10,000 men advanced on Springfield at the beginning of August, finally camping at Wilson's Creek about 15 miles away. Aware of the enemy position, Lyon planned a surprise attack. He would divide his forces, sending Colonel Franz Sigel to attack from the south while he himself led a frontal attack on the main body from the north. Although his strategy was sound, Lyon was outnumbered more than two to one, and the soldiers he did command had almost no battlefield experience.

The resulting battle was a bitter, confused hand-to-hand struggle. It began at about 4 A.M., when the Northern column moved out and drove back the Confederate outposts from the west side of the creek. A flank guard broke away to move against a Confederate force on the east side and was able to drive it back as well. Sigel, however, was having difficulty advancing from the south. At 5:30 A.M., he attacked the Confederate cavalry, then took an intermediate position and regrouped. Troops under Louis Hébert and cavalry under Thomas Churchill managed to send Sigel's poorly trained troops into confused retreat, leaving Lyon's men vulnerable.

However, Lyon's troops were positioned on an incline called Oak Hill, from which they had already repulsed two charges by 10:30 A.M. Lyon

Wounded escaping battle.

himself had been wounded twice, in the head and leg, but stayed alive long enough to rally his troops for yet another defense of the position. After another hour of brutal fighting, the Confederates broke off action and withdrew down the hill.

Samuel Sturgis, who had assumed command after Lyon's death, ordered his exhausted army to retreat to Springfield, thereby making one of the most bitterly contested withdrawals of the war. Had Sturgis pressed the battle, the fight over Missouri might have been won that day. Instead, the state would be the site of bitter fighting throughout the rest of the war.

Wirz, Henry

1822–1865

Commander of the Confederacy's infamous Andersonville Prison, he became the only Civil War figure executed after its conclusion for war crimes. The Swiss-German immigrant came to the United States in 1849 and practiced medicine in Louisiana.

Enlisting as a private in the Confederate army in 1861, Wirz served for a time as clerk at Libby Prison in Richmond. He also saw battlefield action until seriously wounded at Seven Pines in May 1862. His right arm permanently disabled, Wirz was named a staff officer, serving as a purchasing agent in Europe until early 1864. In March, he was appointed commander of a new prison for captured Union enlisted men near Andersonville, Georgia, officially named Camp Sumter. Under Wirz's command, Andersonville soon became the most notorious of the Confederate camps.

Whether Wirz was truly guilty of war crimes is still a controversy. While 12,000 died under his charge of starvation, disease, and neglect, the South by this time was woefully short of food and medical supplies for even its own soldiers. Moreover, Confederate soldiers faced similar conditions in Union camps. Wirz did authorize the shooting of prisoners who tried to escape and those who came too close to the prison wall—hardly unusual orders—but also forbade prisoners from building shelters. Though he certainly allowed appalling conditions in the camp to persist with little or no effort to improve them, accusations of deliberate murder, cruelty, and conspiracy were exaggerated in an overheated post-war atmosphere.

But it was Wirz's misfortune to become the scapegoat as the victors demanded retribution for the dead and the corpselike survivors of the Confederate military prison system. Arrested at Andersonville, he was sent to Washington, D.C. for trial.

Secretary of War Edwin Stanton set up a special military tribunal, presided over by General Lew Wallace, who would go on to greater fame as the author of *Ben-Hur*.

In what amounted to a kangaroo court, Wirz was found guilty and hanged November 10, 1865, before 250 onlookers and four army companies chanting, "Remember Andersonville." In 1909, the Daughters of the Confederacy built a monument honoring the "hero-martyr," which overlooks the former prison camp's cemetery.

Woman Order, Butler's

MAY 15, 1862

Louisiana's military governor, Benjamin Butler, issued an infamous edict, officially known as his General Orders No. 28, threatening to arrest as a prostitute any woman of New Orleans who insulted Union soldiers. To be sure, Butler had a problem on his hands in the South's largest city, occupied by Federal forces in April 1862. He tried to quell resistance from the citizenry through such acts as hanging from the city's mint a man who desecrated the American flag, confiscating the property of those who would not take an oath of allegiance to the Union, and arresting the publisher of the song "The Bonnie Blue Flag," as well as threatening to fine anyone singing it.

The governor had an equally difficult time with the women of the city. They regularly mocked, muttered epithets, and glared hostilely at the occupying forces. Some hoped to incite a violent response from the mostly respectful Yankees, which would lead to an uprising by the town's citizens; others merely vented their hatred. A number of women spat on the soldiers and one topped them all by emptying a chamber pot on Admiral David G. Farragut. Butler's solution was to issue his General Orders No. 28 to "women calling themselves ladies." The order proclaimed, "When any female shall, by word, gesture, or movement, insult or show contempt for any officer or soldier of the United States, she shall be regarded and held liable to be treated as a woman of the town plying her avocation."

The edict managed to alienate people throughout the North and England as well as in the Confederacy. In a speech to Parliament, British Prime Minister Viscount Palmerston declared, "An Englishman must blush to think that such an act has been committed by one belonging to the Anglo-Saxon Race," while Jefferson Davis ordered that Butler be executed on the spot if captured. But the military governor was unrepentant, arresting New Orleans Mayor John T. Monroe when he protested and even issuing an amplification of the edict that managed to offend the townspeople still further.

Yet, the order was undeniably effective; the ridicule of Federal troops ceased almost entirely, and only a handful of women were arrested, although one was held for over two months. While Butler was never forced to revoke his order, it became one in a series of actions that resulted in his removal as military governor in December 1862.

Women In Uniform

In the last few years, historians have become more and more aware of what was previously thought to be a limited phenomenon in the Civil War: the incidence of women disguising themselves as men and enlisting in the army, for any number of reasons.

There were numerous women openly serving with the armies on both sides, but recognized as female; the Union forces, more so than the Confederates, had in their ranks vivandieres, women who marched alongside the men, often going into battle with them, to provide medical assistance, carry water and ammunition down the line, and to carry messages between troops and their commanders. In addition, women such as Captain Sally Tompkins, who ran a hospital in Richmond for the Confederacy and was rewarded with a salaried rank in the Southern army, and Bridget Divers, who served openly in her husband's company of the First Michigan Cavalry, were tireless fighters in their own ways for the aims of their nations and flags.

But as time goes by, more stories are coming to the surface of women who left home disguised as men and passed through the haphazard enlistment process without being detected for what they really were. With few exceptions, these women served gallantly for all or part of the war; some of them, revealed to be women when they fell ill or were wounded, were either honorably discharged or summarily dismissed, depending on the mood of whatever general caught them or had to deal with them. Some of them even drew veterans' pensions in the years following the war.

Their reasons for serving were as different and varied as the women themselves. Sarah Emma Edmonds, a young Canadian girl, ran away from home to avoid an arranged marriage; she impersonated a male bookseller in the United States for a time, then enlisted in the Union army as Frank Thompson. She served with the Second Michigan Infantry until a bout of malaria made her fear she would be caught in her masquerade; she deserted, but was legally cleared of that desertion long after she had been married and had become a mother.

Jennie Hodgers, who stowed away on a ship leaving Ireland bound for the United States in 1844, disguised herself as one Albert D. J. Cashier and served in the Illinois Volunteer Infantry from 1862 until the end of the war. She was never suspected to be anything more than likeable, shy, and very brave. Her masquerade was only discovered long after the war, when at the age of 66 she broke her leg in an automobile accident—and the doctor at the veteran's hospital found her out. The secret was kept, however, and she successfully drew the veteran's pension she was entitled to for her gallant service.

There were others, of course, known and unknown, but one of the women passing for men in the armed forces who seems to have not only served well, but had a good time doing so, was Loreta Janeta Velazquez of the Arkansas Grays, an infantry unit she raised and equipped at her own expense. Velazquez was the Cuban-born widow of a Confederate soldier who died of an accidental gunshot injury early in the war; she left her New Orleans home in search of adventure, with the romantic notion of becoming a "second Joan of Arc." She created a system of wire shields and braces to hide her breasts, put on a Confederate uniform, and adopted the name Harry Buford. She then traveled to Arkansas, where she would presumably not be recognized, and recruited for her new command.

She was elected lieutenant, and her career as the commander of the Grays began at First Manassas (First Bull Run). Eventually she ended up serving with the army in Kentucky and Tennessee, during which service she was twice wounded and cited for gallantry. She did not seem to care for the private behavior of men, finding that when they were reasonably sure there were no women around, their conversation became disgusting and full of "thoroughly despicable" comments about women.

She wound up in Richmond, where someone figured out she was a woman herself. Temporarily arrested as a possible spy, she convinced Confederate authorities that she was a loyal citizen and embarked on a career as a secret agent for the South. Her operations took her to Canada and to the Federal capital at Washington, D. C. Her postwar narrative account of her adventures, amusing, harrowing, and very well written, contains a comment that might well serve as an epitaph for all the women, known and unknown, who chose this unique and dangerous way to serve their country:

"Notwithstanding the fact that I was a woman, I was as good a soldier as any man around me, and as willing as any to fight valiantly and to the bitter end before yielding."

Z

Zouaves

Dressed in colorful outfits, the dashing Zouave regiments of the North and South modeled themselves after the daring—and internationally publicized—French colonial armies of the same name. The original Zouaves were Algerian light infantry who were famous for their ability to fire and reload musketry from prone

A unit of the colorful Pennsylvania Zouaves.

positions. American Zouave units copied every aspect of their Euro-African counterparts, especially their dress, which usually consisted of white canvas leggings, red baggy pants or white trousers, a broad red or blue sash, a dark blue vest and short jacket, a red cape, and a red fez with a blue tassel. Each unit, however, developed its own unique style depending on the material available.

The first American Zouave unit, the U.S. Zouave Cadets, was organized in Chicago by Elmer E. Ellsworth before the war. Ellsworth, who did much to popularize the Zouave units, was killed in Alexandria, Virginia, after removing a Confederate flag from atop a tavern in 1861. As the war dragged on, their uniforms became less colorful and elaborate, but the Zouaves nevertheless served admirably in both the Union and Confederate armies.

Appendix 1
President Abraham Lincoln's First Inaugural Address

Fellow citizens of the United States:

In compliance with a custom as old as the government itself, I appear before you to address you briefly, and to take, in your presence, the oath prescribed by the Constitution of the United States, to be taken by the President "before he enters on the execution of his office."

I do not consider it necessary, at present, for me to discuss those matters of administration about which there is no special anxiety, or excitement.

Apprehension seems to exist among the people of the Southern States, that by the accession of a Republican Administration, their property, and their peace, and personal security, are to be endangered. There has never been any reasonable cause for such apprehension. Indeed, the most ample evidence to the contrary has all the while existed, and been open to their inspection. It is found in nearly all the published speeches of him who now addresses you. I do but quote from one of those speeches when I declare that "I have no purpose, directly or indirectly, to interfere with the institution of slavery in the States where it exists. I believe I have no lawful right to do so, and I have no inclination to do so." Those who nominated and elected me did so with full knowledge that I had made this, and many similar declarations, and had never recanted them. And more than this, they placed in the platform, for my acceptance, and as a law to themselves, and to me, the clear and emphatic resolution which I now read:

"*Resolved*, That the maintenance inviolate of the rights of the States, and especially the right of each State to order and control its own domestic institutions according to its own judgment exclusively, is essential to that balance of power on which the perfection and endurance of our political fabric depend; and we denounce the lawless invasion by armed force of the soil of any State or Territory, no matter under what pretext, as among the gravest of crimes.

I now reiterate these sentiments: and in doing so, I only press upon the public attention the most conclusive evidence of which the case is susceptible, that the property, peace and security of no section are to be in anywise endangered by the now incoming Administration. I add too, that all the protection which, consistently with the Constitution and the laws, can be given, will be cheerfully demanded, for whatever cause—as cheerfully to one section, as to another.

There is much controversy about the delivering up of fugitives from service or labor. The clause I now read is as plainly written in the Constitution as any other of its provisions:

"No person held to service or labor in one State, under the laws thereof, escaping into another, shall, in consequence of any law or regulation therein, be discharged from such service or labor, but shall be delivered up on claim of the party to whom such service or labor may be due."

It is scarcely questioned that this provision was intended by those who made it for the reclaiming of what we call fugitive slaves; and the intention of the law-giver is the law. All members of Congress swear their support to the whole Constitution—to this provision as much as to any other. To the proposition, then, that slaves whose cases come within the terms of this clause, "shall be delivered up," their oaths are unanimous. Now, if they would make the effort in good temper, could they not, with nearly equal unanimity, frame and pass a law, by means of which to keep good that unanimous oath?

There is some difference of opinion whether this clause should be enforced by national or by state authority; but surely that difference is not a very material one. If the slave is to be surrendered, it can be but of little consequence to him, or to others, by which authority is done. And should anyone, in any case, be content that his oath shall go unkept, on a merely unsubstantial controversy as to *how* it shall be kept?

Again, in any law upon this subject, ought not all the safeguards of liberty known in civilized and humane jurisprudence to be introduced, so that a free man be not, in any case, surrendered as a slave? And might it not be well, at the same time, to provide by law for the enforcement of that clause in the Constitution which guaranties that "The citizens of each State shall be entitled to all privileges and immunities of citizens in the several States?"

I take the official oath to-day, with no mental reservations, and with no purpose to construe the Constitution or laws, by any hypercritical rules. And while I do not choose now to specify particular acts of Congress as proper to be enforced, I do suggest, that it will be much safer for all, both in official and private stations, to conform to, and abide by, all those acts which stand unrepealed, than to violate any of them, trusting to find impunity in having them held to be unconstitutional.

It is seventy-two years since the first inauguration of a President under our national Constitution. During that period fifteen different and greatly distinguished citizens, have, in succession, administered the executive branch of the government. They have conducted it through many perils; and, generally, with great success. Yet, with all this scope for precedent, I now enter upon the same task for the brief constitutional term of four years, under great and peculiar difficulty. A disruption of the Federal Union heretofore only menaced, is now formidably attempted.

I hold, that in contemplation of universal law, and of the Constitution, the Union of these States is perpetual. Perpetuity is implied, if not expressed, in the fundamental law of all national governments. It is safe to assert that no government proper, ever had a provision in its organic law for its own termination. Continue to execute all the express provisions of our national Constitution, and the Union will endure forever—it being impossible to destroy it, except by some action not provided for in the instrument itself.

Again, if the United States be not a government proper, but an association of States in the nature of contract merely, can it, as a contract, be peaceably unmade, by less than all the parties who made it? One party to a contract may violate it—break it, so to speak; but does it not require all to lawfully rescind it?

Descending from these general principles, we find the proportion that, in legal contemplation, the Union is perpetual, confirmed by the history of the Union itself. The Union is much older than the Constitution. It was formed in fact, by the Articles of Association of 1774. It was matured and continued by the Declaration of Independence in 1776. It was further matured and the faith of all the then thirteen States expressly plighted and engaged that it should be perpetual, by the Articles of Confederation in 1778. And finally, in 1787, one of the declared objects for ordaining and establishing the Constitution, was *"to form a more perfect union."*

But if destruction of the Union, by one, or by a part only, of the States, be lawfully possible, the Union is *less* perfect than before the Constitution, having lost the vital element of perpetuity.

It follows from these views that no State, upon its own mere motion, can lawfully get out of the Union,—that *resolves* and *ordinances* to that effect are legally void; and that acts of violence, within any State or States, against the authority of the United States, are insurrectionary or revolutionary, according to circumstances.

I therefore consider that, in view of the Constitution and the laws, the Union is unbroken; and, to the extent of my ability, I shall take care, as the Constitution itself expressly enjoins upon me, that the laws of the Union be faithfully executed in all the States. Doing this I deem to be only a simple duty on my part; and I shall perform it, so far as practicable, unless my rightful masters, the American people, shall withhold the requisite means, or, in some authoritative manner, direct the contrary. I trust this will not be regarded as a menace, but only as the declared purpose of the Union that it will constitutionally defend, and maintain itself.

In doing this there needs to be no bloodshed or violence; and there shall be none, unless it be forced upon the national authority. The power confided to me, will be used to hold, occupy, and possess the property, and places belonging to the government, and to collect the duties and imposts; but beyond what may be necessary for these objects, there will be no invasion—no using of force against, or among the people anywhere. Where hostility to the United States, in any interior locality, shall be so great and so universal, as to prevent competent resident citizens from holding the Federal offices, there will be no attempt to force obnoxious strangers among the people for that object. While the strict legal right may exist in the government to enforce the exercise of these offices, the attempt to do so would be so irritating, and so nearly impracticable with all, that I deem it better to forego, for the time, the uses of such offices.

The mails, unless repelled, will continue to be furnished in all parts of the Union. So far as possible, the people everywhere shall have that sense of perfect security which is most favorable to calm thought and reflection. The course here indicated will be followed, unless current events, and experience, shall slow a modification, or change, to be proper; and in every case and exigency, my best discretion will be exercised, according to circumstances actually existing, and with a view and a hope of a peaceful solution of the national troubles, and the restoration of fraternal sympathies and affections.

That there are persons in one section, or another who seek to destroy the Union at all events, and are glad of any pretext to do it, I will neither affirm or deny; but if there be such, I need address no word to them. To those, however, who really love the Union, may I not speak?

Before entering upon so grave a matter as the destruction of our national fabric, with all its benefits, its memories, and its hopes, would it not be wise to ascertain precisely why we do it? Will you hazard so desperate a step, while there is any possibility that any portion of the ills you fly from, have no real existence? Will you, while the certain ills you fly to, are greater than the ones you fly from? Will you risk the commission of so fearful a mistake?

All profess to be content in the Union, if all constitutional rights can be maintained. Is it true, then, that any right, plainly written in the Constitution, has been denied? I think not. Happily the human mind is so constituted, that no party can reach to the audacity of doing this. Think, if you can, of a single instance in which a plainly written provision of the Constitution has ever been denied. If, by the mere force of numbers, a majority should deprive a minority of any clearly written constitutional right, it might, in a moral point of view, justify revolution—certainly would, if such right were a vital one. But such is not our case. All the vital rights of minorities, and of individuals, are so plainly assured to them, by affirmations and negations, guarantees and prohibitions, in the Constitution, that controversies never arise concerning them. But no organic law can ever be framed with a provision specifically applicable to every question which may occur in practical administration. No foresight can anticipate, nor any document of reasonable length contain express provisions for all possible questions. Shall fugitives from labor be surrendered by national or by State authority? The Constitution does not expressly say. *May* Congress prohibit slavery in the territories? The Constitution does not expressly say. *Must* Congress protect slavery in the territories? The Constitution does not expressly say.

From questions of this class spring all our constitutional controversies, and we divide upon them into majorities and minorities. If the minority will not acquiesce, the majority must, or the government must cease. There is no other alternative; for continuing the government, is acquiescence on one side or the other. If a minority, in such a case, will secede rather than acquiesce, they make a precedent which, in turn, will divide and ruin them; for a minority of their own will secede from them, whenever a majority refuses to be controlled by such minority. For instance, why may not any portion of a new confederacy, a year or two hence, arbitrarily secede again, precisely as portions of the present Union now claim to secede from it. All who cherish disunion sentiments, are now being educated to the exact temper of doing this. Is there such perfect identity of interests among the States to compose a new Union, as to produce harmony only, and prevent renewed secession?

Plainly, the central idea of secession, is the essence of anarchy. A majority, held in restraint by constitutional checks, and limitations, and always changing easily, with deliberate changes of popular opinions and sentiments, is the only true sovereign of a free people. Whoever rejects it, does, of necessity, fly to anarchy or to despotism. Unanimity is impossible; the rule of a minority, as a permanent arrangement, is wholly inadmissable; so that, rejecting the majority principle, anarchy, or despotism in some form, is all that is left.

I do not forget the position assumed by some, that constitutional questions are to be decided by the Supreme Court; nor do I deny that such decisions must be binding in any case, upon the parties to a suit, as to the object of that suit, while they are also entitled to very high respect and consideration, in all parallel cases, by all other departments of the government. And while it is obviously possible that such decision may be erroneous in any given case, still the evil effect following it, being limited to that particular case, with the chance that it may be over-ruled, and never become a precedent for other cases, can better be borne than could the evils of a different practice. At the same time the candid citizen must confess that if the policy of the government, upon vital questions, affecting the whole people, is to be irrevocably fixed by decisions of the Supreme Court, the instant they are made, in ordinary litigation between parties, in personal actions, the people will have ceased, to be their own

rulers, having, to that extent, practically resigned their government, into the hands of that eminent tribunal. Nor is there, in this view, any assault upon the court, or the judges. It is a duty, from which they may not shrink, to decide cases properly brought before them; and it is no fault of theirs, if other seek to turn their decisions to political purposes.

One section of our country believes slavery is *right*, and ought to be extended, while the other believes it is *wrong*, and ought not be extended. This is the only substantial dispute. The fugitive slave clause of the Constitution, and the law for the suppression of the foreign slave trade, are each as well enforced, perhaps, as any law can ever be in a community where the moral sense of the people imperfectly supports the law itself. The great body of the people abide by the dry legal obligation in both cases, and a few break over in each. This, I think, cannot be perfectly cured; and it would be *worse* in both cases after the separation of the sections, than before. The foreign slave trade, now imperfectly suppressed, would be ultimately revived without restrictions, in one section; be ultimately revived without restriction, in one section; while fugitive slaves, now only partially surrendered, would not be surrendered at all, by the other.

Physically speaking, we cannot separate. We cannot remove our respective sections from each other, nor build an impassable wall between them. A husband and wife may be divorced, and go out of the presence, and beyond the reach of each other; but the different parts of our country cannot do this. They cannot but remain face to face; and intercourse, either amicable or hostile, must continue between them. Is it possible then to make that intercourse more advantageous, or more satisfactory, *after* separation than *before*? Can aliens make treaties easier than friends can make laws? Can treaties be more faithfully enforced between aliens, than laws can among friends? Suppose you go to war, you cannot fight always; and when, after much loss on both sides, and no gain on either, you cease fighting, the identical old questions, as to terms of intercourse, are again upon you.

This country, with its institutions, belongs to the people who inhabit it. Whenever they shall grow weary of the existing government, they can exercise their *constitutional* right of amending it, or their *revolutionary* right to dismember, or overthrow it. I can not be ignorant of the fact that many worthy, and patriotic citizens are desirous of having the national constitution amended. While I make no recommendation of amendments, I fully recognize the rightful authority of the people over the whole subject, to be exercised in either of the modes prescribed in the instrument itself; and I should, under existing circumstances, favor, rather than oppose, a fair opportunity being afforded the people to act upon it.

I will venture to add that, to me, the convention mode seems preferable, in that it allows amendments to originate with the people themselves, instead of only permitting them to take, or reject, propositions, originated by others, not especially chosen for the purpose, and which might not be precisely such, as they would wish to either accept or refuse. I understand a proposed amendment to the Constitution—which amendment, however, I have not seen, has passed Congress, to the effect that the federal government, shall never interfere with the domestic institutions of the States, including that of persons held to service. To avoid misconstruction of what I have said, I depart from my purpose not to speak of particular amendments, so far as to say that, holding such a provision now to be implied constitutional law, I have no objection to its being made express, and irrevocable.

The Chief Magistrate derives all his authority from the people, and they have conferred none upon him to fix terms for the separation of the States. The people themselves can do this also if they choose; but the executive, as such, has nothing to do with it. His duty is to administer the present government, as it came to his hands, and to transmit it, unimpaired by him, to his successor.

Why should there not be a patient confidence in the ultimate justice of the people? Is there any better, or equal hope, in the world? In our present differences, is either party without faith of being in the right? If the Almighty Ruler of nations, with his eternal truth and justice, be on your side of the North, or on yours of the South, that truth, and that justice, will surely prevail, by the judgment of this great tribunal, the American people.

By the frame of the government under which we live, this same people have wisely given their public servants but little power for mischief; and have, with equal wisdom, provided for the return of that little to their own hands at very short intervals.

While the people retain their virtue, and vigilance, no administration, by any extreme of wickedness of folly, can very seriously injure the government, in the short space of four years.

My countrymen, one and all, think calmly and *well* upon this whole subject. Nothing valuable can be lost by taking time. If there be an object to *hurry* any of you, in hot haste, to a step which you would never take *deliberately*, that object will be frustrated by taking time; but no good object can be frustrated by it. Such of you as are now dissatisfied, still have the old Constitution unimpaired, and, on the sensitive point, the laws of your own framing under it; while the new administration will have no immediate power, if it would, to change either. If it were admitted that you who are dissatisfied, hold the right side in the dispute, there is still no single good reason for precipitate action. Intelligence, patriotism, Christianity, and a firm reliance on Him, who has never yet forsaken this favored land, are still competent to adjust, in the best way, all our present difficulty.

In *your* hands, my dissatisfied fellow countrymen, and not in *mine*, is the momentous issue of civil war. The government will not assail *you*. You can have no conflict, without being yourselves the aggressors. *You* have no oath registered in Heaven to destroy the government, while *I* shall have the most solemn one to "preserve, protect, and defend" it.

I am loath to close. We are not enemies, but friends. We must not be enemies. Though passion may have strained, it must not break our bonds of affection. The mystic chords of memory, stretching from every battlefield, and patriot grave, to every living heart and hearthstone, all over this broad land, will yet swell the chorus of the Union, when again touched, as surely they will be, by the better angels of our nature.

Appendix 2
President Lincoln's Emancipation Proclamation
January 1, 1863

Whereas, on the twentysecond day of September, in the year of our Lord one thousand eight hundred and sixty two, a proclamation was issued by the President of the United States, containing, among other things, the following, to wit:

"That on the first day of January, in the year of our Lord one thousand eight hundred and sixty-three, all persons held as slaves within any State or designated part of a State, the people whereof shall then be in rebellion against the United States, shall be then, thenceforward, and forever free; and the Executive Government of the United States, including the military and naval authority thereof, will recognize and maintain the freedom of such persons, and will do no act or acts to repress such persons, or any of them, in any efforts they may make for their actual freedom.

"That the Executive will, on the first day of January aforesaid, by proclamation, designate the States and parts of States, if any, in which the people thereof, respectively, shall then be in rebellion against the United States; and the fact that any State, or the people thereof, shall on that day be, in good faith, represented in the Congress of the United States by member chosen thereto at elections wherein a majority of the qualified voters of such State shall have participated, shall, in the absence of strong countervailing testimony, be deemed conclusive evidence that such State, and the people thereof, are not then in rebellion against the United States."

Now, therefore I, Abraham Lincoln, President of the United States, by virtue of the power in me vested as Commander-in-Chief, of the Army and the Navy of the United States in time of actual armed rebellion against authority and government of the United States, and as a fit and necessary war measure for suppressing said rebellion, do, on this first day of January, in the year of our Lord one thousand eight hundred and sixty three, and in accordance with my purpose so to do publicly proclaimed for the full period of one hundred days, from the day first above mentioned, order and designate as the States and parts of States wherein the people thereof respectively, are this day in rebellion against the United States, the following, to wit:

Arkansas, Texas, Louisiana, (except the Parishes of St. Bernard, Plaquemines, Jefferson, St. Johns, St. Charles, St. James, Ascension, Assumption, Terrebonne, Lafourche, St. May, St. Martin and Orleans, including the City of New Orleans), Mississippi, Alabama, Florida, Georgia, South-Carolina, North-Carolina, and Virginia, (except the forty-eight counties designated as West Virginia, and also the counties of Berkley, Accomac, Northampton, Elizabeth-City, York, Princess Ann, and Norfolk, including the cities of Norfolk & Portsmouth); and which excepted parts are, for the present, left precisely as if this proclamation were not issued.

And by virtue of the power, and for the purpose aforesaid, I do order and declare that all persons held as slaves with said designated States, and parts of States, are, and henceforward shall be free; and that the Executive government of the United States, including the military and naval authorities thereof, will recognize and maintain the freedom of said persons.

And I hereby enjoin upon the people so declared to be free to abstain from all violence, unless in necessary self-defense; and I recommend to them that, in all cases when allowed, they labor faithfully for reasonable wages.

And I further declare and make known, that such persons of suitable condition, will be received into the armed service of the United States to garrison forts, positions, stations, and other places, and to man vessels of all sorts in said service.

And upon this act, sincerely believed to be an act of justice, warranted by the Constitution, upon military necessity, I invoke the considerate judgment of mankind, and the gracious favor of Almighty God.

In witness whereof, I have hereunto set my hand and caused the seal of the United States to be affixed.

Done at the City of Washington, this first day of January, in the year of our Lord one thousand eight hundred and sixty three, and of the Independence of the United States of America the eighty-seventh.

By the President: Abraham Lincoln
William H. Seward, Secretary of State.

Appendix 3
President Lincoln's Address at Gettysburg, Pennsylvania
November 19, 1863

Four score and seven years ago our fathers brought forth on this continent, a new nation, conceived in Liberty, and dedicated to the proposition that all men are created equal.

Now we are engaged in a great civil war, testing whether that nation, or any nation so conceived and so dedicated, can long endure. We are met on a great battle-field of that war. We have come to dedicate a portion of that field, as a final resting place for those who here gave their lives that that nation might live. It is altogether fitting and proper that we should do this.

But in a larger sense, we can not dedicate—we can not consecrate—we can not hallow—this ground. The brave men, living and dead, who struggled here, have consecrated it, far above our poor power to add or detract. The world will little note, nor long remember what we say here, but it can never forget what they did here. It is for us the living, rather, to be dedicated here to the unfinished work which they who fought here have thus far so nobly advanced. It is rather for us to be here dedicated to the great task remaining before us—that from these honored dead we take increased devotion to that cause for which they gave the last full measure of devotion—that we here highly resolve that these dead shall not have died in vain—that this nation, under God, shall have a new birth of freedom—and that government of the people, by the people, for the people, shall not perish from the earth.

Sources and Further Reading

Sources

Angle, Paul McClelland. *Tragic Years, 1860–1865: A Documentary History of the American Civil War*. New York: Simon & Schuster, 1960.

Baker, LaFayette Charles. *History of the United States Secret Service*. Philadelphia: King & Baird, 1868.

Boatner, Mark M. *The Civil War Dictionary*. New York: Random House, 1988.

Britton, Wiley. *The Civil War on the Border* (2 vols.). New York and London: Putnam, 1899–1904.

Brockett, L.P., MD, and Mrs. Mary C. Vaughan. *Woman's Work in the Civil War: A Record of Heroism, Patriotism and Patience*. Philadelphia: King and Baird, 1867.

Catton, Bruce. *Mr. Lincoln's Army; Glory Road; A Stillness at Appomattox* (3 vols.). New York: Doubleday & Co., 1953.

Cobb, General Howell. "Georgia and the Confederacy, 1865: Letters of General Howell Cobb to Secretary Seddoo and President Davis," *American History Review*, 1 (1896): 97–102.

Culpepper, Marilyn Mayer. *Trials and Triumphs: The Women of the American Civil War*. East Lansing, Mich.: Michigan State University Press, 1991.

Dannett, Sylvia G. Liebowitz. *Noble Women of the North*. New York: Thomas Yoseloff, 1959.

Douglas, Henry Kyd. *I Rode with Stonewall*. New York: Fawcett Publications, 1961.

Dowdey, Clifford, and Louis H. Manarin. *The Wartime Papers of Robert E. Lee*. New York: Bramhall House Publishers/Clarkson N. Potter, 1961.

Edmonds, S. Emma E. *Nurse and Spy in the Union Army: The Adventures and Experiences of a Woman in Hospitals, Camps, and Battlefields*. Philadelphia: W.S. Williams & Co., 1864.

Emilio, Luis Fenallosa. *A Brave Black Regiment: History of the Fifty-fourth Regiment of Massachusetts Volunteer Infantry, 1863–1865*. New York: Arno Press and the New York Times, 1969.

Faust, Patricia L., ed. *Historical Times Illustrated Encyclopedia of the Civil War*. New York: HarperPerennial, 1986.

Foote, Shelby. *The Civil War: A Narrative* (3 vols.). New York: Random House, 1963.

Francis, Julius E. *The Lincoln Memorial Collection: Relics of the War of the Rebellion*. Buffalo, N.Y.: Matthews, Northrop & Co., 1887.

Freeman, Douglas Southall. *R. E. Lee* (4 vols.). New York: Charles Scribner's Sons, 1934.

Furgurson, Ernest B. *Chancellorsville, 1863: The Souls of the Brave*. New York: Alfred A. Knopf, 1992.

Gallagher, Gary W., ed. *Fighting for the Confederacy: The Personal Recollections of General Edward Porter Alexander*. Chapel Hill: University of North Carolina Press, 1989.

Hicks, John Donald. *The American Nation: A History of the United States from 1865 to the Present*. Boston: Houghton Mifflin, 1965.

Hodge, Charles. *The Princeton Review on the State of the Country and of the Church*. Philadelphia: P. Walker, 1865.

Loving, Charles Greeley. *Reconstruction*. Boston: Little, Brown & Co., 1866.

McPherson, James M. *Battle Cry of Freedom: The Civil War Era*. New York: Oxford University Press, 1988.

Moore, Frank. *Women of the War: Their Heroism and Self-sacrifice*. Chicago: S.S. Scranton & Co., 1866.

Schwartz, Gerald. *A Woman Doctor's Civil War*. Columbia, S.C.: University of South Carolina Press, 1984.

Sears, Stephen W. *Landscape Turned Red: The*

Battle of Antietam. New York: Ticknor & Fields, 1983.

Sears, Stephen W. *To the Gates of Richmond: The Peninsular Campaign*. New York: Ticknor & Fields, 1993.

Straubing, Harold Elk, ed. *Civil War Eyewitness Reports*. Hamden, Conn.: Archon Books, 1985.

U.S. War Department. *The War of the Rebellion: A Compilation of the Official Records of the Union and Confederate Armies* (70 vols. in 128 vols.). Washington, D.C.: Government Printing Office, 1880–1901.

Ward, Geoffrey C., Ric Burns, and Ken Burns. *The Civil War*. New York: Alfred A. Knopf, 1990.

Wiley, Bell Irvin. " 'Holy Joes' of the Sixties: A Study of Civil War Chaplains," *Huntington Library Quarterly*, 16 (May 1953): 287–304.

Further Reading

Abel, Annie H. *The American Indian as Slaveholder and Secessionist*. Lincoln: University of Nebraska Press, 1992.

Alexander, Thomas and Richard E. Beringer. *The Anatomy of the Confederate Congress*. Nashville: Vanderbilt University Press, 1971.

Allardice, Bruce S. *More Generals in Gray*. Baton Rouge: Louisiana State University Press, 1995.

American Social History Project Staff. *Freedom's Unfinished Revolution: The Civil War and Reconstruction: A Primary Source Text and Document Reader from the Authors of Who Built America?* New York: The New Press, 1996.

Anders, Curt. *Hearts in Conflict: A One-Volume History of the Civil War*. New York: Carol Publishing Group, 1993.

Anderson, Nancy S. and Dwight Anderson. *The Generals: Ulysses S. Grant and Robert E. Lee*. New York: Random House, Inc., 1989.

Arnold, James R. *The Armies of U.S. Grant*.

New York: Sterling Publishing Company, Inc., 1995.

Barriger, John W. "Railroads in the Civil War," Confederate Historical Society *London Journal*, Summer 1976: 48-66.

Barton, Michael. *Goodmen: The Character of Civil War Soldiers*. University Park: Pennsylvania State University Press, 1981.

Beckett, Ian F. *War Correspondents American Civil War*. Dover, NH: Arcadia, 1993.

Benet, Stephen Vincent. *John Brown's Body* (poem). Garden City, NY: Doubleday, Doran and Co., 1929.

Beringer, Richard E. et al. *The Elements of Confederate Defeat: Nationalism, War Aims, and Religion*. Athens: University of Georgia Press, 1988.

———. *Why the South Lost the Civil War*. Athens: University of Georgia Press, 1986.

Berlin, Ira, Barbara J. Fields, Steven Miller, Joseph P. Reidy, and Leslie S. Rowland, eds. *Free at Last: A Documentary History of Slavery, Freedom, and the Civil War*. New York: The New Press, 1992.

Bernstein, Iver. *The New York City Draft Riots: Their Significance for American Society and Politics in the Age of the Civil War*. New York: Oxford University Press, Inc., 1990.

Beringer, Richard E., Herman Hattaway, Archer Jones, and William N. Still Jr. *Why the South Lost the Civil War*. Athens: University of Georgia Press, 1991.

Beyer, W. F. and D. F. Keydel, eds. *Deeds of Valor: How America's Civil War Heroes Won the Congressional Medal of Honor*. Ann Arbor, MI: Longmeadow Press, 1992.

Bierce, Ambrose. *Ambrose Bierce's Civil War*. Edited by William McCann. New York: Random House, Inc., 1996.

Boritt, Gabor S., ed. *Why the Confederacy Lost*. New York: Oxford University Press, Inc., 1992.

Bosse, David, comp. *Civil War Newspaper Maps: A Cartobibliography of the Northern Daily Press*. Westport, CT: Greenwood Publishing Group, Inc., 1993.

Botkin, Benjamin Albert. *A Civil War Treasury*

of Tales. New York: Random House, Inc., 1960.

Bradford, Gamaliel. *Union Portraits*. North Stratford, NH: Ayer Company, Publishers, Inc., 1977.

Brockett, Linus P. and Mary C. Vaughan. *Women at War: A Record of Their Patriotic Contributions, Heroism, Toils, and Sacrifice During the Civil War*. Stamford, CT: Longmeadow Press, 1993.

Brooksher, William R. and David K. Snider. *Glory at a Gallop: Tales of the Confederate Cavalry*. McLean, VA: Brassey's, Inc., 1993.

Brown, Kent Masterson. *Cushing of Gettysburg: The Story of a Union Artillery Commander*. Lexington: University Press of Kentucky, 1993.

Bruce, Robert V. *Lincoln and the Tools of War*. Champaign: University of Illinois Press, 1989.

Brumgardt, John R. *Civil War Nurse: The Diary and Letters of Hannah Ropes*. Knoxville, TN: University of Tennessee Press, 1992.

Burgess, Lauren C. *An Uncommon Soldier: The Civil War Letters of Sarah Rosetta Wakeman, Alias Private Lyons Wakeman, 153rd Regiment, New York State Volunteers*. Pasadena, CA: Minerva Center, Inc, 1994.

Carmichael, Peter S. *Lee's Young Artillerist: William R. J. Pegram*. Charlottesville, VA: University Press of Virginia, 1995.

Castel, Albert. *Winning and Losing in the Civil War: Essays and Stories*. Columbia: University of South Carolina Press, 1996.

Catton, Bruce. *The American Heritage Picture History of the Civil War*. New York: American Heritage Publishing Company, Inc., 1960.

———. *America Goes to War: The Civil War and Its Meaning in American Culture*. Hanover, NH: University Press of New England, 1992 .

———. *Grant Takes Command, 1863-1865*. New York: Little, Brown and Company, 1990.

———. *Gettysburg: The Final Fury*. New York: Doubleday and Company, Inc, 1990 .

———. *War Lords of Washington*. Westport, CT: Greenwood Publishing Group, Inc, 1969.

———. *Grant Moves South*. New York: Little, Brown and Company, 1960.

Christ, Mark K., ed. *Rugged and Sublime: The Civil War in Arkansas*. Fayetteville, AR: University of Arkansas Press, 1994 .

Clinton, Catherine and Nina Silber. *Divided Houses: Gender and the Civil War*. New York: Oxford University Press, Inc., 1992

Cole, Arthur C. *The Irrepressible Conflict, 1850-1865*. Irvine, CA: Reprint Services Corporation, 1993.

Commager, Henry S. *The Blue and the Gray: The Story of the Civil War As Told by Participants*. 2 vols. New York: NAL Dutton, 1995.

Connell, Moody K. *Rebel Scouts: The Last Ride Home*. Kearny, NE: Morris Publishing, 1995.

Corrick, James A. *The Battle of Gettysburg*. San Diego, CA: Lucent Books, 1996.

Cottrell, Steve. *Civil War in the Indian Territory*. Gretna, LA: Pelican Publishing Company, Inc., 1995.

Cox, Joseph T. *The Written Wars: American War Prose Through the Civil War*. North Haven, CT: Shoe String Press, Inc., 1996.

Crawford, Richard, ed. *The Civil War Songbook: Complete and Original Sheet Music for 37 Songs*. New York: Dover Publications, 1977.

Crook, David P. *Diplomacy During the American Civil War*. New York: John Wiley and Sons, 1975.

———. *The North, the South, and the Powers, 1861-1865*. New York: John Wiley and Sons, 1974.

Current, Richard N. *Lincoln's Loyalists: Union Soldiers from the Confederacy*. Boston: Northeastern University Press, 1992.

Davis, William C. *Concise History of the Civil War*. Conshohocken, PA: Eastern Acorn Press, 1994.

——— and Bell I. Wiley, eds. *The Civil War Times Illustrated Photographic History of the Civil War*. New York: Black Dog and Leventhal Publishers, Inc., 1994.

Ditzel, Paul. *Quantrill: The Wildest Killer of the Civil War and Other Stories.* New Albany, IN: Fire Buff House, 1991.

Donald, David H. *Liberty and Union.* Lexington, MA: D.C. Heath and Company, 1978.

———. *Lincoln Reconsidered.* New York: Alfred A. Knopf, Inc., 1956.

———, ed. *Why the North Won the Civil War.* New York: Simon and Schuster, 1962.

Dudley, William, ed. *The Civil War: Opposing Viewpoints.* San Diego, CA: Greenhaven Press, Inc., 1995.

Dumond, Dwight. *Antislavery: The Crusade for Freedom in America.* Ann Arbor: University of Michigan Press, 1961.

———. *Antislavery Origins of the Civil War in the United States.* Ann Arbor: University of Michigan Press, 1939.

Dupuy, R. Ernest and Trevor N. Dupuy. *The Compact History of the Civil War.* New York: Warner Books, Inc., 1993.

Durden, Robert F. *The Gray & the Black: The Confederate Debate on Emancipation.* Ann Arbor, MI: Books on Demand, 1972.

Dyer, John P. *From Shiloh to San Juan: The Life of "Fightin' Joe" Wheeler.* Baton Rouge: Louisiana State University Press, 1992.

Eaton, Clement. *A History of the Southern Confederacy.* New York: The Free Press, 1965.

———. *Jefferson Davis: A Biography.* New York: The Free Press, 1979.

Eicher, David J. *Civil War Battlefields: A Touring Guide.* Dallas, TX: Taylor Publishing Company, 1995.

Escott, Paul D. *After Secession: Jefferson Davis & the Failure of Confederate Nationalism.* Baton Rouge: Louisiana State University Press, 1992.

Faust, Drew G. *Mothers of Invention: Women of the Slaveholding South in the American Civil War.* Chapel Hill: University of North Carolina Press, 1996.

Fellman, Michael. *Citizen Sherman: A Life of William Tecumseh Sherman.* New York: Random House, Inc., 1995.

———. *Inside War: The Guerilla Conflict in Missouri During the American Civil War.* New York: Oxford University Press, 1989.

Fischer, LeRoy H., ed. *Civil War Battles in the West.* Manhattan, KS: Sunflower University Press.

Fishel, Edwin C. *The Secret War for the Union: The Untold Story of Military Intelligence in the Civil War.* Boston: Houghton Mifflin Company, 1996.

Foner, Eric. *A House Divided: America in the Age of Lincoln.* New York: W. W. Norton and Company, Inc., 1990.

———. *Politics and Ideology in the Age of the Civil War.* New York: Oxford University Press, Inc., 1981.

———. *Slavery, the Civil War, and Reconstruction.* Washington, DC: American Historical Association, 1991.

Forbes, Edwin. *Civil War Etchings.* New York: Dover Publications, Inc., 1994.

Fowler, Robert H. *Civil War Times Illustrated.* Harrisburg, PA: Stackpole Books, 1965.

Francis, Julius E. *The Lincoln Memorial Collection: Relics of the War of the Rebellion.* Buffalo: Matthews, Northrop and Co., 1887.

Franklin, John H. *The Emancipation Proclamation.* Wheeling: IL: Harlan Davidson Inc., 1995.

Fredrickson, George M. *The Inner Civil War: Northern Intellectuals and the Crisis of the Union.* Champaign: University of Illinois Press, 1993.

Freeman, Daniel B. *Lee's Lieutenants.* 3 vols. New York: Scribners, 1977-1985.

Friedel, Frank Burt, comp. *Union Pamphlets of the Civil War, 1981-1865.* Cambridge: Belknap Press/Harvard University Press, 1967.

Gallagher, Gary W. *Chancellorsville: The Battle and Its Aftermath.* Chapel Hill: University of North Carolina Press, 1996.

———. *Stephen Dodson Ramseur: Lee's Gallant General.* Chapel Hill: University of North Carolina Press, 1995.

Golay, Michael. *To Gettysburg and Beyond: The Parallel Lives of Joshua Lawrence*

Chamberlain and Edward Porter. New York: Crown Publishing Group, 1994.

Goodrich, Thomas. *Black Flag: Guerrilla Warfare on the Western Border, 1861-1865.* Bloomington: Indiana University Press, 1995.

Gordon, John B. *Reminiscences of the Civil War.* Baton Rouge, LA: Morningside Bookshop, 1993.

Gragg, Ron. *Civil War Quiz and Fact Book.* New York: Harper and Row, Inc., 1985.

Grant, Julia D. *The Personal Memoirs of Julia Dent Grant (Mrs. Ulysses S. Grant).* Edited by John Y. Simon. Carbondale: Southern Illinois University Press, 1988.

Greene, A. Wilson. *Whatever You Resolve to Be: Essays on Stonewall Jackson.* Baltimore, MD: Butternut and Blue, 1992.

Grimsley, Mark. *The Hard Hand of War: Union Military Policy Toward Southern Civilians, 1861-1865.* New York: Cambridge University Press, 1995.

Groom, Winston. *Shrouds of Glory: From Atlanta to Nashville: The Last Great Campaign of the Civil War.* New York: Grove Atlantic, Inc., 1994.

Guelzo, Allen C. *The Crisis of the American Republic: A History of the Civil War and Reconstruction Era.* New York: St. Martin's Press, Inc., 1994.

Hagerman, Edward. *The American Civil War and the Origins of Modern Warfare: Ideas, Organization, and Field Command.* Bloomington: Indiana University Press, 1992.

Hague, Parthenia A. *A Blockaded Family: Life in Southern Alabama during the Civil War.* Lincoln: University of Nebraska Press, 1991.

Harwell, Richard Barksdale. *Confederate Music.* Chapel Hill: University of North Carolina Press, 1950.

———, ed. *The Union Reader.* New York: Longmans, Green, 1958.

Hauptman, Laurence M. *Between Two Fires American Indians in the Civil War.* New York: The Free Press, 1995.

———. *The Iroquois in the Civil War: From Battlefield to Reservation.* Syracuse: Syracuse University Press, 1992.

———, ed. *A Seneca Indian in the Union Army: The Civil War Letters of Sergeant Isaac Newton Parker, 1861-1865.* Shippensburg, PA: White Mane Publishing Company, Inc., 1995.

Higginson, Thomas W. *Army Life in a Black Regiment.* Gansevoort, NY: Corner House Historical Publications, 1971.

Hoehling, A. A. *Women Who Spied.* New York: Dodd Mead and Co., 1967.

Hubbell, John T. and James W. Geary, eds.. *Biographical Dictionary of the Union: Northern Leaders of the Civil War.* Westport, CT: Greenwood Publishing Group, Inc, 1995.

Jimerson, Randall. *The Private Civil War: Popular Thought During the Sectional Conflict.* Baton Rouge: Louisiana State University Press, 1988.

Johnson, Curt and Mark McLaughlin. *Civil War Battles.* Avenel, NJ: Random House Value Publishing, Inc., 1977.

Jones, Virgil C. *Gray Ghosts and Rebel Raiders.* McLean, VA: E P M Publications, 1988.

Jordan, David M. *Winfield Scott Hancock: A Soldier's Life.* Bloomington: Indiana University Press, 1988.

Jordan Jr., Ervin L. *Black Confederates and Afro-Yankees in the Civil War.* Charlottesville: University Press of Virginia, 1995.

Junt, Harrison. *Heroes of the Civil War.* Avenel, NJ: Random House Value Publishing, Inc., 1990.

Kajencki, Francis C. *Star on Many a Battlefield: Brevet Brigadier General Joseph Karge in the Civil War.* Cranbury, NJ: Fairleigh Dickinson University Press, 1980.

Katcher, Philip. *American Civil War Armies.* London: Osprey Publishing, 1986.

———. *The Army of Robert E. Lee.* New York: Sterling Publishing, 1994.

———. *The Army of the Potomac.* London: Osprey Publishing, 1975.

———. *The Civil War Source Book.* New York: Facts on File, Inc., 1992.

———. *Union Calvaryman 1861-1865.* Mechanicsburg, PA: Stackpole Books, 1995.

Kinard, Jeff. *The Battle of the Crater.* Boulder, CO: Ryan Place Publishers, 1995.

Korn, Bertram W. *American Jewry and the Civil War.* Philadelphia: R. Bemis Publishing, Ltd., 1995.

Lee Jr., Charles R. *The Confederate Constitutions.* Westport, CT: Greenwood Publishing Group, Inc., 1974.

Linderman, Gerald F. *Embattled Courage: The Experience of Battle in the American Civil War.* New York: The Free Press, 1987.

Logue, Larry M. *To Appomattox and Beyond: The Civil War Soldier in War and Peace.* Chicago: Ivan R. Dee, Inc, Publisher, 1995.

Long, E. B. *The Civil War Day by Day.* New York: Doubleday and Co., 1971.

Longacre, Edward G. *The Man Behind the Gun.* Gaithersburg, MD: Olde Soldier Books, Inc., 1977.

———. *Mounted Raids of the Civil War.* Lincoln: University of Nebraska Press, 1994 .

Longstreet, James. *From Manassas to Appomattox.* New York: Da Capo Press, Inc., 1992.

Lonn, Ella. *Foreigners in the Union Army and Navy.* Westport, CT: Greenwood Publishing Group, Inc., 1970.

Loving, Charles Greeley. *Reconstruction.* Boston: Little, Brown and Co., 1966.

Lowe, Carl. *The Civil War Remembered.* New York: Michael Friedman Publishing Group, Inc., 1994.

Lowry, Don. *Dark and Cruel War.* New York: Hippocrene Books, Inc., 1993.

———. *The Fate of the Country: The Civil War from June-September, 1864.* New York: Hippocrene Books, Inc., 1992.

———. *No Turning Back: The Beginning of the End of the Civil War.* New York: Hippocrene Books, 1992.

Macartney, Clarence E. *Grant and His Generals.* North Stratford, NH: Ayer Company, Publishers, Inc., 1977.

Markle, Donald E. *Spies and Spymasters of the Civil War.* New York: Hippocrene Books, Inc., 1994.

McClellan, George B. *The Civil War Papers of George B. McClellan: Selected Correspondence 1860-1865.* Edited by Stephen W. Sears. New York: Da Capo Press, Inc., 1992.

McGuire, Judith W. *Diary of a Southern Refugee During the War.* Lincoln: University of Nebraska Press, 1995.

McPherson, James M. *The Negro's Civil War: How American Negroes Felt and Acted During the War for the Union.* New York: Pantheon Books, 1965.

———. *Ordeal by Fire: The Civil War and Reconstruction.* 2nd ed. New York: McGraw-Hill, Inc., 1992.

McWhiney, Grady and Perry D. Jamieson. *Attack and Die: Civil War Military Tactics & the Southern Heritage.* Tuscaloosa: University of Alabama Press, 1982.

Mitchell, Joseph B. *Military Leaders in the Civil War.* McLean, VA: E P M Publications, 1988.

Mitchell, Reid. *Civil War Soldiers: Their Expectations and Their Experiences.* New York: Viking/Penguin, 1988.

———. *The Vacant Chair: The Northern Soldier Leaves Home.* New York: Oxford University Press, Inc., 1993.

Moe, Richard. *The Last Full Measure: The Life and Death of the First Minnesota Volunteers.* New York: Henry Holt and Company, Inc. 1993.

Mohr, James C. and Richard E. Winslow 3rd, eds. *The Cormany Diaries: A Northern Family in the Civil War.* Ann Arbor, MI: Books on Demand, 1982.

Moneyhon, Carl H. *Impact of the Civil War and Reconstruction on Arkansas: Persistence in the Midst of Ruin.* Baton Rouge: Louisiana State University Press, 1993.

Nesbitt, Mark. *Rebel Rivers: A Guide to the Civil War Sites on the Potomac, Rappahannock, York, and James.* Mechanicsburg, PA: Stackpole Books, 1993.

Nevins, Allan. *Ordeal of the Union.* New York: Simon and Schuster, 1992.

Nofi, Albert A. *A Civil War Treasury: Being a Miscellany of Arms and Artillery, Facts and*

Figures, Legends and Lore, Muses and Minstrels, Personalities and People. New York: Da Capo Press, Inc., 1995

Oates, Dan, ed. *The Hanging Rock Rebel: Lieutenant John Blue's War in West Virginia and the Shenandoah Valley.* Shippensburg, PA: White Mane Publishing Company, Inc., 1994.

Otto, John S. *Southern Agriculture During the Civil War Era, 1860-1880.* Westport, CT: Greenwood Publishing Group, Inc., 1994.

Palfrey, Francis W. *The Antietam and Fredericksburg.* New York: Da Capo Press, Inc, 1996.

Paludan, Phillip S. *A People's Contest: The Union and the Civil War, 1861-1865.* Harper-Collins Publishers, Inc., 1989.

———. *The Presidency of Abraham Lincoln.* Lawrence: University Press of Kansas, 1994.

———. *Victims: A True Story of the Civil War.* Knoxville: University of Tennessee Press, 1981 .

Parish, Peter. *The American Civil War.* New York: Holmes and Meier Publishers, Inc., 1975.

Perry, Lewis and Michael Fellman, eds. *Antislavery Reconsidered: New Perspectives on the Abolitionists.* Baton Rouge: Louisiana State University Press, 1979.

Phillips, Christopher. *Damned Yankee: The Life of General Nathaniel Lyon.* Edited by William E. Foley. Columbus: University of Missouri Press, 1990.

Pula, James S. *For Liberty and Justice.* Gaithersburg, MD: Olde Soldier Books, Inc., 1978.

Quarles, Benjamin. *The Negro in the Civil War.* New York: Da Capo Press, Inc., 1989.

Randall, J. G. and Richard N. Current. *Lincoln the President: Last Full Measure.* Champaign: University of Illinois Press, 1991.

——— and David Herbert Donald. *The Civil War and Reconstruction.* 2nd. ed. Lexington, MA: D.C. Heath and Company, 1969

Rawley, James A. *Lincoln & Civil War Politics.* Melbourne, FL: Krieger Publishing Company, 1977.

———. *Secession: The Disruption of the American Republic, 1844-1861.* Melbourne, FL: Krieger Publishing Company, 1990.

———. *Turning Points of the Civil War.* Lincoln: University of Nebraska Press, 1989.

Reinfeld, Fred. *Civil War Money.* New York: Sterling Publishing Co., 1959.

Rhoades, Jeffrey L. *Scapegoat General: The Story of General Benjamin Huger C. S. A.* New Haven: Shoe String Press, Inc., 1986.

Robertson, James I. *Common Soldier of the Civil War.* Conshohocken, PA: Eastern Acorn Press, 1994.

———. *General A. P. Hill: The Story of a Confederate Warrior.* New York: Random House, Inc., 1987.

Robertson, William G. *The Battle of Chickamauga.* Conshohoken, PA: Eastern Acorn Press, 1995.

Roland, Charles P. *An American Iliad: The Story of the Civil War.* Lexington: University Press of Kentucky, 1991.

———. *The Confederacy.* Chicago: University of Chicago Press, 1962.

———. *Reflections on Lee: A Historian's Assessment.* Mechanicsburg, PA: Stackpole Books, 1995.

Rose, Anne C. *Victorian America and the Civil War.* New York: Cambridge University Press, 1992.

Rosenblatt, Emil and Ruth Rosenblatt, eds. *Hard Marching Every Day: The Civil War Letters of Private Wilbur Fisk, 1861-1865.* Lawrence: University Press of Kansas, 1994.

Rosenburg, R. B. *Living Monuments: Confederate Soldiers' Homes in the New South.* Chapel Hill: University of North Carolina Press, 1993.

Ross, Alexander M. *Recollections and Experiences of an Abolitionist, from 1885-1865.* Temecula, CA: Reprint Services Corporation, 1991.

Royster, Charles. *The Destructive War: William Tecumseh Sherman, Stonewall Jackson, and the Americans.* New York: Alfred A. Knopf, Inc., 1991.

Schutz, Wallace and Walter Trenerry. *Abandoned by Lincoln: A Military Biography of General John Pope*. Champaign: University of Illinois Press, 1990.

Scott, John. *Partisan Life with Col. John S. Mosby*. Gaithersburg, MD: Olde Soldier Books, Inc., 1985.

Sears, Stephen W., ed. *For Country, Cause and Leader: The Civil War Journal of Charles B. Haydon*. Boston: Ticknor and Fields, 1993.

————. *George B. McClellan: The Young Napoleon*. Boston: Ticknor and Fields, 1989.

————. *Civil War: The Best of American Heritage*. Boston: Houghton Mifflin Company, 1993 .

Sheridan, Philip Henry. *Personal Memoirs*. New York: C. L. Webster and Co., 1888.

Sifakis, Stewart. *Who Was Who in the Civil War*. 2 vols. New York: Facts on File, Inc., 1989.

————. *Who Was Who in the Confederacy*. New York: Facts on File, Inc., 1989.

Smith, David P. *Frontier Defense in the Civil War: Texas Rangers and Rebels*. College Station, TX: Texas A and M University Press, 1994.

Spencer, James, comp. *Civil War Generals: Categorical Listings and a Biographical Directory*. Westport, CT: Greenwood Publishing Group, Inc., 1986.

Stampp, Kenneth M. *America in 1857: A Nation on the Brink*. New York: Oxford University Press, 1990.

————. *And the War Came: The North and the Secession Crisis, 1860-1861*. Baton Rouge: Louisiana State University Press, 1950.

————, ed. *The Causes of the Civil War*. 3rd edition. New York: Simon and Schuster, Inc., 1991.

————. *The Southern Road to Appomattox*. El Paso: University of Texas at El Paso, 1969.

Stanton, E.C., Susan B. Anthony, and Matilda Joslyn Gage. *History of Woman Suffrage*. (Vol. 2 of 6 vols.). Salem, NH: Ayer Co., 1985.

Steele, Phillip W. and Steve Cottrell. *Civil War in the Ozarks*. Gretna, LA: Pelican Publishing Company, Inc., 1993.

Stern, Philip van Doren. *Secret Missions of the Civil War*. Chicago: Rand McNally, 1959.

————. *Robert E. Lee: The Man and the Soldier*. New York: Bonanza Books, 1962.

Stiles, Robert. *Four Years under Marse Robert*. Baton Rouge, LA: Morningside Bookshop, 1977.

Stokesbury, James L. *A Short History of the Civil War*. New York: William Morrow and Company, Inc., 1995.

Strode, Hudson. *Jefferson Davis*. 3 vols. New York: Harcourt, Brace, 1955-64.

Sword, Wiley. *Embrace an Angry Wind: The Confederacy's Last Hurrah: Spring Hill, Franklin, and Nashville*. Columbus, OH: General's Books, 1994.

Taylor, John M. *Confederate Raider: Raphael Semmes of the "Alabama"*. McLean, VA: Brassey's, Inc., 1994.

Taylor, Walter H. *Four Years with General Lee*. New York: Bonanza Books, 1961.

Thomas, Benjamin P. *Abraham Lincoln: A Biography*. New York: Random House, Inc., 1979.

———— and Harold M. Hyman. *Stanton: The Life and Times of Lincoln's Secretary of War*. Westport, CT: Greenwood Publishing Group, Inc., 1980.

Thomas, Emory M. *Bold Dragoon: The Life of J. E. B. Stuart*. New York: Random House, Inc., 1988.

————. *The Confederacy As a Revolutionary Experience*. Columbia: University of South Carolina Press, 1991.

————. *Robert E. Lee: A Biography*. New York: W. W. Norton and Company, Inc., 1995.

Thompson, Jerry Don. *Vaqueros in Blue and Gray*. Austin: Presidial Press, 1976.

Time-Life Staff. *Brother Against Brother: Time-Life Book History of the Civil War*. New York: Time-Life, Inc., 1995.

Townsend, William Henry. *Lincoln and the Bluegrass: Slavery and Civil War in Kentucky*. Lexington: University of Kentucky Press, 1955.

Trudeau, Noah A. *Last Citadel: Petersburg, Vir-*

ginia, *June 1864-April 1865*. Baton Rouge: Louisiana State University Press, 1993.

Vandiver, Frank E. *Blood Brothers: A Short History of the Civil War*. College Station, TX: Texas A & M University Press, 1993.

———. *Their Tattered Flags: The Epic of the Confederacy*. College Station, TX: Texas A & M University Press, 1995.

Venet, Wendy Hammond. *Neither Ballots nor Bullets: Women Abolitionists and the Civil War*. Charlottesville: University of Virginia Press, 1991.

Wakelyn, Jon L. *Biographical Dictionary of the Confederacy*. Edited by Frank E. Vandiver. Westport, CT: Greenwood Publishing Group, Inc., 1977.

Wallace, Willard M. *Soul of the Lion: A Biography of General Joshua L. Chamberlain*. Gettysburg, PA: Stan Clark Military Books, 1989.

Ward, Geoffrey C. *Civil War*. New York: Random House, Inc., 1994.

Warner, Ezra J. *Generals in Blue: Lives of the Union Commanders*. Baton Rouge: Louisiana State University Press, 1964.

———. *Generals in Gray: Lives of the Confederate Commanders*. Baton Rouge: Louisiana State University Press, 1959 .

Welsh, Shepherd. *Gettysburg and More from the American Time*. Midvale, UT: Northwest Publishing, Inc., 1996.

Wert, Jeffrey D. *General James Longstreet*. New York: Simon and Schuster, 1994.

———. *Mosby's Rangers*. New York: Simon and Schuster, 1991.

Wheeler, Richard. *A Rising Thunder: From Lincoln's Election to the Battle of Bull Run: An Eyewitness History*. New York: HarperCollins Publishers, Inc., 1994.

———. *On the Fields of Fury: From the Wilderness to the Crater: An Eyewitness History*. New York: HarperCollins Publishers, Inc., 1992.

———. *Voices of the Civil War*. New York: NAL Dutton, 1990.

Whetten, Harriet Douglas. "A Volunteer Nurse in the Civil War: The Letters of Harriet Douglas Whetten," *Wisconsin Magazine of History*, 48 (Winter 1964-1965): 131-151.

White, Christine S. and White, Benton R. *Now the Wolf Has Come: The Creek Nation in the Civil War*. College Station, TX: Texas A & M University Press, 1996.

Whitman, Walt. *Specimen Days in America*. London: W. Scott, 1887.

Wiley, Bell I. *Confederate Women*. Westport, CT: Greenwood Publishing Group, Inc., 1975.

———. *The Life of Billy Yank: The Common Soldier of the Union*. 1971 Baton Rouge: Louisiana State University Press, 1971.

———. *The Life of Johnny Reb: The Common Soldier of the Confederacy*. Baton Rouge: Louisiana State University Press, 1971.

———. *The Road to Appomattox*. Baton Rouge: Louisiana State University Press, 1994.

Williams, T. Harry. *Hayes of the Twenty-Third: The Civil War Volunteer Officer*. Lincoln: University of Nebraska Press, 1994.

———. *Lincoln and His Generals*. New York: Random House, Inc., 1967.

———. *McClellan, Sherman and Grant*. Chicago: Ivan R. Dee, Inc., 1991.

———. *P. G. T. Beauregard: Napoleon in Gray*. Baton Rouge: Louisiana State University Press, 1955.

Wills, Brian S. *A Battle from the Start: The Life of Nathan Bedford Forrest*. New York: HarperCollins Publishers, Inc., 1992.

Wills, Garry. *Lincoln at Gettysburg: The Words that Remade America*. New York: Simon and Schuster, Inc., 1993.

Wilson, Edmund. *Patriotic Gore: Studies in the Literature of the American Civil War*. New York: W. W. Norton and Company, Inc., 1994.

Witt, Jerry V. *Escape from the Maple Leaf*. Bowie, MD: Heritage Books, Inc., 1993.

Woodward, C. Vann and Elisabeth Muhlenfeld, eds. *Mary Chesnut's Civil War*. New Haven: Yale University Press, 1981.

Woodworth, Steven E. *Davis and Lee at War*. Lawrence: University Press of Kansas, 1995.

About the Civil War Society

The Civil War Society, whose headquarters are located in Berryville, Virignia, is comprised of over 65,000 Civil War scholars, students, writers, collectors, and reenactors. The organization's mission is to further historical research and preserve historic sites and battlefields. Its bimonthly publication, *Civil War: The Magazine of the Civil War Society,* disseminates the cutting-edge research and analysis of the Civil War Society contributors throughout the country. Through the Civil War Society's extensive fundraising efforts, the organization has been able to donate monuments to and restore major battlefields throughout the region torn apart by war over a century ago. Its educational outreach program organizes an extensive lecture and workshop series, and sponsors tours of historical sites.